BY·THE
BOOK

BY·THE BOOK

Legal ABCs for the Printed Word

by Martha Blue

This book is lovingly dedicated to
Ollie,
whose understanding, encouragement,
and humor made it all possible.

FIRST EDITION
ISBN 0-87358-491-0
Library of Congress Catalog Card Number
89-42665
Designed by Lisa Brownfield
Cover designed by David Jenney
Manufactured in the United States of America

Library of Congress Cataloging-in-Publication
Data
Blue, Martha, 1942–
    By the book : legal ABCs for the printed
word / by Martha Blue. — 1st ed.
    Includes bibliographical references.
    ISBN 0-87358-491-0 : $45.00
    1. Press law—United States—Popular
works. I. Title.
KF2750.Z9855   1990
343.73′0998—oc20   89-42665
[347.303998]   CIP

5K/10-89/0218

Contents

Caveat

This legal guide assists publishing concerns engaged in producing and distributing the printed word. Neither I nor the publisher make any expressed or implied warranty with regard to the forms' use or freedom from error. Each form must be reviewed by a knowledgable lawyer so that his or her expertise may be applied to your specific legal problem. Some forms, as the text indicates, were prepared by non-lawyers and are included for illustrative purposes.

Permission is granted for copying any of the forms by or under the direction of a licensed lawyer for the use and practice of law. Copying of these forms otherwise is certainly at your own risk. Any other use will infringe the copyright and is not permitted without the express written consent of the publisher.

Acknowledgments

This book bears the imprint of many: my innumerable clients with publishing legal problems, who must remain unnamed; those in publishing, who have taken my classes and workshops; the publishers (newsletter, magazine, and book) and their editors, who have published my work and in the process, continued my publishing education; the Rocky Mountain Publishers Association, the first publishing group who asked me to talk about publishing law at one of their annual conferences.

Jeri Tisdale and Michelle Osborn earned my particular gratitude for their typing skills (and Jeri, for seeing the project to completion), as did Bruce Andresen for his boundless enthusiasm and Susan McDonald for her painstaking editing and piercing questions about form and substance. The chapter on manufacturing, particularly, bears her imprint.

Others deserve mention as well: my law partner, Roy Ward, for encouraging me to develop an expertise in this area; my father, Quentin K. Craft, who in his mid-fifties, started several publications; my daughter, Zoe, for letting me use her room as a writing center while she was at her dad's—the penetrating glares of the guys in her Def Leppard poster kept me on course; my mother, Martha Manning, for her enthusiasm and for keeping my house organized. And last, but not least, Oliver Johnson, the dedicatee.

Excerpts from other works are acknowledged in the text.

Introduction

Basic Concepts

This book's legal information is provided for educational purposes and is not intended as legal advice. It contains a discussion of legal principles and a sampling of publishing legal forms. The forms' variety is impressive, but there is no one form that will accommodate the differences in the law in specific jurisdictions or particular sets of circumstances. The forms are merely illustrative and require selectivity rather than verbatim copying, as there is almost never a situation where your *exact* fact situation will fit. The forms include basic documents that can be modified with the assistance of any lawyer to your particular situation, as well as documents that have been used in actual situations. Some of these overlap.

Many checklists are used. Checklists help you because they:

- save time by outlining the how, what, and when of each legal step.
- simplify decision-making.
- guard against omission of an important factor in negotiating.
- review the subject area.
- serve as general checklists for action, documents, or correspondence.

Remember, users of this guide should consult their own lawyer for preparation of a set of forms tailored to their particular publishing situation. The type of publishing undertaken, i.e., non-profit educational publishing as opposed to magazine publishing, will dictate the use of different form provisions. Some of the factors that may vary include contractual provisions, number of titles, and the editorial process of a particular publishing house; the potential audience and distribution of the publishing house, including marketing of the literary property after book or periodical publication; and the quality of the author's writing as well as the author's reputation and commensurate bargaining position.

While, in many ways, determination of size is relative, in general a small book-publishing concern produces up to ten works each publishing season, while a large publisher releases over a hundred titles every season. A middling-size publishing house obviously falls in between. Book publishing seasons traditionally run from March to June (spring) and August to October (fall), although there are increasing numbers of publishers who have added a third "season," summer.

Teachers can use this book for courses in magazine editing and production, journalism, management of a student magazine, or a newspaper course. This is both an entry-level guide and one appropriate for the more sophisticated, complex organization. Whether you publish a consumer magazine like *Woman's Day,* a business publication like *Consumer Reports,* or a journal like *The Journal of Bacteriology,* you'll find this book helpful.

If there is a sharp division between the requirements of magazine and book production, this volume will guide you, the publisher, through basic legal information related to selected areas. In my own practice, I have observed that informed publishers prevent and/or resolve problems more frequently.

I also touch on legal variations that apply to newspapers (shoppers, dailies, and weeklies), magazines (general trade periodicals, including newsletters, house magazines, and one-shot magazines), catalogues and brochures, and journals.

An example of each of these categories of publishing follows:

Newspapers
- a shopper—*Canyon Shopper,* published in Flagstaff weekly.
- a weekly—*The New Times,* published in Phoenix and reporting on the cultural events in the greater Phoenix area.
- a daily—*The Los Angeles Times.*

Magazines
- general—*SASSY* for teenage girls.
- trade periodicals—the monthly *Arizona State Bar Journal,* sent to Arizona lawyers.
- house magazines—Basha's (a grocery store chain) monthly newspaper.
- one-shot magazines—the Navajo Tribe's annual magazine for its Tribal Fair (biggest Indian fair in the world).

Catalogues and Brochures
- The Nature Company's multipaged catalogue (catalogues are basically stores-by-mail).
- a brochure for prospective advertisers in *Southwest Art.*

A Journal
- the *Journal of Law and the Arts,* with scholarly articles on the arts, entertainment, communications, and intellectual property.

While each entity differs in the number and frequency of its publications, circulation or customers, staff size, and degree of complexity, the general legal procedures still apply. Whether one manages a weekly ad guide or a regional environmental press, a business structure must be chosen; contracting with others for essential services, such as printing and distribution, is necessary; avoidance of copyright problems and extension of copyright protection is critical; postal regulations must be followed; and personnel standards and procedures need to be established and followed.

The purpose of this book, then, is not to define for any particular publishing house a set of state-specific forms, as these should be tailored for use by a lawyer in your jurisdiction who is cognizant of your publishing house's particular actual situation in the publishing world. Nor is it intended to provide precise provisions regarding royalties, advances, and other financial terms, as each publishing house is likely to have slightly different norms, needs, and expectations for literary property. Its goal is to educate the publisher regarding legal business matters so as to minimize legal problems, expedite the handling of those legal problems that may occur, and reduce the amount of money spent on lawyer's fees and costs.

Each chapter contains practice aids for publishing, including references to general texts and, occasionally, case law. Mention of other reference material is frequent.

Since the text's purpose is educational, the provisions of sample forms are divided by explanatory material.

There has been no attempt to discuss the tax implications relative to a particular topic.

Anecdotal, illustrative material, or case incidents, include client matters that have come up in my own practice and in the practice of others, as well as reported court decisions. In some chapters, I have reproduced part of a court decision so that the court's application of legal principles to that area can be understood.

Other References

Should you add other books and periodicals to your publisher's legal-business reference shelf? Yes. Surprised? You shouldn't be. A single topic of this text is often amplified by four-volume works. I counted a half-dozen books alone on how to protect an idea. Some take a different slant or emphasis. Other's value lie in their newsworthiness. A few will be referenced throughout this text.

Some are only for lay persons (although lawyers entering this field could benefit from a quick reading), some are for both lawyers and lay persons, and some for lawyers (plus the lay person who fancies the law). Some present user-friendly information and others are only lawyer-friendly; you may need the lawyer-friendly work for a strictly narrow legal situation. Periodicals and journals contain the most current information, while books will give you background and easily accessible information.

And a Word About Lawyers

If your publishing house, XYZ Company in Moscow, Idaho, or Kitten Paws Company in Bend, Oregon, or the Whale Bound Company in Martha's Vineyard, needs a lawyer (which I hope to convince you that you do), don't expect to easily locate one knowledgable in publishing law. Your choices often boil down to: (1) starting with a lawyer who's never heard of publishing law, or (2) dealing with someone who has, at a distance and by telephone.

If you opt to educate your lawyer, educate yourself at the same time. My business clients with miniscule legal bills are self-educated in their business's legalities. Also, it helps if your lawyer is an avid reader, because he or she may have a natural affinity for publishing law.

Recognizing that legal fees average approximately $100 an hour, you can see that the same amount invested in several reference texts is a bargain. Be on the lookout for additions to your legal–business publishing reference shelf, or order them through interlibrary loan.

Periodicals and Newsletters

Publishers Weekly, the International News Magazine of Book Publishing (249 West 17th Street, New York, NY 10011) contains the most current material. While the subscription nears $100 annually, its "News of the Week" department reports on lawsuits filed, settlements reached, and so forth. The "Rights" column and its feature articles make it the weather-eye of publishing. Occasionally, it runs an in-depth legal article by Carole Rinzer, a publishing lawyer whose style is very readable.

The Committee of Small Magazine Editors and Publishers (COSMEP) publishes a monthly newsletter for members (Box 703, San Francisco, CA 94101), which includes an occasional legal article and always-excellent marketing information. COSMEP also bills itself as the International Association of Independent Publishers. The last time I checked, membership was $50 per year. COSMEP is an excellent organization and provides helpful information.

The Huenefeld Report (P.O. Box U, Bedford, MA 01730) for managers and planners in modest-sized book publishing houses, is prepared twenty-six times a year; again, at last notice, the subscription was $88 annually. Also available from Huenefeld is a hefty and thorough text on business management for a publishing concern.

John B. McHugh (5747 N. Ames, Glendale, WI 53209) runs a management advisory column in the COSMEP newsletter and he also self-publishes.

The Independent Publishers Trade Report (P.O. Box 176, Southport, CT 06490) is another periodical that covers subjects of interest to independent publishers.

In the publication *Small Press* (Department VV, Box 3000, Danville, NJ 07834), author/publisher John Kremer writes a column about publishing reference books.

In one 1987 column, he described books directed to the common legal needs of book publishers and authors. In the next issue's column, he reviewed publishers' resource books on setting up and running a business. His material runs the gamut from business plans to hiring personnel. Consider subscribing to *Small Press* for their occasional legal column as well as for general information.

Reference Books

Several organizations specialize in references for those in publishing.

Writers Digest Books (9933 Alliance Road, Cincinnati, Ohio 45242) created a series called the "Writer's Basic Book Shelf." Order their catalog. Two of their books, *Literary Agents* and *How to Understand and Negotiate a Book Contract or Magazine Agreement,* could be beneficial. In 1989, Writers Digest released the completely revised and updated "bible" for self-publishers, *The Complete Guide to Self-Publishing,* by Tim and Marilyn Ross, which is also available from the Rosses (About Books, Inc., Box 1500, Buena Vista, CO 81211).

Contact NOLO Press, a legal self-help publisher (950 Parker Street, Berkeley, CA 94710), for a list of their publications, which are both readable and informative. NOLO's 1988 catalog includes these useful titles: *A Media Law Handbook, A Partnership Guide, Everybody's Guide to Small Claims Court, Collecting Your Court Judgment, Small Business Start-Up, How to Form Your Own New York Corporation, Legal Research: How to Find and Understand the Law,* as well as a software program entitled *California Incorporator.* Most of these are under $25 (save money by not eating out and buy a reference book instead). Brad Bunnin and Peter Beren's out-of-print NOLO publication, *Author Law,* has been re-released under the title *The Writer's Legal Companion* (Addison Wesley).

Another helpful organization is the Self-Counsel Press Inc. (1301 North Northgate Way, Seattle, WA 98133), which publishes books on probate, small claims court, incorporation, and business reference.

For newsletter publishing concerns, see *How to Start and Print Your Own Newsletter* (Howard L. Shenson, 20750 Ventura Boulevard, Suite 206, Woodland Hills, CA 91364); *Editing Your Newsletter: How to Produce an Effective Publication Using Traditional Tools and Computers* by Mark Beach (Coast to Coast Books) distributed by Writers Digest; and *Success in Newsletter Publishing, A Practical Guide* by Frederick D. Goss (Newsletter Association, Colorado Building, No. 700, Washington, D.C. 20005).

Pressing Business: An Organizational Manual for Independent Publishers is published by Volunteer Lawyers for the Arts (VLA) (1560 Broadway, No. 711, New York, NY 10036). It can't be beat. VLA is a non-profit corporation dedicated to law and the arts. (VLA also publishes the *Columbia-VLA Journal of Law and the Arts,* a quarterly publication of law on the arts, entertainment, communications, and intellectual property. Usually, an article each issue focuses on publishing.) Send for the VLA's publication list, which includes the American Civil Liberties Union's *The Rights of Authors and Artists, The Writer's Legal Guide, A Writer's Guide to Copyright,* and other inexpensive, helpful books.

I like *Publishing Agreements: A Book of Precedents,* edited by Charles Clark

(George Allen & Unwin Ltd., London), which is available (when in print) from Dan Poynter's organization, Para Publishing. Clark's text covers a dozen agreements in detail, with notes on the left-hand side of the page and the agreement on the right-hand side of the page. The agreements include a general book author–publisher agreement, along with a book-club rights agreement. The appendices include permission fees, royalty statements, etc. Dan Poynter's *Publisher's Bookshelf* lists the best books on promotion, marketing, business, product development, and printing. Order from Para Publishing (P. O. Box 4232, Santa Barbara, CA 93103-0232). His bi-monthly newsletter, *Publishing Poynters,* bursts with current information like a cookie chock full of oversize chocolate chips. Relatively new is his computer disk collection, *Publishing Legal Forms;* the twenty-two contracts range from a trade book contract to a special-markets purchase agreement. (I'll say more about this extensive set of forms later.)

My favorite lay-person book about publishing is *How to Be Your Own Literary Agent* by Richard Curtis (Houghton Mifflin Co., 2 Park Street, Boston, MA 02108). This conversational discourse on agents, negotiation, the basic book deal, and related issues includes an excellent chart that lists the elements of a good deal, a poor deal, and an average deal *for the author* (flip-flop for publishers).

University of Washington Press released a revised edition of *A Guide to Book Publishing* by Dalus Smith. The updated book integrates publishing peoples' comments, and includes information on third-world publishing markets.

If you work with periodicals, see *Editorial Forms: A Guide to Journal Management* (CBA Journal Producers and Practices Committee, Bethesda, MD 20814), which contains many forms, as well as text that details their use in publication, including letters of acceptance and tracking forms.

Other helpful books:

- *How to Register a Copyright and Protect Your Creative Work* by Robert B. Chickering and Susan Hartman; Scribner's (McMillan Publishing Co., General Publishing Group, 866 Third Ave., New York, NY 10022).
- *The Copyright Book: A Practical Guide* by William S. Strong; MIT Press (55 Hayward St., Cambridge, MA 02142).
- *Making It Legal: A Law Primer for Authors, Artists and Craftspeople* by Martha Blue; Northland Press (P. O. Box N, Flagstaff, AZ 86002).
- *The Law in Plain English for Writers* by Leonard D. DuBoff; Madrona Publishers (P. O. Box 22667, Seattle, WA 98122).

Most of the non-lawyer reference books are available from mehitabel's catalog (P. O. Box 60357, Palo Alto, CA 94306), a source of books and supplies for writers, editors, and publishers.

A few steps up in textual difficulty and legalese, but still readable for the lay person and indispensable for the professional, are PLI Publications (Practising Law Institute, 810 Seventh Avenue, New York, NY 10019). Get on PLI's mailing list for their catalog and seminar announcements. Bi-annually, PLI sponsors a "Legal and Business Aspects of Publishing" seminar, complete with a companion volume.

The 1988 *Legal and Business Aspects of Book Publishing* includes a literary agent checklist; numerous forms; discussions regarding licensing of subsidiary rights; sample option agreements; copyright development information; publishing agreements, from reprint to trade-book agreements; educational publishing forms; plus a plethora of agreements used by book entrepreneurs (over sixteen agreements). The publication's most useful feature is the updated annotated case list prepared by Richard Dannay, who is a senior partner in a New York City law firm and specializes in book publishing law. His annotated case list covers thirty-four areas of book publishing, which, in 1988, summarized 499 cases.

For any periodical publishing concern, I recommend the latest PLI volume on *Legal and Business Aspects of the Magazine Industry.* The one I use has over twenty-five forms (one of which has over a dozen magazine check endorsements), and also includes reading lists, articles, case law reprints, and outlines.

Each PLI volume is several hundred pages and contains more information, cheaper, and in one volume, than any other publication with which I've worked. PLI publishes texts on copyright infringement, trademark law, computer packaging and technology licensing, movie financing, video production, defamation, and so forth. Every volume that I have is indispensable. You or your lawyer, or both, may find it useful to attend certain seminars (the last Legal Aspects of Book Publishing seminar cost $425); you will benefit by ordering the most recent book publishing law seminar's publication.

Leonard D. DuBoff authored the *Book Publisher's Legal Guide* available through Butterworth Legal Publishers (15014 N.E. 40th St., Suite 205, Redmond, WA 98052). This scholarly text is useful and informative, but is an easier read for lawyers.

Prentice Hall (855 Valley Road, Clifton, NJ 07013) Law and Business's *The Publishing Law Handbook,* by E. Gabriel Perle and John Taylor Williams, is an excellent reference for the practicing lawyer, since it's organized in loose-leaf fashion so that it may be easily updated. With its many legal citations and lawyer hornbook approach, it's a natural companion volume to PLI's publications, and every publishing law lawyer should have it. Its value to lay persons depends on the individual's background and experience.

Following are references that I consider to be strictly for lawyers, or the lay person with a passionate interest in the law. Some specialty publications in the field include:

Melville B. Nimmer, *Nimmer on Copyright,* Matthew Bender & Co. (1275 Broadway, Albany, NY 12201) is the four-volume loose-leaf set for copyright practitioners. The cost is substantial; supplements ran about $250 for 1989, and the basic four-volume set starts at about four hundred dollars.

Entertainment Industry Contracts: Negotiating and Drafting Guide by Alexander Lindey, Matthew Bender & Co. (1275 Broadway, Albany, NY 12201), a bible of contract information, unfortunately contains only a partial volume on book publishing, and the publisher won't separate the volumes. The initial cost is over $300, and the annual supplement is also pricey, but I still recommend it.

Literary Rights Contracts: A Handbook for Professionals, by Richard Wincor,

Harcourt Brace Jovanovich (6277 Sea Harbor Dr., Orlando, FL 32821), may or may not still be in print, but Wincor's theories about literary rights, contracts, and forms are unique and well worth reviewing.

Clark Boardman Co., Ltd. (435 Hudson Street, New York, NY 10014) publishes a yearly *Entertainment, Publishing and the Arts Handbook,* which includes information on a variety of topics. The 1987 table of contents lists copyright, defamation and libel, books, plays, photographs, right of publicity, etc. The articles in the text are timely and informative and for lawyers, it's well worth the $55 or so.

The Entertainment Law Reporter can be ordered from 9440 Santa Monica Boulevard, Suite 600, Beverly Hills, CA 90210.

Entertainment Law & Financing, a monthly publication, comes from a company that publishes many larger publications. Order from Leader Publications (111 Eighth Avenue, Suite 900, New York, NY 10014-0158) for about $135 per year. The information in this newsletter is directed to artists, musicians, and the film world, but many of the articles apply to publishers as well.

A Bare-Bones Bookshelf

If you twisted my arm and made me name five references, I'd choose (in addition to this volume) two books, a software program, and two periodicals:

- PLI's latest Book Publishing text.
- *How to Be Your Own Literary Agent,* by Richard Curtis.
- Dan Poynter's software, *Publishing Legal Forms.*
- *Publishers Weekly.*
- *Small Press.*

Then I'd add a thick three-ring notebook with some whimsical title like *Martha's Rare and Not-So-Rare Collection of Publishing Forms and Trivia.* As you run across a co-publishing agreement or an unusal printer's bid, slip it in the notebook. These items would form the core of my reference library, were I involved in publishing.

A Legal Viewpoint

From a book's conception to the final press run, on into distribution and out of print, publishers face legal issues with the regularity of waves pounding a California beach—adverse libel trends, who owns what in the work, court-found duties to help authors with their manuscripts and promote their books, licensing rights to others, privacy suits, claims of misappropriation of celebrities' names, editorial-products liability issues, erratas or revisions to books, subjective legal threats, and on and on. The afterword outlines the step-by-step process in setting up a legally sound publishing operation and points out the many areas of concern in any publishing venture (you may want to read that now).

In the middle of editing this manuscript, I kicked back and read a paperback, *Apaches* by Oakley Hall. When I finished it, I glanced at the copyright page, and it occurred to me that it provided an excellent short overview of the issues basic to publishing.

This novel is a work of fiction. Names, characters, places and incidents are either the product of the author's imagination or are used fictitiously. Any resemblance to actual events or locales or persons, living or dead, is entirely coincidental.

This edition contains the complete text
of the original hardcover edition.
NOT ONE WORD HAS BEEN OMITTED.

Let's take each component and see what information it conveys.

**This novel is a work of fiction. Names, characters, places and incidents
are either the product of the author's imagination or are used fictitiously.
Any resemblance to actual events or locales or persons, living or dead, is
entirely coincidental.**

This is a disclaimer, which protects the publisher and author from restrictions in
book content claims, that is, defamation and invasion of privacy.

10

This indicates that the author contracted with Simon & Schuster, Inc. (the Inc. indicates that incorporation was their choice of business structure) to publish the original version of the book, which was in hardcover. The author gave Simon & Schuster the right to license the paperback rights to the work. Typically, that happens a year or two after the hardcover publication. The copy of *Apaches* that I was reading was issued under a paperback license, not a condensation license. (In *By the Book,* you'll find contracting in general to be the subject of the first few chapters, and licensing appearing later.)

This notice provides other critical information. "All rights reserved" gives copyright protection in the western hemisphere. The author holds the copyright to the text copyrighted in 1986, but the cover art copyrighted by the artist is Bantam's paperback cover, not the original from the hardcover edition. The Library of Congress number helps researchers locate the work. The statement beginning "No part . . ." attempts to tie up copyright rights tighter than allowed by fair use. The proper contact for permission is indicated. Implied in this provision is an author-publisher contract and an illustrator-publisher agreement. (These provisions can be found in the chapters on contracts, agents, copyright, fair use, and permissions.)

ISBN 0-553-27541-0

ISBN stands for "international standard book number." The numbers identify the language, publisher, and specific edition of the book. It's the number that the larger bookstores use to order by. U.S. publishers are assigned numbers in batches by R. R. Bowker & Co.

Published simultaneously in the United States and Canada

By publishing in Canada, the publisher swept in international protection under the Berne Convention (Berne's covered in the copyright chapters).*

Bantam Books are published by Bantam Books, a division of Bantam Doubleday Dell Publishing Group, Inc. Its trademark, consisting of the words "Bantam Books" and the portrayal of a rooster, is Registered in U.S. Patent and Trademark Office and in other countries. Marca Registrada. Bantam Books, 666 Fifth Avenue, New York, New York 10103.

This tells you that Bantam was part of a publishing merger. (This concept is touched in the buying/selling and entrepreneuring chapter.) Both the name and logo are registered federally (a form of legal protection covered in the next chapter).

PRINTED IN THE UNITED STATES OF AMERICA

O   0 9 8 7 6 5 4 3 2 1

This indicates country of manufacture, as required by law, and the number of times this particular version of the book has been printed.

There: a thumbnail review of one book's legal publishing history and the host of legal protections and structures it used.

Trouble, however, has been known to follow some books.

Consider Ashley Book's release of *Taxi: The Harry Chapin Story,* by Peter Coan, in 1987. Years prior, Coan contacted Chapin about writing Chapin's biography, and a *verbal* agreement was reached. While Coan worked on it, Chapin died, and his widow tried to take possession of Coan's tapes and notes. G. P. Putnam (Coan's first publisher) put the book's publication on hold. Coan sued Putnam for breach of contract and got a settlement, whereupon he turned around and sued the widow for interference with the Putnam contract. When Ashley, the second publisher, released the book, they said they didn't know of the prior contract. In time, the author was not pleased with the lack of press attention the book received through Ashley's efforts, and hired a public relations firm to publicize the book. (*Publishers Weekly,* November 2, 1987). A sloppy beginning led to a sloppy ending.

By now, you realize that the taking of certain legal steps minimizes your legal risks.

---

*The United States joined the Berne Convention in spring 1989.

Experts report that starting any business is risky. So if you know the problems you'll encounter beforehand, and minimize them, your chance of success increases.

Most of you now own and manage a publishing concern. Perhaps you've tangled with legal problems in publishing. Even if you haven't, read this guide through and then go back and set up any legal infra-structures you may be missing. It won't hurt to stop mid-stream and arrange a legal–business foundation.

Your publishing venture has defined its niche, set goals, and drawn up a three-to-five year business plan, right? If not, then utilize basic business references and publishing guides, such as *The Huenefeld Report.* Its subject diversity and basic information ranges from getting a toll-free number to disciplining tardy authors to monitoring and controlling cash flow. Another valuable tool for innovative small businesses (and inventors) is the SBA's *Ideas Into Dollars,* which discusses the process of innovation through to commercialization, along with resources (publications, programs, and organizations).

I assume that a lawyer has checked the lease, zoning, or purchase papers for your work space; that you bought equipment (even if second-hand) with good warranties; and that you hired an accountant to advise you on financial and tax matters, set up your bookkeeping, and prepare financial statements.

If your plans include buying a publishing concern, you can change its business structure if it doesn't meet your needs. (Before acquiring a concern, read the chapter on that topic.)

I Can't Promise You a Rose Garden

I can't promise that you'll never have a publishing legal problem if you follow the guidelines of this book. Anyone can file a lawsuit against another. You can, however, lessen that risk.

Just because a suit is filed against you does not mean that the claimant can recover. It does NOT mean, for example, that:

- you wronged the plaintiff.
- you cheated the plaintiff.
- the plaintiff's theories of recovery are good.
- the claims are fresh.
- the lawsuit was filed in the right county, state, or federal court.
- the claim is good.
- you can't recover attorney's fees.

It means only that someone felt you wronged them and convinced a lawyer to file suit.

Just as you reduce the chances of a heart attack by lowering your cholesterol, you reduce the chances of suit and increase the likelihood of cheap and satisfactory resolution of claims by:

- having a background in (and company policies that incorporate) the legal aspects of publishing.
- keeping good records.
- conducting your affairs in a businesslike fashion, which includes accurate and informative calendars, chronological files of correspondence, letter agreements, and written contracts.
- resolving a complaint when its ugly head first rears and confirming the resolution by letter, letter agreement, or contract, depending upon the complexity of the matter and the sum of money involved.
- involving your lawyer as soon as practical in handling a difficult problem, i.e., one involving big sums of money or difficult people.
- paying attention to your gut reaction to situations and people.

Don't laugh at that last caution. Forewarnings, sometimes verbal or often nonverbal, point to trouble down the line. All professionals recognize this phenomena. Often clients lament that "I should have known this would happen, because. . ."

You prevent legal problems by using basic knowledge.

The 95 Percent Rule

The 95 percent rule? Ninety-five percent of persons and organizations are legitimate, honest, and caring people and organizations with whom you can resolve problems. Only five percent cause business/legal problems. You reduce that percentage by keeping your practices regular and legal.

Stung by Deviations

Don't deviate from your established legal-business policies. You'll most assuredly get stung when you do. No business is so urgent that you can afford to ignore these policies.

Let's apply these principles to a hybrid situation (a combination of legal problems, rolled into one): Gunn Publishers is run by a hard-driven publisher and is approached by the well-known Gun Museum's laid-back director; they decide to co-publish a text on the history of gun collections for a national gun collector-organizer's conference, to be held six months from their meeting. Everyone gears up their normal scheduling, from author to the co-publishers to the typesetter and printer. Neither the author's contract nor the letter of agreement between the co-publishers covered a late and/or unsatisfactory manuscript; neither contained a manuscript schedule, with sanctions; the responsibilities of each co-publisher were ambiguous; and the total author's advance was paid on signing. First, the author's illness slowed down manuscript delivery, then the author delivered a poor manuscript.

Now, this sticky situation is not only unpleasant to deal with but also lacks ground rules for resolution. A tough problem that could have been avoided or lessened if all parties had established clear rules and procedures via agreement previous to starting the project.

A Final Reminder: Shop Around

Shop around before choosing any specialist or professional (lawyer, printer, agent, distributor, and so forth). Check out the person or company's reputation. Ask the specialist for references, and call the references. Meet with the specialist or professional to evaluate the communication level and esprit, and consider how he or she will work with your particular publishing concern. Test their knowledge in their specific field. Pay attention to your gut reaction. *Get the relationship fixed in writing.*

Start With Structure

2

Start at the beginning: business structure. Sole proprietorships, partnerships, corporations for- and not-for-profit, and joint ventures are American business's most common structures.

Business Structure

Sole Proprietorship

Most organic businesses started as sole proprietorships. Sole proprietorships remain the simplest, cheapest, and easiest to begin, manage, and end. In my mind, I visualize a sole proprietor as a scurrier, her hair dangling across her forehead, her glasses askew. She's on the phone, eating lunch, and her desk looks like a cyclone hit the paperwork.

A basic definition: a sole proprietor is one who owns and runs his or her own business. This business-form choice initially saves money and time, as it exists without articles of incorporation or a written partnership agreement. Since it lacks partners or a board of directors, the sole proprietor holds the business's management reins. Business profits (or losses) from a sole proprietorship are reported on Schedule C of the sole proprietor's 1040 Federal Income Tax Return.

With all that going for it, why doesn't everyone choose a sole proprietorship? Because it can lead to heartache. You're personally liable for the debts your business incurs. Put another way, a court judgment can consume a sole proprietor's business and non-business property.

Some restrictions fence this unlimited liability. Court proceedings are required before you can be forced to give up your belongings, property, house, wages, and the like, and certain properties are exempt. Still, the spector of a business liability seriously reducing your personal assets exists. Sometimes, certain risks can be minimized with insurance; premise liability insurance covers liability that results, when someone slips, falls, and is injured at your publishing concern. However, nothing can protect you from bad judgment, bad planning, or bad luck.

Partnership

Another common form of doing business is a partnership. Partnership, in my mind, sparks with the energy that can charge between the partners.

A partnership exists when two or more persons own a business together and the business is not incorporated. This arrangement arises verbally, by written agreement, or by implication from the behavior of one of the partners toward third parties.

The up-side of partnerships: you pool talents, time, effort, and financial resources. The down-side of a partnership: individual partner's assets are liable for payment of partnership debts, up to that partner's interest in the partnership.

The intimacy of a partnership, like marriage, can enhance your business life or lead to disagreements. Partnerships fall apart—sometimes. Don't choose a fox for a partner if you are a little red hen.

Any one of the partners can bind the entire partnership in most matters, even if the partner acted without the approval or knowledge of the other partner(s).

Case Incident:
Two creative geniuses in a wildly successful professional partnership, the creators of *L.A. Law,* had disputes over money, authority, and "lackadaisicalness." Finally, one barred the other from the set of the award-winning series.

Don't try to save money by verbal partnership arrangements. Often, partners' recollections about the substance of a particular term don't match (sometimes, I've wondered if the partners were ever in the same room at the same time). Some terms are never even discussed, such as how to pay a withdrawing partner. In those cases, state laws step in and spell out partnership rules: Beware.

An early partnership case involved the first printing press. Apparently, Johann Gutenberg failed to get a termination agreement with a partner, and when the man died, his heirs wanted in on the secret of Gutenberg's movable press. The high court of Strasbourg, in 1439, ruled for the printer and the heirs got guilders. (Everyone knows about the Gutenberg Bibles, but did you know the University of Texas purchased one for $2.4 million?)

Don't be out on a limb. Put your partnership's agreement in writing. As a minimum, include the following:

- the names, addresses, and legal capacities of each of the parties (married, single, husband and wife).
- name and principal place of the business.
- the purpose of the partnership.
- its term.
- accounting method, that is, cash or accrual.
- original capital contributions.
- capital accounts.
- additional capital contributions.
- drawing accounts.
- profits or losses.
- voting.
- time devoted to the partnership.
- allocation of responsibility.
- restrictions on partners' salaries.
- voluntary dissolution.
- withdrawal of a partner.
- sale or transfer of partnership interest.
- valuation of interest of withdrawing partner.
- terms of payment to withdrawing partner.
- arbitration.
- notices.
- boilerplate (binding effect and applicable law).

A partnership files an informational return on Form 1065, U.S. Partnership Return of Income. The individual partner's income and losses are taken from that form and transferred to individual 1040 forms.

Case Incident:
A very talented sculptor, who later became my client, entered into a verbal partnership with a non-artist sales/business manager. Occasionally, the producing partner got complaints from merchants because of bad checks and notices of penalties for late payment of taxes. By the time the "business" partner got busted for cocaine dealing, he'd done a number on the

19

partnership assets, including cleaning out savings and checking accounts for a foiled flight, leaving Mr. Sculptor with thousands in unpaid tax obligations, not to mention other debts.

Case Incident:
Publishers Weekly (August 10, 1984) reported that after only a year in business, the partners of Richardson & Snyder fell out over the recall of its book *God's Broker* by Antoni Gronowicz, which one partner called an incredible fraud and the other said carried a certain authenticity. The book purported to be the life of Pope John II told in the words of his friends and himself. One partner planned to initiate arbitration proceedings and the other planned to sue the author.

Limited Partner

Can you escape the unlimited liability problem for each general partner for any partnership debt? Yes; this liability for the partner's personal debts vanishes with the "limited partner" structure.

Limited partners don't participate in the business management. They provide economic backing and receive a proportionate share of the partnership profits. These passive investors avoid exposing their personal assets to partnership and individual partner's debts. Hire a knowledgable lawyer to create a limited partnership. If your Aunt Matilda wants to help your publishing concern, make her a limited partner. The paperwork reminds her that she's not a decision-maker, just an investor.

Case Incident:
A publisher of a small press became involved with a hot property authored by a relative. The publisher obtained investment monies through limited-partner offerings, plus paid its lawyer, accountant, etc., on a contingent-fee basis, that is, a percentage of net profit on the book property. This spread the risk of loss, and also the profit.

Joint Venture

The term "joint venture" conjures up a picture of some wizened wealthy wimp in tortoise-shell bifocals bouncing atop a camel across an African desert in a caravan led by his joint-venturers, a handsome couple in safari clothes, on a whimsical search for diamonds.

A joint venture is an association of persons or entities who intend to engage and carry out a single business venture for joint profit. For this single purpose, they combine efforts, property, money, skill, and knowledge, but do not create a partnership or a corporation.

Though legally distinct, a joint venture is akin to a partnership for a single transaction. Joint venture agreements appropriately fit a single book project, as does a limited partnership. Joint decisions on literary or business affairs in a joint venture can be an advantage or a disadvantage, depending on the people involved.

Unincorporated Association

In *Pressing Business: An Organizational Manual for Independent Publishers,* published by Volunteer Lawyers for the Arts (VLA), it is noted that unincorporated associations (utilized by informal groups) are rarely used by a publishing concern, since associations are not oriented toward business ventures. VLA opined that these organizations are probably "pre-corporate and are operating this way on an interim basis." An unincorporated association allows the same exposure to personal liability, because an individual association member's activities can be a source of problems that reflects legally on all members.

Corporations

"Corporation: an ingenious device for obtaining individual profit without individual responsibility." (Ambrose Bierce)

Corporations always conjure up in my mind a sheet of paper with an intricate maze drawn on it—in invisible ink, with a bored board of directors ritualistically going through motions to arrive at a preplanned destination.

The corporate form was created to develop business by protecting the owners from personal liability for corporate debts. A legal fiction, a corporation nonetheless functions like a person: it can make contracts, incur debts, purchase property, sue and be sued. The individuals who make up the corporation, whether corporate officers or employers or shareholders, are not personally liable for any of the corporate transactions even if the corporation is totally bankrupt, as long as the corporation operated within the law.

This corporate limit on liability provided protection for three authors, employees of Ten Speed Press, who wrote *How to Persuade Your Lover to Use a Condom... and Why You Should.* They found it too awkward to publish in-house and too fragile an idea to delay. One of the authors set up a corporation called New York Publishing, "Because I always wanted to be the head of a New York publishing house." (*Publishers Weekly,* May 1, 1987).

A corporation's separate legal entity subjects it to taxation, but the corporate structure allows capital to be raised through the sale of shares. A person who buys shares incurs no personal liability for corporate debt and usually corporate shares can be sold. At a certain point, the number of shareholders (and other factors) triggers state and federal security laws (usually state laws come into play at around ten shareholders, and under the federal law, at thirty-five).

Although corporations retain earnings, there's a double taxation tier: on corporate profits, *and then* on shareholder earnings. Does that spoil it for you? You can gain the corporation advantage and still be taxed as a partnership if you opt for Sub-Chapter S corporate status.

A corporation tunes itself to a defined management structure, more so than partnerships or sole proprietors. It has a longer life expectancy, continuing despite death or withdrawal of its shareholders or directors.

Some disadvantages to the corporate form:

- the time and expense of incorporating.
- attorney's fees involved in incorporating, plus filing fees.
- yearly fees and reports.
- up-to-date minute book records, which must be kept to maintain limited liability.

The procedures for incorporation vary from state to state and include: checking the availability of the corporate name and reserving it; filing articles of incorporation along with a filing fee, and often a certificate of disclosure regarding past criminal conduct of incorporators, officers, and directors; publication of the articles of incorporation in a newspaper of general circulation in the county of the known place of business; and filing the affidavit of publication of articles of incorporation with the state corporation commission.

The articles themselves, at a minimum, must meet statutory requirements on information contained:

- the name of the organization and the original purpose, location, duration.
- names and addresses of incorporators and the initial board of directors.
- name and address of the designated agent for legal purposes.
- information about the shares.

You can get an idea of what your state requires by reading your local newspaper's legal-notice section. Observe the distinct differences between profit and not-for-profit corporations.

Here are some articles of incorporation approved by the Arizona Corporation Commission for a for-profit corporation called Blue Inc. Press:

ARTICLE I
Name
The name of the corporation is BLUE INC. PRESS.

ARTICLE II
Purpose
The purpose for which this corporation is organized is the transaction of any or all lawful business for which corporations may be incorporated under the laws of the State of Arizona, as they may be amended from time to time.

ARTICLE III
Initial Business
The corporation initially intends to conduct the business of publication and wholesale/resale distribution of books, pamphlets, magazines, artwork, prints and posters and related items.

ARTICLE IV
Authorized Capital
The corporation shall have authority to issue One Thousand (1,000) shares of common stock without par value.

ARTICLE V
Statutory Agent
The name and address of the initial statutory agent is MARTHA BLUE, 323 N. Leroux, P.O. Box 789, Flagstaff, Arizona 86002.

ARTICLE VI
Board of Directors
The initial Board of Directors shall consist of one director. The person who is to serve as Director until the first annual meeting of shareholders or until her successor is elected and qualified, is: MARTHA BLUE, 323 N. Leroux, P.O. Box 789, Flagstaff, Arizona 86002, and the number of persons to serve on the Board of Directors shall be fixed by the bylaws.

ARTICLE VII
Incorporators
The incorporators of the corporation are MARTHA BLUE, 323 N. Leroux, P.O. Box 789, Flagstaff, Arizona 86002 and ROY WARD, 323 N. Leroux, P.O. Box 789, Flagstaff, Arizona, 86002. All powers, duties and responsibilities of the incorporators shall cease at the time of delivery of these Articles of Incorporation to the Arizona Corporation Commission for filing.

ARTICLE VIII
Indemnification
Indemnification of officers, directors, employees and agents. The corporation shall indemnify any person who incurs expenses by reason of the fact that he or she is or was an officer, director, employee or agent of the corporation. This indemnification shall be mandatory in all circumstances in which indemnification is permitted by law.

DATED this 21st day of December, 1981.

_____

MARTHA BLUE
Incorporator

_____

ROY WARD
Incorporator

23

STATE OF ARIZONA)
) ss.
County of Coconino   )
    SUBSCRIBED AND SWORN to before me this 8th day of December,
1981, by MARTHA BLUE and ROY WARD.

_____
                    Notary Public

My Commission Expires:
_____

In addition, Arizona requires this certificate of disclosure of a criminal past.

ARIZONA CORPORATION COMMISSION
INCORPORATING DIVISION

Phoenix Address: 1200 West Washington
                 Phoenix, Arizona 85007

Tucson Address: 402 West Congress
                Tucson, Arizona 85701

CERTIFICATE OF DISCLOSURE
A.R.S. Sections 10-128 & 10-1084

PLEASE SEE REVERSE SIDE

_____
EXACT CORPORATE NAME

CHECK APPROPRIATE BOX(ES) A or B
ANSWER "C"

THE UNDERSIGNED CERTIFY THAT:

A. No persons serving either by elections or appointment as officers, directors, incorporators and persons controlling, or holding more than 10% of the issued and outstanding common shares or 10% of any other proprietary, beneficial or membership interest in the corporation:
  1. Have been convicted of a felony involving a transaction in securities, consumer fraud or antitrust in any state or federal jurisdiction within the seven-year period immediately preceding the execution of this Certificate.
  2. Have been convicted of a felony, the essential elements of which consisted of fraud, misrepresentation, theft by false pretenses, or restraining the trade or monopoly in any state or federal jurisdiction within the seven-year period immediately preceding the execution of this Certificate.
  3. Have been or are subject to an injunction, judgment, decree or permanent order of any state or federal court entered within the seven-year period immediately preceding the execution of this Certificate where such injunction, judgment, decree or permanent order:
     (a) Involved the violation of fraud or registration provisions of the securities laws of that jurisdiction; or
     (b) Involved the violation of the consumer fraud laws of that jurisdiction; or
     (c) Involved the violation of the antitrust or restraint of trade laws of that jurisdiction.

B. For any person or persons who have been or are subject to one or more of the statements in Items A.1 through A.3 above, the following information MUST be attached:
  1. Full name and prior name(s) used.
  2. Full birth name.
  3. Present home address.
  4. Prior addresses (for immediate preceding 7-year period).
  5. Date and location of birth.
  6. Social Security number.
  7. The nature and description of each conviction or judicial action, date and location, the court and public agency involved and file or cause number of case.

STATEMENT OF BANKRUPTCY, RECEIVERSHIP OR REVOCATION
A.R.S. Sections 10-128.01 and 10-1083

C. Has any person serving (a) either by election or appointment as an officer, director, trustee or incorporator of the corporation or, (b) major stockholder possessing or controlling any proprietary, beneficial or membership interest in the corporation, served in any such capacity or held such interest in any corporation which has been placed in bankruptcy or receivership or had its charter revoked?   YES _____ NO _____

IF YOUR ANSWER TO THE ABOVE QUESTION IS "YES", YOU MUST ATTACH THE FOLLOWING INFORMATION FOR EACH CORPORATION:

  1. Name and address of the corporation.
  2. Full name, including alias and address of each person involved.
  3. State(s) in which the corporation:
     (a) Was incorporated.
     (b) Has transacted business.
  4. Dates of corporate operation.
  5. A description of the bankruptcy, receivership or charter revocation, including the date, court or agency involved and the file or cause number of the case.

Under penalties of law, the undersigned incorporators/Officers declare that we have examined this Certificate, including any attachments, and to the best of our knowledge and belief it is true, correct and complete.

State of _____)
) ss
County of _____)

Subscribed, sworn to and acknowledged before me this

_____ DAY of _____ , 19_____ .

_____
NOTARY PUBLIC

My Commission expires: _____

BY _____ DATE _____
TITLE _____

BY _____ DATE _____
TITLE _____

FISCAL DATE: _____

Remember, you must follow the steps for incorporation *exactly,* keep the records (minutes) required by law, and manage it according to law, otherwise a court will deny you (as a shareholder or corporate officer) the protection of limited liability. Shareholders share ownership in a for-profit corporation, but a director may also be a shareholder. Dissolution of a corporation, like initiation, requires the services of a lawyer.

To do business in another state, you must often obtain a certificate of doing business in that state and file it with a state official.

Non-profit Corporations

Some small presses opt to form non-profit corporations. While a for-profit corporation can be set up virtually overnight, that is not true for a non-profit corporation with tax-exempt status. Don't set up a non-profit corporation because your enterprise won't make money to begin with. That's not the standard. The purpose of such a corporation *is limited to* certain educational or charitable objectives that benefit the public, and the monies the non-profit earns from the corporate activities must be used to perform these public services. A fair salary can be paid to an individual, say, yourself as editor, but there are no owners or shareholders and no dividends. Further, not-for-profit corporations operate under stricter federal laws.

You can't get tax-exempt status unless you agree that upon dissolution, the non-profit corporation's assets will go to another non-profit organization. Again, *Pressing Business* has a good discussion of the distinction between the two. A tax-exempt status can be just what your small press needs, if your purposes match the legal requirements.

Case Incident:
The Cooperating Associations, which form the private but non-profit arm of our national park and monument systems, are generally organized as non-profits with tax-exempt status. Revenues from the sales of the associations' books, maps, videos, and so forth are used to support their purpose, which is to aid the federal areas with which they are associated in the areas' interpretive endeavors. Some of these associations joined together in a group called a conference, which is an umbrella, non-profit corporation. The articles for that organization follow:

ARTICLES OF INCORPORATION
OF
THE CONFERENCE OF NATIONAL PARK
COOPERATING ASSOCIATIONS

I. Name
The name of the corporation is The Conference of National Park Cooperating Associations.

II. Purposes and powers

The purposes for which this corporation is formed are:

(a) The specific and primary purpose is the promotion of scientific, educational, and literary purposes by in turn advancing the common purposes of the members of the corporation, each member being both a corporation exempt from taxation under state and federal laws, and a "cooperating association" cooperating with the National Park Service of the United States Department of the Interior pursuant to applicable provisions of Chapter 1 of Title 16 of the United States Code.

(b) The general purposes and powers are to have and exercise all rights and powers conferred on nonprofit corporations under the laws of California, including, but not limited to, the power to contract, rent, buy or sell personal or real property; provided, however, that this corporation shall not, except to an insubstantial degree, engage in any activities or exercise any powers that are not in furtherance of the primary purposes of this corporation.

(c) Notwithstanding any of the above statements of purposes and powers, this corporation shall not, except to an insubstantial degree, engage in any activities or exercise any powers that are not in furtherance of the primary purpose of this corporation.

III. Organization

This corporation is organized pursuant to the General Nonprofit Corporation Law of the State of California, Part 1 (commencing at Section 9000) of Division 2 of Title 1 of the Corporations Code and does not contemplate pecuniary gain or profit to the members thereof and it is organized for nonprofit purposes.

IV. Principal office

The County in this State where the principal office for the transaction of the business of the corporation is located is San Joaquin County.

V. Directors

The number of directors of the corporation shall be not less than five (5) and not more than fifteen (15). The exact number of directors shall be fixed, from time to time, by a bylaw or amendment thereof duly adopted by the members or the Board of Directors. The names and addresses of the persons who are to act in the capacity of directors until the selection of their successors are:

Name   *Address*

[all incorporators]

VI. Action by consent of board without meeting

Any action required or permitted to be taken by the board of directors under any provision of law may be taken without a meeting, if all members of the board shall individually or collectively consent in writing to such action. Such written consent or consents shall be filed with the minutes of the proceedings of the board. Such action by written consent shall have the same force and effect as the unanimous vote of such directors. Any certificate or other document filed under any provision of law which relates to action so taken shall state that the action was taken by the unanimous written consent of the board of directors without a meeting and that the articles of incorporation authorize the directors to so act, and such statement shall be prima facie evidence of such authority.

VII. Bylaw provisions

(a) Directors. The manner in which directors shall be chosen and removed from office, their qualifications, powers, duties, compensation and tenure of office, the manner of filling vacancies on the board, and the manner of calling and holding meetings of directors, shall be as stated in the bylaws.

(b) Members. The authorized number, if any, and qualifications of members of the corporation, the filling of vacancies, the different classes of membership, if any, the property, voting and other rights and privileges of members, and their liability to dues and assessments and the method of collection, and the termination and transfer of membership shall be as stated in the bylaws, provided, however, that all members of the corporation shall be corporations which are both exempt from taxation under state and federal laws and are "cooperating associations" cooperating with the National Park Service of the United States Department of the Interior pursuant to applicable provisions of Chapter 1 of Title 16 of the United States Code. The board may elect honorary nonvoting members who do not meet the foregoing qualifications.

VIII. Dedication and dissolution

(a) The property of this corporation is irrevocably dedicated to the scientific, educational, and literary purposes enumerated in Article II, hereof, and no part of the net income or assets of this organization shall ever inure to the benefit of any director, officer, or member thereof or to the benefit of any private persons.

(b) On the dissolution or winding up of the corporation its assets remaining after payment of, or provision for payment of, all debts and liabilities of this corporation, shall be distributed to the National Park Service of the United States Department of Interior, or its successor, for use in augmenting the "interpretive program" of the Service or its successor.

(c) If this corporation holds any assets in trust, or the corporation is formed for charitable purposes, such assets shall be disposed of in such manner as may be directed by decree of the superior court of the county in which the corporation has its principal office, on petition therefor by the Attorney General of California or by any person concerned in the liquidation, in a proceeding to which the Attorney General of California is a party.

IX. Limitation on corporate activities

No substantial part of the activities of this corporation shall consist of the carrying on of propaganda, or otherwise attempting to influence legislation, nor shall this corporation participate in, or intervene in (including the publishing or distributing of statements), any political campaign on behalf of any candidate for public office.

IN WITNESS WHEREOF, the undersigned, including the persons hereinabove named as the first directors, have executed these Articles of Incorporation on _____ , 19_____ .

This chart reviews the advantages and disadvantages of the different business structures.

SOLE PROPRIETORSHIPS

ADVANTAGES	DISADVANTAGES
Ease of formation	Unlimited personal liability
Low start-up costs	Lack of continuity
Least regulation	Difficult to raise money or get grants
Owner control	Tax disadvantage for high profits
All profits to owner	

PARTNERSHIP

ADVANTAGES	DISADVANTAGES
Ease of formation	Unlimited personal liability and liability for partners' debts
Low start-up costs	Lack of continuity
Broader management base	Divided authority—lack of extensive control
Shared responsibility and losses	Difficult to raise additional capital or get grants
Limited outside regulation	Hard to find suitable partners
No direct tax on business	Possibility of personal difficulties
Satisfaction and benefits of working with someone	Tax disadvantages for high profits

CORPORATIONS

ADVANTAGES	DISADVANTAGES
Limited liability	Closely regulated
Possible tax advantages	Most expensive form to organize
Continuous existence	Charter restrictions
Legal entity	Extensive record keeping necessary
Ownership transferable	Double taxation

The law does distinguish between a small, closely held corporation and a large public corporation, with the former less strictly regulated. You can achieve the advantage of a partnership (passing losses through to your individual return) by opting for a Sub-Chapter S corporation. Defamation and invasion of privacy, breach of warranty claims, and author litigation soften in the corporate context. Because of the unusual number and complexities of legal problems facing publishers, often your best form of doing business is corporate. These legal structures play like a deck of cards when entrepreneuring—a non-profit corporation could associate with a for-profit corporation on a book project. As an example, I received this announcement of a publisher–distributor arrangement in a recent Arizona Historical Society (a non-profit corporation) newsletter. (Donning Company, I assume, is a for-profit corporation.)

Order your 'Diamond' and save now

The Donning Company/Publishers has announced the publication of *Diamond in the Rough: An Illustrated History of Arizona*, by Marshall Trimble. In his own inimitable style, Arizona's cowboy historian presents the history, legends and lore of the Grand Canyon State. Over 400 photographs—many from the collections of the Arizona Historical Society and some never before published—highlight Trimble's colorful narrative. Through an arrangement with the Donning Company, the Arizona Historical Society will be the exclusive distributor of this deluxe 9" x 12" volume for 6 months and will offer it to AHS members at a 20% discount.

Business Name: Trademarks and Tradenames

Hand in hand with your business structure goes your business name. What's in a name? Plenty.

Tradename disputes pop up daily:

- the United States Olympic Committee legally barred all commercial and promotional uses of the word "Olympic."
- Miss Piggy's owners squealed when Booth, Maine, celebrated its bicentennial with a Miss Piggy Pageant to locate the "most beautiful" pig.
- two condom companies dickered in court about who had the right to use "Rubber Ducky" to promote its condom sales (National Law Journal, June 27, 1988).
- a Maryland District Court judge stopped Quality Inn's use of "McSheep Inns," despite Quality's argument that it connoted a Scottish thrift theme. This extended McDonald's trademark past the food industry (National Law Journal, October 17, 1988).

Your name's integrity and its public association with your books, creates an important, if intangible, asset: *goodwill.*

American trademark law (a variety of unfair competition theories) protects words, symbols, or other characteristics of work that have become symbolic of the person or company as the source. The terms "trademark" (a product name) and "service mark" (a service name) are used interchangeably. Trademark protection applies to words, symbols, and other markings or design elements that the public associates with a particular producer, as well as other protections.

Historically, trademarks gave information about the maker of goods:

- Etruscan cheese was marked with the sign of the moon.
- pottery at the ancient site of Ur had identifying marks.

- George Washington was granted a trademark for his particular brand of flour.

Attention is focused when you hear some publishing names: Green Tiger, Milkweed, Spinster's Ink, Tor, Orchard, Ten Speed. Through association with their products, they imply a particular image, and the consumer is led to expect a certain type of product based upon that image.

There are both federal and state trademark statutes. Since you do business nationally, depending upon a state registration is like wearing a torn raincoat in a rain shower: it gives some protection, simply and cheaply, and initially, when you have only a little money, it's adequate. But, in the long run, you are exposed to the elements.

You or your lawyer can find a state-by-state summary of trademark and unfair competition law, as well as false advertising practices and related issues, in a new publication guide, *State Trademark*, by the United States Trademark Association, a Clark Boardman Publication (435 Hudson Street, New York, NY 10014).

The advantages of a federal trademark are:

- greater protection.
- nationwide protection.
- broader coverage.
- possibly a treble damage award, if you win a suit for infringement.
- attorney's fees, if the infringer acts in bad faith.

Federal trademarks (the law is called the Lanham Act) require the use of marks in commerce between states, or with foreign nations, or Indian tribes. As stated earlier, a trademark is a visible symbol identifying and distinguishing your goods from the similar goods of another. It also can be a word, name (Sunoco®, Kodak®), a phrase or sign or symbol (flying red horse, muscular arm with hammer). There are also common-law trademark rights, rights you get without registering, that give you some protection.

Federal Trademark

If you sell books or attend book marketing seminars in two or more states, you've established interstate use of your name and eligibility for a federally registrable mark. This interstate name use must be done before you can file an application to register the mark in the United States Patent and Trademark Office. An informational pamphlet and applications can be obtained from the Patent and Trademark Office (Washington D.C. 20231), or the Superintendent of Documents, United States Government Printing Office (North Capitol and H Streets, Washington D.C., 20401). Longevity of use shortens the process.

Don't bother to start the federal application process until you've done a preliminary search to determine whether a conflicting mark is in use. One way to do that is to work through private companies established to service the need. Here's an ad that appeared in the Arizona Bar Journal for such a company.

Only experienced trademark lawyers handle the federal application process. A search report for identical or similar marks can result in a $100 to $250 charge; in my experience, the searchers want the client to have chosen more than one name. The application process itself requires the first dates of use of the mark anywhere, a filing fee of $175 per class, and an examination by a trademark lawyer on the Patent and Trademark Office staff, which can take six to twelve months after filing. Sometimes there might be technical objections or a refusal to register because of a previously registered mark. When the application is approved, it is published in the U.S. Patent and Trademark Office Official Gazette in order to allow anyone to oppose the registration if he or she believes the mark will damage them.

Getting the green light sometimes takes a couple of years.

State Tradenames

The state registration fees vary from $10 to $25, a cheaper way initially.

Two state applications for name registration are reproduced here. Often these applications are not examined for prior conflicts, although the State of Arizona does a limited examination. State registration evidences (although it is rebuttable) exclusive trademark rights in that state. The forms and information can be obtained from your Secretary of State.

If most of your sales occur in the four Southwestern states (Arizona, New Mexico, Utah, Colorado), you could achieve some protection by registering in

ARIZONA

APPLICATION
FOR REGISTRATION OF TRADE NAME
(A.R.S. Title 44, Chapter 10, Article 3.1)

Telephone_____   Approved_____

Be it known that, _____
_____
(Name of Applicant)

check one

☐ Person   ☐ Firm   ☐ Foundation   ☐ Foreign Corporation licensed to do business in this state
☐ Partnership   ☐ Association   ☐ Federation
☐ Corporation   ☐ Society   ☐ Organization

hereby makes application for registration of the name, title or designation under which such applicant is operating by filing the following statements with the Secretary of State of Arizona:

1. a. Name of applicant(s) _____
_____

   b. Arizona business address _____
     (Street No. or Box No.)   (Street Name)

   _____
     (City)   (State)   (Zip)

2. If incorporated, state of incorporation_____

3. Name, title or designation to be registered _____
_____
_____

4. General nature of business conducted _____
_____

5. The date the name, title or designation was first used by the applicant in business operations within this state is_____
   (Month)   (Day)   (Year)

_____
(Applicant's Printed Name)

Subscribed and sworn to before me this_____day of _____19_____

_____
(Applicant Sign Here)   (title)

My Commission Expires: _____   _____
    Notary Public

those states. One of the most common legal problems I handle for businesses seems to be appropriation of a business name by another organization in the same state. When businesses have state-registered their tradename, that resolves most intrastate conflicts.

If another company begins to use your business name, have your lawyer send a letter to the effect that your rights in the name are being infringed and the continued use of the name will confuse the public. Like anything else, you have to maintain this right by use. Do not abandon it. Be particularly careful if you license someone else to use your mark; trademark rights have been lost when a trademark became synonymous in the public's mind with the product itself, that is, it became generic.

Some words began life as a trademark brand name, then acquired a generic meaning for a type of product or service, such as aspirin, kleenex, cellophane, escalator. Be sure the public distinguishes between your name and a common descriptive name. (Xerox® repeatedly runs ads addressing this issue.)

For more information, read two excellent articles by William M. Buchard, "How to Get and Keep a Tradename," in *Law and the Arts* (Volume 8, No. 2, 1983) as well as "Solving Common Problems Arising from the Use of Trademarks in the Arts," by William M. Buchard and William M. Hart in *Law and the Arts* (Volume 10, No. 2, Winter 1986).

Additional Comments for Periodicals, et al.

Even if you're not publishing books, but instead publish a weekly give-away or a magazine, the same considerations regarding legal structure and tradename apply. In the case of tradenames, your good name is literally worth money.

Acquisition & Contract Basics 3

T he editor first inspects the literary property to discover the nature of that property. Second, the editor estimates the literary property's potential by mentally transforming it from one form to another. A sample literary property best illustrates this process.

This proposal, along with a few chapters, lands on an acquisitions editor's desk (yours, perhaps) one Monday morning. It looks like a hot property, with its themes of land disputes, ceremonialism, witchcraft, and the like.

> This story begins near an old Navajo forkstick hogan, which was crumbling to the ground. Anthropologists and archaeologists identified this ancient primitive dwelling as being built around the years A.D. 900 to 1,000 by the ancestors of the great Navajo chief, Zarcillos Largo. It contained many objects: a wolfskin, a Navajo medicine bundle, a hand-written record of the Navajos' migration over the Bering Strait as told to a possessed Navajo in 1980, a slab of rock with a recent pictograph of Spider Woman, a buckskin sack of rare corn kernels from the Four Corners area, and a sash of aboriginal design.
>
> By the hogan is a *yei* (Navajo god-figure) dancer, his neck ruffed in juniper boughs. He is stamping his feet to the beat of a non-existent drum. He bears an uncommon resemblance to the Navajo Tribal Chairman. His companion, a black-painted-faced, long-haired kachina dancer from Hopi,

bears a resemblance to the Hopi Tribal Chairman. The Hopi kachina said to the *yei* dancer "when that old hogan goes, the Navajo land claims vanish and Hopis win." An old Navajo woman, a tribal politician and recipient of the Nobel Peace prize, Annie Wauneka, watches the activity.

A medicine bundle, loaned to the author only for carbon dating by a living medicineman, Beshikii Estitie, is proposed by the author for use on a jacket cover that incorporates a drawing of the medicine bundle's contents, the two dancers, the medicineman wearing the wolf skin, and Annie Wauneka.

You, the acquisition editor, know (or learn) the following:

- the Navajos and Hopis have been involved for centuries in land disputes.
- Spider Woman is a ceremonial figure involved in Navajo weaving.
- the author's proposed title is *Beshikii Etsitie's Hogan*
- a wolfskin is associated with witchcraft.

This work is riddled with legal problems. The acquisitions editor must think about this project's market potential and must also pinpoint the work's legal problems. Any contract for this property must include a wide grant of rights; an iron-clad warranty, indemnity, and permission clause; and absolute publisher control of the title and text.

Before contracting for this work, the editor must consider whether it will be too overrun with legal problems to be worthwhile. A few of the potential problems are: the use of a living person's name in the title; the question of whether the medicineman is a collaborator or informant on the project; whether the bundle use or information exceeds the author–medicineman agreement; the defamatory nature of the wolfskin; the commercial appropriation of the likeness of the individuals depicted on the cover; invasion of the medicineman's privacy; the pictograph and the handwritten record, which could infringe a copyright; and more. The editor learns that the author, an ex-hippie, lives in a hogan near the reservation and is supported by his veteran's disability check. Not much indemnification available there, regardless of the strength of the warranty. If these issues can be resolved, and the market potential is promising, however, the acquiring editor may choose to contract with the author for its publication.

Once the publisher has contracted for the work, it can commercially exploit various subsidiary rights and licenses, after the legal problems are cleaned up.

A license is a spin-off agreement that gives another a slice of the literary pie. That term can include an appropriation of character rights to do a screenplay, film, musical, television movie; translations in foreign countries; and book clubs or anthology rights, among others. The proposed title could follow the work into a screenplay, television, movie, or film. The *yei* and kachina figures could be merchandised on t-shirts, posters, and so on.

I admit this is a wild example, but it should get you brainstorming when a proposal hits your desk.

Introduction to Contracts

A contract is an exchange of promises between two or more people, enforceable by law. The spectrum of contracts a publishing concern makes includes those with authors, agents, printers, typesetters, fulfillment companies, translators, artists, partners, distributors, book clubs, motion picture studios, to name just a few. Contractual clauses differ, depending on the product or service contracted for.

There are five essential ingredients to a legally enforceable contract:

- offer.
- acceptance.
- consideration.
- competence.
- legality.

An *offer* sounds like: "I will pay you $150 to write an article on the humor of Evan Mecham." An *acceptance* sounds like: "Okay." Sometimes, you can accept an offer only by taking action; that's what happens with reward offers. An offer can be withdrawn at any time before acceptance. Once an offer is accepted, a contract is formed and the offer cannot be withdrawn.

Consideration is what the parties to a contract promise to give each other. This usually has a dollar-and-cents value. For example, "*Small Words* will give you $1,000 to develop a new type font within six months."

Beware of making a contract with the insane or demented, and those rendered mentally incompetent by reason of excessive use of drugs or alcohol. These people lack the "capacity" to make a contract. Age is also a factor in determining *competence.* As the rights and responsibilities of minors have increased, some states hold minors to business contracts, but some states still do not.

Obviously, contracts to break the *law* will not be enforced by the courts. If your state law forbids pornography, a contract between an author and a publisher to write and publish such a book would be unenforceable.

Case Incident:

The owner of *Small Words* fueled up the jeep to drop off publications at the local McHenry's newsstand. On the way, the owner stopped off at and snacked on doughnuts and then went into the local newspaper office to order some reprints of a recent overview of *Small Words.*

Several contracts were made that day: a gas contract with the station, a consignment contract with the magazine stand, breakfast contract with the doughnut company, and a special-order contract with the newspaper company.

Written and Oral Contracts

In some cases, a contract must be written in order to be enforceable:

- contracts for sale of goods valued at over $500.
- contracts that cannot be completed within one year (Statute of Frauds).
- contracts for sale of land.
- leases for longer than one year.
- certain other situations.

Case Incident:
When co-authors tried to force a publisher to honor an oral agreement to spend $30,000 on promotional advertisement, a New York court dismissed the author's claim as barred by the parole evidence rule, since the written agreement made no reference to a sum of money and only obligated the publisher to take out three ads (*Frankell v. Stein & Day, Inc.,* 470 F.Supp. 209 [1979].) The parole evidence rule disallows oral modifications to a written contract.

Under certain circumstances, even oral contracts for the sale of goods valued at over $500 are enforceable. (See DuBoff's *Book Publisher's Legal Guide,* p. 91 et seq., for a detailed discussion of the problems in this area and the Uniform Commercial Code.) If production of the order has begun, if the agreement is between "merchants" (people who are earning regular income from their work), and if the oral agreement is confirmed in writing and the confirmation is not objected to within ten (10) days of receipt of the writing, it may be enforceable. Too, if the buyer accepts goods valued at $500 or more, the agreement can be enforced.

Bear in mind that cables, letters, memos, and telegrams—informal as they are—can be treated as a contract as long as they are dated, signed by the party to be charged, identifies the parties, the price, and the goods or services. There are varying views on written versus oral contracts.

A lawyer wrote his son (a third-year law school student) this about contracts (excerpted from the Texas Bar Journal, November 1963):

Remember, there is no sure way to bind men together and keep them bound by any written instrument.

The only thing that binds men together is the fact that under all circumstances most men, without knowing what the other will do, will reach for the golden rope of justice, truth, decency and fairness and thereby bind themselves to every other person who grasps the same rope. This is the only combination that will endure.

That's one viewpoint.

Another opinion was expressed by Sam Goldwyn, the famous Hollywood movie producer, who said, "an oral contract isn't worth the paper it's written on."

Always follow this principle: put your contracts in writing. Problems abound in proving an oral arrangement, even if it's one that's enforceable. Even an incomplete written contract can promote understanding about who is to do what, when, and how. And if the parties to an oral contract can't agree on its terms, guess who decides? A court.

Martha's Maxims About Contracts

Keep these maxims in mind when you are thinking about, looking at, or considering a contract.

Maxim #1: Any written contract proposed and drafted by the other party is in their favor.

Maxim #2: Nobody looks at a contract after it's signed unless a problem develops between the two parties.

Maxim #3: Enforcement of oral contracts boils down to a swearing contest.

Maxim #4: A standard contract can always be changed—well, almost always.

Maxim #5: A party in a hurry to get you to sign their contract usually wants to hide something.

Maxim #6: A rushed contractual deal falls apart at the same rate of speed.

Before Contracting

Before entering into any contract for services, whether of an agent, printer, bookbinder, typesetter, or publicist, do the following:

- determine what's available.
- network with others who obtain services in that field.
- visit and talk with the potential providers.
- compare price quotations and look for hidden costs.
- check them out with current customers.
- weigh your criteria (price, quality, style, knowledge).
- define the service you are looking for and the level of quality.
- review the work done for others.

Read the fine print and if it refers to trade customs, read those. Read the fine print on the back of your suppliers' purchase orders, the printing order, and the advertising quotation you're about to sign.

Before you begin negotiations on any contract, weigh these factors:

- the parties' respective power.
- whether one or both of the parties is a rising star, falling star, or in the limelight.
- the parties' respective knowledge about contracting.
- desire of each to be associated with the other.
- the parties' negotiating skills.
- the financial condition of each party.
- the availability of goods and services elsewhere.
- the status of each of the parties.

- the work itself.
- the reasonableness of any time-lines.

If someone you plan to do business with proposes a contract to you, insist that you receive the contract prior to the commencement of the business relationship.

Do not be rushed into signing a contract someone else has drafted. This telephone conversation repeats itself at least once a month in my office:

> My secretary: "Mr. Doitnow has to talk to you."
> "Now?"
> "Now," she says, suppressing a giggle in her voice. I only have a second or two to wonder what Mr. Doitnow is up to now.
> "Hello," I say.
> "Oh, I got you. Boy, it's a good thing. Mr. Osaha's flying in at 1:00 today to sign off on these contracts, and that only gives us an hour or two to look them over."
> I interrupt and glance at the note my secretary passes me that my next appointment cancelled. Am I glad or not?
> "What contract? Who's Mr. Osaha?"
> There's a sigh at the other end.
> "Well, I'd been meaning to get over to your office but I've been out of town." He pauses. "My gopher's on his way over to deliver the papers. You see, I didn't know if it would happen or not, so, well, like, I didn't want to take up your time if it wasn't going to happen."
> My secretary puts the papers on my desk. I note that the draft typing symbol in the left corner is three weeks ago, and the thing is twenty-three pages, without exhibits. Mr. Doitnow's had it at least a week, I guess.
> "It just came."
> "Oh good. Well, you've got it now," as if he was suddenly relieved of all responsibility.
> I found one of the parties is Mr. Doitnow's brother-in-law who's boon-doggled him before. "Noitall's involved?" I ask incredulously.
> "Well, sort of." He pauses. "But there's a provision in the contract someplace, can't remember where, that he only puts up the money."
> "Do you remember what clause?"
> "Oh no, you've got the contract," he says confidently.
> "You didn't keep a copy?"
> "Nope. Never even read it all the way through."

And so on. Mr. Doitnow is one of those clients who complains about the amount lawyers charge for their services.

Proposed Contracts

You should read the proposed contract without the other party there. Make a copy, then highlight or underline any terms that you do not understand. Sometimes, if you read aloud the unclear sections, or type those sentences double-spaced, the terms become clear. If there is a reference to a trade practice, find out what the trade practice is. Once the cloud lifts from the ambiguous terms, go back (do I hear groans and mutters?) and read the entire contract again.

Next, list the involvement you expect to have with the other party regarding this project. Then play devil's advocate and see how the contract terms might adversely affect these plans. Maybe they aren't even covered. Consider how the contract resolves any conflicts. Finally, determine what areas of the contract you object to, why you object to those various clauses, and what your alternative term would be.

Remember, if you can't strike an onerous term from the contract, you *can* water it down. Usually, a watered-down provision:

- is shorter in duration, i.e., one year instead of three.
- covers a smaller geographic or other area, i.e., the Southwest instead of the United States.
- has a condition attached to it, i.e., failure to do X results in a dollar penalty and a forfeiture of the contract.

A simple way to change a contract without having it reprinted or retyped is to put one line through the deleted areas and print or type in the additions. Each of those should be initialed. The purpose of the single line is so that the parties can see what has been changed.

3. The Manuscript. The Author agrees to deliver to the Publisher not later than _____ , an original ~~and a carbon~~ of a complete typewritten script $\mathscr{SM}$ M.B. **of the Work in final form satisfactory to the Publisher, and it is mutually agreed that the minimum and maximum lengths of the Work shall be from _____ to _____ words.**

In the matter of contract interpretation, written additions will take precedence over conflicting printed provisions. Almost every contract (except perhaps a General Motors Credit Company agreement) contains agreed-upon individualized changes.

DO NOT sign a contract simply because the other party says that this or that problem can be taken care of later. That person could leave the company and you would still be bound by the terms left unresolved.

Try to be in the position of proposing your own contract to the other party. Standard contracts serve several purposes:

- they protect the publishing house's expenses and risk in a work.
- they provide an initial framework for discussion.
- they control the negotiation.

Unless it is a one-person operation, the financial manager(s) needs to evaluate the standard contracts for continued profitability and to fine-tune the *maximum* royalties and advances that can be met.

Know this by heart: don't utilize a form contract until it is adapted to your particular needs and you understand each term and why it is there.

A Summary of Contract Contents

Contract contents (and this includes documents entitled "assignment," "lease," "license," "agreement," or "contract") include the following:

- parties (mailing address along with correct names and the status of the party, where the party is not an individual—that is, corporate, partnership, or representative capacity).
- statement of the consideration to be paid.
- a description of the property to be involved, which should be as specific as possible.
- duration of the agreement.
- payment and other performance, including any security for performance, interest, amount, method of payment and terms, and sometimes time and place of payment.
- excuses for non-performance or failure of consideration, such as acts of God, war, civil disturbance, or death.
- default or breach, including provisions that time is of the essence, remedies, anticipatory breach, what acts or omissions equal breach, and the effect of a waiver.
- miscellaneous matters, such as accounting, bonds, definitions, insurance, indemnification, risk of loss, passage of title, time for taking possession of property, costs and attorney's fees, liquidated damages.
- arbitration.
- choice of law.
- severability clause.
- modification of contract.
- termination of the agreement.

Be very careful to put in the effective date of the instrument at the beginning of the instrument. Often, the effective date is prior to the actual signing by all the parties.

If you include other documents as part of that instrument, mark them with consecutive letters, i.e., Attachment A, B, C. Refer to them in that fashion in the agreement, attach them, and incorporate them by reference. Be sure that persons signing for a corporation or in a representative capacity indicate their status and authority to sign the same, i.e., XYZ Publishing Corporation by Susie Q., Publisher. Where authority is a touchy situation, be sure to examine the board resolution that authorizes signatories. (For most formal contracts, I prefer to have the signatures acknowledged.)

Be sure each party has an executed copy of the document. Keep this within reach and in a safe place. Put it in a file that includes papers involving this particular transaction. If you're not organized by nature, or your operation is too small for a secretary, use accordian files with broad subject categories. If there's been legal involvement, give the lawyer an executed copy, or the original, as well. Lawyers can usually locate their files on old matters more easily than publishers.

Get the details of every major transaction in writing. For example, a publishing concern should not engage a firm or person to design, distribute, or package a book or other publication without a written, signed document setting forth the rights, job requirements, fees, delivery date, and the rest. This protects you and informs the other party of exactly what you expect. Put all of it in writing *before* the first task is undertaken and any money paid. This avoids the horrible incidents that contribute to lawyers' stock of war stories.

Many of the contract provisions relative to a literary property are the same as those of any other contract:

- party description.
- the recitals describing the project or subject matter in general terms.
- assignments.
- law to govern.
- arbitration of disputes.
- date of execution.
- signatures.

Repetitive Contract Provisions

Let's cover *now* those repetitive provisions found in more formal contracts. (Other covenants [absolute, unconditional promises], conditions [a possible duty to perform], and warranties appear in following chapters.)

To begin:

> **AGREEMENT made** _____ , **19**_____ , **between** _____ **referred to as Publisher, a corporation having its principal place of business at** _____ , _____ **and** _____ **of** _____ , **City of** _____ , **County of** _____ , **State of** _____ , **referred to as Author (copyright owner, photographer, graphic artist, cartoonist, book distributor, fulfillment service, and so forth).**

> ### RECITALS
> **1. Publisher desires to (describe project) referred to as** _____ **subject to the terms and conditions hereafter.**
> **2.** _____ **desires to perform this service for publisher.**
> **3. For these reasons and for other good and lawful reasons and in consideration of the covenants set forth below and these Recitals which are incorporated therein, the parties agree as follows:**

The parties' description identifies them and facilitates future contact. It also indicates the parties' particular capacities so it is clear that the proper signators executed the contract and bound the parties. The shorthand designation throughout the contract of "Author" and "Publisher" is amplified in the recitals, as do the terms "Book" or "Work," which encompass the entire job concept without restating it. Sometimes the recitals need to be part of the contract's terms rather than outside of it. Therefore, add language that indicates that the contract incorporates the recitals.

I use the term "boilerplate" to refer to "standard and usual" contract provisions. (The dictionary refers to boilerplate in journalism as syndicated copy in the form of stereotype plates, used especially by weekly papers, while my *Black's Law Dictionary* does not define it—I now have more than a passing concern about my use of the term boilerplate.) Still, utilizing my definition, all contracts should end with boilerplate clauses:

> **This Agreement shall be interpreted according to the law of the State of**
> _____ **.**
>
> **This Agreement shall be binding upon the heirs, executors, administrators, and assigns of Author [or other term] and upon the successors and assigns of the publishers, but no assignment except to an affiliate of the publishers shall be binding on either of the parties without the written consent of the other.**

Or (preferably):

> **This Agreement shall be binding upon the heirs, executors, administrators and assigns of Author and upon the successors and assigns of the Publishers as well as any publishing imprint subsidiary to or associated with the Publishers.**
> **This Agreement constitutes the complete understanding of the parties. No modification or waiver of any provision shall be valid unless in writing and signed by both parties.**
>
> **Interpretation**
> **Regardless of the place of its physical execution, this Agreement shall in all respects be interpreted, construed, and governed by the laws of the State of _____ .**
> **Arbitration.**
> **If any difference shall arise between the Author and the Publisher touching the meaning of this Agreement or the rights and liabilities of the parties thereto, the same shall be referred to the arbitration of two persons (one to be named by each party), or their mutually agreed umpire, in accordance with the Rules of the American Arbitration Association; judgment on the award rendered may be entered in any court having jurisdiction thereof.**
> **Disputes-Attorneys' Fees**
> **In any action upon this agreement, including litigation and arbitration,**

the party which prevails will have all attorneys' fees and costs paid by the losing party.

IN WITNESS WHEREOF the parties hereto have executed and duly witnessed this Agreement as of the day and year written below.

Name: _____   Name: _____

              Author   Publisher

The applicable-law provision becomes important if you're located in New Mexico and the printing's done in Nevada. It's legally sensible to interpret the contract by your state laws, as your lawyer is likely to be the most familiar with them. On the other hand, if you're talking about a book publishing contract, New York has the greatest body of law relating to this subject; sometimes, when the choice of law becomes an issue, parties opt to follow New York law.

The binding of others becomes important if, for example, your printer (who has a sole proprietorship) dies. Then, that particular event does not require contract renegotiation. "Successor" means someone who purchases or otherwise acquires the business (such as a creditor in bankruptcy). An assignment means a transfer or giving over to another of the whole of any property, except that it usually means the rights in or connected with the property, as distinguished from the particular item of property.

You can't give a court power it does not have. Therefore, a state court couldn't hear a copyright infringement case; only federal courts have that power.

I like to add "reasonable" attorney's fees, because that's the court's standard for assessing attorney's fees to a losing party. In fact, in most states, there's a law that allows the prevailing party to recover reasonable attorney's fees for *any* breach of contract, regardless of whether it's stated in the contract or not; it doesn't hurt to have it in there. However, I've had clients ludicrously hang their litigation hat on this provision in a dispute with the other party by taking the "I'm right and you're totally wrong," and the "I don't care what my attorney's fees are, you'll end up paying them," attitude. If there's a dispute, usually each party considers itself to be right. The prevailing party may be difficult to determine unless the problem is exceedingly simple.

Case Incident:
A dispute arises between a printer and a publisher regarding the quality of the print job (from the publisher's perspective) and the change orders the publisher gave the printer. A court could award each some monetary relief.

Arbitration Provision
Consider adding an arbitration clause to your standard contracts. Remember Abraham Lincoln's comment on litigation:

Discourage litigation. Persuade your neighbors to compromise whenever you can. Point out to them how the nominal winner is often a real loser—in fees, expenses, and waste of time.

As you may recall, there is a suggested arbitration clause in the boilerplate discussion. Here are others:

> **The parties agree that, should a dispute arise between them in any manner concerning this contract (except to matters that involve copyright), and said involves the sum of $10,000 or less in money damages only, exclusive of interest, costs, or attorney's fees, they will submit the matter to binding arbitration pursuant to the _____ Rules for Compulsory Arbitration and the decision of the arbitrator(s) shall be final and binding upon the parties.**

or:

> **The parties agree that, should a dispute arise between them in any manner concerning this contract, the parties agree to a private, voluntary process whereby a mutual third party decision-maker is selected by the disputants and renders a decision that is binding up to the sum of $_____ or less in money damages exclusive of interest, costs, or attorney's fees pursuant to the American Arbitration Association's dispute resolution guidelines.**

or:

> **The parties agree that should a dispute arise between them in any manner concerning this contract (except for copyright matters), a court-annexed arbitration, which must be resorted to in the jurisdiction whose law applies to this contract prior to going to court, shall be exhausted by the parties.**

These suggested provisions on arbitration are tricky. Arizona requires compulsory arbitration, and under some new Supreme Court rules, a certain amount of money must be involved in order to begin arbitration. Arizona law requires each Superior Court to have arbitration on cases filed where the parties agree that the disputed amount does not exceed $50,000. There's also a serious question as to whether an arbitration clause could divest federal courts of copyright jurisdiction. You may be sued for performance, for instance, to get a book published sooner than planned (or to get it published at all), rather than just monetary damages. The arbitrator's decision is final and binding upon the parties. For further discussion, order the American Bar Association (1800 M Street, N.W., Suite 200–S, Washington, D.C. 20036) Standing Committee on Dispute Resolution's publication, *Alternative Dispute Resolution Primer.*

A problem with arbitration is that you pay the arbitrators as well as the lawyers. However, arbitration lessens the threat of a lawsuit.

Signatures and Initials

Here's a signature line from a major publisher's contract. Some other contracts include a line for the author's social security number and the publisher's employer I.D. number.

AUTHOR

_____

(Signed)   Social Security Number

_____   _____

     Citizenship   Date of Birth

By _____

     Contracting Officer

Date _____

Initial each page of a multipage contract and ask the other party to do the same. Also initial individual typed or handwritten provisions or riders.
Example:

Sm 60 M.B.

The Author shall receive copies sold at a discount of 55 percent or more of the catalog retail price, the prevailing royalty less one-half of one percent for each one percent discount of more than 54 percent.

M.B. 59 Sm

If you later need to modify the contract or waive any provision, propose this by a letter agreement, specifying the paragraph of the original agreement that is to be modified or waived, and spell out how it is to be changed. Ask the other party to sign both the original and one copy of the letter agreement and return to you; retain the other copy.

Dear Typesetter:

Clause 2 of our contract, dated May 1990 for a *Legal Guide for Small Presses* provides a deadline of May 31, 1990, for the typesetting for that project. This clause is extended to June 15, 1990, per your request, and a reduction in the price to be paid for your services, from $750 to $570, is agreed upon. Please execute the letter at the bottom, date it, and return the original to me; keep the copy for your file.

Sincerely,

XYZ Publishing

Literary Property Checklist

Before I attack the cornerstone of any publishing concern—the author's contract—glance through this checklist of matters to consider when drafting an agreement relative to any literary property.

_____ PARTIES PRESCRIBED
- Names and addresses
- Status and capacity
- Designation

_____ RECITALS (Describes project in general terms)

_____ GRANTS OF RIGHTS
- Copyright released to publisher?
- Copyright retained by author?
  - types of rights?
    - hardcover, full-length edition
    - paperback edition
    - licensing rights
      - serializations
      - book club and secondary publishing rights
      - foreign licensing
      - book clubs, condensed forms
      - programmed instruction
      - dramatizations, stage, etc.
      - advertising
  - where publisher exercises these rights?
  - languages published in and approval of translation?
  - duration of rights granted publisher?
  - exclusive or joint rights?
  - reservation of some rights to author (commonly dramatizations)?
  - author's approval over licensing contracts by publisher and receipt of copies?

_____ DELIVERY OF WORK, etc.
- Delivery of manuscript, date and length
- Retyping of manuscript
- Illustrations
- Permission for inclusion of copyright material
- Termination
- Time of essence

_____ WARRANTIES AND INDEMNITIES
- Author owns work, not libelous, doesn't infringe other's copyrights
- Author agrees to indemnify publisher
- Infringement of work

_____ CORRECTION OF PROOF

_____ PUBLICATION OF WORK AND COPYRIGHT
- Time within which to publish

- Use of copyright notice and registration

_____ ROYALTIES AND OTHER PROCEEDS TO AUTHOR

- Advances
  - amount and method of payment
  - policy of recoupment
- Royalties
  - percentage
  - basis for percentage
    - net
    - wholesale
    - discounts
  - licensing percentages
    - book club, condensations, etc.

_____ FREE COPIES

_____ ADVERTISING AND PROMOTION

_____ STATEMENTS AND PAYMENTS

- When Reports Made
- Reserves

_____ REVIEW COPIES

_____ OPTION

_____ COPIES OF AGREEMENTS

_____ ASSIGNMENTS

_____ LAW TO GOVERN

_____ BANKRUPTCY

_____ DISCONTINUANCE OF PUBLICATION

- Publisher's right
- Notice to author
- Purchase by author
- Payment to author

_____ ARBITRATION OF DISPUTES

_____ NOTICES

_____ WAIVER OR MODIFICATION

_____ RIDERS AND ADDITIONAL CLAUSES

_____ DATE OF EXECUTION

_____ SIGNATURES

To repeat myself, a preliminary consideration when drafting any contract concerns itself first with parties: participation and involvement by all essential parties, the parties' capacity to contract (if corporate or similar identities, the authority and power to contract; if an agent or guardian or other party acting in a representative capacity, their authority and power to do the same). A deceased poet's surviving husband may not be her only heir.

Beware of special property interests in certain states, such as community property. In Arizona, either spouse can bind the community property by their business act.

Determine if there are federal, state, or local laws governing a contract's form and content, and the underlying business transactions. For instance, if your small press decides to develop an educational text for use in secondary schools, you must be aware that nearly half the states buy educational texts through an adoption process and that these procedures vary statewide.

About Authors

The starting pitcher in publishing is the author, even in self-publishing.

The term "author" is deceptively simple. Varieties include collaborators creating (*plural* authors) a joint work; an author who later adapts the first author's material to a different medium, or translates it, or adds illustrations or music; and a corporate author. Each may have a literary agent. The publisher can be both author and agent. Sometimes, there's a book packager, who plays several roles simultaneously. This octopus-like structure ends with the ultimate user of the literary property; its tentacles can be barnacled with lawyers.

My bottom-line position is, always trust your author.

And never trust your author.

Both of these precepts are necessary to a healthy and vigorous relationship with your author (or *anyone else with whom you do business*). If you seek out an herbalist to cure your shingles and he gives you a blend of herbs and who-knows-what to infuse, that relationship requires both trust and skepticism. It's the same with publishing. On the one hand, the author is an experienced writer, knowledgable about fair use, restriction-on-materials rules, responsive to deadlines, efficient to work with, and so forth. But authors can also be unrealistic, perhaps expecting a monograph on *The Navajo Witch Purge of 1878,* published by a scholarly press, to be on the bestseller list. Authors are human.

Publishing concerns are run by humans.

Don't forget, too, the publishing range: self-publishing to Warner Books. This includes a spectrum of competence, experience, financing, and support staff. No one takes an entrance exam to become an author or a publisher, or applies for a license, nor is required to attend any special training or school. Thus, the standards of performance can vary greatly.

Authors fail to deliver manuscripts on time; turn in lousy manuscripts, or ones riddled with defamation or invasion-of-privacy problems; demand marketing input; neglect their own work while they tell the publisher what he or she should be doing; and sell something that they don't own.

Publishers, likewise, fail to publish manuscripts, skimp on copyediting, fail to exploit the work, fail to print it, or publish it with errors.

Even if you've worked with an author on numerous publishing projects on the basis of an oral agreement and a hug, things can change with a new spouse or illness or real/perceived offensive behavior of the publisher to the author.

Thus, if you go into the arrangement trusting your author, but utilize your contract as a backup for unsettled disagreements and the unknown, you're protected.

If you're a self-publisher, order Dan Poynter's *The Self Publishing Manual, How to Write, Print and Sell Your Own Book.* Poyntner has written over twenty books related to publishing and he explains things simply; that's why he's sold to book clubs, and had his books translated and condensed. Most importantly, he refuses to take a jerry-rigged approach to publishing.

Order his *Publishing Forms*, a collection of applications and information for the beginning publisher, which has one hundred-plus pages of forms and instructions, such as directory and copyright listings; *Business Letters for Publishers*; and lastly, for the purpose of these contract discussions, *Publishing Contracts on Disk.* The disk product covers twenty-two types of contracts, including:

- book contract
- co-publishing agreement
- book distribution contract
- agreement for sale of translation rights
- contract writer agreement
- agreements between:
  - publisher and translator.
  - publisher and illustrator.
- international book packaging agreement.
- sales representation agreement.
- literary agency agreement.
- partnership agreement.
- permission agreement.
- release forms.
- agreement for sale of merchandising rights.
- special markets purchase agreement.
- copyright agreement between author and magazine editor.
- agreement for paste up, layout and book design.
- writer–magazine agreement.

These form contracts *need to be customized* for your particular situation, but they save you a great deal of typing.

(Since Poynter's diskette works on IBM and workalikes using Microsoft Word, Wordperfect, and Wordstar, the customizing of a contract after you have read through the discussion is greatly enhanced. Not to niggle, but some minor inconsistencies exist in the forms. For instance, in contract number 19, paragraph 6, the artwork is treated as a work-for-hire, with the publisher owning the copyright, but later, in paragraph 14, the illustrator retains the ownership of the copyright.)

Legal Variations for Magazines, et al.

Newspapers, magazines, newsletters, and journals contract in a manner similar to publishers, and for many of the same services. Differences exist primarily as to the size of a job and its frequency. The concepts of work-for-hire, ownership of material, and use limits with regard to periodicals is discussed in later chapters.

Part I

The Generic Book Contract

Contracting for Work and Author's Responsibilities

4

Here's a thought-provoking quote about book contracts:

> The agreement between author and publisher is the cornerstone of their relationship. Care taken by them together to ensure that the contract really reflects in detail the nature of the book they are discussing pays off time and time again, not only in focusing early attention on the points of real substance, not only in avoiding subsequent unsettling disputes, but in giving the author the confidence he needs to let the publisher get on in equal confidence with his job to their mutual advantage. (from *Publishing Agreements,* by Charles Clark)

Your decision to publish is reached at an editorial meeting, by informal discussions, or just spur-of-the-moment, and needs to be recorded.* That's where the book contract comes into play.

Before you flip through these chapters looking for a complete contract, from recitals to signature, stop. My approach is to provide and discuss illustrative clauses.

---

*Not many manuscripts will experience the tortuous path from decision to publish to publication of Marvin Kitman's book, *I Am A VCR* [Random House 1988]: three title changes, six editors, three agents, two contracts, and two publishers. See the article in *Publishers Weekly* [July 22, 1988] "Idiotic Flip Side: The Kitman-Vaughan Letters," which excerpts the humorous and not-no-humorous letters between the publisher and the author, spanning the eighteen-year history of the project.

For a different slant, and complete contracts, see Lindsey on *Entertainment, Publishing and the Arts: Agreements and Law*. For other complete book publishing contracts, see the DuBoff and Perle–Williams texts. Here, you're provided with a spectrum of book contract provisions from which to pick, choose, and adapt to your publishing concern. I avoid setting forth a complete contract, because someone might not read the text, typeset the contract, and use it as their form. (I know that wouldn't be you.) Moon-shaped quilt pieces won't interlock with stars unless an overall plan carefully fits them in place.

With a standard provision, establish your negotiating jump-off point, which prevents your acquisitions editor from committing you to an unprofitable deal. A big publisher may have the ability to absorb a lost advance, plus the direct or indirect editorial costs that were poured into a quashed publishing project, but a small press that publishes only a few titles a year can founder under such a loss.

Before negotiating, know your maximum royalty and advance figures.* Establish an in-house requirement that standard contract variations be approved by your management group, not just a particular editor. If you commonly run into specific proposals from your prospective authors, which may be debatable as far as you're concerned, let your lawyer draft alternate contract provisions.

Your standard contract gets negotiations rolling. If the author wants changes, then the author's counter-proposal should be specific. By using a standard contract and approved variations, your publishing house controls the bargaining process.

If the author's clout leads you to add "reasonably satisfactory" to a particular contract, add a simple arbitration provision to cover disputes over both manuscript quality and marketing considerations. In arbitration, each party chooses an arbitrator and the two arbitrators select a third. Except from the arbitration process those situations where the manuscript exposes the publisher to legal liability, as there should be no obligation to arbitrate in that particular instance.

Recitals

Be sure to incorporate recitals in the agreement's body by some language to that effect:

> **For these reasons and others and in consideration of the covenants in this Agreement which incorporates these recitals, the parties agree as follows:**

In a book contract, consider setting forth in the recitals the project's parameters:

> *Recitals*
> **1. The Author has submitted for Publisher's consideration a book proposal, _____ chapters of a book, __ page outline. The working title of**

---

*Royalties are commonly based on either list price or net receipts; the percentage for the former is usually lower than for the latter. Also, advances are often calculated by figuring the total royalty the author will be likely to receive in the first year, and then offering half of that amount.

the proposed book is _____ and it is referred to in this Agreement as "the Book" (*preferably add more descriptive identification of the project*) _____.

2. Publisher desires to publish the completed book subject to the terms and conditions hereafter.

Delivery of a Satisfactory Manuscript

A critical element of any publishing agreement is the "satisfactory manuscript" clause:

> **The author agrees to deliver two complete copies (original and clean copy) of the manuscript of the work in the English language of approximately ____ words in length, satisfactory to the Publisher, together with any permissions required by this Agreement, and all photographs, illustrations, drawings, charts, maps, and indexes suitable for reproduction and necessary to the completion of the manuscript, not later than _____, *and* the author agrees to repay within sixty (60) days all amounts which may have been advanced under this Agreement if he/she does not deliver an acceptable manuscript.**

or:

> **The Author agrees to deliver a work original to the Author and provisionally titled _____, the complete manuscript, which shall be approximately (not less than, not more than) _____ words and shall be delivered in duplicate to the Publisher ready for the printer, together with any illustrations and/or other material as agreed between the Author and the Publisher under the terms of this Agreement not later than _____.**
>
> **The Publisher shall accept the work, provided that the manuscript meets the technical requirements of this Agreement and conforms, to a reasonable extent, to the book proposal and sample chapter through which the Author and the Publisher agreed upon the nature, scope, and style of the work, and as a result of which this Agreement was entered into.**

Emphasize the delivery of a satisfactory manuscript by placing this provision at the beginning. Without a satisfactory manuscript, the grant of rights (which often comes first in an Agreement) means nothing. With some projects and some writers, the work's length should be agreed upon to avoid excessive publication costs and editing haggles.

I recollect one consultation with a gentleman who wrote (as a ten-year retirement project) a 1,400-page manuscript on the subject of a Colorado bandit. He consulted me about copyright permissions.

A: "Ya' know I'm not goin' to let any publisher change a word, mind ya', not a word."

MB:	"But it's 1,400 pages long."
	Author nodded happily.
MB:	"That's a two-volume work."
A:	"I know; it's got every detail of his life in it."
MB:	And also numerous spelling and punctuation errors, passive voice, flawed syntax, long paragraphs, I thought. Still, buried in all that, was a thoroughly fascinating life story. "Are you interested in getting this published?" I asked, innocently.
A:	"Of course I am. Why else would I be sitting here talking to you?" he said to me in a tone that implied I was dense and maybe deaf.
MB:	"Do you want to know how to increase the chances of getting it published?"
A:	"Yes, yes," he said impatiently with a look like, lady, why do you really think I came in here?
MB:	"Then you'll need to do at least two things—one'll take time and the other, a little money."
A:	"Time I got a lot of—money's a different matter." He looked at his wife when he said money. They'd spent years traipsing over the West to find biographical material on the outlaw.
MB:	"First, reduce the manuscript to half its present length," I said, and, at his look of disbelief, I decided, What the hell, "and second, once it's a manageable size, pay a professional copyeditor to edit it for you."
A:	There was a long pause. A thunderbolt did not strike either of us. We chatted a bit more and then to my surprise, he asked me to show him what I meant.

I did—we copied a page, cut the text to half, and then edited it.

This story's point: an author's conditions about manuscript can spell trouble for any publisher who produces quality publications. And the lesson I learned: don't be so hasty to prejudge a person's potential response.

There're other fish to fry in the satisfactory manuscript arena. Agree early about the number and form of the graphic material (such as photographs, drawings, maps, tables, charts), indexes, and other front or back matter. Require that photographs, drawings, and maps be suitable for your retouching and reproduction. Be able to set type from tables and charts. Determine whose responsibility it is to provide the material; sometimes you'll provide some or all of that material, or you may elect to divide the costs and fees with the author.

I do not recommend adding the following chart *as printed matter* in your contract. Add it as a rider or side letter of agreement once you determine the money division. (An author or agent, seeing a blank list, will assume that the percentages are up for grabs.) Who provides photos and pays for same may not be negotiable depending upon your company policy, the scope or costs involved in the particular work, the project itself, or other factors.

The following additional materials shall be provided and paid for as indicated below:

	Provided by: (insert Publisher, Author, or mark N/A)	Costs & Fees Paid by:	
		Publisher	Author
photographs	_____	_____%	_____%
drawings	_____	_____%	_____%
maps	_____	_____%	_____%
tables	_____	_____%	_____%
charts	_____	_____%	_____%
index	_____	_____%	_____%
other illus.	_____	_____%	_____%

If it's a children's book, the author may expect you to pay for the illustrations. If the author's also the illustrator, then the author may ask for separate payment as illustrator. (See the graphic artist's contract in a later chapter.)

Since most contracting is based on a proposal and sample chapters, traditionally, the publishing commitment pivots upon the acceptance of the completed manuscript. It's advantageous to clearly define the manuscript you expect to receive, because that encourages the author's understanding and ability to meet those requirements. On this issue, authors have been known to howl and turn on the waterworks. The Author's Guild organized a panel titled "A New Look At Contracts," reported *Publishers Weekly* (November 20, 1987). Letty Cottin Pogrebin, an author-panelist, called the satisfactory manuscript clause "risk-free publishing." One agent, George Borchardt, likened the rejection of manuscripts under the satisfactory manuscript clause as "telling an editor that all the books he had worked on for four years were not really the books initially discussed and he must now return his past four years of salary." This agent opined that most publishers are not gougers, even though among them there may be "con men, crooks, and fools." Other panelists felt that the number of publishing staff involved with an author's project paved the road to rejection.

Earlier, in 1980, an Author's Guild Contract Committee Report concluded that the satisfactory manuscript clause victimized authors, since publishers used it to terminate contracts and to compel authors to repay advances, *regardless* of the manuscript's fitness for publication. The committee grouped the situations in which publishers terminated contracts using the lack of a "satisfactory manuscript" as the reason into:

- the manuscript's lack of professional competence and fitness for publication.
- a new estimate of the book's financial prospects.
- changes in the publisher's management, business policies, or financial conditions.
- diminuation of the book's appeal.

The term "satisfactory manuscript" is not clearly defined in most contracts. The *general rule*: it is the publisher's sole option to reject a manuscript as unsatisfactory and terminate the contract. (See *Random House, Inc. v. Gold*, 464 F.Supp 1306 [New York]. For a detailed discussion of this provision, see also "The Satisfactory Manuscript Clause of Book Publishing Contracts," by Mark Fowler, Columbia VLA *Journal of Law on the Arts*, Volume X:119.)

Some argue that the clause's legal effect is to "transform the contract into an option to publish."

Not a bad argument.

Developing case law has reduced, in some jurisdictions, the arbitrary use of satisfactory manuscript clauses. Some cases require that the publisher provide the author with either editorial criticism or assistance, and an opportunity to remedy the deficiencies; this approach focuses "unsatisfactory manuscript" rejection on literary factors rather than the publisher's financial situation. Be aware that the publishing house has a duty to edit, although few contracts are conditioned on the presence of a specific editor; publishing staff have been known to move around like gypsies.

Some authors request that the word "reasonable" qualify "satisfactory manuscript," or specify that "the manuscript is deemed acceptable if it is in substantial conformity with the quality of the proposal, which is incorporated by reference," or that the manuscript must be "in style and content, professionally competent and fit for publication." (See *Author's Guild Bulletin*, January-February, 1981.) Avoid these changes, as all dilute the publisher's standard.

Preserve your freedom to reject a manuscript for marketing and financial reasons, regardless of case-law trends, by adding "if supervening events or circumstances since the date of this agreement have, in the sole judgment of the publisher, materially adversely changed the economic expectations of the publisher in respect to the work, the publisher may reject the work."

Whatever your contract provision, don't mollycoddle your authors on this issue. Whether they submit the work in pieces or all at once, state manuscript problems explicitly and clearly *in writing*, and withhold payment of the next installment of the advance until you get a satisfactory manuscript. Some excellent proposals are followed by inferior manuscripts.

If you can't sit tight with the "satisfactory manuscript" clause, the law review article cited previously suggests several contract variations including:

The publisher shall be the sole judge of whether the manuscript is satisfactory; except the author shall be entitled to retain all sums advanced and paid, if the manuscript delivered is in substantial conformity with reasonable professional standards.

or:

The publisher may reject the manuscript if the publisher is honestly dissatisfied with its form or content, but the author may retain all payments received prior to rejection.

Some authors will propose that he or she be notified within thirty days after a manuscript's receipt as to its acceptability, and if it is not, that he or she is provided with a written explanation. Additionally, it is usually requested that he or she be allowed a reasonable time to cure the publisher's dissatisfaction with the work.

Piecemeal out your advances and give a small amount on contract signing. On occasion, when a manuscript has been rejected after the first advance, larger publishers (although this is not universal) allow the author to keep the signature advance. Still, the decision is the publisher's.

Depending upon the author's clout and your house's financial situation, you may demand full repayment of the advance, or allow the author to keep part (or all) of it if you reject the manuscript. Sometimes, contracts or settlements will allow the author to keep the advance until he or she sells the project to another house; the time lag between your rejection of a manuscript and placement with another publisher, however, can be substantial. Consider adding a provision for a non-discretionary kill fee if you cancel the contract because of economic considerations.

Some authors may ask for a deadline delay for author's military service, illness, accident, or other unforeseen circumstance.

Permission to Use Copyrighted Material

Some author-oriented contracts provide that the publisher secures and pays for the permissions, some specify that they are the author's responsibility, and some split both the responsibility and the payment. Permissions take time to obtain and can be costly, especially for art books, anthologies, or similar works. Costs depend on the term of license, the status of the author, and the territory requested (United States or North America only as opposed to the World, in English language, or all languages, etc.).

> **If the Author incorporates in the work any copyrighted material, the Author shall procure, at the Author's expense, written permission to reprint it.**

or:

> **Written permission to use any copyrighted material not original to the Author, for which permission is required, shall be obtained for all languages and editions which are the subject of this agreement by the Author, who agrees to bear all fees for the use of such material, or to promptly reimburse the Publisher for any fees paid by them in respect of such copyright material.**

Don't overlook permissions. Develop permission *guidelines*. Include a disclaimer to the effect that these guidelines are *not* the definitive, authoritative, final word on the subject of permissions. (See the fair-use chapter for ideas for permissions guidelines.)

You might provide sample permission forms, as well as a sample record of permission requests, for your author's use, and require the return of both with the completed manuscript. If there's trouble later about a permission, and the author's deceased, ill, or otherwise unavailable, this record will allow you to defend any claim. Otherwise, you will have no way of knowing what was done or not done.

My reservations about the small publisher taking on the permission responsibility are two-fold. First, it's time consuming, and most small publishers are understaffed. Second, the sufficiency of a particular permission, or the need for it, may not be apparent from form or text. Let the author run the risk.

Be sure to allow your authors enough time to get permissions. This can take from a few weeks to six months. Also, expect to run into problems if you want your author to adapt the material significantly.

For your protection, be sure that the permission to use certain material in the work is not just a one-time publication right, and includes the entire grant of rights from the author to you. Otherwise, you might be legally unable to reprint the book or license subsidiary rights without substantial editing.

In preparing this work, I requested permission to utilize a one-page chart from a pamphlet on agents, published by a periodical. The periodical responded, offering non-exclusive, one-time printing rights in the United States only, for a fee. Although the non-exclusive clause was fine, and the charging of a fee was predictable, the United States restriction negated the value of the permission, since Canadian distribution was already planned. Also, the one-time limit made the permission next to worthless.

Grant of Rights

The Author grants to the Publisher during the term of copyright, including renewals and extensions thereof:

a. Exclusive right in the English language, in the United States of America, the Philippine Republic, and Canada and a non-exclusive right in all other countries (subject to b. and c.) to:

    i. Print, publish and sell the work in book form;

    ii. License publication of the work (in complete, condensed or abridged versions) by book clubs;

    iii. License publication of a reprint edition by another publisher with the consent of the Author. The Author shall be deemed to have given consent if within twenty (20) days after the forwarding of written request Author fails to notify the Publisher in writing of his refusal to consent;

    iv. License publication of the work (in complete, condensed, adapted or abridged versions) or selections from the work in anthologies and other publications, in mail-order and schoolbook editions, as premiums and other special editions and through microfilm and with the Author's consent Xerox® or other forms of copying;

    v. License periodical publication including magazines, newspapers and digests prior to book publication;

    vi. License periodical publication after book publication to the extent that any such right is available;

vii. License, subject to the approval of the Author, adaptation of the work for filmstrips, printed cartoon versions and mechanical reproduction;

viii. License, without charge, transcription or publication of the work in Braille or in other forms, for the physically handicapped;

ix. For publicity purposes, publish or permit others to publish or broadcast (but not dramatize) by radio or television, without charge, such selections from the work as in the opinion of the Publisher may benefit its sale.

b. Exclusive right to license in the English language throughout the British Commonwealth (other than Canada), the rights granted in subdivision a. above, are revocable by the Author with respect to any country for which no license or option has been given within eighteen (18) months after first publication in the United States.

c. Exclusive right to license in all foreign languages and all countries, the rights granted in subdivision a. above, revocable by the Author with respect to each language or country for which no license or option has been given within three (3) years after first publication in the United States.

d. Exclusive right to use or license others to use, subject to the approval of the Author, the name and likeness of the Author, the work and the title of the work, in whole or in part, or any adaptation thereof as the basis for trademark or tradename for other products or for any other commercial use in connection with such other products.

This particular provision does *not* provide the publisher a grant of rights in all languages and all countries, but directs itself to a small publisher's marketing capabilities. Some grants of rights add "and a non-exclusive right in all countries except the British Commonwealth (other than Canada), the Republic of South Africa, and the Irish Republic." The minimum you should insist upon are North American, English-language rights. The potential for export of the work and translation differs from book to book; actually, before tying yourself down in a Grant of Rights provision, consult your marketing staff, and brainstorm the possible spin-offs with your editorial staff.

Another sample provision:

The Author grants to the Publisher the sole and exclusive right of license to produce and publish themselves, further, to license the work or any abridgment of the work or any substantial part of the work in volume form in all languages for the legal term of copyright throughout the world.

or:

The Author conveys to the Publisher exclusive rights to reproduce and/or publish (in book or other form), to adapt to other media, to license other parties to publish in whole or in part or adapt to other media, and

to distribute and sell a license of the parties to distribute and sell, this work and all the contents of it. This exclusive right to publish, adapt, license, distribute and sell shall be applicable to the original English language version of the manuscript and to any translations into all other languages and shall extend to all nations and territories of the world without exception.

As you can see, the first alternative secures print rights only, while the second alternative, which *is very broad*, encompasses all rights, print and other media. Again, a happy medium is realistic, or you could secure all rights and then shed them, like a reptile's skin, each year or so.

Let me make a few preliminary comments about the grant of rights and licenses. Many publishers expect to acquire rights for the duration of copyright, which now is an author's life plus fifty years. Knowledgable authors often insist that publishers can keep the rights for a specified number of years only, or switch them to a non-exclusive license after a period of time. Some say, for example, that a hardback book's average life is three years and a paperback's, less than ten. A non-exclusive license or rights grant allows both the publisher and the author to market those pieces of the property. A compromise suggestion follows:

The publisher has the sole and exclusive right and license to produce and publish themselves and further to license the work or any abridgement of the work or any substantial part of the work in book form in all languages for the legal term of the copyright throughout the world except after a period of ten years the publisher shall obtain the consent of the author (such consent not to be unreasonably withheld or delayed), supplying the author with a copy of the sublicense before it is executed.

Run any time period in your contract from the date of book publication. Some authors' groups recommend limiting periods in areas such as translations rights to no longer than 36 months, and British Commonwealth rights to between 12 and 24 months. As with most contract provisions, limits occur by duration, geography, and proceeds share.

A kid's cookbook utilizing peanut butter probably does not need a grant of translation rights for third-world countries, nor video rights. It's another story with a children's book that is colorfully or unusually illustrated and has a lively main character. In that case, you may want to control not only the work in printed form, but translations, commercial uses of the illustrations for t-shirts or cartoon strips, etc. A book of Navajo place names may generate interest in a German translation because of the Indian clubs there, but beyond that, you may be fantasizing if you project other, more exotic, uses.

These subsidiary rights can be licensed either by the publisher or the author, depending on the contract, and can include abridgements, book clubs, first and second serializations (which are periodical publication rights before and after publication), advertising, syndication, films, plays, radios, commercial uses, television, reprints by another publisher, and so forth.

What you are defining, then, is control, the length of that control, perhaps a veto power, and division of monies received from the licensing of subsidiary rights. Some publishers give first and second serialization rights to the author, and often agree to varying percentages based on the first $10,000 of income, with subsequent steps of $10,000 for other licensing revenues. Various author-advocacy groups recommend that the author receive not less than 80 percent for television, and film rights and no less than 50 percent from hardcover rights. Some contracts specify deductions (agent commissions and so forth) from the gross proceeds prior to the division between publisher and author. Small publishers often rely upon agents to license the subsidiary rights, so spell out these deductible costs. If an author wants the right to receive copies of any licensing or subsidiary rights agreements negotiated by the publisher, that's reasonable.

It's not fair to either party for the publisher to control all rights forever if the publisher doesn't have the ability to exploit the manuscript. A reasonable compromise would be to split earnings from marketing those rights for x period of time, and then if the publisher failed to exploit the subsidiary rights (as these are called), those rights pass to the author, with the publisher receiving a token percentage, i.e., 10 or 20 percent or so. (I refer you to the Appendix in Richard Curtis's *How to Be a Literary Agent* for an analysis of what is a good deal and what is a bad deal in the division of subsidiary rights monies.)

If you change your standard book contract, examine the grant of rights section against any other section in the book contract that may discuss subsidiary rights or licensing.

Author Warranties

Provision A:

The Author represents and warrants to the Publisher that the Author has full power and authority to enter into this Agreement and to grant the rights granted in this Agreement; that the Work is original except for material in the public domain and those excerpts from other works as may be included with the written permission of the copyright owners; that the Work does not contain any libelous or obscene material or injurious formulas, recipes, or instructions; that it does not infringe any trade name, trademark, or copyright; and that it does not invade or violate any right of privacy, personal or proprietary right, or other common law or statutory right.

The Author agrees to indemnify the Publisher and its licensees and assignees under this Agreement and hold them harmless from any and all losses, damages, liabilities, costs, charges, and expenses, including reasonable attorneys' fees, arising out of any breach of any of the Author's representations and warranties contained in this Agreement or third-party claims relating to the matters covered by the representations and warranties in this Section 3 which are finally sustained in a court of original

jurisdiction. If any action or proceeding is brought against the Publisher with respect to the matters covered by the representations and warranties in this Section 3, the Publisher shall have the right, in its sole discretion, to select counsel to defend against this action or proceeding. In addition to other remedies available to the Publisher, the Publisher may charge the amount of these losses, damages, liabilities, costs, charges, and expenses against any sums accruing to the Author under this Agreement or any other agreement currently existing between Author and Publisher.

If there is an infringement of any rights granted to the Publisher or rights which the Publisher is authorized to license or in which the Publisher is to share in the proceeds, the Publisher shall have the right, in its sole discretion, to select counsel to bring such action or proceeding, and the Author and the Publisher shall have the right to participate jointly in the action. If both participate, they shall share equally the expenses of and any sums recovered in the action, except that if the Author retains separate legal counsel, the Author shall be solely responsible for the legal expenses of the Author's counsel. If either party declines to participate in the action, the other may proceed, and the party maintaining the action shall bear all expenses and shall retain all sums recovered.

The provisions of this Section shall survive any termination of this Agreement.

Provision B

The Author represents and warrants to be the sole Author and proprietor of this Work, and to have full power to make this agreement and grant of rights, and that—to the best of the Author's knowledge—it in no way infringes upon any copyright or proprietary right of others, or contains anything libelous or in violation of any right of privacy. The Author agrees to exempt the Publisher from penalties and hold the Publisher harmless against all liabilities, losses, damages, and expense of any kind whatsoever resulting from any claim, action, or proceeding asserted or instituted and sustained on the ground that the said Work violates any copyright or proprietary right, or contains anything libelous or in violation of any right of privacy. The Author further agrees to cooperate fully in the defense thereof.

In case of any infringement of the copyright of this Work by others, the Author shall have the right to bring action based on such infringement. In such event the legal costs and the net proceeds of any recovery shall be divided equally between the Author and Publisher. If the Author does not take action within fifteen days of being notified of the infringement, the Publisher may at his discretion, sue or employ such remedies as deemed expedient; all such suits or proceedings shall be at joint expense, and the net proceeds shall be divided equally. However, the Author shall not be liable for any expenditure in excess of $500 undertaken by the Publisher for such purposes without his previous written consent.

Provision C

The Author warrants that he is the sole author of the work; that he is the sole owner of all the rights granted to the Publisher; that he has not previously assigned, pledged or otherwise encumbered the same; that he has full power to enter into this agreement; that except for the material obtained pursuant to Paragraph _____ the work is original, has not been published before, and is not in the public domain; that it does not violate any right of privacy; that it is not libelous or obscene; that it does not infringe upon any statutory or common law copyright; and that any recipe, formula or instruction contained in the work is not injurious to the user.

In the event of any claim, action or proceeding based upon an alleged violation of any of these warranties (i) the Publisher shall have the right to defend the same through counsel of its own choosing, and (ii) no settlement shall be effected without the prior written consent of the Author, which consent shall not unreasonably be withheld, and (iii) the Author shall hold harmless the Publisher, any seller of the work, and any license of a subsidiary right in the work, against any damages finally sustained. If such claim, action or proceeding is successfully defended or settled, the Author's indemnity hereunder shall be limited to fifty percent (50%) of the expense (including reasonable counsel fees) attributable to such defense or settlement; however, such limitation of liability shall not apply if the claim, action or proceeding is based on copyright infringement.

If any such claim, action or proceeding is instituted, the Publisher shall promptly notify the Author, who shall fully cooperate in the defense thereof, and the Publisher may withhold payments of reasonable amounts due him under this or any other agreement between the parties.

These warranties and indemnities shall survive the termination of this agreement.

These three warranties represent: (A) a fairly standard major book publisher's contract, (B) a provision from a book publishing agreement for small presses, published by Dust Books (P. O. Box 100, Paradise, CA 95969), and (C) a major publisher's warranty and indemnity provision, which strikes a balance between the author and publisher's respective concerns.

Example A's warranties-and-indemnities provision places the entire financial burden squarely on the shoulders of the author. In some cases this may be laughable. A professional mountain biker who lives out of her saddlebags may be judgement-proof if it turns out that she infringed another's copyright in her book, *Mountain Biking in Bali*, which A Great Risk Press published.

Example B's author warranties-and-indemnities clause is a greatly diluted version of the first. It qualifies the warranty by a very subjective and personal standard, to wit, "to the best of the [this] Author's knowledge." (The word "exempt" should be "indemnify," and is an error.) Also, I would have eliminated the phrase "from penalties," so that indemnification isn't limited to penalties. This provision also does not extend to licensees, assignees, and sellers of the work. Its

$500 cap on litigation expenses is unrealistic; at least triple it, or add another zero.

Provision C requires that the author participate in any settlement, and the author's financial contribution is dependent on the successful defense or settlement of the matter. A percentage cap expense is a more equitable limit than a money cap.

A publisher's nightmare: multiple libel, defamation, or copyright violation claims as a result of publication of a work, claims that eat up the profits from that book, the next book. . . You, as a publisher, need assurances that:

- the work is not unlawful, and that it is neither libelous nor obscene.
- it does not infringe on another's copyright.
- it does not violate any other statutory or proprietary right.

You want the author, who has violated these provisions, to pay any costs that you incur defending yourself—and him or her—from these claims. It is not necessarily an industry practice to hold authors to the letter of this provision, but small presses may have to do so, since their financial capabilities are not as great. Attorney's fees, costs, or payment of damages can quickly gobble up any profit from the first edition of a book. If you only publish three books a year—well! Even a provision allowing you to withhold all royalties if there's a claim or lawsuit may not help if the book's a flop.

Another way to put it, and to repeat, your author *must* warrant that:

- he or she is the sole author of the work.
- the work is original with him or her and does not infringe statutory copyrights or common law literary rights of others.
- the work is not obscene or scandalous.
- the work does not defame, libel, or violate the right to privacy of other persons.
- the work is not injurious.
- the work has never been published.

The Author's Guild opposes heavy-duty warranty and indemnity clauses; a prospective author may try to minimize this clause's impact by requesting that he or she not pay costs arising from controversies caused by unapproved editorial changes or inserts. This is not unreasonable.

Further, some prospective authors may balk at indemnification, except where claims are reduced to judgment. I suggest that you not allow this dilution. A claim or demand may be merely Nancy Smith calling and stating that your author's Bali book violated her copyright and she wants five thousand dollars. You may not go to court but you still need to deal with the claim. (Once you've read the chapter on legal procedures and review the steps on litigation, you'll have a better appreciation of the difference.)

Under the standard clause, if a publishing concern has to pay a settlement, the author must repay the publisher, either from his or her pocket, or future royalties. Although very few claims end up as lawsuits, and even fewer lawsuits go to trial, still, the matter could drag first through a trial court, then into one or more levels of appeals courts—all at great time, cost, and attorney's fees to you. You could grow old, and poor, waiting for that final judgment on which you agreed to base recovery from the author. Don't change the language of your standard warranty and indemnity clause to require that you prove an actual breach before you can charge the author with repayment. Such standards are subjective and difficult to prove.

Prospective authors will sometimes push to cap the publisher's costs, or to allow the author to participate through a lawyer of his or her own choice, or to exclude your lawyer's fees if the author uses his or her own attorney. Some try to delete the provision that you withhold royalties in the event of a controversy, or try to reduce the amount withheld.

Who puts the words to paper? The author. The publisher, in turn, pays to publish those words. Therefore, some opine that there is no justification in moving the burden of responsibility to the publisher.

The most reasonable contractual course of action, if your author is solvent, is to stay with stringent warranties and indemnities, modulated on a case-by-case basis. For instance, if, in the previous Bali example, 25 percent of the total text of the infringing book was taken from the first book, the author should absorb the entire loss. On the other hand, if the percentage of copying was negligible, but because of the changing legal decisions, these result in a finding of infringement, the costs and damages could be shared. Other factors that affect this decision include:

- other author's works published by you.
- the degree author promotion affects sales of his/her works.
- present works-in-progress with that author.
- house identification with that author.
- whether the situation arose intentionally or negligently.
- the length of the publisher/author arrangement.
- projected future dealings between the two parties.

Even if you're a small publisher, your pocket's likely to be deeper than that of most authors. A litigious claimant not only ties up your author's royalties, but your precious time and money, and, even if the book's out of print, you can still be sued, so the warranty-indemnity must survive the contract's end. Further, if you've licensed editions in Zimbabwe, Yugoslavia, Japan, and China, the license arrangements with the foreign publisher probably required you to indemnify them. You, in turn, must try to keep this responsibility in your author's court.

Some manuscripts scream out that lawsuits and legal claims lurk around the corner: first novels, unauthorized biographies, diet and exercise books, and certain cookbooks. In that event, you should plan on a legal manuscript review by your lawyer (discussed later), negotiate a smaller advance, keep reserves of royalties for claims, and require changes in the legally offensive material. *Don't change it for the author.* Most authors willingly change problem passages; further, if *you* make these changes, you, as publisher, may assume liability. Cancel the contract if the author is uncooperative and get back your advance investment.

If you intend to do a legal manuscript review, consider adding this statement:

If the publisher makes an independent investigation to determine whether the warranties and representations are true and correct, such investigation shall not constitute a defense to the author in any claim or action based upon a breach of any of the foregoing warranties and/or indemnification.

Remember my earlier *caveat*: any party can reduce the effect of a tough contract provision by time, scope, money, and so forth, but the author turns the table on you if he or she is successful in incorporating the suggestions mentioned in this chapter. Leave your contract tough and soften its application only for compelling reasons.

Some publishers insure themselves against claims and suits for libel, invasion of privacy, and the like, and this insurance sometimes can be extended to cover the author. The Author's Guild keeps track of the companies that provide insurance to authors, and you could suggest that your author contact them.

Let's stop here in this discussion of generic book contracts and look at the potential problems with a work's content that make the warranty-indemnification clause so important.

Restrictions on Content

Watching the Author's Words

5

There are a host of legal theories that can create problems for your work's content, or, on the other hand, can protect it:

- obscenity.
- invasion of privacy, including:
  - the appropriation of a person's name or likeness for commercial purposes (right of publicity).
  - the disclosure to the public of embarrassing private facts.
  - placing a false image of the person before the public (false light).
  - intrusions into a person's seclusion or private life.
- protection of a character from misappropriation.
- defamation: libel and slander.
- infliction of emotional distress.
- unfair competition or misappropriation.
- infringement of a trademark, tradename, or trade secret.
- product liability.

These theories, particularly the first five, relate to *content,* while copyright infringement and balance of the items listed relate to economics; copyright provides the financial incentive to publish, and product disparagement and liability, trademark and tradename infringement and unfair competition can affect economic expectations.

Almost all the restrictions on printed works center around content. (Be careful if your prospective author is a federal employee. Reagan passed an administration directive requiring prepublication review of the writings of high-level federal employees.) Other creative work, such as art, textiles, and toys, have restrictions on the work's materials: feathers, lead glazes, fur, and fabrics. By extension, these concerns could apply to books—if you bind your special edition in the hide of some endangered species, you may run afoul of the law.

An Obscenity Yardstick

Not every "erotic" work is legally obscene. A variety of laws regulate the sale, display, and transportation of "obscene" materials in the United States. Many obscenity arrests occur on the state or local level; for instance, Larry Flynt of *Hustler* magazine was prosecuted under a state law. Whereas some states prohibit obscene materials from being either publicly displayed or sold to minors, others prohibit only the *sale* of such materials to minors. Cities, too, adopt anti-obscenity laws, some of which prohibit *any* commercial dealings in pornography. If you're curious about the anti-obscenity laws in your area, ask your lawyer or the local chapter of the American Civil Liberties Union.

Because obscenity laws dilute a citizen's essential right of free expression, the United States Supreme Court has ruled that these laws must be clear and specific in their language. An old New York State law that prohibited the showing of "sacrilegious" films was deemed too vague a yardstick by which to judge and restrict free expression.

The Supreme Court developed a three-pronged test for judging obscenity:

- as that which expresses sexual conduct in a patently offensive way and, taken as a whole,
- appeals to the prurient interest in sex (both applying contemporary community standards),
- does not have a serious literary, artistic, political, or scientific value (applying a reasonable-person standard of redeeming value).

The film *Carnal Knowledge* was held to be *not* obscene under the test described above. The Supreme Court also has ruled that material must be truly "obscene" in order for the distributor to be jailed.

Where borderline "obscene" materials were sold to minors, publicly displayed so that minors and members of the public couldn't avoid them, or promoted with an emphasis on the prurient aspects of the work (like *Eros* magazine), the Supreme Court dealt more harshly with the distributor and used a looser interpretation of *obscene*. Ralph Ginsburg discovered this when he was sentenced to five years for the publication and sale of *Eros*.

Across the country, states have adopted Minor's Access Laws (general distribution and display of obscene materials to minors). These "kiddie porn" laws, as they're called, are designed to discourage child abuse, and generally prohibit the distribution of books and other materials depicting sexual performance by children, even if the materials do not fit the legal obsenity definitions. The kiddie-porn law, signed by Reagan in 1984, makes the shipment of books that depict sexual activities involving minor children through the mail or interstate commerce a crime.

Publishers, booksellers, and authors have agreed that this has a chilling effect on the right of free speech. In response to these laws, a major publisher cancelled three books that had language that was objectionable, particularly the word "goddamn." Both the Authors League of America and the American Society of Journalists and Authors protested that action.

During Banned Books Week in the fall of 1988, the American Library Association reported 105 school censorship attempts in 42 states, with a one-third success rate. The successes included the removal from the shelves of Saul Silverstein's *A Light in the Attic* because of its "violent content, idealization of death, and light treatment of manipulative behavior" (*Publishers Weekly,* September 30, 1988).

Possession of "obscene" material in the privacy of your home is your business. Federal law forbids transporting it across a state line or national border for personal use, however, U.S. Customs held up the appearance in the 1976 New York Film Festival of an entry titled *In the Realm of the Senses.* It was later released. It is also a crime, punishable by a jail term, to send "obscene" material through the U.S. mail.

Since only local, state, and federal governments and their representatives are prohibited from violating a citizen's First Amendment right to free expression, a privately sponsored art show can legally refuse to hang any works showing bare skin, or activities of a questionable nature. On the other hand, Straitown City Museum cannot legally refuse to hang a so-called obscene work until *after* a hearing determines that the work violates the local anti-obscenity law; no agency of government can legally prohibit a showing *prior* to such a hearing. For a city to do otherwise would violate the artist's First Amendment rights. For example, the Supreme Court ruled that a theater leased by the City of Chattanooga violated free-speech rights by flatly refusing its use for the production of the musical *Hair,* because of the play's allegedly "obscene" content.

For those adventuresome souls who still find themselves running afoul of the authorities for violation of obscenity laws, the National Coalition Against Censorship (New York City) or your local branch of the American Civil Liberties Union may be able to provide assistance.

Obscenity Canadian Style
Canadian courts tend toward a contemporary judgment of morality. This view is illustrated by a United States case quoted by the Canadian court, in which a federal court judge, in the case of the *United States of America v. One Book Called "Ulysses,"* refused to find *Ulysses* obscene because "the words, which are characterized as dirty, are old Anglo-Saxon words known to almost all men . . . and are such words as would be naturally and habitually used, I believe, by the type of nature whose life, physical and mental, Joyce is seeking to describe. In respect of the recurrent emergence of the theme of sex in the minds of his characters, it must always be remembered that his locale was rural and his season Spring."

In 1961 in England, and in 1962 in Canada, D.H. Lawrence's book, *Lady*

Chatterly's Lover, was held not to be obscene. The Canadian decision rested on the definition of obscenity in the Canadian Criminal Code. When the Ontario Court of Appeals held that *Fanny Hill: Memoirs of a Woman of Pleasure* was not obscene, it looked at the book as a whole to assess the author's purpose and to judge its serious literary purpose or baseness.

First Amendment Situations

The First Amendment to our constitution guarantees the right of free speech. It's this constitutional protection that runs smack into content restrictions.

An unusual freedom-of-speech issue involved Hustler Magazine, Inc. A U.S. Circuit Court of Appeals ruled that an article in *Hustler* called "Orgasm of Death," would not be considered an incitement to an unlawful act. The article described masturbation while hanging oneself, which temporarily cut off the blood supply to the brain at the moment of orgasm. The article warned readers at least ten times that auto-erotic asphyxiation is deadly. In a suit brought against *Hustler,* by the mother of a teenager who had died while trying this technique, a suit based on grounds of negligence, product liability, dangerous instrumentality, and attractive nuisance, the court reasoned that freedom of speech does not protect obscenity, child pornography, fighting words, incitement to imminent lawless activity, and reck-lessly made false statements; it concluded the *Hustler* article fit none of those and the plaintiff would have to prove that auto-erotic asphyxiation is a lawless act. She could not. Later, the United States Supreme Court let stand an appellate ruling that a $182,000 jury verdict against *Hustler* violated the magazine's free-speech rights.

Publishers Weekly (February 24, 1984) reported another twist on freedom of speech. The American Way's Freedom to Learn (formed to counter conser-vative groups like the Moral Majority) and a former executive of the National Association of Biology Teachers accused publishers of giving decreasing atten-tion to Darwin's theory of evolution, and cited Silver–Burdett's *Biology* and Win-ston's *Modern Biology* textbooks. Texas purchases ten percent of all biology text-books, so, the critics argue, publishers bow to the Texas Board of Educator's adoption requirements.

Mrs. Onassis got a 1975 court order restricting a photographer, described as a "camera-kaze," from getting within twenty-five feet of her and thirty-one feet of her daughter, Caroline; this order was issued *over* the photographer's First Amend-ment argument that he had a right to pursue her photographically. In the 1980s, she pressed contempt charges against him for violating the restraining order by ruining her son's, and then her daughter's, graduation.

Invasion of Privacy

Invasion of privacy is what Ron Galella did to Jacqueline Kennedy Onassis when he poked his camera lens too closely into her life.

State law spells out the areas protected from invasion. Most living persons have a right to privacy, which is basically the right (with qualifications) to be let alone. If invasion of privacy could be a problem in your author's work, get good legal advice concerning your state's privacy laws.

A state privacy law usually prohibits commercial exploitation of the name or portrait of a living person without consent. It does not apply to the commercial use of photographs of animals, buildings, and so forth, although other restrictions (copyrights, ownership rights) could prohibit the commercial use of these.

The many cases in this area focus on whether the use of the plaintiff's name or image is for commercial and trade purposes or for news purposes. The line between the public's right to know and the individual's right to privacy is a fine one.

A participant in a St. Patrick's Day Parade lost his invasion-of-privacy case against *New York* magazine. The court ruled that printing the marcher's photograph on the front of the magazine to illustrate an article called "The Last of the Irish Immigrants" was published "in connection with the presentation of a matter of legitmate public interest to readers," and therefore no recovery for invasion of privacy was available. Since anyone thrust willingly or unwillingly into the public eye is considered a "public figure," he or she, as such, is fair game for comment. A "public figure" will have a hard time winning an invasion-of-privacy suit unless a clear commercial purpose can be demonstrated.

What about a sneak street shot of that gorgeous bikini-clad tuba player in last year's Independence Day Parade? Don't sell it to a tuba company for their next big advertising campaign. Without a release (written permission), you might get sued for invasion of the tuba player's privacy. But the local gazette could print the photograph of the tuba player alongside an article on the Independence Day festivities with no problem, because the photograph was not used for commercial purposes but rather as part of a news story.

Here's a real-life question that came up when hindsight drove an artist to my legal doorstep.

Memorandum
To: Client
From: MB
Re: A pictorial-narrative text about a Hispanic artist.
Background: This book was published by XYZ Publishing, who holds the copyright. The book is apparently in its second printing. The authors saw the subject and used a tape recorder for interviews. It is unclear whether a stipend or check was received for subject's interview time, although one press staff member recollects checks and that an art show featuring subject's work was sponsored by the press. The subject is pleased with the textual material in the work, but is less than satisfied with the representative selection of his art work.

The concern now by the subject is whether his privacy was invaded.
Elements of tort involving invasion of privacy: Whenever facts are generally available to the public because the facts are observable in a public place, are matters of public record, are generally known in the community, or have been otherwise disclosed to and are available to the public, there can be no cause of action for invasion of privacy. However, when the facts are not generally available to the public, such as facts that take place in a private

setting, are not matters of public record, are not generally known in the community, or have not otherwise been disclosed or made available to the public, a cause of action exists. Further, the matters published must be "highly offensive to a reasonable person," matter published must not be of "legitimate concern to the public."

It is not my understanding that the matters published would be highly offensive to the subject, nor did he consider the matters not of legitimate concern to the public. Further, there are certain defenses to the tort of invasion of privacy: expressed or implied consent. In *Neff v. Time, Inc.,* 406 F. Supp 858 (W.D. Pa. 1976), the plaintiff's "hamming it up" for the photographer, knowing who the photographer was, constituted "implied consent." Note that under *Virgil v. Time, Inc.,* 527 F.2d 1122 (9th Cir. 1975) *cert. den.* 425 U.S. 998 (1976), the express consent can be revoked prior to publication if done in a timely manner.

Given the circumstances of this case, that is, the cooperation by subject with author and press and the arrangement for a show on his behalf, there would appear to be both express and implied consent.

Publicity that places an individual in a false light: "False light" is similar to defamation, but it does not usually involve the same level of injury to reputation. An individual can be placed in a "false light" by distorted facts, by omission of relevant facts, by embellishment of facts, and by fictionalization. Unless subject can show that the selection of work makes him out to be a folk artist rather than a Southwestern impressionist, it seems that the subject's claim of "false light" [based on the fact that his selection of works would differ] is flimsy at best.

Again, an express or implied consent is a defense to that particular tort. And the statute of limitations may have run, although at the very least a strong affirmative defense of laches (due to the second printing) could be made. Laches means that you can't sit on your haunches and wait to make a complaint while the other relies on your acquiescence.

Conclusion: The circumstances of this arrangement seem to indicate that subject gave his express and implied consent to the preparation of the book about him. Further, consideration seems to have been paid subject indirectly, due to the arrangement of the exhibit.

A photographer should pay at least a dollar and obtain a release from any subject of a portrait or photograph that may be used for advertising or other commercial purposes. (See the sample release form, which should be tailored to your specific needs.) When photographing or drawing identifiable human subjects, it is a good idea to get a release whenever possible, as who knows what might be done with the photograph or drawing. As mentioned, a photographer does not need a release to publish or distribute a photograph of someone involved in a truly newsworthy event, but because of the great gray area between the clearly newsworthy and the clearly commercial, when in doubt, get a release.

A magazine that uses reader-"as told to"-success stories, as well as reader photographs, demands this release form:

Some photographers never get releases, or if they do, they do not provide them to their publishers. The following case study shows the disastrous consequences that can follow what appeared to be an undocumented photo release, fifty-two years after the original image was taken.

Case Incident:
A Laura Gilpin photograph taken in 1932, titled "A Navajo Madonna" and featuring a traditional bejewelled Navajo woman holding a child in a cradleboard, became the subject of a lawsuit in federal court in New Mexico in 1984, against a book publisher, a distribution company, an art magazine, a marketing company for another magazine, and a museum of western art for the publication and dissemination of the Gilpin photograph, based on misappropriation of likeness and public disclosure. The complaint sought damages and an injunction.

Sometimes, people are sensitive about the use of their names for characters in a piece of fiction, and will file suit to stop the project.

Case Incident:
The use of real-life people, still living, as novel characters, garnered a victory when a New York court refused a preliminary injunction against the novel, *In the Name of the Father,* by A.J. Quinnel, published by New American Library; an Archbishop sued to stop the use of his name as a violation of his rights of privacy under New York law, which requires obtaining written consent before using the name of a living person "for advertising purposes, or for purposes of trade."

Character protection under other legal theories is discussed later in this chapter.
The right of publicity, as a species of invasion of privacy, states that a person with a public reputation has a right to benefit from the commercial value associated with that person's name or picture. The right to publicity can often be assigned or enforced by heirs.

Case Incident:
An interesting right of publicity case, i.e., *Carson v. Here's Johnny Portable Toilets, Inc.,* 698 F.2d 831 (6th Cir. 1983) protected entertainer Johnny Carson's commercial interest in the words "Here's Johnny" against a distributor of portable toilets called "Here's Johnny," and the slogan "the World's Foremost Commodian."

Case Incident:
Another is *Hirsch v. S.C. Johnson & Son., Inc.,* 280 N.W.2d 129 (1979), in which a state supreme court held that "Crazy Legs," a football player's nickname utilized on a woman's shaving gel, violated the football player's right of publicity.

Years ago, our office handled a case involving an elderly Tohono O'odham basketmaker who displayed her demonstrated craft skills at an educational institution. At first, after seeing a painting of her, we thought the artist had rendered her likeness from a photograph acquired from the institution, although it appeared later that the photographer-artist may have taken the photograph. The matter was settled (for cash and some of the valuable prints) before litigation. Part of the demand letter is reproduced to illustrate important concepts:

Dear Photographer-Artist:

Our office has been retained by _____ and her family to pursue their claim against you for your unauthorized use of _____ likeness in the "_____." The contents of this letter are in furtherance of compromise and settlement and this letter shall not be introduced as evidence in any proceedings.

This misappropriation of _____ likeness is a violation of her right to be let alone and her right to publicity. Generally, persons have a proprietary interest in their own identities and this right explicitly recognizes that identities have economic value which cannot be appropriated without compensation. It has long been recognized that there is a commercial value in an identity; the likeness or representation of an individual, if identifiable to others, is also part of identity and therefore is protected. Your appropriation of her identity obviously indicated that it had some economic value to you.

This misappropriation was discovered this past spring when certain family members saw a "_____" print in a gallery and readily identified _____ .

_____ has never authorized, either expressly or impliedly, the use of her likeness. Nor has she consented to photographs by the general public. For several years, _____ was a basketmaker and basketmaking demonstrator at the tribal museum. The tribal museum customarily took a photograph of the exhibitors for their archival records and provided copies of those photographs, according to the museum, only to the exhibitors. Apparently, you somehow managed to obtain a copy of a photograph of _____ from the tribal museum archives or surreptitiously took your own photograph of her. The tribal museum policy is that they do not make those photographs available to the public. The print clearly represents the basket room at the tribal museum, and undoubtedly, the print is an accurate and identical representation of _____ . Again, we repeat, that at no time has _____ agreed that her photograph be taken or a drawing or a painting be made of _____ that was intended for publication. Neither has she signed a release for said use. Not only the family, but others have carefully examined the print and agreed that it depicts _____ . It portrays identically _____ facial features, hands, clothing and paraphernalia.

The print edition for "_____" was nearly one thousand, thus your commercial purpose is clear and convincing. Further, the use of _____ likeness is substantial as opposed to incidental.

It is apparent that you either photographed _____ or somehow you had access to the tribal museum's photograph collection of _____, which in essence was her personal property even though stored at the tribal museum, since her consent to be photographed by the tribal museum was implicitly conditioned upon the tribal museum retaining the photograph. The gravamen of your offense is that the commercial value in our client's identity has been appropriated by you. Obviously, if it were not for the realistic image of a basketmaker making baskets, you would not be able to sell the prints. In all probability, you chose _____ as a subject for your print due to inherent special qualities in her personal appearance, which lent credibility and authenticity to your print. While the _____ Press indicates that you have spent hundreds of hours with the Tohono O'odham observing, sketching, and listening, it is undoubtedly clear that in order to render the detail in the print, you were working from a photograph either taken by you without her consent or taken from the tribal museum archives without their consent or _____ consent.

In short, you are basically selling her identity; hence, we are demanding the total gain from the sale of the prints and any paintings. Otherwise, there would be unjust enrichment. In our opinion, there is a constructive trust on the profits you have received from the sale of prints and any paintings.

The photographer–artist's lawyer wrote to us defending the use of our client's image. Our response to the photographer–artist's lawyer's letter:

Be advised that the claim is being asserted by _____, who is extremely upset over the appearance of her exact likeness in over 900 print reproductions. Even though she is elderly, she is acutely alert. The reference in your letter to greedy relatives was not only insulting and inappropriate but is also totally erroneous.

We disagree with your conclusion that there is no claim for invasion of privacy. As stated, there is a dual claim: invasion of privacy and/or commercial appropriation of likeness. The use of a likeness of a Plaintiff who has developed a commercially valuable persona (as you neatly set forth in the agreement in your letter) gives rise to damages akin to property damages, as in copyright and trademark violations, the unauthorized use of an unknown person's name or likeness for commercial purposes constitutes a good claim for the violation of her right to be left alone without further showing of harm.

Obviously, the question of whether _____ is a "public figure" is one for the trier of facts. Either way, this presents a Catch-22 dilemma for your client.

While you have attempted to show the educational and artistic purposes of _____ appropriation of _____ likeness, the indisputable fact is that your client is a well-known and accomplished "commercial"artist whose work is touted commercially, for instance by _____. To quote, "_____spent hundreds of hours with... and became intimately attached to their life style...."By commercial, I do not mean that your client's work is not fine art but rather, that she makes her living as a painter and in developing a following for her work.

This appropriation is an affront to social custom. Nearly any person who has lived or worked among the _____, as _____ purportedly has done, knows that this culture, as well as the individuals, are extremely sensitive and reluctant to have likenesses made of themselves as well as of their villages, whether for personal or commercial use.

Your client's commercial purpose was clear and primary, and the use was substantial, as opposed to incidental.

While there is a balance between privacy and disclosure to be achieved, this is restricted by the society's culture and the particular individual's status and life situation. Anthropologists would readily testify that _____ abhor this type of invasion of privacy.

The appropriation for the artist's advantage of the Plaintiff's name or likeness has been recognized in Arizona as a tort, *Cluff v. Farmers Insurance Exchange,* 460 P2d 666, 10 AZ App 560 (1970) and *Reed v. Real Detective Publishing Company* 162 P2d 133, 63 AZ 294 (1945).

Your categorization of _____ as a public figure is inaccurate. Yearly, the tribal museum takes photographs of the demonstrators for archival purposes—if a photograph appeared in a museum publication, the purpose of the publication is clearly non-profit and educational.

_____ recollects allowing an individual to photograph her at the museum, and was given $10.00. She assumed the photograph was for the photographer's personal use. In fact, the photograph used by _____ as an aid in the painting depicts the very floral blouse that _____ wore. It is our position that her demonstration at an educational facility for educational purposes was not sufficient to make _____ a public figure. We would request further information regarding the photographs, dates, and witnesses.

Irrespective, as we've said before, of whether her right to privacy has been violated, certainly her right of publicity has.

We would disagree regarding inherent values of the work—true, it is a work of art but _____ poses as someone familiar with _____ cultures, whose paintings accurately depict _____ life. The print caption does not say "rendition from photograph of _____, demonstrating _____ at an educational facility." No, the public is led to believe otherwise. The gravamen of this offense is commercial exploitation.

Canadian Law—Privacy

In 1982, the Charter of Rights and Freedoms was annexed to the Canadian Constitution. Until then, Canada was cast as a consumer's society, with accommodation and compromise and concern for the general welfare, rather than the American model of individualism and its liberties. The Charter affects the laws on defamation, but that extent is beyond the scope of this book.

In an old privacy case in Quebec (1879), the court said the doctor who sued his patients for fees, and set forth in his complaint the nature of their malady, violated confidences. Canadian legal theory on privacy and commercial appropriation of a likeness is best illustrated by a photograph of a police constable mopping his brow on traffic duty; this photograph later appeared in an ad for a foot-bath, captioned, "Phew! I am going to get my feet into a _____ foot bath." The Canadian courts held this to both violate the constable's right to privacy and be an unallowable commercial expropriation of a likeness. Many of the provinces have also passed privacy legislation.

Libel and Slander

Defamation laws are as old as Moses and are designed to protect a person's reputation (including artistic reputation) from the taint of falsehood. Under defamation laws, private citizens can sue to recover money damages for the harm caused by any oral or written misrepresentation of their name, personality, or behavior (so don't depict your worst enemy with an unnatural or obscene deformity). When the defamatory statement is verbal, it is called *slander;* when it is written, it is called *libel.* Libel is essentially a fight about reputations. Most defamation cases concern libel but not slander. The definition of defamation is about the same in Canada as the United States, as a defamatory statement is one that lowers a person in the estimation of others.

Publishers Weekly (September 23, 1983) reported that five defendants paid $150,000 in settlement to a psychiatrist–author, and his co-author wife, of the bestseller, *I'm O.K.-You're O.K.,* for slanderous speech broadcast by an evangelist, who said Thomas Harris (the author) committed suicide two years after the book came out. The broadcast damaged sales as well as the psychiatrist's reputation and his income, as revenues were lost due to cancelled speaking engagements.

The defamatory material can be a drawing or photograph as well as the printed or spoken word, and a business entity can be defamed as well as an individual. California's libel law, enacted in 1872, looks like this:

Libel, what? Libel is a false and unprivileged publication by writing, printing, picture, effigy, or other fixed representation to the eye, which exposes any person to hatred, contempt, ridicule, or obloquy, or which causes him to be shunned or avoided, or which has a tendency to injure him in his occupation.

The person making a defamatory statement is liable to the defamed person, as is anyone else who participates in its distribution—publisher, newspaper editor, gallery owner. Remember, the indemnification clause in most licensing agreements runs from you, the publisher, to everyone associated with the work.

A federal court judge dismissed a libel complaint filed by a California deputy district attorney, who claimed F. Lee Bailey libeled him in *How to Protect Yourself Against Cops in California and Other Strange Places* (Stein & Day). That left pending the suit against author, publisher and television stations (*Publishers Weekly,* January 27, 1984).

In order to win a defamation suit, the defamed person must prove that the defamatory statement was *communicated* to others; that the statement clearly *identified* the plaintiff (the person bringing the suit); that the plaintiff suffered *injury* because of the statement; and most important, that the maker of the statement was somehow *at fault* with regard to the statement. Because each state has its own definition of defamation, these requirements will vary. The traditional rule that the dead can't be libeled was upheld in 1984, when the survivors of Errol Flynn, purportedly defamed by *Errol Flynn: The Untold Story* by Charles Higham (Dell), a 1981 biography, were thrown out of court.

Publishers, editors, and authors may be sued for libel in any state in which their material is circulated and may be forced to travel to another state to defend libel charges, even if neither the plaintiff nor defendant has any other involvement with that state. The two Supreme Court cases responsible for this rule involved *Hustler* and the *National Enquirer.* This means that the plaintiff can forum-shop—look for a state with a longer statute of limitations or liberal punitive damages.

A notorious falsehood whispered to a friendly tree would not be defamation, nor would a statement calling the mystery man a thief and a philanderer. You *can,* however, defame a person without using his or her name—"All the members of the RMA are swindlers." The requirement of showing injury is complicated slightly by the fact that if the defamer *knew* that the statement was false or at least entertained serious doubts as to its truth, no actual injury has to be shown in order to win a defamation case.

The last few years, in order to strengthen the constitutional right of free speech, the Supreme Court adopted two standards of fault, one that applies to public officials and figures and another that governs private persons. A public figure must prove that the defaming statement was made either with knowledge of its falsity or with reckless disregard for the truth. Barry Goldwater recovered $50,000 from *Fact* magazine and $25,000 from its editor, who ran a story portraying Goldwater as a latent homosexual, a "cruel" practical joker, a paranoid, and so on. But a deputy sheriff who had been falsely accused of bribery lost his defamation suit for lack of proof that the defamer acted with reckless disregard for the truth. Erma Bombeck complained (in a January 1988 column) about a biography written about her by a man she doesn't know and had never met. She said "once you enter the Public Domain [she means becomes a public figure], you'll be misquoted [and] misunderstood . . . [about] all those things you've supposedly said and done."

Private persons only have to show that the defamers acted negligently in failing to check the truthfulness of the statement. Thoroughness is important—a "lick and a promise" won't do. A lawyer accused of framing a Chicago policeman and of being a "communist fronter" by the John Birch Society magazine won his libel case; because he was not a public figure, he only had to prove that the magazine was negligent in not checking out the statements made about him. Mrs. Firestone, a Palm Beach socialite, also recovered a $100,000 libel judgment from Time, Inc., for defamatory remarks concerning her divorce. The Supreme Court refused to throw out the judgment, saying that Mrs. Firestone's divorce case was not of sufficient *legitimate* public interest to apply the test for public figures.

An author once called me and related this problem:

A: "I've just published my life story, called X. And a friend of mine gave a copy to a doctor who's in the book, but he's not depicted very, well, very flatteringly."

MB: "By name?"

A: "I changed it from Smithe to Smith."

MB: "Did you change anything else, like his place of practice, specialty, . . .?"

A: "Oh no, he's a _____." So specialized, I groaned to myself, that I didn't know what kind of specialist he was.

MB: "What bad things did you say about him?"

A: "Well, I said he was double-gaited, that he smoked giggle sticks between patients, that he went to a drag party as Mae West . . ."

MB: "Stop. What's your documentation of these?"

A: "Documentation?" She paused, "Oh, his ex-wife told me everything, except I saw him at a Halloween party dressed as Mae West and . . ."

MB: "Was it a drag Halloween party?"

A: "Of course not," she huffed. "I wouldn't attend such a party. It just made the book more interesting. Well anyway, he just called me and threatened to sue me."

MB: "I'll bet. And so you're looking for a lawyer?"

A: "Maybe, if he sues. I mean, I want to line one up." She responded thoughtfully and then sprightly added, "But think how that would boost the sales of my book!"

In a recent Supreme Court case, the Court ruled that the trial judge must apply the "clear and convincing evidence" standard to the public-figure libel plaintiff's documenting proof, and thereby required a lesser standard of preponderance of the evidence. The Author's Guild periodical (Winter 1987 issue) reported that this could increase the use of summary judgments to shorten and resolve libel litigation. The Guild further said that the legal fees to prepare a summary judgment are $45,000, as compared to $400,000 to prepare a case for trial. Makes you think, doesn't it?

The Iowa Libel Research Project reported that between 1974 and 1984, only one in ten plaintiffs in libel suits prevailed, while another fifteen percent settled out of court, often without any cash payment. The profile: A libel plaintiff is most typically an upper-income male, a professional (public figures make up fifty-five percent of the suits), while the defendant is usually a newspaper.

However, the plaintiff's post-publication contact with the publishing concern also influenced the bringing of a suit. The plaintiff usually contacted the concern (before contacting a lawyer) to ask for a retraction or an apology, and was shabbily treated.

Martin Garhus, a trial lawyer who specializes in publishing issues, wrote that libel's many costs included high insurance rates, cautious publishers, and stifled voices. Eighty percent of the costs for a case are lawyer's fees; a Los Angeles libel lawyer, he reports, charges $300 an hour for a libel read. As a result, insurance companies sometimes want a say in what can and cannot be published (*Publishers Weekly*, September 5, 1986).

Resolution of a libel action may not be final. *Publishers Weekly* (June 3, 1988) reported that *Maxwell: A Portrait of Power* by Anthony Delano and Peter Thompson (Transworld), was whipped off bookseller shelves twice—once after legal action for libel removed the purported libelous matter, then a second time, when the back cover's blurb declared it to be "the [almost] complete story" of Maxwell's life. Back in court, Maxwell claimed the bracketed word suggested that the removed material was, in fact, accurate. A law that makes book retailers responsible for the contents of books sold encouraged the publisher to withdraw the book a second time.

Usually, truth is a defense to a lawsuit for libel. However, the truth is sometimes hard to prove, especially in the controversial areas in which libel suits usually occur. Retraction of the libelous statement is not a defense to libel, but can serve to reduce the amount of damages recovered.

Fiction authors are not immune from libel actions. As fact becomes stranger than fiction, and fiction writers create "faction" (fact plus fiction), this area raises a whole list of new questions concerning libel that have not yet been considered by the courts. In *Bindrim v. Mitchell*, (157 Cal. Rptr. 29 [1979]), the defendant authored a fiction book about a nude encounter group. The doctor–leader of the actual groups in which the author participated won a verdict against her and her publisher, even though the book's character's physical characteristics were opposite of those of the real person. The defendant–author signed a contract when she attended the plaintiff's nude encounter group weekend not to reveal anything (no pun intended). That, with a statement that the author made to a friend that she had "devastated Paul Brindim" in her book, did her in legally.

The motion picture version of Sylvia Plath's classic novel, *The Bell Jar,* like a perpetual hangman's noose, reminds novelists, publishers, and motion picture producers that an individual who claims to be depicted in a defamatory manner as a character can sue for libel years after the book has been released.

Case Incident:
Anderson v. Avco Embassy Pictures Corp., **No. CA 82-0752K (Barton, Mass.,1987). The plaintiff asserted that a character in the novel and motion picture was "of and concerning" herself and this portrayal included homosexual and suicidal inclinations, which defamed her and caused her sub-**

stantial emotional anguish. She argued that the producer was negligent, in that with the exercise of reasonable care, they could have determined the Joan Gilling character was her. The novel, when published, had a biographical note that the author "worried about the pain publication might cause to many people close to her whose personalities she had distorted and lightly disguised in the book," and then the note concluded with a statement by Plath's mother that the publication would cause personal suffering, for each character represents someone. Later, a biography of Plath identified the character as the plaintiff, although disclaimed she tried to commit suicide. Anderson threatened to sue the biographer but no notice was given to Plath's estate administrator or the publisher, Harper & Row.

After the sixth day of trial, the defendants agreed to a judgment of $150,000, that the film unintentionally defamed the plaintiff, and that future film distributions contain two disclaimers.

Dropping of a book, article, etc., by a publisher because of libel claims does not always eliminate the publisher's financial obligations. Harcourt Brace Jovanovich paid author Deborah Davies for an unauthorized biography, *Katherine the Great,* that was cancelled by HBJ; she received $100,000 for breach of contract and for destruction of unstamped copies; the rights were reverted to her; she was also compensated for HBJ's conduct not in accordance with the contract (*Publishers Weekly,* November 18, 1983).

I know authors whose publishers demanded that they change not only the name, physical characteristics, and residence but also gender of even minor characters to avoid libel problems in fiction based on fact.

To avoid lawsuits for defamation, have your authors, and in some cases, your employees, follow these rules:

- Research factual material very carefully.
- Any potentially defamatory statements should be confirmed and verified and the notes of this research retained.
- In fiction, carefully disguise beyond recognition any real-life persons who are used as models for characters.
- Obtain a release if possible.
- Avoid accusations of dishonesty or professional incompetence if you cannot prove them.
- Avoid remarks regarding unchastity, a criminal act or crime, physical or mental disease, if not provable.
- Avoid associating an individual with a cause or group that's generally held in disrepute.

Educate your employees on the issues of libel and privacy. Be aware of the libel problems common in certain types of books—first novels, non-fiction, investigative journalism, and biographies of living persons. Not only may your author be skidding into liability (and taking you along) if he or she writes untruths that injure a person's reputation on business, competence, chastity and sexual preferences, health, honesty, and so forth, but going a step further, even if these words are truthful, they could invade the privacy of a person who is not a public figure. This right to be left alone centers around publishing embarrassing or disagreeable facts, ordinarily offensive, about a private person whose activities are not matters of public interest; if the unpleasant facts are well-known, then they aren't private. One protection from these charges is to not only change the name of the subject, but make sure the person is not recognizable.

Book recalls to rectify mistakes or problems are common. Random House recalled approximately 58,000 copies of a biography, *Poor Little Rich Girl: The Life and Legend of Barbara Hutton,* because of erroneous statements about a doctor who puportedly treated Hutton. According to the doctor, he would have been fourteen at the time, obviously not old enough to have a medical degree, much less to have seen Hutton as a patient.

Our law firm once stopped the release of a book and required its revision when a graduate student in sociology wrote about a family she had lived with for a summer; her text was written in such a way as to allow the family to be easily identified, and we alleged that the work invaded the family's privacy and required revision.

Employers' Libel

A mushrooming defamation area covers employment relationships that fall apart. Some estimate a third of defamation lawsuits now are by disgruntled employees (see *National Law Journal,* May 4, 1987). The allegations made by former employees concern references, allegedly defamatory, given to prospective employers that prevent them from getting job offers. While a qualified privilege traditionally protects most employment situations, a showing of actual malice eliminates the privilege. Some actions or remarks during the untangling of and after the employment relationship could be construed as malicious, and ex-employees pull at jury's heartstrings.

Unfair Competition and Misappropriation

Another source of protection from misuse of your work by others (or potential claim against you) is the remedy of unfair competition. Imitators regularly get sued, as these two articles reprinted with permission from the *National Law Journal* (June 8, 1981) show:

Beastly and Curious Products Draw Imitators

Flies in the Face
Of the Competition
ARTCRAFT Novelty Corp. of Abilene, Texas, was doing a buzzing business selling tourists giant plastic flies and oversized Texas fly swatters. It seems that visitors to the Lone Star State like to bring home evidence that everything is bigger in Texas.

Business was so good that Baxter Lane Co. of Amarillo got into the act and began selling the immense insects and their ponderous nemeses.

Bugged by the move, Artcraft called up lawyers Jerry Mills and James Ryndak of Dallas and Charles Scarborough of Abilene to sue for patent infringement.

85

The case came to trial in federal court in Abilene. Jurors, who deliberated about two hours, found Baxter Lane's products were likely to cause confusion among prospective customers and that Baxter Lane's practices constituted unfair competition. The copycat company was ordered to pay $40,000 in damages.

U.S. District Judge H. O. Woodward said he would issue an injunction prohibiting further sales of the 3-foot fly swatters and 8-inch flies by Baxter Lane.

Court Bags
Monster Lawsuit Claim

THE KING OF MONSTERS, they call him. He's Godzilla, a fictitious, gigantic, green, lizard-like monster who has raged in movies, TV, comic and coloring books, sheet vinyl toys, a game and slides.

A likeness of Godzilla also appeared on garbage bags sold by Sears, Roebuck & Co., under the name "Bagzilla." The bags depicted a "comic, helpful, personified reptillian creature" plugging "Monstrously Strong Bags."

This unauthorized emergence made Toho Co. Ltd., the Japanese corporation that has been responsible for all the grade B Godzilla films, quite unhappy. The company contacted its lawyers at Fulwider, Patton, Rieber, Lee & Utecht in Los Angeles and filed suit in federal court charging trademark infringement, unfair competition and unjust enrichment. Sears called up Nilsson, Robbins, Dalgarn, Berliner, Carson & Wurst in Los Angeles to defend it.

The district judge dismissed the case and the monster matter came up before the 9th U.S. Circuit Court of Appeals. After carefully comparing bag and beast, Judge J. Jerome Farris affirmed for Sears.

"The contention that Sears intends to confuse consumers is implausible," the judge stated soberly. "Sears means only to make a pun," much as Montgomery Ward & Co. did when it made trash compactors called "Jaws Two" and "Jaws Power," borrowing from the hungry movie shark.

"Sears' use of 'Bagzilla' has not impaired the effectiveness of the name and image of Godzilla," Judge Farris wrote. "Neither does Sears' use of the reptilian monster character on its garbage bag packages link Godzilla with something unsavory or degrading."

Unfair competition has been found by the courts in the following cases:

- passing off the product of another as your own.
- false or misleading advertising.
- running down a competitor's goods or reputation.
- trade secrets in unpatented and unpatentable items.
- interference with the business growth of another.
- unfair use of written works.
- obstruction of competitor's suppliers.
- bribing customers of competitors.
- unfair usage of imported products.
- boycott.
- price wars.
- unfounded patent litigation.
- copying or simulating a trade name or title.

If you think that you have a claim for unfair competition, ask yourself the following questions:

- Has the design of the offending article been taken from yours?
- Has the offending work been compared to your original work?
- Does the overall appearance of the offending copy strike you as an attempt to pass it off as the original?
- Does the copy have the same design but inferior workmanship, and are the materials the same as the original?
- Has there been trade libel or price cutting?
- Would the average person be taken in by the similarity?

Titles cannot be copyrighted, but sometimes have protection through the theory of unfair competition, fraud, or misappropriation. Hemingway prevented the use of one of his titles, *The Fifth Column,* from utilization as the title for a motion picture, *The Fifth Column Squad,* using those legal theories. Other titles garnering protection are:

- *Sex and the Single Girl,* against *Sex and the Single Man.*
- *Sesame Street,* against use on commercial goods, unless a disclaimer indicated that the product was not connected with the television show.
- the name *Frank Meribell,* which appeared in the title of a thousand stories.
- *The Story of O,* against *The Journey of O.*

But *Alice in Wonderland* the title of an expensive Walt Disney motion picture, was not protected from use for another movie with the same name, as the original work by Lewis Carroll was in the public domain. On the other hand, courts denied the title *Test Pilot* protection because it was purely descriptive and had not acquired a secondary meaning. In order for unfair competition to protect titles, the title must have acquired a secondary meaning, that is, title must have been used for a sufficient length of time to become connected to the work in the public's mind.

Litigation with a triad of issues—copyright infringement, character and title rights—involved a bestseller:

Case Incident:
Judith Rossner, author of the bestselling *Looking for Mr. Goodbar,* sought to enjoin CBS from using "Goodbar" in a television movie, *Trackdown: Finding the Goodbar Killer* (although Rossner licensed the title and movie rights to Paramount). Another writer wrote *Trackdown,* a less successful novel, on the Quinn murder (on which Rossner's was also based). The parties negotiated a settlement to include a disclaimer in credits, but when the movie aired, credits appeared in the commercials.

Litigation commenced, and the court found that any similarities between the characters in the movie and the novel existed because Rossner drew fictional inspiration from an actual event. Rossner could not build a story and characters around an historical incident and then claim the exclusive right to use of the incident. The court did not find a violation of the Lanham Act under the principles of the title acquiring a secondary meaning and likelihood of confusion.

There should be a clear distinction between *copyright,* "works of authorship fixed in any tangible medium of expression," and *trademark,*"a word, name, symbol, or device... used to identify his goods and to distinguish them from those manufactured or sold by others." Remember, a trademark can be a work of authorship, i.e., a fanciful design to label a product, or characters from films, or titles of songs. (See David J. Meyer's "Misapplication of the Misappropriation Doctrine to Merchandising, *Law & the Arts,*" vol. 11, no. 4, Summer 1987.) A popularized symbol, phrase, title, symbol character, or personality image used in association with a product—look at the bumper sticker fad, t-shirts, and so forth—becomes a merchandising property. Often, the Lanham Act is invoked as a legal weapon to prohibit competition, based on the likelihood of consumer confusion as to the origin of goods. Some disputes over merchandising rights resolved in the claimant's favor include:

- posters bearing the likeness of King Kong.
- beer cans bearing the logo of school football teams.

A rather amusing case involving multiple-plaintiff theories of copyright, trademark infringement, and unfair competition was brought against my favorite macaroni company, Kraft:

Case Incident:
McDougal, Littell and Company, a textbook publisher sued Kraft, Inc., for cheapening its product by using a photograph of their textbook, *Building English Skills,* in a special offer on a package of Macaroni and Cheese Dinner, on the theories of copyright, trademark infringement, and unfair competition. The textbook was used in a $1.50 special offer of a pencil box designed to look like a box of Kraft Macaroni and Cheese. The publisher asked unspecified damages, that Kraft be enjoined from using the photograph, and that it deliver to impoundment all the boxes with a photograph.

In one case, unfair competition protected a character from misappropriation: the exclusive right of the cartoonists who created Mutt and Jeff to use the characters was upheld. Dashiell Hammett was ultimately successful in arguing that his rights to the character Sam Spade, of the famous *The Maltese Falcon,* were not lost with the sale of a right to publish a copyrighted story. Since the sale did not specifically include the character Sam Spade, which was his property, the character could be reused by him. While Sam Spade was really given protection as a matter of contract, the court mentioned that copyright protection extends to the character when the character "constitutes the story being told" or when it is so developed that it leaves the realm of idea and becomes the expression. Hopalong Cassidy and Tarzan were protected under this theory. The Naval Institute Press and the authors of *The Hunt for Red October* and *Flight of the Intruders* mediated, through the American Arbitration Association, on the issue of who owned the characters in these works of fiction. (See the discussion in the copyright section about the protection of characters by copyright.)

Trade Secrets

A trade secret is usually technical information generally not known by others engaged in a trade. Trade secrets that have been protected by the courts are chemical formulas, customer lists, customer credit ratings, blueprints, architectural plans, patterns, unpatentable or unpatented designs, inventions, and advertising slogans. Examples of long-standing trade secrets are the formulas for Coca-Cola ® and Smith's Black Cough Drops ® (which are over one hundred years old). Trade-secrets protection can last longer than the terms for copyright or patents.

Some trade secrets have died away—for example, knowledge of pigment compositions used by painters in the fifteenth and sixteenth centuries. The Romans controlled knowledge of trade secrets by enslaving those who possessed the knowledge, while the Anglo-Saxons accomplished the same control through guilds.

In modern times, you can file a lawsuit against a person who discloses or uses your trade secret without your permission. Usually, the person would have acquired the secret improperly, either by theft or by receiving the information in confidence, with the understanding that he or she would not disclose it.

If you think your publishing business involves valuable trade secrets, pay attention to the number of persons with whom you share the secret; have employees, at the time of hiring, sign a written contract that they will not disclose the secret(s).

Publishers have more trade secrets than they may at first think. When you consider the hopscotching from one publishing house to the next that occurs among editorial staff, the protection of these secrets by contract is something to consider.

Canada has both civil and criminal law on trade secrets—the Trade Secrets Production Act—with definitive statutory torts and criminal offenses.

Freedom of Information Act and Sunshine Laws

Two federal acts give publishers rights that may affect the content of a published work.

Facts are a basic stock-in-trade for many publishers and writers. The federal and state Freedom of Information Act (FOIA) and Sunshine Act are relatively new tools with which publishers and their writers can pry information out of federal, and some state, governments. The FOIA rules apply only to information held by administrative agencies of the federal government; it does not cover documents belonging to the legislative or judicial branches. Also, the act exempts nine separate categories of documents to which agencies can deny public access. (For more information on FOIA request procedures, refer to *Making It Legal.*)

The federal government's Sunshine Act became law on March 12, 1977. The policy behind the act was that "the public is entitled to the fullest practicable information regarding the decision-making processes of the Federal Government." To implement this policy, the act declares a presumption in favor of open meetings and requires publication of notices of meetings. Some states have also passed similar laws.

Not all states have enacted laws concerning public access to information. Check with your local chapter of the ACLU or your lawyer to see if your state has a Freedom of Information Act (FOIA) and/or a Sunshine Act.

In Canada, there are two federal acts of which you should be aware: the Access to Information Act, which gives the public a right to receive government-held information; and the Privacy Act, which protects the privacy of personal-nature information in government information.

According to the *Canadian Corporate Law Reporter* (vol. 2, Issue no. 9, July 1985), the Canadian Access to Information Act is a two-edged sword for businesses (as it also is in the United States). It is estimated that about eighty percent of requests under FOIA are made by businesses seeking information about competitors' secrets (exclusive of FBI/FOIA). One suggestion to prevent this abuse is to make the government aware that certain information is a trade secret, or confidential and commercially sensitive. The Canadian Bar Foundation in Ottawa, Ontario, has a series of booklets, some of which could be of use to you, for instance, *Privacy Law and the Media in Canada* and *The Charter in the Media*.

Shield laws protect the nondisclosure of a journalist's confidential sources, because nondisclosure outweighs public and private interest in compelled testimony, as it would deter undercover investigative reporting and threaten press freedom and the public's need to know. New York's shield law has not been extended to authors.

"Son of Sam" laws are directed to situations where criminals earn monies for writing or collaborating on a book about his or her own criminal activities.

Case Incident:
New York's Son of Sam laws do not apply to victimless crimes, and therefore did not apply to a book by Sydney Biddle Barrows, *Mayflower Madam*, a woman who claimed to have pilgrim ancestors and who pled guilty to promoting prostitution.

Check with your lawyer if you propose to publish this type of work.

Other Legal Theories

The theories of products liability, negligence, and tortious interference with a contract sometimes pop up, and lawsuits can drag on. When the underdog U.S. hockey team got an unexpected gold medal in 1980, J. B. Binelli stepped in and negotiated an exclusive contract for team poster and print rights. Volkswagen distributed 120,000 free posters of the gold-winning team, destroying Mr. Binelli's market and eight years later, a state court of appeals upheld the $1.6 million jury verdict for tortious interference with his exclusive rights.

The *National Law Journal* (July 25, 1988) reported a lawsuit against Pacific Bell Smart Yellow Pages, brought by a dissatisfied advertiser whose travel agency specialized in exotic travel. The ad read "Specializing in International Erotic Travel." Since the ad had appeared, the $1 million business dropped by more than fifty percent. The $10 million suit alleges gross negligence and emotional distress.

You need to be wary of editoral products liability claims for damage caused by publication of erroneous material, or material with a foreseeable degree of risk. Diet and exercise books are prime candidates for this problem, as are certain types of children's books—those with zippers, buttons, or other attachments that can be broken off, swallowed, or otherwise injurious to children. Attention was focused on this potential exposure by the more than $1 million jury verdict in the Rand McNally "exploding chemistry experiment" litigation, and the lawsuit against NBC for a rape allegedly caused by the made-for-television movie, *Born Innocent.*

Disclaimers are often used when use of information in a book could cause injury.

Memorandum
To: XYZ Publishers
From: MB
Re: Sample disclaimers regarding self-treatment for life-threatening
        physical disorders

You've asked what kind of disclaimers, if any, you should use for the "as told to" story of the miracle recovery through self-treatment of Ms. X from her life-threatening illness.

Yes, use a disclaimer. Read the examples listed below, and then give me a call.

1. from *The F-Plan Diet: Lose Weight and Live Longer:* "Before starting any diet, you should consult your doctor to discuss the reducing plan you intend to follow."

2. from *Life Extension C:* "Disclaimer . . . this set of comments is usually called a disclaimer, that is, our attempt to provide certain principles which govern what we consider reasonable use of our book. This is not a mere formality. We really mean what we say.

"Don't be careless with new knowledge. As you read this book, it is important to keep in mind these factors: (1) we are research scientists, not physicians, and (2) we are not infallible. See your doctor for treatment of serious disorders such as heart disease, etc."

3. from *Holistic Health:* "Our intent as staff is to act as tour guides. We provide information and share the maps or tools that can lead to high-level wellness . . . as tour guides, it is important for us to recognize and utilize the integrated interdisciplinary approach which is available to us."

4. from *Jane Brody's Nutrition Book:* "This book is a guide to good nutrition throughout your life. Although the emphasis is on eating to preserve health, it does not contain dietary prescriptions for specific medical problems. Do not use any of the advice herein for self-treatment without your physician's knowledge and okay."

Part II

The Generic Book Contract

The Publisher's Rights

6

So much for restrictions on content. Now, draw a long breath and we'll go through the generic book contract, up to post-publication matters.

Parameters of Publisher's Control

These provisions, too, vary:

> **Upon delivery and acceptance of the manuscript, index and graphic materials, the Press shall manufacture, publish and sell the work at its own expense and in such style and manner and at such prices as it deems suitable. The Press may edit the work to ensure that it is consistent and conforms to a style of punctuation, spelling, capitalization and usage the Press considers appropriate. The Press shall have the right to distribute copies of the work and to grant permissions to produce excerpts from it free of charge to promote sale of the work.**

Note that this provision lacks a publishing date. Over half of the book contracts I've examined fail to indicate the work's publication date. (This shocks most author-clients, who missed this detail.) In terms of publisher's editorial work on a manuscript, however, the above clause is more explicit than most.

There have been numerous cases regarding changes not consented to by the author. The European doctrine of *droit morale* (that is, the right of a creator to have his work attributed to him in the form in which he created it) has not taken hold in the United States, where the courts look to the contract. Since the United States joined the Berne Convention in 1989, the concept of *droit morale* will likely become more important (see Copyright Chapter Ten). Already in existence is a New York law that grants artists a legal right to insist that their works not be displayed or reproduced in a manner that might damage their reputation—consider this if you publish art books.

Calls from disgruntled authors come in monthly regarding publisher rewrites (most of these refer to magazines rather than book publishers). Where the author grants rights to sell condensed or abridged editions, and there is no clause forbidding changes without the author's consent, the courts haven't been seriously concerned with the author's screams of breach of contract or other legal issues regarding publisher's changes in the manuscript. If you use a contract, be sure to provide for editorial changes consistent with your publishing boundaries, i.e., grammatical corrections, omissions, or total rewrites.

Another simple provision is:

Publisher agrees to publish the work, at its own expense, within _____ months after acceptance of the final copy, in a style and manner, and at such price as it deems best suited to the sale thereof.

Or this alternative provision:

Publication of the Work
After giving written notice to the Author that it has accepted the Work for publication, the Publisher shall within 12 months of written acceptance of the manuscript publish the Work at its own expense and in such style and manner and with such trademarks, service marks, and imprints of Publisher, and sell the Work at such prices, as it shall deem suitable. The Publisher shall publish the Work with a copyright notice and register the Work in accordance with the United States copyright laws in the name of the Publisher or Authur as the Author may elect.

Both provisions need to have added, at the very least, the following: "The Publisher shall not be liable for delays in performance due to causes beyond the Publisher's control."

The publisher usually retains the right to put the publication together in its own way, under the theory that the publisher is the professional in this area. However, depending upon your author's clout and his or her personality, you might want to agree to a minimum retail price, and to consult with the author on format, style, graphic material, and dust jacket decisions. It's generally a good idea to formally commit to nominal print runs and promotional efforts, so that good faith is demonstrated to the author.

Each contract implies an obligation of good faith and fair dealing. In some contracts, the publisher agrees to use its "best efforts" to promote the author's book.

In the case of *Van Valkenburgh, Nooger & Neville, Inc. v. Hayden Publishing Co.* (281 N.E.2d 142 [1972]) the court found that the publisher breached this duty. The author and publisher agreed to produce a multi-volume set, which sold well; after two years, they became involved in a royalty dispute and the publisher discontinued magazine ads, hired writers to produce two multi-volume sets similar in style and content to the original author's, and predictably, the sales of the first set dropped.

In *Zilg v. Prentice-Hall* (717 F.2d 671 [1983]) the court failed to find a breach when the publisher printed thirteen thousand volumes, had an advertising budget of $5,500, distributed six hundred free copies to reviewers, purchased ads, and tried to sell the paperback rights. The Book of the Month Club was prepared to handle the book through its subsidiary, the Fortune Book Club, but when the book, a critical historical account of the Dupont family, became too controversial, the Book of the Month Club dropped it.

Proofreading and Author's Corrections

From an English publishing agreement:

> **The author undertakes to read, check and correct proofs and to return them to the publishers within _____ days of their receipt, failing which the publishers may consider the proofs as passed for press. Cost of all alterations and corrections made by the author in the finished art work and in the proofs (other than correction of artists', copy editors' and printers' errors) above 10% of the original costs of composition shall be borne by the author. Should any charge arise under this clause, the amount may be deducted from any sum which may become due to the author under this agreement.**

Or from an American one:

> **If requested by the Publisher, the Author shall correct proof of the Work and return it promptly to the Publisher. If the Author makes or causes to be made any alterations in the type, illustrations, or film which are not typographical, drafting, or Publisher's errors and which exceed 15 percent of the original cost of composition and artwork independent of the cost of these Author's alterations, the cost of the excess alterations shall be charged against any sums accruing to the Author under this Agreement.**

Another provision, which basically states what is set forth above, adds that:

> **The cost of all changes requested and made by the author at any subsequent stage of book production shall be assumed by the author and paid within thirty days of receipt of an itemized invoice. The author agrees to prepare an index, if suitable and requested by the publisher, at the author's own expense, or may ask the publisher to have one prepared, in which case the cost will be deducted from future royalties.**

Do you see the common threads that run through these provisions? First, there is only a short time allowed to the author for checking of proofs, because the next step is printing. Second, publishers want to avoid the all-too-frequent situation in which the author does a final edit on the galley proofs, as *all* proof alterations are expensive. While proof alterations for illustrations and visuals cost more than for typesetting, still, extensive galley alterations are expensive. One publisher's final typesetting cost for a manuscript ran $6,000 instead of the $3,000 bid, because the author did her final edit on the galleys.

Delays in returning galleys and excessive alterations preclude your meeting the publication schedule. Some publishers, burned by authors editing at the galley stage, require that the cost of alterations be paid within thirty days, rather than be charged against future royalties—future royalties seem unlikely to materialize.

The last illustrative clause can be a problem, for it implies that the author can insist on changes (as distinguished from corrections) as long as he or she is willing to pay for same. There's a psychological advantage to you if the author knows that once the grimy, tattered manuscript leaves her ink-stained hands, that's it—it can't be changed. Redefine that provision if you add it to your contract.

It's okay to require the author to prepare an index, but it's wise, always, *to put a timeline on any request from publisher to author.*

Copyright

One provision on copyright reads:

> **Upon first publication of the work, the publisher shall duly register the copyright in the name of _____ in the United States of America**
> **(publisher/author)**
> **under the Universal Copyright Convention, and shall insert the requisite copyright notice on all copies of the work that are distributed to the public. The author shall furnish promptly any authorization or other document necessary for this purpose.**

or:

> **Publisher shall register the copyright in its name in the United States (including renewals and extensions thereof) and at its option may secure a copyright on same in any countries covered by this Agreement. Author shall furnish the Publisher promptly with any authorization or document necessary for this purpose. If the Work is out of print, then the copyright shall revert to the Author.**

or:

> **The PUBLISHER shall register the copyright of the work and all renewals of such copyright name in any and all countries of the world. It shall also have the right to any assistance from the AUTHOR as may be necessary to protect the copyright and renewals thereof.**

Under the Grant of Rights, the author gives certain rights and licenses to the publisher regarding the work. Sometimes, the breadth of these encompasses a copyright owner's total rights, but not always. Standard publishing practice allows the author to retain the copyright. Occasionally a publisher insists on copyright, but agrees that the copyright will revert to the author on certain conditions, such as contract termination.

As a copyright junkie, I check the copyright page of each book or publication I pick up to see who owns the copyright. I've discovered a number of interesting facts: that an author credited on the jacket cover is writing under a pseudonym, that an author is deceased and the copyright is owned by his or her heirs or estate, or that a group of persons owns the copyright. Unusual copyright pages end up in my collection.

Contracts are also written as "work-for-hire," and so the employer (publisher) owns the copyright. This work-for-hire concept is extended by California's law, which considers authors contracted with by publishers as employees entitled to full state benefits. Thus, California writers need to be covered by the same insurance provided by the publisher to their regular employees.

Reread these contractual provisions after you read the copyright chapters.

Advance Payments

The industry standard is a recoupable advance, which allows the publishing house to somewhat offset the risks inherent in advancing money on unearned royalties. If the work doesn't get published, would you have your lawyer sue for return of a $500 or $1,000 advance? No. But can you afford to lose even a $1,000 on a project? No.

A major publisher's contract that I examined for an author provided for the following regarding advances, manuscripts costs, and permission costs:

> **The Publisher will pay the Author an advance of Five Thousand Dollars ($5,000.00) on account of all income accruing to the Author from the Work, payable as follows: One Thousand Dollars ($1,000.00) upon the signing of this Agreement; Two Thousand Dollars ($2,000.00) upon delivery to and approval by the Publisher of one-half (½) of the manuscript; and Two Thousand Dollars ($2,000.00) upon delivery to and acceptance by the Publisher of the complete final manuscript (including portions previously approved). It is understood and agreed that approval of portions of the manuscript shall not be deemed acceptance or conditional acceptance of the complete final manuscript.**

> **The Publisher shall reimburse the Author up to One Thousand Dollars ($1,000.00) for typing, photocopying, and other similar expenses incurred in the preparation of the manuscript. Such funds will be disbursed by the Publisher based on the submission of paid invoices or other reasonable verification of expenses incurred by the Author.**

> **The Publisher agrees to advance and make all payments required for the cost of securing permission to use copyrighted material of others in the Work. The Publisher shall absorb fifty percent (50%) of the amount of such**

payments up to a total contribution by the Publisher of Three Thousand Dollars ($3,000.00). All payments in excess of the Publisher's share shall be applied as an advance on account of income accruing to the Author from the Work. The Author will obtain written permission for use of all material that is the property of others and is incorporated in the Work by the Author, and will deliver the permissions to the Publisher by the delivery date with the final revised manuscript. The Author shall make no commitment on the Publisher's behalf for any such permission fee without prior written approval of the Publisher. If the Author is unable to obtain permission satisfactory to the Publisher for any material, mutally agreeable material will be substituted.

Another, simpler, provision that makes no promises regarding permissions or typing costs states:

> Publisher shall pay to the author as a fee under this agreement, the sum of $ _____ , payable one-half on signing the publishing contract, and one-half upon the publisher's determination that author has delivered a satisfactory manuscript of the work to the publisher."

Small presses rarely give advances, or if they do, they're often modest and disbursed in three increments: upon signing, upon receipt of a satisfactory manuscript, and upon publication. If legal objections or other problems keep a work off the market at the last minute, the unpaid advance could be a financial advantage to your small press. While Richard Curtis, in his book *How To Be Your Own Literary Agent,* lists any advance under $5,000 as a poor deal for the author, his figures are based on advance amounts from major publishing houses. The various Author's Guild trade book contract surveys also usually include conglomerate publishing companies, with only a handful of university presses or small presses represented. In my experience, advances given by small presses, if any, are under fifteen hundred dollars.

Authors frequently seek the highest advance they can get because royalties are both a long time coming and may be negligible. Authors believe that the bigger the advance, the higher the publisher's stake in the work and the harder the publisher works to market and promote the work. Small presses argue that they cannot afford to let *any* of their products sit; they do relatively few and have substantial investments (proportionately) in each, and they need that money back.

Some authors contend in a no- or small-advance situation, the publisher is using "their" money interest-free. Small presses point out that an advance is unearned and that publishers loan the money in expectation of sales sufficient to repay. Some presses, such as university presses, never pay advances because (they say) they don't have the money. The financial realities of small press-publishing often given publishers no choice but small (or no) advance payments, and authors must recognize that.

The financial realities from the author's perspective can be daunting, as well. Many support themselves from advance to advance. You figure that if an author writing for a small press gets zero advance, and it takes twenty-four months to publish the work, and finally, the earnings aren't reported until the next accounting period, it may be three years or more before the author sees any money from that book.

In determining the advance, some publishers rely on whimsy, hunches, or instincts. Others estimate the first year's sales and from that, project the author's royalties and pay all or part of that as an advance. Richard Balkin's small press book-publishing agreement guideline sets advances by small presses at $250 to $2,000; his rule of thumb for calculating a fair advance is to figure out the royalties from the book's first-printing or first-year sales and then deduct 20% to 25% from that amount for returns. If production costs for the work are scaled up due to color reproductions, or you want to spend significant sums on advertising a book, an early hefty advance affects your cash flow. Further, do not automatically pay the next advance installment because you physically receive the manuscript; wait until you've determined that the manuscript is satisfactory. Unfortunately, it is common for a publisher to get finished manuscript that is not equal to the quality of the proposal and must be extensively reworked.

Too often, the author demands, and is granted, the total advance on contract signing. Then the publisher has to attempt to wrench a satisfactory text from the author, which is comparable to fishing for sardines with a tuna net. Some publishers, by sheer ingenuity, perseverence, and legal "threats," finally get a satisfactory manuscript, but the energy required is substantial and can be expensive, both financially and creatively.

While on big deals, "bonus advances" (sometimes called "escalators") become payable in the event of certain contingencies—such as the appearance of the book on the bestseller list, a screenplay or a movie based on the book, or a book club purchase—most publishers of a small-to-medium size do not view those as real possibilities. They are occasionally surprised, though. North Point Press published Evan Connell's *Son of the Morning Star,* which was on the bestseller list; I understand that just keeping the work in print taxed the publisher's resources. An example of success almost doing you in.

The more money you pay out in advances, the more reluctant you are to drop the project if trouble turns up later. Whether a problem is worth losing an advance over depends on the parties, the possible solutions, the cost of these, and the project's stage. An heir who interferes with the deceased's unfinished work may be too difficult to tackle, but an invasion-of-privacy charge that can be satisfied by a little manuscript tinkering might work.

A landmark "advance" case involved an ex-presidential candidate, Barry Goldwater of Arizona. In *Harcourt Brace Jovanovich, Inc. v. Goldwater* (532 F.Supp. 619 [1982]), Harcourt, after rejecting Goldwater's book of political memoirs as unsatisfactory, sued to recover the $65,000 advance paid to Goldwater and his collaborator. They, in turn, counterclaimed for the balance of the advance, $135,000, due if the manuscript had been accepted as satisfactory. Goldwater took the same manuscript to another publisher, who gave him a little editorial assistance.

Viola! A bestseller. The court ultimately rejected Harcourt's argument, on the grounds that Harcourt breached its contract by failing to provide the author with editorial assistance. The court let Goldwater and his collaborator keep the $65,000 and directed the publisher to pay them the balance of the advance, plus interest, but mitigated those damages by deducting from them the amount of the advance and royalties paid by the second publisher.

An expensive lesson, both in calculating advances and "duty to edit."

Not all famous personages prevail. When Doubleday sued Tony Curtis, *Doubleday v. Curtis* (763 F.2d 495 [2nd Cir. 1985]), for return of advance on a manuscript novel that they rejected as unsatisfactory, the court allowed Doubleday to recover the $50,000 advance and dismissed the author's counterclaims for the balance. The court determined that Doubleday acted in good faith in rejecting the manuscript, even though editorial assistance was given somewhat late.

If you've invested in an author and developed a steady backlist of his or her books, consider joint accounting; this enables you to balance money lost on an unprofitable book with income on those that are profitable. A provision on joint accounting for multiple books follows:

> **If the Author shall have received amounts in excess of the royalties due under this Agreement, then the Publisher may recoup such overpayment from any further royalties or advances payable to the Author for the work or due under any other agreement between the Author and the Publisher for any other work.**

Royalties

The yin and yang of book accounting: royalties and licensing revenues. A royalty represents proceeds from the sale of copies of the book, while licensing revenues are derived from licensing parts of the grant of rights.

Here's a simple royalty clause:

> **Publisher shall pay to the author a royalty of _____ % of retail price of all units sold, less actual returns and a reasonable reserve for returns except as set forth below:**
> **a. No royalty shall be paid on copies sold below or at cost including expenses incurred or furnished gratis to the author, or for review, advertising, sample, remainder books, destroyed books or damaged books found to be unsaleable, or like purposes.**
> **b. Fifty percent (50%) of the amount received from the disposition of licenses granted pursuant to paragraph _____ , subdivisions _____ through _____ .**

Or this variation from a university press's contract:

> **The Press shall pay to the author the following royalties:**

On sales of the work in hardbound editions, ten percent (10%) on the first three thousand copies; fifteen percent (15%) thereafter of all monies paid to and received by the Press from the sale of the work, less shipping and handling charges (if included in amounts billed) and sales or equivalent taxes, less returns, less allowances and discounts.

On sales of the work in paperback editions, five percent (5%) of all monies paid to and received by the Press from sales of the work, less shipping and handling charges (if included in amounts billed) and sales or equivalent taxes, less returns, less allowances and discounts.

On sales, licenses, transfers or assignments to third parties of rights of any kind in the work or any part thereof, fifty percent (50%) of all monies paid to and received by the Press.

The rather detailed advance, reimbursement of expenses, and permissions from a major publisher's contract (already noted) included the following provision on royalties in its contract:

Royalties
The Publisher will pay the Author a royalty on the amount received by the Publisher for all copies of the Work sold by the Publisher (less copies credited for return) as follows:

fifteen percent (15%),

except as specified below;

10% for copies of any edition of the Work sold for export, or outside the United States, or at less than the established wholesale price;

5% for copies of any edition sold through the medium of mail order, coupon, space, radio or television advertising, direct by mail circularization, or any other direct to consumer mail order methods;

5% with respect to copies sold as overstock, provided that no royalty will be payable with respect to any copies sold or disposed of at or below the per unit cost of manufacture.

No royalties will be paid for copies of the Work or any component of the Work disposed of at or below cost, or copies furnished for review, publicity, promotion, sample or similar purposes, or for charitable or other public purposes for which the Publisher receives no proceeds in excess of the cost of manufacture, or for copies furnished to the Author or gratis to others at the Author's request. No royalty will be payable with respect to manuals, keys, tests, teaching aids, audio programs, or other materials related to the Work and prepared for use as an adjunct to the Work.

As used herein with respect to the Publisher's sales, the "amount received by the Publisher" will mean the net cash amount actually received by the Publisher from each copy sold and not credited for return, after discounts, and excluding postage, shipping and insurance costs or charges, and sales, excise, value added, and similar taxes, if any.

These terms—"amounts received," "actual proceeds," "net sales," or "gross receipts"—are appearing more frequently in book contracts superseding the previously common phrases, "cover price" or "list price" of the work.

Generally, for hard-cover, trade book publishing, the royalty is five percent of the list or cover price or ten percent of the net proceeds, of the first 5,000 copies sold, escalating by two to two-and-a-half percent on the next 5,000 sold, and so forth. Mass-market and trade paperback publishing involve more complex and larger discounts, and as a result, the royalties start lower and don't go as high; they usually escalate on the basis of hundreds of thousands of copies sold.

As book-merchandising techniques become more ingenious, and more competitive, publishers must sell their books at a variety of discounts and deals. Book-buyers who take substantial quantities merit larger and larger discounts. Therefore, some publishers have found it useful to build in a percentage relationship between discounts and royalties. Also, mail-order royalties are sometimes half of the standard rate because of high marketing costs—newspaper and magazine ads, mailing lists and printed solicitations, shipping, and handling.

A small publishing concern, without salespeople or commissioned representatives, often relies heavily on wholesalers, thus requiring the sale of its books at a high percentage of discount. The first royalty in the sample publishing agreement (previously cited on page 101) grants an initially generous royalty percentage with an escalation clause, but the rest of the clause reduces the royalty under different sales circumstances. The rationale for this is that if you have to use a wholesaler to sell books to certain markets, at a discount that is often ten percent to twenty percent more than the normal bookstore discount, you thus end up with a lesser share of the sales dollar, even though you sell more books, and you want to share that reduction with the author. Publishers often base royalties on the net receipts for special sales, *but* define terms so you don't have to fall back on "industry practice" in case of a dispute.

If you give full credit for unsold books, add a provision dubbed "reserve against returns." Sometimes the contract provides for a "reasonable" reserve, which industry practice has determined to be twenty percent to twenty-five percent of the cost of books shipped. It is not uncommon, however, for actual returns to run much higher. The author may want to cap the reserve against returns by a certain percentage sum, or period of time; consider your normal return rate and respond accordingly.

Authors may also ask you to pay interest on late royalty payments, or to treat late royalty payments as a breach of contract. While there have been few court cases reported for non-payment of royalties, the number of royalty issues between author and publisher is staggering. In one case, it was determined that payment- and statement-default was a basis for rescission and accounting on the contract. One court indicated that there was no breach when twenty-six percent of the royalties due were paid, while in another situation, it was held that failure to pay two-thirds of the total owed was a fundamental breach.

Other recurring problems between publishers and authors regarding royalties are:

- different interpretations of royalty provisions.
- definition of special sale.
- differences between gross income, gross receipts, and gross sales (if any).
- restriction of sales to heavily discounted markets.
- royalty on books sold by the author.

Your publishing concern's pricing formula, projected budget, and overhead set your royalties. Give your editor ranges to utilize when negotiating with an author. Obviously, establish these in conjunction with your financial person or accountant. Don't forget to also have your financial advisor determine your royalty breaking-points for discounted sales, foreign sales, remainders, and direct-mail sales. Small presses often find it better to pay royalties on net receipts rather than list price, particularly if they rely on wholesalers, while some literary publishing concerns pay royalties only on a percentage of copies from each print run.

The minimal exceptions to your standard royalty rate include:

- mail order sales.
- large orders discounted more than fifty percent.
- export sales.
- sale of overstock (remainder sales).
- sales from a small reprinting done to keep the book in circulation.

Some contracts make the author and publisher joint-venturers, with the author providing the manuscript plus some money, and the publisher providing its publishing expertise, as well as other costs. The parties then divide the net income derived from sales. If you operate this way, fine-tune the definition of costs (see the discussion of co-publishing in a later chapter).

Some small publishing concerns unwisely ignore primary subsidiary rights or secondary subsidiary rights (primary rights include book club, reprint, second serialization, and selections and abridgments, while secondary rights include those for the British Commonwealth or international market, commercial exploitation, dramatization, first serialization, and foreign translation rights).

The usual split on primary subsidiary rights is 50/50, although an author might propose an escalating split depending upon the revenue collected. Subsidiary rights sales are essentially "gravy" and can mean the difference between a profitable and unprofitable book. The sale of subsidiary rights means more money to divide between the author and you. *If* your publishing concern *doesn't have* a subsidiary rights person, or a rights agent, *then* you need to look long and hard at acquiring British Commonwealth rights, and foreign, first serial, and even performance rights for the copyright term.

Consider the type of book first. A monograph about a historical view of the witch purge of 1878 on the Navajo Indian Reservation, published by a Native American college press, has only regional appeal, and wouldn't warrant haggling over rights. If you don't have the capacity to sell sub-rights, let them go after a time, or flip-flop the percentages so that if the author sells them on his or her own, you still get a small percentage from the sale of material that you brought to public attention.

If your publishing concern has expertise, or an agent, or wants to control more of the rights, and if the subject matter of the book dictates it, you will probably want several variations of the subsidiary rights clause that apply to special conditions beyond those indicated in the samples. For contrast, here's a provision from a major publisher's agreement, with fourteen variations.

> **The Publisher shall pay to the Author a royalty on the retail price of every copy sold by the Publisher, less actual returns and a reasonable reserve for returns (except as set forth below):**
>
> **_____ percent (_____ %) up to and including _____ copies; _____ percent (_____ %) in excess of _____ copies up to and including _____ copies; and _____ percent (_____ %) in excess of _____ copies. Where the discount in the United States is forty-eight percent (48%) or more from the retail price, the rate provided in this subdivision a. shall be reduced by one-half the difference between forty-four percent (44%) and the discount granted. In no event, however, shall such royalty be less than one-half of the rate provided herein. If the semi-annual sales aggregate is fewer than 400 copies, the royalty shall be two-thirds ($^2/_3$) of the rate provided in this subdivision a. if such copies are sold from a second or subsequent printing. Copies covered by any other subdivision of this Paragraph shall not be included in such computation.**
>
> **Five percent (5%) of the amount received for copies sold directly to the consumer through the medium of mail-order or coupon advertising, or radio or television advertising.**
>
> **Five percent (5%) of the amount received for copies sold by the Publisher's Premium or Subscription Books Wholesale Department.**
>
> **Ten percent (10%) for hard-cover copies and five percent (5%) for soft-cover copies sold with a lower retail price as college textbooks.**
>
> **For a School edition the royalty provided in subdivision a. of this Paragraph but no more than:**
>
> > **i. Ten percent (10%) of the amount received for a Senior High School edition;**
> >
> > **ii. Eight percent (8%) of the amount received for a Junior High School edition;**
> >
> > **iii. Six percent (6%) of the amount received for an Elementary School edition.**
>
> **Five percent (5%) for an edition published at a lower retail price or for an edition in the _____ (regular or giant size) or in _____ Books; and two percent (2%) or two cents (2¢) per copy, whichever is greater, for an edition in the _____ College Editions.**
>
> **Ten percent (10%) of the amount received for the original edition and five percent (5%) of the amount received for any lower-price edition for copies sold for export.**
>
> **For copies sold outside normal wholesale and retail trade channels, ten**

percent (10%) of the amount received for the original edition and five percent (5%) of the amount received for any lower-price edition for copies sold at a discount between fifty percent (50%) and sixty percent (60%) from the retail price and five percent (5%) of the amount received for copies sold at a discount of sixty percent (60%) or more from the retail price, or for the use of the plates by any governmental agency.

No royalty shall be paid on copies sold below or at cost including expenses incurred, or furnished gratis to the Author, or for review, advertising, sample or like purposes.

Fifty percent (50%) of the amount received from the disposition of licenses granted pursuant to Paragraph 1, subdivision a., ii, iii, iv, vi and vii. At the Author's request his share from book club and reprint licensing, less any unearned advances, shall be paid to him within two weeks after the receipt thereof by the Publisher. If the Publisher rebates to booksellers for unsold copies due to the publication of a lower-price or reprint edition, the royalty on such copies shall be the same as for such lower-price edition.*

Ninety percent (90%) of the amount received from the disposition of licenses in the United States and Canada granted pursuant to Paragraph 1, subdivision a., v.**

Eighty percent (80%) of the amount received from the disposition of licenses granted pursuant to Paragraph 1, subdivision b.***

Seventy-five percent (75%) of the amount received from the disposition of licenses granted pursuant to Paragraph 1, subdivision c.†

Fifty percent (50%) of the amount received from the disposition of licenses granted pursuant to Paragraph 1, subdivision d., provided that all expenses in connection therewith shall be borne by the Publisher.‡

*   book club reprint, anthology, after-periodical publication, filmstrips, etc.
**   pre-periodical publication.
***British Commonwealth.
†   translation rights.
‡   author's likeness, title of work, etc.

This contract reduces the royalty on small printings. (Even though short runs are more expensive per unit, authors often object to a royalty reduction, as it raises in their minds the spector of publisher abuse.)

If you reverse a small part of Richard Curtis's "good deal" discussion for authors, a good deal for a publisher consists of hardcover, world rights in all languages, and control of movie and television rights, with royalties under ten percent on the first 5,000 copies sold, escalating in two-and-a-half percent increments for the next 5,000, and so forth. Twenty-five percent or more of the British and translation licensing revenues would go to the publisher; more than ten percent of first serial, movie, and television revenue, and more than fifty percent of reprint, book club, and other primary and subsidiary rights revenue would also go to the publishing house.

Warner Books, according to *Publishers Weekly* (May 6, 1988), gambled when it acquired, for a nearly $5 million guarantee, the hard- and softcover rights to the sequel of *Gone with the Wind.* The royalties are set at seventeen and one-half percent until the guarantee is paid out, then drop to fifteen percent on the hardcover; softcover royalties are set at a straight fifteen percent. For Warner to recoup its investment, 250,000 hardcover sales (at $25 each) and 3 million soft-cover sales are necessary.

There are those who contend that book club rights, electronic rights, reprint, and second serial rights should be shared equally, while the split for publication in the United Kingdom, or in a foreign language, or commercial rights should be split 75/25, with first-serial rights and performance rights either retained by the author or split 90/10 to 80/20, if controlled by the publisher.

If your publishing concern handles subsidiary rights in a timely manner or has a subsidiary rights agent, you need a fair percentage of the income from this additional exploitation of the work. From the publisher's perspective, this represents a return on your promotion and marketing of the work, which increases the overall value of the book rights. If the publishing concern controls these rights for two or three years and produces nothing, yet has made an investment in promoting these rights, the author who takes over should not cut you out financially. The mere act of publication gives birth to the other rights; these rights wouldn't have come into play without your publication of the underlying work.

Most publishers deduct the agent's fee on the sale of subsidiary rights before splitting the proceeds. After the split, establish how long you need to hang on to the author's share; it seems unfair to delay paying until royalties are paid, if you've received the money; in a sense, the author's share then becomes an interest-free loan to you. On the other hand, be realistic about the speed with which proceeds run through your internal accounting procedure. Remember, when you receive payment on the subsidiary rights, you are the author's agent. This creates a fiduciary relationship, which legally imposes extra care.

Accounting, Reports, and Payments

These provisions, like the others, run from A to Z. A major publisher in romance genre accounts as follows:

> **Royalty accounts as herein provided shall be rendered and paid quarterly viz. in February, May, August, November as of December 31, March 31, June 30, September 30. The AUTHOR agrees that any accounts, bills, and amounts of any nature that may be due the PUBLISHER by the AUTHOR on the date when royalty accounts are rendered, may, at the discretion of the PUBLISHER, be deducted from the AUTHOR'S royalty account before payment.**

A simple provision found in a university press contract provides that:

The Press shall render statements of accounts annually in August, as of June 30 of each year, and shall make settlements in cash within one month after the date of each statement. Royalties of less than $25 in any given year shall be accrued for the author until the end of the accounting period in which the total exceeds that amount.

And, from a major mass-market paperback publisher:

Statements and Payments

The Publisher shall render to the Author semi-annual royalty statements commencing one year after the publication of the first or any subsequent or reprinted edition, accompanied by a remittance of the amount shown to be due thereon, subject to a reasonable reserve against returns, on or before
(i) May 31 of each year covering the last six months of the preceding year
(ii) November 30 of each year covering the first six months of the year.
All royalty statements shall set forth in detail the various items for which royalties are payable and the amounts thereof, including the number of copies sold in each royalty category.

If the total royalties due are less than $100.00 the Publisher may defer the rendering of statements and payment of royalties until at least $100.00 are due.

Examination of Accounts

The Author shall have the right upon written request to have his accountant examine the Publisher's books of account insofar as they relate to the Work. Any such examination shall be conducted at the place where the Publisher maintains such books of account. It shall be conducted during reasonable business hours in such manner so as not to interfere with the Publisher's normal business activities. A true copy of all reports made by the Author's accountant shall be delivered to the Publisher at the same time such respective reports are delivered to the Author by such accountant. In no event shall an audit with respect to any statement commence later than twelve (12) months from the date of dispatch to the Author of such statement nor shall any audit continue for longer than five (5) consecutive business days nor shall examinations be made hereunder more frequently than twice annually, nor shall the records supporting any such statements be audited more than once. The expenses of such examination shall be borne by the Author, unless errors of accounting of 10 percent or more of the total sums paid to the Author shall be found to his disadvantage, in which case, the expenses thereof shall be borne by the Publisher. All royalty statements rendered under this Agreement shall be binding upon the Author and not subject to objection for any reason unless such objection is made in writing stating the basis thereof and delivered to the Publisher within twelve (12) months from delivery of such statement, or, if an examination is commenced prior thereto, within thirty (30) days from the completion of the relative audit.

The Publisher shall not be required to retain supporting records after any statement of royalties has become binding upon the Author.

Think about adding to your accounting provision a time limit for author objections. Although it won't hold up in court if you engaged in fraudulent conduct, it creates a "put up or shut up" situation that favors you.

Because of the recent author attacks on the definition of a "reasonable return on reserve," be sure to indicate your preference in your royalty statements. Reproduced below are three different royalty statements, the first from a major publisher, the second from a small publisher; and the last from a university press:

Royalty Statement			Period Ending: 06/30/86	
			Page No.: 1	
			Account No.: 14333 959	
DETAILED STATEMENT BY PRODUCT				
RATE COPIES RECEIPTS			DUE AUTHOR	DUE PUBLISHER
TITLE-CODE 015431				
LEGAL GDE FOR ARTISTS WRITERS & CRAFTSPEO				
BALANCE FROM PREVIOUS STATEMENT				111.03
EARNINGS FROM SALES				
DOMESTIC $.6713	28		18.80	
EXPORT $.3356	1		.34	
MAIL SALES $.4475	2		.90	
GROSS TOTAL—CODE 15431			20.04	111.03
NET TOTAL—CODE 15431				90.99
015431 NET AMOUNT CARRIED TO SUMMARY STATEMENT				90.99
SUMMARY STATEMENT				
PRODUCT CODE TITLE DETAIL PAGE			DUE AUTHOR	DUE PUBLISHER
015431 LEGAL GDE FOR ARTISTS WRITERS & CRAFTSPEO		1		90.99
ADVANCES DEFERRED TO FUTURE ROYALTY PERIOD				90.99

Date: _____
To: All _____ Authors
FROM: _____, Customer Service/Royalties
RE: Royalty Checks and Statements

Enclosed is your royalty statement reflecting sales for the period February 1988 thru August 1988. I would like to remind you of two things. First, if you have any trouble interpreting your statement or have any questions regarding royalties paid, please contact me. The editorial department will not have the answers to your questions.

Second, you are entitled to a 40% discount on any publication. The cost of purchases may be paid for in one of three ways. They can be charged against your royalty account(s), paid at the time of purchase (with a check or chargecard number), or billed to you on net 30-day terms. You must specify at the time of purchase the method of payment preferred. All invoices outstanding after 60 days will be charged against royalties and the entire invoice amount (including tax and shipping) will be subtracted from your next royalty check. Please note: If your charges exceed your royalties, you will be notified in writing and no further charges will be allowed.

MARTHA BLUE   (1184)
FLAGSTAFF, AZ 86002

Tax ID:

Royalty Statement for Period through 8/88   Page 1

Type	Level	Price	Period	Sold In Calculation Base	Royalty Rate	Share %	$ Earnings
Book:	MAKING IT LEGAL		(0174/LEGAL)				
CHG	ROY. AD. CK #013882 12/87						−375.00
CHG	ROY. ADV. CK #14294 3/88						−375.00
CHG	ROY. ADV. CK #14974 8/88						−375.00

***** Book Total: −1125.00

Author Total: −1125.00

(Minimum payment per author is $00. This statement is NOT ELIGIBLE for payment.)

Explanation of the Royalty Statement

CHARGES AND CREDITS:
   —CRD is a credit, frequently for secondary rights.
   —CHG is a charge, frequently for books purchased.
RULE:
   The figures in parentheses are the numbers for the base and rule being used by the computer to calculate the royalty.
COLUMN 1: "TYPE"

The computer separates sales into the five different types specified in most of our contracts:

AUTH   sales to the author

DIS1   sales at a discount less than either 47% or 51%, depending upon your contract.

DIS2   sales at a discount greater than 46% or 50%

FRGN   books sold for export

MFG   books sold at a price below the original manufacturing unit value

COLUMN 3: "PRICE"

The list price at which the book was sold.

COLUMN 4: "SOLD IN PERIOD"

The number of copies sold minus any returns. A negative figure indicates that returns exceeded sales.

COLUMN 5: "CALCULATION BASE"

This is either the net dollar value of sales (if your contract specifies a royalty based upon net sales) or the list price of the book multiplied by the number of copies sold (if your contract specifies a royalty based upon list price).

COLUMN 6: "RATE"

The total royalty rate for the book as stated in the contract.

COLUMN 7: "SHARE"

Your share of the royalties earned, as a percentage.

Royalty Statement for Period through 6/88   Page 1

Type	Level	Price	Sold In Period	Calculation Base	Royalty Rate	Share %	$ Earnings
Lifetime net sales through 6/88: 1899)							
sale:	(3-11)						
S1	2	19.95	10	75.80 NET	15.00%	57.50%	6.54
S1	2	24.95	508	7186.96 NET	15.00%	57.50%	619.88
GN	2	24.95	4	69.86 NET	10.00%	57.50%	4.02
						*****Book Total:	630.44
						Author Total:	630.44

Remember, many authors really believe that publishers cheat on royalties. To forestall this, determine what information goes into your royalty statement and be very clear in explaining it. At this time, there is no custom, tradition, federal statute, or uniform code that defines what a royalty must contain. Agents' and brokers' beefing and barking about royalty statements, as well as increasing legal problems, should encourage your publishing concern to adequately and accurately report a book's financial activities in a given period. The details of licensing income should be reported separately; many authors request, if not approval, at least copies of any subsidiary rights licenses and agreements to check the accuracy of income reported to the author from that source.

Consider including the following if you want to keep the hounds at bay:

- the print run from the work.
- copies sold.

- copies furnished gratis.
- copies shipped.
- copies otherwise unsaleable (given away, destroyed, lost, or stolen).
- royalty rate for each type of royalty in your contract reflected in the sales.
- copies returned.
- reserve against returns. (If you have, as many small concerns do, a non-return policy, omit the space on your accounting statement for reserve for returns).

Authors often balk at the twice-a-year accounting, preferring quarterly payment. One of my clients reported that a well-known author accepted twice-a-year accounting, provided she received interest from the time the payment was earned until it was paid; this came to a staggering amount. A nice gesture is to report and pay quarterly, if you can. It's good business to treat the authors of your books as suppliers.

Sometimes something happens to alert the author that all is not right on the accounting statement and an audit is demanded. Audits consume time and money, and the author may ask for a contract provision that requires you pay if the errors exceed a specified amount or percentage. The arbitration of accounting disputes could be beneficial.

I urge you to double-check all of your accounting statements on a rotating schedule, at least once every few years. Further, if you bought a publishing house, don't start your calculations with the last royalty statement, but go back and read the contracts and see if the statements are in accord with contract provisions. Don't carry-over some kind of error.

Strive for clarity, simplicity, and completeness in your royalty statements to alleviate many of the problems authors regularly bring to their agents, lawyers, or other authors, usually to the detriment of the publishing house.

An author might express a wish to spread income forward into future tax years, but avoid that situation. The dangers are:

- one or more of the parties going through bankruptcy or other financial problems.
- one or more of the parties changing his or her mind—a common area of litigation.
- one or more of the parties changing hands or merging with another company.

Copies to the Author

One of the more complete and interesting provisions on author's copies reads as follows:

Upon publication, the publisher shall give _____ copies to the author. The author may purchase additional copies of the work at a discount of _____ % for resale or personal use; no royalties shall be paid on these copies.

> Shipping costs are to be paid by the author. Payments for author's purchases are to be subtracted from the royalties of the same accounting period or paid within 90 days of date of invoice, whichever comes first.

or:

> *Author's Copies* The Press shall furnish to the Author, free of charge, twelve (12) complimentary copies of the edition of the Work as first published. So long as the Work is in stock, the Author may purchase from the Press, at a discount established by the Press from time to time, additional copies of the Work intended for her own use or free distribution, but not for resale.

In my first book contract, my co-author and I negotiated a provision that gave us a trade discount schedule, as well as royalties on our purchases. Our argument: "What difference does it make to the publisher who sells the book—a book wholesaler, a book rep, a bookstore, or us?" When we ordered a thousand copies of the book from the publisher's warehouse, the warehouse was more than a little startled, since my check did not represent the forty percent discount usually allowed to authors; when we provided them with a copy of the contract, the warehouse staff said it was the first one they'd seen. The discount, if I recollect correctly, was fifty-five percent because of the size of the order. The royalty statements reflected royalty credit for the books purchased under that agreement. We sold all the books that we ordered.

It is often the case that authors, particularly with small publishing concerns, are the best salespersons, and it's to your advantage to work with them on this issue. If your author is a lecturer and runs workshops, he or she will want the best price available. As a publisher, you may be concerned that the author will sell the book at less than the suggested list price of the book; therefore, I recommend that, if you agree to give the author the best price available to others, you add a statement to the contract that requires the author to sell those books only at the publisher's list price. There are publishers who view allowing authors to buy at trade discounts in order to sell books themselves as a form of unfair competition; authors, after all, have no overhead and can, in theory, undercut the publisher's own market.

The decision on this issue turns on two factors:

- your sales force's response to the practice.
- your author's book options with your company.

Publishers who regularly encourage author sales report occasional difficulties in collecting payment for the books if the author's royalties don't exceed or equal the amount of purchase, or if the purchase is in February and the next royalty statement isn't due until August. Protect yourself by conditioning the sales on payment in sixty days (or whatever your house practice is), or as a debit against royalties when due, whichever comes first. For large orders, follow your usual credit procedures.

Author's Property

Here's a clause on author's property:

Except for loss or damage due to its own negligence, the publisher shall not be responsible for loss of or damage to any property of the author.

Better yet, vary that by inserting the term "gross" before negligence. Negligence means carelessness, while "gross negligence" requires a higher degree of inattention or carelessness.

Or best, eliminate "Except . . . negligence" and avoid any responsibility for loss or damage to any property of the author. This puts the author on notice that he or she is responsible for keeping copies of any materials given to you. See the following clause:

Loss and Return of Manuscript

A. The Author shall prepare his manuscript in triplicate, and all drawings, charts, designs, photographs and other illustrations in duplicate, and shall deliver to the Publisher two copies of the manuscript and one copy each of the drawings, charts, designs, photographs and other illustrations as is provided by paragraph 4 hereof. The Publisher shall use due care in safeguarding the same. If the originals are lost or destroyed from any cause whatsoever whilst in the Publisher's or the printer's possession, the Publisher shall not be liable therefor, and the Author shall thereupon deliver to the Publisher the copy of the manuscript previously retained by him together with the second copy of each of the drawings, charts, designs, photographs and other illustrations.

B. After publication, and on the written request of the Author, the Publisher agrees to return to the Author one copy of the original manuscript and/or galley and page proofs thereof, with the printer's corrections. If the Author does not request such return in writing within one month following the date of such publication the Publisher may destroy.

When you consider the number of other entities who handle the property of the author—perhaps a translator, certainly a printer, a color separator, or maybe an outside copy editor, multiple copies and a clear definition of responsibility become important. The loss of artwork or photographic material can be extremely expensive. Some authors may request the return of the original manuscript and any other graphic material within a certain time after publication. I see no problem with returning the original manuscript, but in terms of applying the warranty and indemnity provisions, if you substantially edited the work, keep copies of the author-submitted material.

Case Incident:

A publishing concern and a Canadian author had a falling out prior to the publication of a work under contract with the publisher. The original manuscript was returned to the author with an agreement that the author would not use the substantial editorial changes provided at the cost of the publisher. The second publisher, a Canadian company, did not check the termination of the first agreement (always terminate relationships in writing, signed by both parties) and had no idea that the author's manuscript as presented was the result of the former publishing house's work. When the work appeared in print with substantially all the editing changes paid for by the first publisher, the first publisher made claims not only against the author but against the second publishing house. Both author and second publisher were difficult to access legally because of their Canadian status.

The next chapter deals with the balance of normal contract provisions, and their variations.

Part III

The Generic Book Contract

Post-Publication

7

Work relationships, which a publishing contract memorializes, begin, run a course, and end. In the process, there may be a revision, a copyright infringement suit, an option, all of which are post-publication matters. A publishing relationship ends because the life of the work naturally fizzles out, the parties disagree, or the publishing concern folds.

Let's discuss some post-publication issues first.

Competing Work

A non-competition clause can range from the following simple one:

> **The Author agrees that he will not, at any time during the continuance of this Agreement, prepare any manuscript, or cause or permit any book by him, to be published that will directly compete with the book herein mentioned.**

to a more complete provision such as:

> **COMPETING WORKS**
> **While this Agreement is in effect, the Author shall not, without the prior written consent of the Publisher, write, edit, print, or publish, or cause to be**

written, edited, printed, or published, any other edition of the Work, whether revised, supplemented, corrected, enlarged, or otherwise, or any other work of a nature which might interfere with or injure the sales of the Work or any grant of rights or licenses permitted under this Agreement by the Publisher, or permit the use of the Author's name or likeness in connection with any such work.

These provisions define "competing work" to mean any publication that decreases sales of the work the author sold to you. Here again, a balance must be struck between the publisher's interest and the author's. For example, an author who works in a narrow field—Native American basketry, walking canes of eighteenth-century America, or southern cooking—doesn't want the door sealed when related specialty writing projects crop up. If the author raises this issue, require him or her to conceptualize potential writing projects for the next decade; consider whether these projects would impede the sale of the work you contemplate publishing. Consider too, that often, a new work enhances or complements the older book and renews interest in it, a very positive attribute.

Knowledgable authors may ask you to restrict this provision by time (say, for three years), types of publication (such as scholarly, trade, mass market), geographic area (canes of America as opposed to canes of New England), or may wish to otherwise tightly define subject matter considered competitive. You'll have to weigh those proposals against your press's interest in building a backlist. If the proposed work is on popular, present-day Indian basketry, you could exclude scholarly periodicals or books on this subject, exclude popular works on baskets other than Indian baskets, or exclude a work specially directed to a single tribe (such as Hopi basketry) if the subsequent work's introduction mentions your press's publication.

Some authors will insist that a closely similar work gives the small press a remedy for copyright infringement. Not so, if the author owns the copyright. The protection publishers seek here is not from literal copying, but from conceptual copying.

Competing-work problems fall into two categories: an author who writes about the same subject from different angles over a different time frame, and the author who's dissatisfied with your publishing house and wants to rewrite the book and get it to *another* publisher elsewhere while your contract's alive and kicking and preventing him or her from doing so.

The other side of this coin is that the publisher may release books that compete with one another. I recommend that, if your publishing niche is narrow (such as accounting or investment advice for lay persons), you add this provision to your book contract:

> **Author acknowledges that publisher produces and sells works related to _____, some of which may now or hereafter be competitive to this work and author agrees to said practice.**

If you publish Native American theme books, then in reference to the Indian basketry book discussed previously, you could put "Indian basketry" in the blank. The purpose of this addition is to protect you if the author complains that you are producing and marketing works that compete with his or hers.

Options

Option clauses run the gamut from:

> **The author gives to the publisher the right to publish the author's next full-length manuscript, of which he will submit to the publisher. In no case shall the publisher be required to exercise this option before publication or within three months following publication of the work which is the subject of this agreement.**

or:

> **The author grants the publisher exclusive option to publish his next book. It is understood that such option shall be exercised within sixty days after the receipt by the publisher of the complete and final manuscript; provided, however, that in no case shall the publisher be obligated to accept or decline such manuscript sooner than ninety days after the publication of the work contracted for.**

to:

> **The publisher has an option on the author's next work.**

Are options important to you? The answer: it depends. If you're investing not only in that particular book but a long-term, profitable relationship with an author, the option clause represents one spoke in the wheel of the relationship.

The other spokes, equally important, are:

- production of a quality of work each accepts.
- a cordial resolution of disagreements.
- meeting respective deadlines.

From the author's point of view, an option clause can seem unfair because it:

- reinforces an erroneous theory abounding in the publishing world that it hurts to bring out more than one or two books a year by the same author.
- fails to address the prolific author who may write books that don't fit the needs of the contracting press.
- fails to recognize that authors live from advance to advance.
- fails to recognize the length of time from book production to royalties.
- penalizes authors who want to improve their advances and royalties with

each contract; the penalties imposed by standard option clauses allow acquisition of the next work "on the same terms and conditions" as those paid for the present work.

- formalizes a publisher's reluctance to proceed with contracting for a new work until sales figures are in from the first book.

Some agents opine that "options are made to be broken." An author may suggest that the option cover narrowly defined future books, or exclude books produced under a pseudonym. An author may also suggest that you add "except that the amount of the advance and the royalties shall be subject to negotiation." This clause is worthless to you *unless* you cap it in some way, i.e., not to exceed 25% of the last advance and one-half percent of each royalty category. A provision that requires your press to match any offer on advance and royalties your author secures from another publisher to retain the work is better. It may be hard to compare terms, however. You offer your author $2,500 with an eight percent royalty, and promise to publish the book in one year, while your competitor offers a $1,000 advance against a ten percent royalty but promises to publish the book in nine months—which is the better deal?

Fairness to both parties dictates certain considerations. Limit the time it takes you to consider the author's material. Agree to tie the option clause to a detailed outline, book proposal, and a sample chapter or two, or enough to make a publishing decision. Of course, you run the risk that the manuscript may not be what the "tickler" indicated.

Lawsuits abound involving "first-refusal" under an option clause. Farrar was knocked down in *H.B.J., Inc., v. Farrar Strauss and Giroux, Inc.,* (4 Media Law Reporter 2625 [Supp. T.N.Y.C.O., 1979]), when a court held that a clause giving the publisher the option to acquire publication rights "on terms to be mutually agreed upon" was merely an agreement to agree.

Competing works, options, and so forth tie into your publishing concern's master plan, whether you're investing in authors, specific subject matters, geographic areas, or all of the above.

Revisions

In educational and textbook publishing, the name of the game is "revisions." If a book isn't revised periodically, students keep recycling the same book through the college bookstore's used book department, or another book comes along that provides up-to-date information. Sample provisions on revision follow:

Revisions

When and if the Publisher, in its sole discretion, considers revision of the Work necessary to render its continued publication profitable, the Author agrees, at the Publisher's request, to revise the Work within a reasonable time in accordance with the recommendations of the Publisher. The provisions of this Agreement will apply to each revision of the Work

upon which the Author has performed the requested services as though such revision was the Work being published for the first time under this Agreement.

Failure to provide revision

If the Author does not provide an acceptable revision within a reasonable time, or should the Author be deceased, disabled, or unwilling, the Publisher may have the revision prepared and may deduct the authorship cost thereof from the Author's royalties.

Choice of revision author

If the Author is unable or unwilling to provide such, the Publisher will have the right in its sole discretion to select a new author or authors to prepare a revision, and the Publisher may deduct the cost of such new or additional authorship from the Author's royalties.

The revision author's name shall be indicated in the revised Work.

or:

The Author will revise the work when the Publisher deems it necessary. Except as set forth below, all the terms of this Agreement will apply to revisions and any derivative works related thereto.

If the Author refuses, fails, or is unable to deliver a revision acceptable to the Publisher within the Publisher's schedule, the Publisher may have the revision prepared or completed by others, give them authorship credit, and the Publisher will pay the Author, or the Author's legal successors, one-half of the applicable royalty and payments specified in paragraph _____ with respect to the first revision in which the Author does not participate or so deliver, and one-quarter of the designated royalty and payment with respect to the second revision in which the Author does not participate or so deliver. If the Publisher elects to publish any further revisions, the Publisher need not give the Author further author's credit and will pay the Author no further royalties or other compensation in respect of any such revisions.

Add, where appropriate, that "the provision for payment of an advance to the Author shall not apply to revisions."

Some contract clauses provide: "if the author and the publisher agree that a revision of the work is necessary" and then complete the revision scenario. The utility of this provision is problematical, because it puts the decision of whether the work requires revision in the hands of two parties with competing and widely differing interests.

One contract I looked at provided that "any future work for which Publisher fails to exercise his option is deemed a non-competitive work." Not bad, *except* that if the author gives you a revision of the current publication, there could be problems with interpretation.

Suits for Infringement of Copyright*

Suits for Infringement of Copyright

If the copyright of this work is infringed, and if the parties proceed jointly, the expenses and recoveries, if any, shall be shared equally, and if they do not proceed jointly, either party shall have the right to prosecute such action, and such party shall bear the expenses thereof, and any recoveries shall belong to such party; and if such party shall not hold the record title of the copyright, the other party hereby consents that the action be brought in his or its name.

Discontinuance of Publication

A sample provision of discontinuance of publication:

Discontinuance of Publication

a. When in the judgment of the Publisher the demand for the Work is no longer sufficient to warrant its continued publication, the Publisher shall have the right to discontinue the publication and declare the Work out of print, in which event the Author shall be so advised in writing.

b. If the Work is not for sale in at least one edition (including any revised edition or reprint edition) published by the Publisher or under license from the Publisher and, within eight months after written demand by the Author, the Publisher or its licensee fails to offer it again for sale, then this Agreement shall terminate and all rights granted to the Publisher in it shall revert to the Author (except for material prepared by or obtained at the expense of the Publisher which shall remain the property of the Publisher).

c. The termination of this Agreement under this Section 7 or otherwise shall be subject to (1) any license, contract, or option granted to third parties by the Publisher before the termination and the Publisher's right to its share of the proceeds from these agreements after the termination and (2) the Publisher's continuing right to sell all remaining bound copies and sheets of the Work and all derivative works which are on hand at the time of termination.

Or consider the following:

Discontinuance of publication

If the Publisher fails to keep the Work in print and the Author makes a written demand to reprint it, the Publisher shall, within sixty (60) days after the receipt of such demand, notify the Author in writing if it intends to comply. Within six (6) months thereafter, the Publisher shall reprint the Work unless prevented from doing so by circumstances beyond its control. If the Publisher fails to notify the Author within sixty (60) days that it intends to comply, or, within six (6) months after such notification, the Publisher declines or neglects to reprint the Work, then this Agreement

---

*Please see the previous discussion of warranties and indemnities, in addition to the discussion of infringement of copyright in Chapter 13.

shall terminate and all rights granted revert to the Author, subject to licenses previously granted, provided the Author is not indebted to the Publisher for any sum owing to it under this Agreement. After such revision, the Publisher shall continue to participate to the extent set forth in this Agreement in monies received from any license previously granted by it. Upon such termination, the Author shall have the right for thirty (30) days thereafter to purchase the plates, existing sheets and bound stock, if any, at cost (including typesetting).

Definition of "in print"

If the Work is under contract for publication or on sale in any edition in the United States, it shall be considered to be in print. A Work shall not be deemed in print by reason of a license granted by the Publisher for the reproduction of single copies of the Work.

If the Publisher should determine that there is not sufficient sale for the Work to enable it to continue its publication and sale profitably, the Publisher may dispose of the copies remaining on hand as it deems best. In such event, the Author shall have the right, within thirty (30) days of the forwarding of a written notice from the Publisher, to a single purchase of copies at the "remainder" price. Author forfeits royalties in the remaindered books and in any single purchase made by Author.

Define what "keep the work in print" means for type of a specific book and your publishing house.

These provisions come into effect when sales slow so dramatically that inventory exceeds the publisher's needs. The publisher then takes steps to sell off the remaining stock, often at huge discounts, recovering some of the manufacturing costs if possible, and achieving liquidity from stagnant stock, a move otherwise known as "remaindering." Authors will occasionally ask for a clause that prohibits remaindering until a predetermined time after first publication, which may not be unreasonable from your perspective.

The thrust of this provision is that once you determine, using your commercial judgment, that the book is not selling at an adequate rate, then you need to dispose of the book, and possibly the plates and negatives as well. The manner in which you do this should be spelled out in the contract. Years ago, one California publisher donated books that weren't moving, took a substantial deduction for these charitable contributions, and gave the author nothing. This caused an uproar. If the author is willing to buy the publisher's inventory at the same price the remainder house offers, then in all fairness, in my opinion, give the author the opportunity.

The provision quoted earlier gives the author the right to purchase these materials at the publisher's cost, not at scrap value. Depending upon how your publishing house defines costs, the provision can be amplified. There is nothing, of course, that precludes you from negotiating a lower amount for the manufacturing materials with an author at the time of disposal; you can defray some of your loss on a particular book while keeping author goodwill.

Avoid any provision that allows the author to obligate you to produce a new edition on short notice. Pay careful attention to any written notices or time-lines from authors concerning this particular provision.

If you're no longer interested in the book, return the rights to the author. Define the contract out-of-print provisions to take into account your reprinting budget, warehousing possibilities, and new lists, so that demands for return of rights don't surface as soon as sales taper off. Authors will occasionally push for their work to be out of print; once they get the rights back and revise it a little, it can be presented to a new publisher. New people, new publishers, and a newly revised work: sometimes this is good for everyone involved, and pumps life back into the book.

As a gesture of goodwill, refer authors to Buckley-Little Book Catalogue Co., Inc. (Kraus Building, Route 100, Millwood, New York 10546). William F. Buckley Jr. and Stuart W. Little started the company to provide a way for authors to sell books they'd gotten back from publishers, and to keep their books in print. Kraus, who bought out Buckley-Little, will sometimes print as few as one hundred books.

If you plan to jump on the bandwagon of publishing reprints of out-of-print books (some were big sellers on the last year or two: *If You Want to Write* by Brenda Ueland [Gray Wolf]; *West with the Night* by Beryl Markham [North Point]; and *Their Eyes Were Watching God* by Zora Neale Hurston [University of Illinois], all favorites of mine), be sure that the party who sells you the reprint rights now owns them and that you don't pay for something they don't have.

Arbitration

There's a trend toward the use of arbitration in the business–legal communities because of the technique's speed in resolving issues, lack of publicity, and purported economy. Publisher–author disputes, though, often go beyond strictly money issues: changing publication dates, enforcing editorial changes in the text, interpreting the option clause, and establishing termination terms. With major publishers, the expense and trouble to take disagreements to court discourages some author-initiated litigation, but you shouldn't count on that to protect you.

Perhaps because authors and publishers are so intimately involved with words, disputes seem to be settled with minimal lawyer involvement—not always, but usually. I jokingly call this an "industry practice." I have had several book contract termination disputes that were resolved just a hair short of litigation, however. Since neither party knows whether the arbitrator will be as knowledgable, fair, and patient as a judge, you still might be looking at the luck of the draw. Consider mediation, which is less formal than arbitration, for minor contract disputes. The parties could select someone knowledgable in the field to mediate a settlement dialogue between them.

Some publishers use arbitration clauses in their contracts. I mentioned arbitration in an earlier chapter (see pages 45–46). Here are a few provisions:

Arbitration

Any claim or dispute between Publisher and Author concerning questions of fact or law arising out of or relating to this Agreement, its performance or alleged breach, which is not disposed of by agreement of the

parties shall be arbitrated pursuant to the Rules of the American Arbitration Association and an award rendered pursuant to such arbitration shall be final and binding on all parties.

This arbitration provision is a complete defense to any suit, action or proceeding in any court or before any administrative tribunal with respect to any controversy or dispute between the parties arising from this Agreement. The arbitration provisions survive the termination or expiration of this Agreement.

Or this one from a university press:

The parties agree that should a dispute arise between them, in any manner, concerning this contract, and said dispute involves the sum of ten thousand dollars ($10,000) or less in money damages only, exclusive of interest, cost, or attorneys' fees, the parties will submit the matter to binding arbitration pursuant to the Supreme Court Rules for Compulsory Arbitration and the decision of the arbitrator(s) shall be final and binding upon the parties.

or:

A. Any claim or controversy arising among or between the parties hereto pertaining to those matters contained in this Agreement shall be settled by arbitration by three (3) arbitrators under the then prevailing rules of the American Arbitration Association.

B. In any arbitration involving this Agreement, the arbitrators shall not make any award which will alter, change, cancel, or rescind any provision of this Agreement, and their award shall be consistent with the provisions of this Agreement. Any such arbitration must be commenced no later than ninety (90) days from the date such controversy arose.

C. The award of the arbitrators shall be binding and final, and judgment may be entered thereon, in any Court of competent jurisdiction.

Publishers Weekly (September 30, 1983) reported that arbitration was used to resolve a dispute involving ex-partners in the firm that published the "Sweet Pickles" juvenile books. One ex-partner charged that the others violated her departure contract by creating a new company, diluting licensing monies by failing to acknowledge her creative role, and not paying royalties.

Bankruptcy and Liquidation

Most contracts omit any discussion of bankruptcy or liquidation, but authors ask for some protection of their materials in the event this situation arises. A backlist can be worth quite a bit; a New York bankruptcy court valued Stein & Day's (in a Chapter 11 bankruptcy) 1,200 title backlist at $5 to $6 million—or over $4,000 per title (*Publishers Weekly,* October 7, 1988). See the Author's Guild article in the Spring-Summer 1987 issue, "An Author's Primer on Bankruptcy, or What To Do

When Publishers Go Bust," for its excellent explanation on bankruptcy, and its discussion of principles that authors should incorporate in book contracts, so you'll know where authors are coming from.

As a practical matter, once a company moves into bankruptcy, the creditors (which include authors) hammer at the assets to get a share, and this provision may not have much effect.

Bankruptcy and Liquidation

If (a) a petition in bankruptcy is filed by the Publisher, or (b) a petition in bankruptcy is filed against the Publisher and such petition is finally sustained, or (c) a petition for arrangement is filed by the Publisher or a petition for reorganization is filed by or against the Publisher, and an order is entered directing the liquidation of the Publisher as in bankruptcy, or (d) the Publisher makes an assignment for the benefit of creditors, or (e) the Publisher liquidates its business for any cause whatever, the Author may terminate this agreement by written notice and thereupon all rights granted by him hereunder shall revert to him. Upon such termination, the Author, at his option, may purchase the plates as provided in Paragraph ____ and the remaining copies at one-half of the manufacturing cost, exclusive of overhead. If he fails to exercise such option within sixty (60) days after the happening of any one of the events above referred to, the Trustee, Receiver, or Assignee may destroy the plates and sell the copies remaining on hand, subject to the royalty provisions of Paragraph ____.

A National Writers Union grievance officer opined, in the bankruptcy case involving Stein & Day, that the federal bankruptcy code nullifies contract terms that revert rights to a book to the author if the publisher goes bankrupt.

Case Incident:

A published author's new Gothic hit the bookstores for only three weeks before publisher X was forced into bankruptcy by its printer, who in turn sold X's contracts to Y company. The new president of Y company was the former president of X company. This new company wrote its authors advising them that Y would reissue the book when it was good and ready. My client had retained copyright to her book. After much correspondence charging, from our end, a whole litany of illegal acts on X and Y's part, the publisher agreed that the rights reverted to my client and amazingly found some 2,000 or so books; instead of shipping them to my client pursuant to our agreement, however, Y company shipped them to my law office—a real inconvenience to us.

Termination

Termination clauses provide a smooth and graceful end to the relationship—or at least, that's the goal.

Some sample termination provisions:

In the event of the termination of this agreement as elsewhere provided, any rights reverting to the author shall be subject to all licenses and other grants of rights theretofore made by the publisher to third parties, and to the rights of the publisher to proceed with such licenses and grants. Rights of the publisher under the warranty and indemnity clause, as well, survive the termination of this Agreement.

or:

The Publisher reserves the right, if in its judgment its editorial assistance or intervention will not result in an acceptable manuscript, to terminate this Agreement, or the Publisher may terminate this Agreement if the complete manuscript is not acceptable. Upon termination by the Publisher under this Paragraph ____, all rights in the work granted or transferred to the Publisher under this Agreement will automatically revert to the Author, the Author will have the right to retain all sums previously advanced in full consideration hereof, but the Author will be entitled to no other or further compensation, remedy, or damages. It is understood that requests for changes and approvals of outlines, of portions of the manuscript, or of draft materials are intended only to indicate that the Publisher deems it appropriate to continue the editorial process and are not intended to affect the Publisher's right to determine if the complete finally revised manuscript is acceptable or to obligate the Publisher to accept the final revised manuscript.

or:

The Press shall hold its rights as long as the Work is kept in print with copies available for sale. However, if at any time after two years from the date of publication the Press fails to keep the Work in print in any edition licensed in the United States and does not reprint it within six months after the Author's written request to do so, then the Author has the right to terminate this agreement by written notice. Thereupon the Author shall have the right within sixty (60) days to purchase all remaining copies of the Work on hand and the printer's negatives, at the cost of manufacture. If the Author fails to make such purchase, the Press may dispose of any and all manufacturing materials and all copies of the Work on hand at any price obtainable therefor, without payment of royalty. Upon termination of the agreement, all existing rights in the Work will revert to the Author and the Press will assign the copyright to the Author.

If you reach a point with one of your authors that termination of the contract is your only viable option, don't do it in anger—well, not total anger—and leave no ragged edges. From the publisher's perspective, a parting of the ways often arises from an author's:

- unreasonableness.
- failure to meet deadlines.
- failure to cooperate with the book marketing and strategy.
- failure to complete a satisfactory manuscript.
- disagreements over royalties.
- disputes about a work's "out-of-print" status.

When parties reach the end of a complex relationship, that ending must be carefully orchestrated. Until that time, and as long as things were going well, probably neither party referred to the contract at all. When things fall apart, and distrust and suspicions rampage, your book contract's clause on termination needs to be crystal clear.

Yes, I'm jumping ahead to dispute resolution—and no, I'm not. Practically speaking, all business arrangements and procedures require fine-tuning along the way (if you only hear a scramble of sounds from your radio, if it can't be tuned or fixed, you'll dispose of it). You may also need to do this thirty days after you sign a contract with someone.

Include the termination provision in your contract and cover it thoroughly. To ignore this contract clause, which memorializes the ending of a business relationship, is like not making a will because you refuse to recognize death is inevitable.

The Author's Guild provides authors with a sample termination agreement. It may be insufficient in most situations for either party.

Use a written termination contract in all troublesome situations including:

- works unpublished but contracted for, plus licenses and subsidiary rights already granted.
- a work or works already published, along with licenses.
- disputes over disposition of existing copies of the work and plates.
- disputes over existing licenses, unsold rights, and options.
- disputes about royalties and license fees.

Here's a worst-case scenario, the kind lawyers love to conjure up. It involves multiple works by one author. An extensive royalty dispute arises about book A, for which the publisher licensed translation rights. Book B is out of print and you don't plan an immediate printing, but the author wants the rights back now. Further, your contracts with this author require the author to deliver a satisfactory manuscript for book C, which the author has not done, and now owes you the manuscript or the advance back. The author gave you a synopsis, two sample chapters, and a book proposal on a hot subject, D, under the option clause in the contract for C, which you *do* wish to publish. Due to the present situation, however, the author has withdrawn the submission of this material from your consideration. You want your money back for book C, payment for the film and so forth for book B, a resolution of the royalty dispute for book A, and some consideration for optioned work D. These numerous matters could be resolved by contract. Were you to reach this point, there would be little or no goodwill left to recommend recapture, *unless* the publisher's option clause is tight.

When a publisher acquired a house with a line of *genre* fiction, which was discontinued, the publisher started its proposed letter of agreement with the *genre*-line authors thus:

The market has changed considerably, and simple business necessity has forced us to make this difficult decision. In discontinuing the line, we are making every reasonable effort to be fair to our authors.

Then the publisher reminded the author that he was a party to a contract for a specific novel and that they had an option on the next work, tentatively titled such-and-such. After a few additional remarks, the publisher stated:

Upon our receipt of a copy of this letter signed by you releasing us, we will pay you the sum that would have been due to you on signing the contract for the option book, had we gone that far, but not any installments that would have been due thereafter. In addition, we will pay you that amount that would have been due under the contract upon our acceptance as satisfactory the manuscript that you just turned in for _____, had acceptance occurred . . . you will then be free to sell the rights to both of these books elsewhere without any further obligation to us with respect to such books, and our contract for _____ (including our option to publish your next work) will be deemed terminated.

If you are willing to accept this offer, please sign below and return a signed copy of this letter to the undersigned; the second copy is for your files. Your signature will constitute your release of us and your acknowledgment of the payment described above will discharge us from any further obligations to you with respect to said books.

This arrangement will not affect any contracts that may exist between you and us other than the contract for this last book. Those other contracts will continue in full force and effect.

The letter accompanied the returned manuscript. A corporate officer signed the letter and below his signature was typed "Agreed:" a line, and the name of the author typed below.

Be sure your termination agreements specify what contracts exist between the author and yourself. If no publication of any work by the author has occurred, and no licensing, then the agreement might follow this format:

Termination Agreement

THIS AGREEMENT, between _____ referred to as AUTHOR, residing in _____, and _____, referred to as PUBLISHER, whose address is _____, is made this _____ day of _____, 19_____ .

1. **AUTHOR** entered into a contract with **PUBLISHER** for a book tentatively titled "_____" in _____.

2. The parties have disagreed about each other's performance under the contract and therefore, the parties agree to mutually terminate the contract.

3. **PUBLISHER** warrants that it, and no other person and/or entity, has acquired the rights, title and interest in "_____."

4. Effective this date, the contract is terminated, and all grants to **PUBLISHER** of rights, title and interest to the work are terminated and said rights, title and interest revert to the **AUTHOR** except that the warranty and indemnity provisions of the contract survive this termination agreement. **AUTHOR** is entitled to exercise and authorize others to exercise all rights in the work; **PUBLISHER** shall not be entitled to share proceeds from any uses of said rights.

5. **AUTHOR** is entitled to retain the _____ Dollar ($____) advance received by **AUTHOR**, while **PUBLISHER** agrees to waive **AUTHOR'S** liability for repayment of same now, or in the future. **AUTHOR** waives any further liabiity or obligation by **PUBLISHER** for payment of any outstanding advances and/or royalties.

6. Both parties, **AUTHOR** and **PUBLISHER**, mutually release the other from any and all claims which may have arisen from the Publishing Contract and this release extends to corporate officers of said corporation.

Publisher:

By: _____

Author: _____

Date: _____

Some agreements add a clause that the parties are not admitting liability by entering into this agreement.

If there are outstanding licenses for subsidiary rights for paperback, book club, or others, you need to type in the names of the licensees and the date and type of license.

For published works, there are a number of issues to be considered: the publisher wants to be sure that the warranty and indemnity provision survives the termination agreement. Make provision for disposal of existing copies of the last print run of the work and payment of royalties, along with disposal of the plates and other material, if the author decides not to purchase them pursuant to the publishing contract. In regard to existing licenses, which often have five-year renewable terms, the publisher should make an effort to have the opportunity to renew those. Require any payments from the author at the time of signing to be by cashier's check.

Of course, if the author had assigned the copyright to the publisher, that also needs to be reassigned.

Following the provision that states that the agreement or agreements are terminated and there are no further obligations, add "except that publisher shall continue to account to author for any royalty or other payments earned under said agreements and the warranty and indemnity shall continue to be enforced." A standard general release provision, which you would have occasion to use in a variety of contract termination situations, follows:

This Agreement is a complete settlement of all existing and potential disputes between author and publisher based on any events or agreements prior to the execution of this Agreement. Author and publisher have no further obligations to or claims upon the other except as stated in this Agreement. Author and publisher mutually release each other from all claims, actions, suits and causes of action, known or unknown, actual or contingent, which either now has, ever had, or may have against the other because of any event, agreement or other thing occurring or existing at any time prior to the execution of this Agreement.

What does this mean? If the author defamed you by accusing you of cheating him, you release your defamation claim. Likewise, if the author discovers some additional unpaid royalties up to the termination date (which resulted from publisher negligence rather than fraud), the author agrees to release that claim.

Finally, be sure to add a provision binding those who stand behind the author and yourself. (See the boilerplate provision on heirs, successors, and assigns in interest, page 44).

Miscellaneous Credits

If another author or editor, ghost writer, or collaborator works on the book, define the exact nature of each person's credit in the publishing agreement, including the appropriate name, placement, and size of the credit. The lack of attention to that detail has hampered more than one project.

Case Incident:
A small publisher planned a work written by a rather obscure scholar on a world-renowned archaeological object. The publisher found a well-known expert on this object who agreed to write a chapter for inclusion in a twenty-chapter work. The expert wanted his name, credentials, and photo to be two-thirds the size of the author's. An accord was not reached.

Advertising

The previous Grant of Rights provision provided that the publisher could use the author's name and likeness in advertising and promotion of the work. This may be extended to include the physical participation of the author in promoting the book.

Here's a provision that I found in my book contract file on author appearances:

> **The Author agrees, provided that the same shall not interfere with his regular employment or business matters in which he is then engaged, and provided that the Author is not then in such poor health as to prevent cooperation, the Author shall give, without charge (unless the Publisher, or its licensee or sublicensee shall be enabled to obtain a fee for the same), any and all newspaper and/or magazine interviews, and will make such radio and/or television as well as book and department store appearances as the Publisher, its licensee or sublicensee may be enabled to arrange in connection with the promotion and sale of any edition of the Work. Any fee which the Publisher or its licensee or sublicensee shall be able to obtain for such interview and/or appearance shall belong and be paid to the Author. If the interview and/or appearance shall be out of the city or town in which the Author shall then reside, reasonable travel costs (and hotel accommodations, if necessary) required to enable the Author to fulfill the engagement shall be paid by the Publisher or its licensee or sublicensee.**

Advertising also becomes an issue in considering whether or not you include mention of other books in your list on the jacket or interior of the book. Some authors will object to this, and you should decide upon a general policy and response to this objection.

Agency

If your author is represented by an agent, the agent will insist on an agency clause that indicates the agent's authority to act on behalf of the writer and to receive compensation. Due to the increasing number of cases against agents, it's wise, in the event that you add such a provision, to provide that the publisher shall be authorized, once it receives notice from the author, to send any sums (their respective shares) directly to the author and the agent upon the termination of the author-agent agreement.

> **The Author hereby authorizes his agent _____ to collect and receive all sums of money payable to him under the terms of this Agreement and the receipt by agent shall be a good and valid discharge in respect thereof. Such agent is authorized and empowered to act on behalf of the Author in all matters in any way arising out of this Agreement.**

> *Case Incident:*
> A publisher was reluctant to send separate payments to an author and his ex-agent, even though the author requested it, because the ex-agent held onto the author's share for a long time before transferring it. A lawyer's letter did the trick.

Security Interest

A security interest allows one party, in exchange for any sums due under the contract by another party, to keep property of the second party's that is in the first party's possession. If all you (as the publisher) have is the manuscript, your local lawyer may recommend that you obtain a security interest in the author's more valuable property. This would most likely arise in the case of potential litigation based on a manuscript's contents, against which the author contractually indemnifies the publisher.

Letter Agreements

These are short contracts. One of my author–clients had this abbreviated contract proposed to her, and she asked me to supplement it, using no more words.

> This is to formalize our discussion about publishing _____ .
> We plan to have a press run of 1,000 copies on sepia-tone paper of good stock. There will be approximately 5 half-tones of your paintings in the text as section dividers; 1 painting in at least 3-color separation (4, if possible) will be used for the cover of the book, subject to your approval. You agree to supply a finished manuscript by _____ , and we will target the book for spring ____ . This includes advertising and distributing through our normal channels for the _____ series, including _____ as a distributor. We will supply you with 50 free copies of the book.
>
> I'm very pleased to move toward the completion of the book. Please let me know if you accept these terms in writing. This letter and your acceptance constitute a contract between us.

I provided this supplementation to my client, which was accepted by the publisher after some minor tinkering.

> ### Amendment to Letter Agreement
> It is further agreed that _____ is granted the primary rights to publish and sell the work in the United States, the Philippines, and Canada and all rights not specifically transferred are reserved to the Author. The book shall be copyrighted in the Author's name and the Publisher agrees to properly and promptly register the copyright and to place the Author's copyright notice on the work; that if the work is not published by _____ , then Author is free, at her option, to seek publication of the work elsewhere. The Author shall receive a standard royalty of _____ , payments to be made pursuant to _____ payment schedule which is attached and incorporated by reference. That if the Publisher discontinues the publication of the work at any time or if the work is out of print, then all of the rights revert to the Author and the Author has the right to purchase plates, sheets or bound stock of the book at cost. Further, Author has

control of the form and content of the final product except for pricing and marketing procedures. Author may purchase an unlimited number of copies for personal use or resale of at least a 40% discount.

Date: _____ _____

Date: _____ _____

Modifications

Remember, innovative drafting can solve problems and resolve issues fairly on all sides. Use side-letter agreements (see example following) as the project changes, or to clarify and amplify the publishing agreement.

If you are willing to accept this offer (change), please sign below and return a signed copy of this letter to the undersigned; the second copy is for your files. Your signature will constitute your release of us and your acknowledgement of the payment described above will discharge us from _____ (any further obligations) to you with respect to said books.

This arrangement will not affect any contracts that may exist other than this last book.

A Final Warning

It is to be hoped that your publishing concern's book contract addresses the potential problem areas, unlike the agreement a Canadian judge reviewed over fifty years ago, and lamented:

I cannot but wonder if publishers and authors enter into agreements as indefinite as this. It is so vague and general in its terms that it is hard to say what it means. It contemplates a book being published and copies of it being sold; but nothing is being said about the number of copies to be printed, nothing about the price at which they are sold, or the time of publication.

Negotiation: Beginnings and Stumbles

Now that you understand the various elements and functions of the publishing contract, you are ready to make an offer to an author.

Before you begin negotiating, establish the following:

- a key-word list, tied to your contract.
- the royalty range, verified with the appropriate person.
- a list of all the possible forms a successful work could take.
- the author's primary interests (money, early publication date, etc.).
- notes for a specific work project.
- your best offer, which you should never give first.

Further,
- be enthusiastic about the work.
- don't change your warranty and indemnification clauses.

- extend advance payment installments.
- keep negotiating bones handy to toss when needed to sweeten the pot.

If contract negotiations with a prospective author wobble or collapse, consider improving the deal with offers such as:

- additional free copies.
- absorption of mail costs (book rate) of up to X number of copies for the authors.
- defraying copying costs up to one hundred dollars.
- providing author with X number of dust jacket covers to use for his/her own promotion.
- a sliding discount on books purchased.
- registration of copyright in author's name.
- payment of royalties on the copies the author purchases.
- reduction of the decision-making period regarding the option clause (stay at thirty days, at least).
- author purchase of the stock on hand and production materials at a percentage of cost.
- publisher subsidy of, say, twenty-five percent of the cost of revisions, if same needs to be done and author doesn't do it.
- payment of typing costs, up to X amount, for the manuscript.
- provision of a bonus payment if the work receives a recognized literary prize or award.
- payment of a portion of the permission fees, or advance all or part of the costs of same against royalties.

Most of these give the author a little more and won't do you in.

Collateral Contracts

8

The generic book contract discussed in the previous chapters is foundational. Collateral agreements include those for graphic art, collaborations, contract writer (that's a work for hire), textbook or educational publishing, magazines, and translations.

Graphic Art

The graphic art or illustrator agreement, as it's sometimes called, affects more than art book publishers. Consider comic books, the new graphic novels, children's books, textbooks, cookbooks—and what every book has—cover art. Len Leone's introduction to a Society of Illustrator's catalogue says that some "paperback houses [were] commissioning thirty to seventy paintings a month and paying fees upwards of $7,000 per cover to illustrate a particular title" (*Publishers Weekly,* October 2, 1987).

As does any contract, a graphic artist-publisher agreement describes the conduct of business between parties and covers issues critical to both artist and publisher. Don't make any payments or let work begin without a signed written agreement.

This particular type of contract starts out with a clear work description: the size, number, medium, materials, and subject matter; deadlines for delivery of the preliminary and final work, along with any penalties for delay; a specification that the work be satisfactory to the publisher; and indication of who has authority to change the work.

The following contract clauses define the term "artist" broadly and allow the insertion of the term "work," whether it's cover art, interior illustrations, photographs, charts, or other graphic material. *Specify. Specify.* For some projects, you'll need finished mechanicals ready for the printer. Be sure to indicate the need for review of the rough or design concept, the semi-comprehensive design, finished work, as well as the number of illustrations, artwork, photographs, the color, the size, the medium and so forth.

Some draft initial clauses follow:

> **The term "Artist" is intended to encompass either a professional photographer, illustrator, fine or graphic artist who is knowledgeable in his/her field of work. The Artist in this contract engages in the following field(s) _____ . Work in this agreement refers to _____ .**
>
> **_____ intends to publish a book tentatively titled _____ , a _____ of about _____ pages in _____ and referred to as Book.**
>
> **Artist has read _____ and understands that _____ desires _____ , which shall be _____ . _____ also desires that Artist prepare the jacket design for the cover of the Book and submit a proposed jacket design based on _____ and the general nature of the book.**
>
> **Artist shall submit to _____ prior to _____ at least _____ more particularly described as follows: _____ .**

Graphic artists sometimes object to the publisher's liberality in altering, editing, or changing their work. If the artist insists on consent to any changes, be sure that consent cannot be unreasonably withheld. Also, most artists want the first shot at execution of changes. Some demand additional money if the publisher's changes amount to more than ten percent of the total project. All of these demands can balloon if you, the publisher, release the reins of artistic control.

Dan Poynter's publisher–illustrator contract procedure starts with rough, then a second rough, then a semi-comprehensive design, and finished artwork. Here's part of it. (Be sure to check out the whole contract on the Poynter diskette).

Schedule

> **The Illustrator agrees to the following delivery schedule and will make every effort to honor and meet these deadlines. However, these delivery dates are estimates only and Illustrator shall not be held responsible for any damages for failing to deliver by these dates.**
>
> **The Illustrator shall provide roughs not later than _____ , 19____ , in case the first rough is not acceptable and a second rough is required.**
>
> **The Illustrator shall provide a semi-comprehensive design and type selection not later than _____ , 19____ . It is recognized that Illustrator may make minor design improvements as the work progresses.**

The Illustrator shall provide the finished Artwork not later than
_____ , 19____ .

Work for hire
This is a "work for hire" in which Publisher owns all copyright interests in the Artwork as it relates to the Work, and Illustrator assigns all of same to Publisher.

Exhibition rights
The Illustrator shall allow the Publisher free of charge full use of the Artwork to promote the Work in (but not limited to) catalogues, advertisements, paperback editions, foreign editions, publicity and exhibitions.

Illustrator shall make the Artwork available free of charge to the Publisher for any subsequent publishing purposes and shall not sell or otherwise dispose of the Artwork without imposing such conditions on the purchaser, donee or third party.

Credit
The Illustrator's name shall be printed either on the Title page of the Work, on the Half title page, the Reverse of the title page, the Acknowledgement page and/or in the Colophon at the discretion of the Publisher.

The Publisher shall use their best endeavors to ensure that the Illustrator is given full acknowledgement in any edition of the Work sub-leased by the Publisher to a third party.

The Illustrator shall ensure that any exhibition of the Artwork shall make full acknowledgement to the Work, its author and to the Publisher.

Final Acceptance of Work
Determine, within a reasonable time, whether the work meets with your approval. A clause directed to that situation:

_____ may require artist to perform alterations or revisions of the work chosen for publication, or may arrange for same to be done by a third party at _____ expense.

Within _____ days after receipt of the work or after alterations pursuant to Paragraph ____ , _____ shall either:

(a) Reject the work by returning to artist all material submitted as the work, whereupon the contract and the rights and obligations of the parties terminate and if the Artist has received an advance upon signing of the contract, Artist keep said advance including expenses provided that same do not exceed one-third of the total advance and expenses under the contract; or

(b) Accept the work, whereupon this contract and the rights and objections of the parties shall be a full force and effort.

Establish a deadline for the finished graphic art. The first step (except for photographic work) is preparing a "rough"; roughs are design concepts sketched on tissue or other types of art paper. After you look at the rough and approve it, the graphic artist prepares a semi-comprehensive design, which includes color and other variables. The final piece should be fully completed and camera-ready. Each stage moves by steps into the final piece's time schedule.

Grant of Rights

Don't get into a quagmire on the grant of rights. Copyright and work-for-hire issues (discussed in a later chapter) can mire you down in your negotiations, so be very clear about your needs. Determine by contract clauses the following:

- Who is going to own the original artwork?
- Under what circumstances can the original artwork be possessed for varying purposes (such as reprinting when the book is translated, promotional schemes, and so forth)?
- What licensing is available?
- Who exploits the copyright?
- Who owns the copyright?

Beware of situations where you have no relationship with the graphic artist, for instance, when an author asks a friend to do the artwork, and tells you "not to worry about it." *Always* have an agreement, or insist that the author formulate an acceptable one with his or her friend.

Grant of Rights provisions range from simple to complex.

The Artist grants the Publisher all rights to the work.

or:

The Artist grants one-time, non-exclusive rights in the book for first and future printings of the book in the English language throughout the world including one-time, non-exclusive rights in the work for uses in a book club edition, film version, paperback edition, foreign edition plus exclusive reproduction rights for packaging, advertising, publicity or promotional materials.

or:

The Artist grants one-time, non-exclusive rights in the book for first and future printings of the book in the English language throughout the world plus exclusive reproduction rights for packaging, advertising, publicity or promotional materials. All other rights remain with the Artist and additional use rights by _____ shall be negotiated with Artist at a price not to exceed average industry standards.

Traditionally, the publisher received "all rights" to graphic art, sometimes described as "exclusive world rights in perpetuity." These rights are in two parts: the basic right of the publisher to publish and sell the work, and rights subsidiary to the work. Subsidiary rights include paperback, book club, foreign, reprint, performing, and other. Nowadays, graphic artists try to retain the copyright and agree to only a slim grant of rights in order to retain control of their work. Sometimes, the graphic artist wants to add that "all the rights that are not specifically transferred to the publisher are reserved by the graphic artist," and/or that the grant of all rights to the publisher is limited to the use of work for the purposes related to the publication of the book or magazine in which the art is incorporated. In that situation, the graphic artist retains most subsidiary rights for him- or herself.

Case Incident:
The jacket cover for my book *Making It Legal* features a clever notary seal stamped over blotches of primary colors. Northland printed that partial title, in other words, the upper third of the jacket cover, on t-shirts. Northland's employee art director, David Jenney, did the jacket cover, which is copyrighted in Northland's name (appropriately). If a freelancer did the artwork, and it wasn't a work for hire, the t-shirt use could be wrong.

It is best to obtain "all rights." Anything less should at least include the concept that covers are used for promotion, posters, and so forth.

_____ **shall be deemed to have transferred to Artist, after first publication in _____ of any work, all rights in the work except for:**
(a) The right to reproduce any published work in advertising and promoting the issue of _____ in which it is published, without additional payment;
(b) The right to reproduce whole pages or parts of pages that include published work, without additional payments;
(c) The right to reproduce any published work in other _____ publications of and additional payments;
(d) In the event the work is used on a _____ book cover, the right to reproduce said work as a _____ book cover for any purpose _____ may choose, without additional payment. In addition, Artist may not authorize the reproduction of any work that has been used in the book without _____ prior consent.

Publishing Agreements, by Charles Clark, lists some of the subsidiary rights for graphic art:

- paperback.
- book club.
- condensed book.

- first and second serial and syndication rights.
- anthology rights.
- strip cartoon rights.
- foreign hardback/paperback and book club rights.
- translation rights.
- merchandising rights.
- film strip rights.
- film and television rights.

Clark points out that some of the monies earned from work may be divided three ways, based on the respective contributions of the parties: the graphic artist, the author, and the publisher.

Flat Fees, Advances, and Royalties

Payments can be made either on a one-time basis (more commonly used here) or through a combination of advance and royalty. Some graphic artists want to treat any advance as non-refundable and not chargeable against other work. A "kill fee" (usually a percent of the total) may be required, if you contract for work that you ultimately don't use. Again, as with a book contract, you have to calculate the total royalties to be paid, what they're based on, and the division of monies from the sale of subsidiary rights. The same considerations apply here as discussed earlier for author contracts.

If the illustrations are half of the book, such as in a children's book, incorporate the royalty scale from the book contract into the artist's contract, since each will probably receive one-half of the total paid. Sometimes the two may sign the same contract, and a collaboration contract as well. The following clauses propose a variety of fee arrangements for graphic artists:

_____ will pay to Artist an assignment fee of $____ per day for a total number of ____ days of photographing plus expenses as set forth in the attached exhibit and marked expenses as if set forth in this agreement.

or:

_____ will pay to Artist $____ for the work created by Artist and timely submitted to and accepted by _____ payable as follows:

or:

If the work submitted by Artist is used in the published book, artist shall be paid the following royalties:
(a) ____ cents ($.____) per copy of hard-cover copies sold;
(b) ____ cents ($.____) per copy of soft-cover copies sold;
(c) For any other use of the illustrations, ____ percent (____%) of the net profit accruing to _____ from such use.

140

or:

> **If the work submitted by the Artist is used in the published book, Artist shall be paid the following rates on _____ retail list price for the work:**
>
> **(a) The amount of ____ percent sold by _____ through its retail sales outlets or catalogue distributions in book form;**
>
> **(b) One-half (½) of the above royalty percentages for copies of the work in digest form, at a discount, in a foreign language edition and the other grant of rights in Paragraph ____ of the _____ standard book contract, a copy of which is attached hereto and incorporated by reference.**
>
> **(c) No royalty shall be paid on copies of the book sold below or at cost including expenses incurred, or furnished gratis to Author or Artist, or for review, advertising, sample, remaindered books, destroyed books or books found to be unsaleable, or like purposes.**
>
> **_____ shall pay to the Artist, as an advance on monies accruing to Author under this agreement, the sum of _____ dollars ($_____), payable in three equal installments at the time of signing this agreement, delivery of satisfactory work and publication.**

Few contracts provide for a flat payment per copy to the artist (see above); this type of schedule should usually be avoided. In one case, the amount paid to the artist per book exceeded the combined author royalty share and publisher's profit. This imbalance led to the book going out of print. An amended agreement clause on the artist's percentage of royalty could have eliminated this problem.

If you're paying a flat fee, that fee may be paid within a specific period from receipt of the graphic artist's invoice (usually thirty to sixty days), or it may be paid out over a period of time, in equal or unequal installments. For instance:

- one-third on signing the contract agreement.
- another one-third on approval of graphic artwork.
- the last one-third on delivery and acceptance of finalized graphic artwork.
- or skip the second step and pay the last third on publication.
- or one-third on the roughs, a third on the semi-comprehensive, and the last third on publication.
- or any combination of the above.

Refer to the book contract section for boilerplate clauses to conclude the graphic artist's contract, including law applicable, assignment, modification, notices. Don't forget a warranty provision.

Graphic Artist's Lost Work

The most common dispute with graphic artists, particularly with photographers, is over lost or damaged work. They argue that each photo stands on its own, regardless of whether it's part of a sequence, because each photo is an accounting of a specific time and place.

Professional photographers sue clients who lose original photographic material. The American Society of Magazine Photographers (ASMP) (205 Lexington Avenue, New York, NY 10016) publishes *Professional Business Practices in Photography,* a manual that lists industry norms. In the form contract recommended to its members, it sets a standard value of $1,500 for each transparency. ASMP specifically provides for liquidated damages and the resolution of disputes before the American Arbitration Association. "Liquidated damages" means the parties agree ahead of time on payment for loss or damage to property.

Case Incident:
In *Rattner v. Geo,* (N.Y.L.J., March 16, 1987, page 39), the court ignored the publishing company's signed receipt that the transparencies were worth $2,000 each, and assessed, for thirty-nine slides that the publisher lost, $39,000 plus a $12,000 penalty.

In *Entertainment Law and Finance* (September 1987), Marc Jacobson noted in his article, "How to Place a Value on Lost Photographs," that in *Ackerson v. Stragrya* (13489-79 [1983]) a default judgment for $474,747.55, including costs and interests, was awarded by a New York lower court to a photographer. In this case, a design firm failed to return two hundred thirty original transparencies, shot in a foreign land. The judge considered the ASMP value, plus the cost of reshooting the transparencies in foreign places. (Read the article if you're a photographer, or work with them).

In 1987, a New York court awarded a photojournalist $486,000 ($1,500 per image) for three hundred twenty-four negatives lost by a Manhattan professional lab that "has since shuttered its doors and disconnected its phones" (*Photo District News,* October 1987).

One New York court struck down the stipulated provision for photographs because it didn't meet the standard required for a liquidated damage provision, and ASMP instructed its photographers to amend its provision.

The Poynter contract adds a provision to the effect that "the graphic artist shall insure the artwork against loss or damage." If you have a photographer who won't bend on these provisions, and you need his or her photographs, consider some variation of the following:

The artist agrees to keep a duplicate original transparency of any and all items submitted to the publisher. In the event that any or all of the transparencies are lost or damaged while in the Publisher's possession or control (including printers or anyone the Publisher lawfully provides with same), Publisher shall pay the cost for duplicating same within six (6) weeks after a receipt of a bill or invoice from the artist.

Beware of proposed clauses that incorporate a schedule purporting to be the reasonable value of the graphic art (at least negotiate it down to what *you* think it is), or high liquidated damages, or other language.

If push comes to shove, add:

Except for loss or damage due to its own negligence while in Publisher's actual possession, the Publisher shall not be responsible for loss of or damage to any property of the Author and the loss shall be the fair market value of the goods or $500 whichever is less.

Remember, Man Ray received $15,000 for eleven transparencies lost by the American Museum of Natural History.

Case Incident:
In the rush of mailing for overseas shipping of photo transparencies for a photographic-essay book (contracted for practically on a handshake), several transparencies were lost. Proper inventorying had been neglected. Each—publisher, print broker, printer—insisted the other had them. The photographer threatened suit against the United States publisher, as this was simplest and cheapest for her. Then, the publisher scurried about trying to resolve this matter. After a great deal of wrangling, the printer finally paid the claim, as its records were the least defensible.

Rights and Releases for Photographs

ASMP has publications with information and forms that benefit photographers, including a model submission/holding form, sometimes called a delivery memo. This form can be used for any artwork, not just photographic negatives or transparencies. Its provisions cover:

- what is being submitted.
- insurance.
- objection or response to terms required in so many days.
- notification that submission is for selection purposes.
- submission is returnable in X number of days.
- fees for keeping the materials too long.
- specified damages if lost.
- no use without transfer of cash.
- copyright notice.
- ownership.

This memo accompanies shipments (solicited or unsolicited) to a publisher, who needs to examine the work to reach a decision. When contracting for use, remember that photographs should be described, and the size they will be in the publication should be indicated.

Most photographers will grant you only one-time, non-exclusive, North American rights to photographs. The magic words to express the sale of *all rights to the photographs* are the words "exclusive rights." The customer then has the right to unlimited use of the photographs, including the right to:

143

- the photograph itself.
- reproduce the photograph.
- crop or retitle the photograph.
- copy the photograph in another medium.
- make any other use of the photograph.

It is not clear at this time if the copyright would be included in the list of "exclusive rights." If you wish to acquire the copyright, then go a step beyond the term "exclusive rights" and specifically indicate in the contract that "the graphic artist transfers copyright."

Under trade practice, a publisher receives only the right to a limited use of the photograph, that is, the right to rent it. Magazines buy "first rights," which means the right to be the first to publish the photograph. "One-time rights" means the photographer retains all rights to the photograph except for the right of the publisher to use the photograph one time. If the photograph is sold as a part of a limited edition, the customer has the right to *possess* one print out of the total number of the edition—no more and no less. One reason photographers are so rigid is that the medium allows multiple prints from a single transparency.

Under some circumstances (salary, costs, etc.), a publisher employs a photographer, who gives the publisher all rights to the photographs taken, except for possession of the negatives. On the other hand, if the photographer is freelancing and covering all his or her expenses, he or she retains full rights to the photographs.

Photographers, and sometimes visual artists, have to recognize and deal with the issues of invasion of a subject's privacy or the libelous use of the photograph. Photographic releases should be written, signed, and as broad as possible. One should exist for every individual, group, or entity whose name, likeness, image, photograph, performance or story is depicted or recorded. There are, of course, *exceptions* to using releases (see the chapter on content and material restrictions).

The release serves to negate a right, claim, or privilege and insulates the other from claims asserted after the work is finished. The indemnification provision between subject and photographer or photographer and publishing house needs to be specific because if the publisher, in its use of the photograph, retitles it, crops it, or places it in a particular way, the release would not be effective. The photographer may ask that the publisher indemnify him or her in that situation. (Some photographers prohibit the publisher from cropping, retitling, or otherwise changing the photograph.) In one matter, the publisher's caption aroused some concern.

Case Incident:
A page from a textbook discussing anger illustrated its point by a photograph of an umpire at a game. The umpire contacted the publisher, objecting not to his inclusion in the book but to the misdesignation of his motive. The caption was changed to reflect the umpire as caring for the other participants in the photograph.

Print Contracts
With art books, prints are often struck and sold in conjunction with the book.

Here's a contract a publisher proposed for a one-print deal, and another proposed for a multiprint deal*:

This Agreement is made this ____ day of _____, 19____, by and between _____ doing business as _____ referred to as the Publisher and _____ referred to as the Artist. The Publisher desires to offer a limited edition of a _____ print in order to promote the book _____ during the _____, therefore it is mutually agreed as follows:

1. The Artist grants to the Publisher any and all rights he may have to print a limited edition of one hundred and fifty (150) prints of the paintings entitled _____ measuring approximately 20 by 24 inches.

2. Publisher shall be solely responsible for and pay all costs of printing, publicity material and descriptive material.

3. Publisher will create one hundred and fifty (150) prints for the limited edition, twenty-five (25) artist's proofs and twelve (12) publisher's proofs. Nine (9) of the publisher's proofs will be made available to _____ employees at cost, two (2) of the publisher's proofs shall remain in _____ archive, and one of the publisher's proofs shall be hung permanently in the _____ offices.

4. That the limited edition of one hundred and fifty (150) prints will retail for ninety-five dollars ($95.00) per unit with the Publisher having the option of selling the prints at one hundred percent (100%) retail or their standard forty percent (40%) discount.

5. The Artist's royalties shall consist of ten percent (10%) of the retail price regardless of whether the Publisher sells the print units at retail or wholesale. No royalties shall be paid to the Artist on artist's proofs or publisher's proofs.

6. Publisher will insure all work for at least the retail price. Publisher will insure that the work is printed by methods and materials suitable for a limited edition print. Insurance proceeds, if any, shall be equally divided. Artist will sign and number prints if requested by Publisher.

7. Artist warrants that she is the creator of the work but Artist will not indemnify the Publisher against any suit, claim, demand, recovery by judgment by reason of any alleged violation of proprietary right in said work. Copyright shall remain in the Artist's name and the appropriate notice shall be affixed to all prints in the edition.

8. Publisher shall render semi-annual statements of the account to the Artist on the first day of March and the first day of September, and shall mail such statements during the April and October following, together with checks in payment of the royalties due on the sale of the print.

9. In case of bankruptcy, receivership, assignments for the benefit of creditors, or liquidation of any kind of Publisher, all rights granted herein

*Please see form contracts for direct sales, commission agreements, agreements with galleries, museums, and agents in *Making It Legal: A Law Primer for Authors, Artists and Craftspersons.*

to the Publisher shall at the option of the Artist, revert to the Artist.

10. This agreement shall be binding on and to the benefit of the executors, administrators, heirs, successors and interests and assigns of the Artist. The Publisher shall provide to the Artist a certification of a cancellation of the plate or other image used to make the print.

11. The term of this agreement shall be for two years, and after two years this agreement shall continue unless terminated upon either party giving sixty (60) days written notice and termination to the other party. Upon termination the inventory remaining shall be equally divided between the Artist and Publisher.

The next print contract ties up the artist for a period of years, regarding production of prints:

Dear

This letter is to outline our agreement to produce limited edition prints and original stone lithographs with you, beginning with a series of ten of each to accompany our publications series entitled _____ .

It is our plan to produce and sell all of these works as soon as the market will allow. The exact schedule also depends on the availability of workshop time at the lithographic studio. We will use several workshops as their time and your schedule permit.

In consideration for your work on the lithographs, you will receive 20% of the total edition that is offered for sale on both of the first and second lithographs, 20% of the total saleable edition on both the third and fourth, 25% on both the fifth and sixth, and 33% on the seventh through the tenth. For example, if the first work is an edition of 100, plus the usual artist's proofs (10% of the main edition) you will receive 17 lithographs taken from the main numbered edition and artist's proofs. The quantity of 17 lithographs is based on being 15% of the total saleable edition ($100 + 10 = 100 \times 15\% = 16.5 = 17$). All trial proofs and color trial proofs will be split evenly between you and Publisher. Progressive proofs, if any are made, and any other impressions in addition to these will be the property of Publisher.

At your option, Publisher will sell any part or all of your royalty lithographs at the wholesale issue price, and pay you monthly as the sales progress. The sale of your share would be made along with ours, so if in one month we sold 30% of the edition, you would receive 30% of the value of the lithographs you authorize us to sell.

The lithographic studio will make the usual record impressions, printer's proofs, roman impressions, presentation proofs, and museum impressions in keeping with their shop policy.

It is understood that Publisher shall be the exclusive publisher for your original lithographs and reproductions during the life of this agreement, and that you will not authorize, produce, or sign other prints or lithographs without prior written approval from Publisher.

If a second state of any of the ten lithographs is produced, the resulting lithographs will be split according to the same formula used on the main edition from which the second state was generated. In the event of any guest editions, the resulting lithographs will be split evenly between you and Publisher. When more than one lithograph is created on the same series of stones and/or plates, all of the images created, for the purpose of this agreement, will be counted as one lithograph, although they need not be marketed as such.

We will pay all of your necessary and reasonable expenses incurred during the production of each lithograph, and transportation for you from your home to and from the workshop, as required by the production process. Publisher will pay all workshop and promotional costs for all prints and lithographs, and in no event are you liable for any of these costs.

The exact number of lithographs in each edition and the retail issue price will be set by Publisher after consultation with you and the lithograph workshop, at the time a satisfactory _____ has been pulled. We plan to offer your lithographs in editions ranging from 40 to 100 and at retail issue prices ranging from $160.00 to $400.00, depending on the saleability of each work.

We will produce limited edition prints of selected paintings if you create and offer them for sale, and you will receive 20% of each print edition as royalties. You agree to sign and number these prints at our convenience, and we agree to pay all necessary and reasonable expenses incurred in this process. You will agree to assign the copyright for each painting to Publisher. No other prints or reprints will ever be made, except for the usual advertising and promotional uses. The life of this agreement is through the completion of ten lithographs, but will in no event exceed three years. This agreement may be renewed at any time by mutual consent.

I am looking forward to working with you on this project, and I hope that it provides you with some new opportunities not only for market exposure and added income, but also for some new areas to use your remarkable creative talents.

Sincerely,

Director
Accepted and Agreed:
Date:

Collaborations in Book Publishing

In late-summer 1988, several non-fiction books on *Publishers Weeklys'* hardcover bestseller list were collaborations between public figures and professional authors: *Talking Straight*, by Lee Iaccoca with Sonny Kleinfield (Bantam) and *Trump and the Art of the Deal*, by Donald J. Trump with Tony Schwartz (Random House) were two prominent entries.

These arrangements involve your author working with someone else. Sometimes, the author doesn't have the time, energy, credentials, or writing skills to complete a work alone. The author may write anonymously and be unknown, or be a ghost for a public figure, or be listed as a subordinate co-author with the subject—"with" or "as told to" are commonly used. These designations may also be eliminated, and the secondary author may be credited as an equal co-author. Each requires tailored contract provisions.

As a publisher, avoid like the plague any work on a living individual not subject to specific contractual arrangement between the author and the subject, unless it is an unauthorized biography (which creates different problems). Because each has differing responsibilities, and receives (perhaps) non-equal credit and payment and compensation rights, the subject must be available and cooperative.

Provision of Agreement

If presented with an opportunity to publish a work with joint authors, a ghost writer, a collaboration between subject and author, or some variant of these, *insist* that the parties provide you with a copy of their underlying agreement. Larry Bond collaborated with Tom Clancy on the bestseller *Red Storm Rising;* even though his name does not appear as author, his work is mentioned in the acknowledgments. Their only contract "was a handshake." The copyright is held jointly (*Publishers Weekly,* October 2, 1987). Lucky, weren't they?

The parties' agent or lawyer can put together a written contract or letter agreement. This structure often offers resolutions to problems. Have the parties refer to *Lindey on Entertainment, Publishing and the Arts: Agreements and the Law* (Chapter 50, "The Ghostwriter," and Chapter 51, "Subject and Collaborator.") Also, refer the collaborators to *The Writer's Legal Companion* by Brad Bunnin and Peter Beren, published by Addison-Wesley. A briefer discussion appears in my book, *Making It Legal.*

Because you, as the publisher, want to obligate both parties to the maximum under your contract with them, don't involve yourself in their problems. Avoid assisting the parties with that underlying agreement so that your own publishing agreement with them is not tainted.

Contract-Writer Agreement

The advantage of the contract-writer agreement is that one of the authors controls decision-making if a dispute erupts. The author employs someone to assist him or her in the writing project and pays that person a flat fee for their work on the project, rather than a percentage of the royalties. The only person, then, who contracts with you is the author and not the hired writer, who would be paid directly by the author.

Dan Poynter's forms include contract number 10, a collaboration agreement, and contract number 11, a contract-writer agreement, through which one writer hires another to work with him/her.

Here's a sample contract in which a flat-fee arrangement covers a writer updating and rewriting an author's self-published book. This agreement should have included a warranty from the collaborator to the author, as during a legal manuscript review, it was found that much of the rewrite lifted substantial portions of text from a recent book. Also, the agreement should add the publisher as a party, so the warranty covers the publisher as well.

IN CONSIDERATION of the mutual covenants contained in this Agreement, the parties agree as follows:

1. That _____ is the author of a book entitled _____ , and _____ is the proprietor of said book. That the Author and Proprietor have entered into a contract with _____ regarding the rewriting, editing and updating of said manuscript.

2. The Author and Proprietor are not professional writers and need assistance in editing, updating and revising said manuscript.

3. The Collaborator represents that she/he is a professional writer and is ready, willing, and able to collaborate on the manuscript. The Collaborator also agrees to follow and utilize the editorial and revision directions of Publisher to Author dated _____ , which letter is attached hereto and incorporated by reference as if fully set forth herein. The Collaborator will work with the Author to prepare and deliver to the Publisher on or before _____ , one complete, clean copy of the manuscript for the work in double-spaced typewritten form on $8\frac{1}{2} \times 11$ sheets or as may otherwise be specified by the Publisher. The manuscript for the work must be satisfactorily acceptable to the Publisher in both form and content for publication.

4. The Collaborator shall also include in the manuscript a title page, table of contents, index, tables, bibliographies, maps, illustrations and charts as may be necessary for the manuscript.

5. The Author shall supply the Collaborator with one copy of the present manuscript along with materials, documents, tables, illustrations, notes, etc., that will be necessary in rewriting the manuscript.

6. Time is of the essence in this Agreement and any extension of any time period herein is not meant to waive or extend any other time period.

7. The Author shall be treated as the creator of published material for all purposes including reservation of copyright, which Collaborator transfers to Author by this agreement if Collaborator has any copyright interest in the work, and the Collaborator shall not be mentioned except if the Publisher opts to mention _____ as a Collaborator, the Publisher may do so, but otherwise, the work shall not be attributed to the Collaborator in any form.

8. That the funds payable to the Collaborator under this agreement shall be as follows: _____

_____ . The Collaborator shall have no interest in royalties or other payments between the Publisher and Author.

9. The Author agrees to present to the Collaborator two free copies of the regular edition of the work.

10. This agreement shall be binding on and enure to the benefit of the executives, administrators, and assigns of the Author and Collaborator, but no assignment, voluntary or by operation of law, shall be binding on either of the parties without the written consent of the other party hereto.

11. The Collaborator shall not write, edit, collaborate on, ghostwrite, print or publish, or cause to be written, edited, elaborated on, ghostwritten or published, any magazine articles, books or manuscripts, whether revised, supplemented, corrected, enlarged or abridged or otherwise, or any other work of a nature which relates to the subject of this work.

12. This Agreement shall be interpreted regardless of where executed, as though executed within the State of _____ and shall be governed by the laws of the State of _____ and of the United States of America.

13. This Agreement constitutes a complete understanding of the parties and no waiver or modification of any provision shall be valid unless in writing and signed by Author and Collaborator. Waiver of a breach or of a default under any provision hereof shall not be deemed a waiver of any subsequent breach or default. In the event that the manuscript is not acceptable to the Publisher in both form and content for publication, then the Collaborator on written notice by the Author or Publisher shall form corrections and revisions of the manuscript.

14. It is understood that the Author shall have the right to cancel this agreement in the event that the time limit for submitting the manuscript to the Publisher is not met, and/or in the event that the manuscript is not satisfactory to the Publisher, and/or in the event that the Collaborator does not timely make revisions and changes requested by the Publisher or Author. In the event of such cancellation, neither party shall have any obligation hereunder to the other party, after the effective date of the cancellation including payment of any sums still due the Collaborator.

15. Upon the completion of the edited manuscript, the Collaborator will return to the Author any notes, documents, and other material provided by the Author to the Collaborator for the use in collaboration.

Ghostwriters & Subject Collaborators

In the ghostwriter contract or the subject–collaborator contract, obligate both the subject and author. Revelations from the subject's personal life experiences could be defamatory, invade privacy, or otherwise contribute to legal problems. The provisions through which each party warrants that the materials supplied by them do not violate any copyright or any personal right of any third person are important. Usually, a ghostwriter is paid a flat fee and does not share in any other way in the proceeds of the book. In a subject-collaborator contract, the parties often split any advances, royalties, and subsidiary rights equally, but each must agree before the sale of subsidiary rights. Their signatures to subsidiary rights agreements constitute written consent and their agreement to licensing.

The subject–collaborator agreement contains a clause that if the work is sold, the agreement between the parties lasts for the life of copyright. If the work is not sold within a certain period of time, each contributor takes what he or she contributed and goes their own way, and the author cannot use the information supplied by the subject for another project.

You might need to add this provision to your contract if your author–subject is involved with a ghostwriter:

> **Publisher understands that _____ is the writer of the material to be published under author's supervision and pursuant to a written agreement between author and _____ . Pursuant to that agreement, author shall be treated as the creator of the published material for all purposes, including reservation of copyright and _____ shall not be mentioned nor shall the work be attributed to _____ .**
>
> **[If ghost writer is being paid a percentage of the royalties]. Whenever funds are payable to author pursuant to this agreement, they shall be paid by publisher in two checks, one for ___% payable to author and the other for ___% payable to _____ .**

To summarize, proceed cautiously in a co-author or collaborator situation. Look over the parties' contract before contracting with them, and beware of situations that require collaborators to "mutually agree." Some potential problems:

- If you require revisions and only one collaborator does the revisions, would you charge off any of the cost to the other?
- To the extent that the authors have a say in licensing subsidiary rights, what happens if they don't agree?
- If sequel, character, format, or trademark rights develop from the collaborated book, can one of the collaborators go off on his or her own for a new book, using the same subject matter or material?
- What happens to time deadlines when one of the collaborators is prompt in delivering materials but the other is not. Do you penalize both?

In short, when you add another party, there's potential for a rainbow of disagreements. Favor contract clauses that keep publishing details, liability, subsidiary rights and so forth within your control, and that obligate both authors individually and collectively as to any standard author obligations.

A man and a woman approached me about a contract for a collaborative effort on a text partially written by the woman and more-or-less based on the man's time-management seminars. This first draft of the collaboration covered both potential publishing routes, normal trade and self-publishing.

Collaboration Agreement

This agreement is between Martha of _____ , Arizona and George of _____ .

1. The parties have collaborated in the writing of a non-fiction book ("the Book"), tentatively entitled _____ . The manuscript of the book is attached to this agreement and made part of it by this reference.

2. Each Party agrees to cooperate in efforts to secure publication of the Book and to market other rights in it to the maximum extent possible.

3. Subject to the exception in this agreement, all decisions of all kinds affecting the Book and its commercial use and value shall be jointly made. Specifically, no decision about the employment of professional advisors and representatives, or about the style and content of the Book, or about agreements and contracts concerned with the Book, shall be made unless both parties agree, except as provided otherwise in this Agreement.

4. The parties shall work together in the following way: George shall have final authority over the technical contents of the manuscript and Martha shall have final authority over the style and manner of presentation of the material in the manuscript. Each party shall keep the other notified of any absence of more than three (3) days from their respective residences which residence addresses are _____ and _____ . All notices mailed to these addresses shall be considered received one week after mailing unless the party has advised the other of the change of address.

5. The parties intend to have a written signed contract with a major publisher for regular publishing on or before 30 days after executing this agreement. If they do not, they may mutually agree to extend the deadline for publication. If they do not mutually extend the deadline for regular publication then Martha shall handle and make all the arrangements for self-publishing including, but not limited to, arrangements for copyrighting, editing and design, content, printing, binding and sales. In the event the book is self-published, the parties shall open a joint checking account for the Book project with Martha as signator. Regular publishing is defined as the situation where a publisher pays publication costs and the author(s) receives royalties.

Any costs in excess of _____ to obtain bound copies of _____ number of books, in the event of self-publication, shall be a joint decision. If George does not wish to pay the additional costs then Martha's share of the book, if she pays these costs, shall increase. [Should cover distribution costs, marketing, author sales, subsidiary rights, etc.]

The parties shall bear the expenses of self-publication on a 60–40 percent ratio with Martha bearing 60 percent of the expenses.

6. Once the Book is complete, the parties shall hold joint copyright in it.

7. The parties shall work together to find a publisher for the work during the time allowed. Neither may enter into an agreement for publica-

tion of the Book without first obtaining the other's consent and signature on the publication agreement. This provision does not apply to the self-publishing course of action. Under that course of action, Martha has authority to execute documents and take other action to accomplish self-publication.

8. All payments, of whatever kind, resulting from the regular publication of the Book and the license, sale, or other disposition of subsidiary rights in the Book shall be divided equally between the parties. If possible, each party's share shall be paid directly to that party. The division of profit on self-publication is set forth elsewhere in this Agreement.

9. Authorship credit for the book shall be equal for the parties, and their names shall appear in alphabetical order.

10. Neither party may make changes in the Book after it has been typeset without the written consent of the other. That consent shall not be unreasonably withheld.

11. Either party may assign his/her rights to income from publication of the Book or rights to income from the disposition of subsidiary rights to a third party, but no third party shall have any other rights in or to the Book. Neither party may assign any other rights or obligations of this agreement without first obtaining the other party's written consent.

12. During the time the parties pursue the regular course of the publishing option and in the event the parties publish the work as a regular publication, the parties must agree before incurring any expenses in connection with the Book after this date which are to be reimbursed from the book proceeds which exceed $_____. Those expenses shall be shared equally by the parties.

13. Nothing in this agreement shall be deemed to create a partnership or a joint venture between the parties, who are collaborators on only this single work.

14. Unless this agreement is first terminated by a settlement agreement or arbitration award, or by the death or disability of one or both of the parties, its term shall equal the copyright in the Book, including all extensions.

15. If either party is unable to complete work on the publication of the manuscript, for any reason, the survivor may complete it, alone or with another, as if the survivor were the sole author. The party who is unable to complete the work shall nevertheless receive credit as a co-author of the Book and that party, or the estate, shall receive that party's prorated share in the income from publication of the Book and disposition of subsidiary rights in it, taking into account the parties' respective contributions to the completed Book, after deducting expenses incurred in completing the Book, including any salaries, fees, or royalties paid to another to complete the Book.

16. During the first year after publication of the Book, neither party may publish or allow the publication of a sequel to the Book without the

prior written consent of the other. A work is a "sequel" if it is substantially based on the material in the Book, deals with the same subject, is similar in style, development, and presentation as the Book, and is pointed toward the same market as that for the Book.

17. Material collected by either party in preparation of the Book (i.e., tapes, reference books, equipment, etc.) shall belong to that party if acquired at his/her sole expense. If acquired at the expense of both parties, that material shall belong to both parties and shall be disposed of only by the parties' agreement.

18. Each party represents and warrants that he/she has full power to enter into this agreement and that any material provided for the Book does not infringe or violate the rights of any other person, including but not limited to copyright, and further is original. Each party shall hold the other harmless from, and indemnify the other against, all damages and costs, including reasonable attorneys' fees, from any breach of these warranties and representations.

19. Any dispute or claim arising out of or relating to this agreement or any breach of this agreement may be submitted to mediation under terms to be agreed on by the parties at the time. Should the parties fail to agree on a mediation procedure or should a mediation session be held and fail to produce agreement, the dispute of claim shall be submitted to arbitration in accordance with the rules of the American Arbitration Association; judgment on the award rendered may be entered in any court having jurisdiction thereof.

20. This agreement constitutes the entire understanding of the parties and may be modified only by a written statement signed by both of them.

21. This agreement shall benefit and bind the successors, personal representatives, and assigns of the parties, but neither party may assign rights, except the right to royalties or other income from the Book, without first obtaining the other party's written consent, and the assignment of royalties or other income shall be effective only if the assigning party first notifies the other party of the assignment in writing.

22. The parties agree to perform all acts and execute all documents necessary or desirable to carry out this agreement.

23. This agreement is executed in and shall be subject to the laws of the State of _____.

Translation Agreements

Translations occur either simultaneously with production of a work, or more commonly, after a work is in print. Some poetry and periodicals run the work in English side-by-side with the foreign language. An international translators' organization equates the status of translator with author. If this occurs, the financial arrangement may need to include the author, foreign publisher, translator, and yourself.

Be sure to acquire copyright in the translation.

Consider the quality of the translation. *The New Yorker* (May 23, 1988), in a review by Clive James of Primo Levi's last book *The Drowned and the Sword* (Summit), a translation, reported that "the book has not been as well translated as one could wish—Levi's supreme mastery of prose is reduced to something merely impressive. . . ." The article goes on that the translator got things sidewise and trusted his ear too much, rendering *promiscuita* as *promiscuity* instead of *propinquity,* for instance—a glaring error tantamount to a bad joke, for it referred to people's lives in the ghetto. The recitation of errors careened on for two columns.

A contractual requirement should provide that "the translation must be rendered into good, accurate, literary English and remain faithful to the work." (See Clark, p. 16, et seq., and his discussion of the positive and negative effects of designating the translator as a secondary author; such a status infers both rights and responsibilities.) As far as compensation is concerned, from the publisher's point of view, a flat fee arrangement is most practical.

Anthologies and Adaptations

Conceptually, anthologies and adaptations concern the editing of work in existence as to the selection of the author, the subject matter, and exact text.

Educational textbooks are often anthologies or adaptations. A glance at book club selections shows this format's popularity with the general reader, as well. The bookshelf nearest my writing desk contains three such works: Neil Perrin's *A Reader's Delight,* published for Dartmouth College by University Press of New England; *Deep Down: The New Sensual Writing by Women,* edited by Laura Chester, Faber & Faber (both QPBC selections); and a Mentor Book from New American Library, *American Indian Mythology,* by Alice Marriott and Carol K. Rachlin, a compilation of auditory archaeology, or oral histories.

If an individual author is contracting with you to put together a book consisting of selections from other works, use a special agreement with a larger-than-usual permission clause, due to the length of some contributions. (See Form 52-1 in Lindey, Author-Contributor Contract with commentary. Note that the form omits the requisite signature line that would normally make the original author a party to that agreement.)

Permissions and acknowledgments play star roles in anthologies. (See page 256 for permissions from the copyright viewpoint.) The permission trail can be complex and expensive (depending on the contract), not only in actual fees, but author and/or staff time and processing costs. Since the author selects someone else's material to incorporate in the anthology, it makes sense that this task, as well as the cost, rests with the author. The author can control, to an extent, the selections. The author's royalty for an anthology is the same as for other works, even though the author did not write the text. Remember, your contract already makes the author financially responsible if a legal problem occurs, under your contract's warranty and indemnity provision. You may need to assist the author by providing forms, information, and perhaps networking to obtain a difficult permission.

Try to get permission to use the material for all editions, book rights, and subsidiary rights. At the very least, establish the fee for future use, for other editions, foreign publications, and associated book and subsidiary rights, if possible. If not, consider substituting another selection. Avoid the time and expense of negotiating each of them as they arise.

Here's a sample permission request from an educational publisher for material to be included in an anthology. (I added the sentence on editing.) The contract that goes with this permission appears in the discussion of education contracts:

Dear Permissions Editor or _____:

I am currently preparing a book on the subject of _____ which will be published by _____ Publishers. I request permission to use the material described below in that book: _____. The only editing that will be done to the material, if any, is to shorten the selection by the deletion of certain words, phrases or sentences. I request non-exclusive world rights in all languages for this edition and all future editions. Agreeing to this request will in no way restrict republication of your material in any form by you or by others authorized by you. If you do not control these rights, please let us know where to write for permission to use this material.

I will, of course, give full acknowledgment to author, title, and publisher. If you require a specific credit line, please indicate the proper credit below.

To grant permission, please sign and return this letter; the duplicate is for your records. Your prompt consideration of this request will be greatly appreciated.

Author's name
Title
Company Address
_____
I (we) hereby grant permission for the use of the material requested above and request this specific credit line: _____
_____ .

_____   _____
(Signature)   (Date)

_____
Title (Permissions Editor
   or Author or _____)

Consultant Contracts

When you use an outsider to complete a definite task, that person is operating as a freelancer or consultant, i.e., a financial advisor, staff trainer, copy editor, artist, assistant on a special project. Reduce that arrangement to writing.

Be sure to cover the following points:

- non-employee status.
- scope of services and acceptance.
- schedule of payment.
- ownership of copyright (work for hire).
- warranties.
- performance time.
- dispute resolution.
- termination.
- boilerplate.

Here's a short consultant agreement offered to me when I conducted an educational workshop.

Consultant Agreement

THIS AGREEMENT entered into this _____ day of _____, 19_____, by and between (_program or project_), party of the first part, hereinafter referred to as "_____", and (_name of consultant_), party of the second part, hereinafter referred to as the CONSULTANT. WITNESSETH:

In consideration of the undertaking hereinafter set forth the parties hereby agree that:

1. "_____" hereby retained CONSULTANT for the following purpose:

2. The period for which CONSULTANT is to be employed shall be:

3. The compensation of CONSULTANT to be employed shall be:

4. CONSULTANT hereby agrees that at no time during the time or times when party of the second part serves "_____" as a CONSULTANT, or hereafter, will party of the second part disclose or make any other use of information about the business methods, operations, costs, proposals, budgets and projections or any other information of a confidential nature pertaining to "_____".

5. Upon termination of party of the second part services to the program, CONSULTANT agrees to return all written and other materials, which are not matters of public record, furnished to him by the project.

157

6. This AGREEMENT may be terminated at any time, with or without cause, by either party, upon notice in writing. Written notice shall be deemed sufficiently given if posted by registered or certified mail.
7. This AGREEMENT constitutes the entire understanding between the parties and no amendment or modification hereof shall be effective unless reduced to writing and executed by both parties.

IN WITNESS WHEREOF, the parties hereto have executed this AGREEMENT as of the date first above written, in duplicate, intending the duplicate to be an original.

APPROVED: ACCEPTED:

_____   _____

Conclusion

Once you understand the principles and intent of contracting, any arrangement can be memorialized in the contract form—just as "Twinkle Twinkle Little Star" can be played on any musical instrument and in any key.

Contracts for a Variety of Publishers

9

The generic book publishing agreement is the backbone of book publishing. There are other varieties of publishers, as well—subsidy or vanity, self, desktop, software, educational, and periodical publishers (magazines, newsletters, weeklies, journals and the like). Regardless of your particular niche, you must understand business structure, contract basics, content restrictions, manufacturing, and marketing matters to operate successfully.

Paying for a Book You Authored

So far I've talked about publishing situations in which an author writes a manuscript that a publisher pays to publish. Sometimes, the quality of a manuscript, a small anticipated market, or other modest commercial possibilities thwart the publication of a work by a trade publisher, and so an author decides to become a self-publisher—an entrepreneur in the American way. For some, the road leads to subsidy or vanity publishing. This quote by Sir James M. Barrie illustrates why authors take these steps:

> For several days after my first book was published I carried it about in my pocket, and took surreptitious peeps at it to make sure the ink had not faded.

In self-publication, a business structure is established, and either you or an independent contractor design, typeset, print, bind, market, promote, fulfill, and account for the work. (See all of Dan Poynter's publications, including the self-publishing manual, *How to Write, Print and Sell Your Book.* Also, review the *Publish It Yourself-Handbook: Literary Traditions and How To* by Bill Henderson [Push Cart Press] and other self-publishing how-to texts for business guidance in that area).

The same legal considerations that apply in an author/publisher arrangement are also of importance to self-publishers. You still must be knowledgable about your structure. Louise L. Hay, author of *You Can Heal Yourself,* published the book through her corporation, Hay House, Inc. She still had to protect the privacy of her student-clients in the book's text and worry about fair use of material quoted or referenced from other texts. She dealt with a jacket illustrator, a printer, a bindery, a distributor—who knows who else! (Note: at last estimate, more than 400,000 copies of the book are in print.)

Subsidy presses publish an author's work at the author's expense. A pure vanity press, to me, is merely a printer: give them the work and they'll print it as it is. A subsidy press offers more services.

Subsidy-Vanity Publishing

Lindey on *Entertainment, Publishing and the Arts* has a subsidy-vanity press contract with comment (Form 48-1). That particular contract favors the subsidy press in that it excludes services the subsidy press will not provide, emphasizes full payment due to the publisher before the book's printed, but reserves a percentage of subsidiary rights for the publisher as well as granting the publisher the option of reprinting copies at its cost. If this occurs, the agreement shifts to a straight publisher-author contract, with a much lower percentage of royalty to the author (forty percent is the norm for subsidy-vanity publishing). If the work is a sleeper, the press can still share in the pie.

Here are some subsidy-vanity press provisions from a contract that I reviewed for an author:

Sales Promotion, Distribution, Advertising
Sales promotion, distribution, advertising and publicity shall be at the Publishers' election and discretion as to the extent, scope and character thereof and in all matters pertaining thereto, and same shall be at no extra cost to the Author, unless otherwise provided for. It is specifically understood and agreed, however, that the promotion, publicity and advertising recommendations in the *Author's Promotion and Production Report,* a copy of which is being submitted to the Author with this agreement, will be performed by the Publishers within a reasonable period of time following completion of the said Work, provided that the Author has fully and completely performed each and every term, covenant and condition to be performed by him under the terms of this agreement. It is agreed, furthermore, that the recommendations in the said *Author's Promotion and Production Report* represent the minimum promotion program allocated to the said Work and will constitute the Publishers' full and satisfactory compliance as provided for in this agreement.

Design and Production
The Author agrees that all matters dealing with the design and production of the said Work shall be at the discretion and election of the Publishers, unless otherwise provided for.

No Sales Guarantee
This agreement is entered into by both parties hereto in good faith, it being distinctly understood that neither party has guaranteed, or intends to guarantee, the sale of any specific number of copies of the said Work, or receipts from possible subsidiary rights, it being mutually recognized and acknowledged that it is impossible to predict what success any book may attain.

Complete Contract
The Author acknowledges that the Publishers have not made any prior pledges, promises, guarantees, inducements of whatever nature, either in writing or by word of mouth, or in any other form except as may be contained in this agreement. This agreement constitutes the whole and complete understanding of the parties, and no representations other than those expressly contained herein shall be binding. No alteration, modification, amendment, or waiver of any provision hereof shall be valid and enforceable unless it be in writing and signed by both parties.

PMA's newsletter (July 1988) reported on a business periodical article that touted vanity publishing, and compared it to complaints PMA had received about vanity publishers. One author whose work had been published in this manner told PMA that the vanity publisher convinced him that his World War II memoirs were marketable. The author spent $20,000 to publish a 450–plus page book. The author got:

- a book.
- an $8.60 per volume price tag to author.
- an unedited work.
- a book without an ISBN.
- no marketing, although it was promised.

Don't take nearly illiterate Old Henry's entire retirement savings to publish a book of rhymed poems about his experiences as a janitor at a grade school in Joliet, Illinois; do a lousy "publishing" job; and dump the books in his lap. You may end up tangling with the state attorney general's consumer fraud office or a legal aid attorney.

Certain kinds of work suit subsidy publishing, provided the author understands and can afford the risk. Some examples:

- A self-made businessman in the auto industry for seventy years, now on social security but with an ongoing business, has a ghosted autobiography relative to the development of the automobile.

- A retired high school English teacher who has written haiku in her spare time wants to publish a small, tastefully done, chapbook to distribute to her professional acquaintances and former students.
- A small junior college has a seventieth anniversary coming up and the present board of trustees would like to publish a photo documentary and text that commemorates the college's growth and staff.

As a subsidy publisher, you should be sure that your contract spells out:

- the total payment, the payment schedule, and what the author gets.
- the form in which the manuscript is transmitted.
- editorial services provided (or not).
- minimal production, art sources, design, selection of typeface, and assembly provided, and if any can be purchased separately.
- printing specifications (general or specific depending on the expertise of the author).
- types of binding, jacket cover, dust jacket (if any).
- quantity of bound copies and press sheets to be published, and ownership of same.
- who establishes the retail price, what it will be, and the author's royalty.
- subsidiary rights granted, and the fee for marketing same.
- publication date and excusable delays.
- who pays for shipping.
- how the books will be stored, how long, and for what charge.
- warranties and indemnifications.
- what advertising you will do, and in what media.
- what samples or reviews will be sent out.
- your sales obligations.
- any extra-charge schedule.

Some authors will pointedly require specifics. They may want to see a dummy, some sample books, or the names of bookstores that handle your books.

Keep your responses simple, and don't puff. Avoid a litany of legal claims like fraud, fraud in the inducement, misrepresentation, breach of warranty, breach of contract, and so forth by being short, direct, and specific. Disclaim any representations regarding sales potential or market recognition.

The big problem in this area is quality, both in the text and in the produced book. If I were setting up a subsidy publishing house, I'd establish quality categories for the finished product and let the author select. As companies that sell corporate record books have the practical, no-frills; the executive; and the senior executive set, you could also offer varying types of quality, reduce author–consumer complaints, and possibly make more money. After all, if I looked at the no-frills model and compared it to the super-deluxe dummy, the one with an elegant cover and quality paper, wouldn't I opt for the more costly package for *my* memoirs?

Co-Publication

Co-publishing is also a co-production: one book is produced at the same time for two or more publishers. Here I use the term "publisher" loosely, to encompass any party to an arrangement to publish a work with another party (excepting authors).

Publishers Weekly (June 3, 1988) reported that Toppan and Dai Nippon (Japanese printers) have solicited co-publishing ventures for a decade. Their goal in doing this is to make a profit in the domestic market and co-publish abroad for both prestige and profit. *Helga,* printed by Dai Nippon for Abrams, had sales of 20,000 to Japanese publishers for release during the Japanese Wyeth exhibit, with the remainder of the print run going to Abrams.

Sometimes the co-publishing venture is structured as a partnership, and sometimes as a joint venture. The 1988 PLI Book Publishing Handbook devotes nearly two hundred pages to various formats of structuring a deal.

Bookmaking discusses the use of co-production to save on plant costs—one-time expenses, such as those for separations, film work, etc., not affected by the size of the run—plus the costs of labor and materials, which vary according to the number of copies printed and bound (see pp. 366 et seq., for a detailed discussion of savings on high plant costs associated with production of an art book).

The shortest co-publishing arrangement I've ever seen is this:

The _____ (First Party) and _____ (Second Party) desire to publish the book, "_____," derived from _____ of the same name, commissioned by _____. Specifications, time-frame and responsibilities are as follows:

Mechanical Specifications: _____ **pages plus cover, 6⅞″ × 9½″, body stock equivalent to 80# (basis 25″ × 38″) Quintessense, cover stock equivalent to 10 pt. Kromokote (CIS), with Smyth-sewing and glued cover. 10, 12–page signatures will be printed in 4/color process (unrestricted bleed) averaging 2 color separations per page, totally 120 pages and 240 color separations. The remaining 54 pages shall be printed in 1/color (black) with text and halftones. First printing shall be 17,500 copies.**

Camera-ready art shall be produced by Second Party in concern with _____ with completetion by (date). Such camera-ready art will be turned over to (printer) on (date), for camera work, separations, press and bindery production, to be completed with delivery in (city) by (date). Second Party will execute the financial contract with (printer) and be financially responsible for production costs.

Financial Breakdown: **(by unit)**

$_____ . . . Retail price
(-) _____ . . . Discount
_____ . . . Subtotal
(-) $_____ . . . Royalties

_____ ... **Subtotal**

(-) $_____ ... **Advertising Budget**

_____ ... **Subtotal**

(-) $_____ ... **Manufacturing Cost (includes pre-press, separations, presswork, binding materials and shipping)**

$_____ ... **Second Party**

By now you've read enough about contracts to imagine a laundry list of problems with this. Assuming that the work exists already in some format:

- what about the authors?
  - who pays them?
  - who owns copyright?
- term?
- subsequent editions?
- warranties?
- termination?
- copyright infringement?

Poynter's contracts include a co-publishing agreement (contract 4) that covers a situation in which a small publisher sells a title to another, larger, publisher. A different slant is taken in Lindey's Publisher-Packager Contract Form 44-1, in which a packager engages in some of the same entrepreneurial activities as the publisher–agent, copy editor, managing editor, compositor and printer—on a one-time arrangement for a particular book.

Obviously, the packager (referred to as the proprietor in these contracts) can't grant more rights than are transferred to it by author. A host of arrangements can be made with the author in such a complex book-making deal:

- a flat fee for commissioned work and no part of profits.
- split of proceeds in some form.
- royalties to the author, with the packager making its money on the manufacturing side.

Co-publishing arrangements are as various as Dutch tulips:

- one party can advance prepublication expenses in exchange for royalties or a percentage of the profit.
- one party invests prepublication expenses up to an agreed-upon figure, and then is paid a royalty based on net receipts.
  (Both of these arrangements allow the publisher to make all decisions on publication, style, price, distribution, and marketing, underpinned by the investor's money.)
- one party acts as agent, advisor, business, and financial consultant, and the other as publisher-distributor.

- one provides the work and printing materials (film, separations, plates) and the other pays the actual printing costs.
- the printer may wish to buy in (one of my clients, about to self-publish, was offered a co-publishing arrangement by the printer).
- a foreign publisher wanting a translated edition printed at the same time (a subsidiary right in a co-publishing context).
- in a premium sale, a membership association, such as Rafters of America, sells to its members and gives a distributor access to other customers.

One of my clients was approached by another small press with an offer to jointly publish a manuscript; the agreement proposed by the initiating publisher failed to indicate its rights to the manuscript, so I suggested adding that "it [the originating publisher] owns all rights to the book; attached is a copy of the contract by which these rights were acquired," along with a "warranty and indemnity" clause from the first press to the second.

The contract proposed this allocation of income and expense:

3. *Allocation of Income and Expenses:*
   a. _____ shall contribute one-third of the cost of printing and publishing the Work, but _____'s total contribution shall not exceed _____ Dollars ($_____) regardless of total printing, marketing, distribution or other costs.
   b. _____ shall give _____ sixty (60) days advance notice of the date by which the _____ Dollars ($\_\_\_\_\_) contribution shall be made, and _____ shall deposit the _____ Dollars ($_____) with _____ on or before the date stated in the notice.
   c. In return for _____'s contribution of capital and of the Work to be published, _____ shall be entitled to receive from _____ one-third ($33^{1}/_{3}\%$) of the gross profits from the sale of the first printing of the Work. The parties agree that the first printing shall consist of approximately three thousand to three thousand five hundred copies (approximately 1,000 hardcover and 2,000 softcover copies, the exact mix to be determined by _____).
   _____ shall pay _____ one-third of the gross profits from any printings subsequent to the first printing, provided that _____ shall have the right to request a contribution from _____ of one-third of the cost of each subsequent printing and publication, not to exceed _____ Dollars ($_____) per each printing.

The definition of the "costs of printing and publishing" and "gross profits" needed to be clearly stated. I suggested a formula, and that the publishers talk to their respective accountants. I changed the last sentence to read:

As well on each subsequent printing, _____ shall, after _____ days notice, contribute if it desires up to but not exceeding $^{1}/_{3}$ of costs or

$_____ whichever is less, of each subsequent printing and in the event _____ makes the requisite contribution then it shall share in the gross profits from each such subsequent printing.

Under warranty, I added "that the work has not been previously assigned, pledged or otherwise encumbered," "that except for permissions, the work is original" (add that before that the work had not been previously published). The warranty provision lacks a section on indemnification.

In the event of any claim, action or proceeding based upon an alleged violation of any of these warranties _____ shall have the right to defend the same through counsel of its own choosing and to settle same without the consent of _____ and _____ shall hold harmless and indemnify _____ and/or any seller of the work, and any licensee of a subsidiary right in the work against any loss or expenses including counsel fees incurred, arising from any breach or alleged breach by _____ of this Agreement or any of _____'s warranties and representations in this Agreement. These warranties and indemnities shall survive the termination of this agreement.

or:

In the event of any claim, action or proceeding based upon an alleged violation of any of these warranties (i) _____ shall have the right to defend same through counsel of its own choosing and (ii) no settlement shall be effected without the prior written consent of _____ , which consent shall not unreasonably be withheld, (iii) _____ shall hold harmless _____ Press, any seller of the work, and any licensee of a subsidiary right in the work, against any damages including expenses finally sustained, and (iv) if such claim, action or proceeding is successfully defended or settled, _____'s indemnity hereunder shall be limited to fifty percent (50%) of the expense (including reasonable counsel fees) attributable to such defense or settlement; however, such limitations of _____'s liability shall not apply if the claim, action or proceeding is based on copyright infringement or is not successfully defended or settled or _____ withholds consent to settlement.
If any such claim, action or proceeding is instituted, _____ shall promptly notify _____ , who shall fully cooperate in the defense thereof, and _____ may withhold payments of reasonable amounts due _____ under this or any other agreement between the parties until said matter is finally resolved. These warranties and indemnities shall survive the termination of this agreement.
If the copyright of the work is infringed, and if the parties proceed jointly, the expenses and recoveries, if any, shall be shared equally, and if they do not proceed jointly, either party shall have the right to prosecute such

action, and such party shall bear the expenses thereof, and any recoveries shall belong to such party; and if such party shall not hold the record title of the copyright, the other party hereby consents that the action be brought in his or its name.

The proposed warranty read:

Warranties: _____ covenants, represents and warrants that it is the sole owner of the Work; that the Work has not previously been published in whole or in part in book form; that the Work is original; that the Work may be copyrighted in the United States and under the Universal Copyright convention; that the Work does not violate the copyright, right of privacy or any other personal or property right of any other person or party whatsoever; and that the Work contains no libelous material.

And I suggested adding:

Permissions: The permissions could be elaborated further by stating that "it is _____'s sole responsibility for obtaining written permissions to reprint in the work any copyrighted material with _____ bearing the costs of permissions for photographs to a limit of $_____ for _____'s share and _____ bearing all other permission costs". (Of course, you could advance _____'s share of those costs and deduct it from their share of the gross receipts.)

The first press proposed these terms on reports and payments and copies:

Reports and Payments: _____ shall render semi-annual statements of accounts to the first day of February and the first day of August and shall mail such statements during the April and October following, together with checks in payment of the amounts due thereon. Upon its written request, _____ may examine, or cause to be examined, during regular business hours, through certified public accountants, the books of account of _____ insofar as they relate to the Work.

In response, I suggested:

Under Reports and Payments, add (after the first sentence) "Should _____ receive an overpayment arising out of copies reportedly sold but subsequently returned, _____ may deduct such overpayment from any further sums due _____". I would add to that provision "Upon _____'s written request, but not more often than once every _____ months, _____ may examine or cause to be examined during regular business hours through certified public accountants at _____'s expense the books of account of the _____ insofar as they relate to the work, provided, however, if such examination establishes errors of accounting (arising from causes other than by interpretation of the terms hereof) amounting to $_____ or more to _____'s disadvantage, then the cost of such examination shall be borne by _____ ."

Add: on copies to _____ "That _____ may purchase further copies at a discount of _____% of the retail price, except for special, limited, numbered and signed copies; however, _____ in reselling same needs to follow _____ discount schedule and return policy." I have a question as to how many books _____ can have out at one time, and do you charge that cost against the division of gross profit? Wouldn't that division be easier with less money changing hands?

In short, always establish what I call "the worst-case scenario." This means that you need to think of the worst problem that could happen and determine if the proposed contract answers it.

As you can see, the variety of arrangements are almost endless, and the roles are dependent on the activities assumed by the parties, i.e., financial investment, creative efforts, design requirements, manufacturing details, marketing, and distribution.

Minimally, all agreements should cover the following issues:

- a clear identification of the parties and each party's responsibilities (product development—making the work, marketing, etc.).
- the work or works covered.
- terms.
- editorial control.
- promotion and publicity.
- advertising and promotion.
- delivery of books.
- additional printings.
- subsidiary rights.
- payments.
- warranties.
- out-of-print clause.
- buy-back.
- non-competition clause.

Summary

Co-publishing can be a boon or a boondoggle. While you may enhance funds and expertise available for a project, you've also added yet another party to the process.

Desktop Publishing

There are those who say that desktop publishing should be called desktop typesetting. In desktop publishing, you connect a personal computer with a quality, high-speed printer to produce type of varying quality.

The technology includes transmitting by modem or delivering to a typesetter an uncoded, edited disk that's been keyboarded on your word processor, or inserting variable or exact coding for the typesetter. After keyboarding the copy, you can design a page layout and print camera-ready copy.

Several companies offer electronic mail and typesetting via local access numbers and a data upgrade communication network, which allows receipt of camera-ready pages by return mail. You can also have typesetting done from page layout programs. However, even if you telecommunicate or send a disk, typesetters still need complete, written specs and a hard copy of the manuscript to let the typesetter know how the job should look and to check for accuracy on the disk.

Potential glitches, which could spell problems, include:

- compatibility between your desktop publishing file and the service bureau who will typeset for you.
- appearance problems, such as spacing and mismatched screen fonts.
- gray tint blocks (screens) between laser-printed page proofs and typeset material, which can vary.
- careless proofreading.

This sort of type is generally not the same as professionally set type. There are limits to desktop equipment's capacity to kern, as well as a restricted number of type faces and type sizes. The relatively low dots-per-inch resolution of most laser printers cause many publishers to seek true typesetting, because of higher resolution (which translates into cleaner, crisper type) and a wider font selection.

Find a typesetter who can interface with your computer system by looking at Ronald A. LaBuz's *How to Typeset From a Word Processor: An Interfacing Guide* and *The Interface Data Book for Word Processing/Typesetting,* co-authored with Paul Altimonte (R. R. Bowker). Beware of long-term typesetting contracts until you have a trial period to determine not only the price (and savings) but quality and timeliness of the work.

Arrange for sample documents to be telecommunicated and produced, and incorporate in any agreement that the type you get is sharp and clear.

Steve Roth, author of *Small Press Guide to Computers in Publishing* (Meckler Corporation), reports in *Small Press* magazine in the "Technically Speaking" column on programs for desktop publishing. Read his column and his book. See also *The Illustrated Handbook of Desktop Publishing and Typesetting,* by Michael L. Keeper (TAB Professional & Reference Books, 1987). In December 1987, an article by Jesse Berst, "Desktop Publishing Service Bureaus," appeared in *Small Press,* directed to economy and efficiency without the expense of an in-house desktop publishing system; his June 1987 article on "Offset Printing from Laser Mechanics" is excellent, plus he discusses improving laser print.

Beware of desktop laser printers used as a substitute for offset printing; problems can include amateurish page design, broken letters, washed-out areas, and out-of-place artwork.

My personal gripe about desktop publishing and certain self-published books concerns the quality of the production of the book. A $15.00 retail book, *Beyond Your Fat: A Practical Guide to Obtain and Maintain Your Ideal Weight for Life*, by Ilana H. Damian, M.A., touts on the copyright page "This edition has been printed directly from camera-ready copy." This statement is separated from the copyright notice, and slants down. The book's content is excellent, but its layout, type (some letters fuzzy), double-spaced text, page-long paragraphs, sloppy title page (white spots in thick letters and broken typeface) all detract from the message. This amateur appearance takes away from a very original, thought-provoking, and excellent text. In self-publishing and desktop publishing, you need to hire experts to train or track you, or do those aspects of book-making that you don't want to or can't do well.

Some estimate that six to ten percent of a corporation's gross revenue dollars are spent on printing and publishing documents. While a company may use a desktop publishing set-up to issue newsletters, in-house advertising, and marketing brochures, you need to be aware of the pitfalls. As one marketing communications president complained: "I see some terrible, terrible copy coming out of some companies. When it comes to doing brochures or work that needs design expertise . . . it shouldn't be done in-house."

These sorts of publications face the same considerations in acquiring rights to the copy, avoiding defamation and invasion of privacy, getting permissions, and entering into agreements for outside services (such as electronic typesetting). Further, the proliferation of gadgets for use in desktop publishing is extensive; a tool-box-size color transfer machine and a complete system for making signs are only two of this burgeoning medium's accessories; warranties are thus important.

Warranties

Most states have adopted the Uniform Commercial Code (UCC), which governs warranties, both express and implied. The law implies at least three warranty terms in a contract for the sale of consumer goods. One is that the product is "fit for the ordinary purposes for which such goods are used"; in the case of a book, this would mean that the book remain intact and the spine not fall off on first reading, or that the sign program for your desktop publishing works.

Another warranty implied by the law is fitness for a particular purpose. If your company sells, as part of its miscellany, Chinese silk book covers that fit no standard size book, you may have breached that implied warranty.

The third implied warranty of sales contracts is a guarantee that the seller has the authority to transfer the title or ownership to the buyer, and that the items sold are not burdened by lien or other clouds on the title. In order to avoid the application of this warranty to a sale, the seller must alert the buyer that the seller does not claim to have good title. If you are selling a very limited edition of a hand-printed and -colored medieval text for $50,000 each, you are implying that no one else has claims against the work, or in other words, the printer won't show up on my doorstep to recover that piece in lieu of payment of his bill.

In addition, by placing your name on the work, you expressly guarantee your authorship of the piece—this is also called "warranty of authorship." For instance, if you release an art book on Bulgarian national parks, with hitherto undiscovered photographs by Ansel Adams, they had better be Ansel Adams's photographs (and you had better have permission to publish them).

Software Publishing

Many print publishers are moving into the software product market to service the estimated thirty-three million personal computers that are in operation. Practising Law Institute, referred to previously, has several publications in this area: *Software Protection and Marketing: Computer Programs and Databases; Video Games and Motion Pictures,* Volumes I and II (1983); and *Book Publishing 1988,* Barbara Schlain's "New Technologies: Some Key Issues for Book Publishers and Software Publishing and the Licensing of Electronic Rights." One of NOLO Press's publications, John Remer's *Legal Care of Your Software,* is an excellent and thorough reference to software publishing.

Some ways in which you can acquire rights to a computer program include:

- purchase of a software company.
- in-house development (is the person an employee? is it a work made for hire?).
- via publishing agreement with the software author (a much more specific and detailed agreement, as compared to a print/publishing agreement, with exhibits and many specifications).
- joint venturing with the software author.

In software distribution, your primary concern is the protection of proprietary rights in the product against commercial piracy, as well as private or hobbyist software duplication. Other concerns are:

- the scope of protection offered by U.S. Copyright Law.
- the use of license agreements to clarify the end-user's rights to copy and use the software.
- protection against liability for errors (disclaimers, limits of liability, federal and state laws and regulations).
- acquisition and compensation for electronic rights given the rapid technological changes in the field.

Software publishers have the same legal concerns as other publishers. The *National Law Journal* (January 2, 1989) reported that filmmaker George Lucas filed suit against Solar Systems, Inc., which publishes a software game, "Templates of Doom." This program teaches the use of financial spreadsheets using Ohio Smith, a parody of Indiana Jones. The package's title framed the image of a leather-jacketed, fedoraed adventurer, which Lucas complained would confuse the purchaser. Solar System's owner said that Lucas was "2,300 times bigger than I am and there's no question he can lawyer me to death." Lucas's lawyer worried that the suit's publicity would boost the sales of the software program.

While software publishers utilize a contract similar to that used by book publishers, software contracts spell out the author's grant of rights in computer software form on a particular computer. Software publishers have been known, though, to adapt book publishing agreements without fine-tuning them to software sales. Notice the confusion by the drafter in the following contract, particularly in its grant of rights, between manuscript requirements and computer materials. (Why the termination clause is blank is a mystery to me.) Here it is:

_____ (herein "the Author")
in connection with a work of the Author's tentatively referred to as
_____ (herein "the Work").

WHEREAS, the Author and Publisher have discussed and agreed upon the terms pursuant to which the Publisher shall have the right to publish the Work in printed form and/or computer diskette form and otherwise make it available in other forms and media, and

NOW THEREFORE, in consideration of the mutual covenants set forth below, the parties agree as follows:

1. AUTHOR'S GRANT

2. DELIVERY AND PUBLICATION

(a) The Author shall deliver to the Publisher two copies of the complete manuscript of the Work, which shall consist of <u>computer diskettes/documentation</u>, including all illustrations, pamphlets, discs, and other non-textual matter, in form and content satisfactory to the Publisher, not later than: _____, time being of the essence. The manuscript shall be in a form suitable for the Printer, and all illustrations, photographs, drawings, charts, graphs, maps and other matter not to be set in type shall be delivered in a form suitable for reproduction as determined by the Publisher and all computer materials in a form suitable for reproduction as determined by the Publisher. If any of the material to be included in the Work is not submitted in acceptable form, the Publisher may have the material put in acceptable form at the Author's expense. The Publisher shall have the right to determine the style, number and placement of any and all illustrations in the Work.

(b) Subject to the provisions of this Agreement, the Publisher shall publish the Work at its own expense in such style and manner, and at such time and price, as it shall in its sole discretion determine.

(c) The Author shall pay all fees and expenses necessary to authorize the inclusion in the Work of text, illustrations or other material not owned or controlled by the Author and shall obtain and furnish to the Publisher on

delivery of the manuscript the original copies of all written authorizations obtained by the Author for the inclusion thereof in the Work.

(d) The Author shall read and correct all proofs or other forms of the Work sent to him or her by the Publisher and shall sign and return the proofs or other forms of reproduction of the Work within the period of time provided therefor by the Publisher. If the Author fails to thus return the proofs, the Publisher may proceed with the manufacture and publication of the Work and charge the Author for any expense incurred by it as a result of his or her such failure. The cost of Author's alterations to the type and/or plates of the Work (other than corrections of printer's errors) in excess of ten percent of the original cost of the composition shall be borne by the Author except that in the case of illustrations the full cost of such corrections shall be borne by Author.

(e) If in the opinion of the Publisher the Work should include an index, the Author shall, if so requested by the Publisher, prepare such an index and submit two copies thereof to the Publisher within the period of time provided therefor by the Publisher, or, if the Publisher so determines, the Publisher shall have such an index prepared at the Author's expense.

(f) The Publisher shall not be responsible for any loss or damage to any manuscript, illustration or other material placed in its hands by the Author.

(g) The Author shall provide Publisher with all computer materials in a form suitable for reproduction, as determined by the Publisher, it being agreed and understood that the information for computer use may vary in form depending upon the targeted ultimate user.

3. COPYRIGHT

4. ROYALTIES

The Publisher shall pay to the Author royalties as follows:

_____

_____

_____

The terms "sales" and "sold" shall include all Work sold during any statement period less any Work returned for credit and less any Work payment for which has been declared uncollectible by the Publisher, provided, however, that if such uncollectible accounts are thereafter collected such collections shall be considered sales in the period of collection. If returns and Works for which payments are declared uncollectible shall exceed the number of Works sold during a statement period the difference shall be carried forward to the next period or periods until offset by Works sold.

No royalty shall be paid on copies furnished without charge or for review, advertising, sample promotion or other similar purposes or on copies sold as remainders at cost or less. The Publisher may publish or permit others to publish or broadcast without charge and without royalty selections from the Work for the purpose of promoting its sale, and the Publisher shall also be authorized to license publication of the Work without charge and without royalty in Braille or by any other method primarily designed for the handicapped.

5. SUBSIDIARY RIGHTS

Except for matters covered in paragraph 4, the following shall govern all disposition of rights in or exploitation of the Work: The Publisher shall pay the Author fifty percent (50%) of the net amount it actually receives, less any commissions, fees or other charges incurred in connection therewith, from exploitation of the Work or any rights therein by third parties, provided, however, that no payment shall be required for any use by the Publisher of portions of the Work in other works published or produced by the Publisher, provided that such portions do not exceed twenty-five percent (25%) of the Work.

6. STATEMENT AND PAYMENTS

(a) The Publisher shall mail to the Author, ninety (90) days after the first of July and the first of January in each year, semiannual statements of account of all earnings accruing to the Author, covering the six (6) months preceding the said dates. The balance shown on such statements to be due the Author shall be paid by the Publisher to the Author at the time of rendering such statement, provided that the Publisher shall be authorized to withhold therefrom such sums as may be necessary or appropriate to comply with the laws of any state or country applicable thereto.

(b) The Publisher may withhold annual payments to the Author which total less than twenty dollars ($20.00) until such time as the total payment due the Author equals or exceeds that amount. Should the author receive an overpayment of royalty on copies of the Work reported sold, but subsequently returned, or should the Author otherwise be indebted to the Publisher, the Publisher may deduct the amount of such overpayment or debt from any earnings of the Author otherwise due under this Agreement. If, in the opinion of the Publisher, there is a risk that a substantial quantity of unsold copies will be returned, the Publisher may withhold a reasonable reserve against such returns.

7. REPRESENTATIONS, WARRANTIES AND INDEMNITIES

The Author represents and warrants to the Publisher that he or she is the sole owner of the Work; that except for matter in the public domain or for which the Author has obtained authorization as provided in subparagraph 2(c) of this Agreement, the Work is original and has not previously been published in any form; that the Work does not infringe upon any statutory copyright or upon any common law, proprietary or any other right of any kind; that the Work contains no matter which is scandalous, obscene, libelous, in violation of any right of privacy, or otherwise contrary to law; that he or she is the sole and exclusive owner of the rights herein granted to the Publisher; that he or she has not previously assigned, pledged or otherwise encumbered the same; that following any regimen, recipe, or instructions contained in the Work will not cause injury to the user or others; and that he or she has full power to enter into this Agreement and to make the grants herein contained.

The Author shall indemnify the Publisher for, and hold it harmless from, any loss, expense (including attorneys' fees and expenses) or damage occasioned by any claim, demand, suit, recovery or settlement arising out of any breach or alleged breach of any of the foregoing warranties or arising out of any other failure on the part of the Author to fulfill any of his or her representations, warranties or covenants contained in this Agreement.

The Author shall make such changes in the Work as the Publisher or its legal representatives recommend in order to lessen the risk of the Publisher's liability to third parties or of governmental action against the Publisher and/or the Work.

The Publisher and the Author shall promptly inform each other of any claim, demand or suit made against them in connection with the Work. The Author shall fully cooperate with the Publisher in the defense of any such claim, demand or suit asserted against the Publisher. The Publisher in its discretion shall have the right to settle any claim, demand or suit brought against it in connection with the Work.

In the event of any claim, demand or suit asserted against the Publisher, it shall have the right to withhold payments due the Author under the terms of this Agreement as security for the Author's obligation as stated herein.

The Author's representations, warranties and indemnities as stated herein may be extended by the Publisher to third party licenses and grantees and the Author shall be liable thereon as if such representations, warranties and indemnities were originally made to them. The Author's representations, warranties and indemnities herein shall survive the termination of this Agreement.

8. TERMINATION

9. REVISIONS

In consideration of the earnings accruing to the Author hereunder, the Author agrees, upon request of the Publisher, and without charge therefor, to revise the Work and supply any new matter which in the judgment of the Publisher may be appropriate to keep the Work current. If the Author refuses or is unable to make such revisions within a reasonable time provided therefor by the Publisher, the Publisher may engage others to do so and may deduct its expense therefor from royalties or other moneys due to the Author hereunder. If any revision is made by third parties, the Publisher shall so indicate in the revised edition. All of the terms and conditions of this Agreement except those which clearly apply only to the first edition of the Work shall apply to all revisions of the Work. It is further agreed that for the purpose of royalty computation the revised edition shall be considered a new Work and the same scale of royalties shall apply to it as was applied in paragraph 4 of the original edition.

10. PROMOTION AND PUBLICITY

The Publisher shall have the right to use the name, likeness and biography of the Author for the purpose of promoting and/or publicizing the Work and any exploitation thereof.

11. AUTHOR'S COPIES

The Publisher shall furnish the Author six free copies of the Work upon its publication. The Author shall be entitled to purchase additional copies for resale at the list price less twenty-five percent (25%).

12. INFRINGEMENT BY OTHERS

If the copyright in the Work is infringed, the Publisher may institute suit or seek other remedies as it shall determine and the Author agrees to cooperate fully with the Publisher in connection therewith. The proceeds of any recovery therefrom shall belong solely to the Publisher except that if the Author on request of the Publisher agrees to share equally with the Publisher all expenses incurred in connection therewith, then the net proceeds of any recovery thereafter obtained shall be divided equally between them.

13. NON-COMPETITION

The Author agrees that during the life of this Agreement he or she will not without the prior written consent of the Publisher directly or indirectly prepare or participate in the preparation of any work of similar character which may interfere or compete with the sale of the Work.

14. OPTION

The Author hereby grants to the Publisher the irrevocable option to accept for publication (on the same terms as set forth in this Agreement) the next Work written by the Author. This option, if not exercised by the Publisher with respect to any particular option Work, shall not apply to any succeeding option Work.

15. ADDITIONAL PROVISIONS

(a) The Author is in no respect an agent or employee of the Publisher.

(b) The waiver of breach of, or a default under, any of the terms of this Agreement shall not be construed as a waiver of any subsequent breach or default. No waiver or modification of this Agreement shall be valid unless in writing and signed by all the parties to it.

(c) This Agreement contains the entire understanding and agreement between the parties. There are no representations or undertakings other than those expressly set forth herein.

(d) This Agreement shall be deemed to have been executed and delivered in the State of _____ and shall be interpreted and construed in accordance with, and governed by, the laws of the State, regardless of the forum in which this Agreement or any part thereof may be submitted for construction, interpretation, or enforcement.

(e) **This Agreement shall be binding upon and inure to the benefit of the heirs, executors, administrators, assigns and successors of both parties.**

(f) **Any notice to be given hereunder by either party to this Agreement to the other party shall be deemed to have been delivered if deposited in any United States Post Office in a sealed envelope, with registered postage prepaid, addressed to the Author or the Publisher at their respective addresses heretofore recorded in the Agreement or at any other addresses of which due notice has been given by either party as above specified.**

16. SPECIAL PROVISIONS

NONE

_____

_____

The next contract has been carefully structured to software distribution, and the publisher took care in Exhibit A to provide a _full page_ (single spaced) software description, which I imagine came from the author's proposal. It covers the users, the equipment it runs on, how it works, its options, test modes, and a quantitative statement of the number of disks and informational equivalents. The software publisher promises too much, however, when it says it has "unique abilities and opportunities to market the software. . . ."

WITNESSETH

WHEREAS, Author has developed and is the owner of all the rights, title and interest in and to certain software (which is hereinafter more particularly described on Exhibit "A" attached hereto) (the "Software") ; and

WHEREAS, _____ has unique abilities and opportunities to market the Software and put the _____ label on the software and is desirous of entering into an agreement pursuant to which it would have the right to market the Software; and,

WHEREAS, Author is likewise desirous of entering into an agreement pursuant to which Distributor would market the Software;

NOW, THEREFORE, for and in consideration of the mutual covenants contained herein the parties hereby agree as follows:

Section 1. _Distribution Rights._ **Author hereby grants unto _____ the exclusive right to market the Software for the three (3) year period commencing with the effective date set forth above (unless this Agreement shall be earlier terminated in accordance with the provisions hereof), subject to all other terms and conditions contained herein.**

Section 2. _Duties of Distributor._ **During the term hereof, _____ agrees to actively market the Software. _____ hereby acknowledges that its relationship with Author is that of independent contractor and further agrees that any and all costs, expenses or other obligations of any nature or kind incurred by Distributor in connection with its performance hereunder shall be solely its cost, expense or obligation and it shall hold Author harmless from any such cost, expense or obligation. _____ further agrees that it shall**

not conduct its marketing efforts or affairs in such a manner which shall have the effect of creating any adverse image, reflection or reputation of or on the Author.

Section 3. *Procedures.* All orders obtained by ____ for the Software shall be reported in a timely manner to the Author. All collections for sales made shall be solely the responsibility of ____ . ____ agrees to pay the Author as hereinafter defined quarterly upon the receipt of payment for the software units sold during the quarter. Following is the stated commission schedule for software sold: 10% on each unit sold.

Section 4. *Duties of Author.* Provide ____ with a complete and fully tested program ready for distribution. Provide complete and accurate documentation of the program to be put in manual format and packaged by ____ . Provide Distributor with support and updates as need may arise due to changing technology, program error, or general support information regarding any portion of the program. This support shall continue through the three (3) year period commencing with the effective date set forth (unless agreement shall be earlier terminated in accordance with the provision hereof), and applies only to the ____ version of the "Software."

Section 5. *Termination.* This agreement shall continue for three (3) years from the effective date first written unless terminated in accordance herewith. This Agreement may otherwise be terminated as follows:

    a. By mutual agreement of both parties;

    b. By either party upon notice to the other party of such other party's breach of the agreement or its failure to perform its duties hereunder, and such other party shall fail to cure such breach out of failure to perform its duties within 10 days of such notice;

    c. By ____ if Author shall fail to achieve the following schedule.

        i. Documentation completed by ____

        ii. Complete and fully tested program by ____

        iii. If significant program error is found and not corrected within a reasonable time.

Section 6. *Governing Law.* This Agreement is being executed and delivered, and all obligations herein are performable, in ____ and the laws of such state shall govern the validity, construction, enforcement and interpretation of the Agreement.

Section 7. *Multiple Counterparts.* This Agreement may be executed by one or more of the parties in several counterparts and all such counterparts so executed shall together be deemed to constitute one final agreement as if signed by all parties, and each such counterpart shall be deemed to be an original.

Section 8. *Notices.* Any notices to be provided hereunder by either party to the other may be a return receipt requested. Mailed notices shall be addressed to the parties at the following addresses:

Any party may change his or its address by written notice in accordance with this paragraph. Notices delivered personally shall be deemed provided and communicated as of actual receipt. Mailed notices shall be deemed provided and communicated as of the date of mailing.

Section 9. *Assignment.* This Agreement may not be assigned by either party hereto without the advance written consent of the other. Any purported assignment without advance written consent shall be null, void and of no force or effect and shall entitle the other party to immediately terminate this Agreement.

Section 10. *Amendment.* No amendment or modification of the Agreement shall be deemed effective unless and until executed in writing by all of the parties hereto.

Section 11. The author retains Copyright to the "Software."

The royalties are based on gross receipts. I would have suggested that Section 3 specifically set that out, i.e., ten percent of the gross receipts from each unit sold. From the publisher's perspective, the agreement lacks:

- a warranty and indemnity provision.
- indication of how returns will be handled.
- a specific time after the end of the quarter for payment.
- mention of author's copies, options, or non-competition.

I would combine the best parts of the two contracts into one that covers the special needs of software publishing.

Educational Publishing

Educational publishing is a merger of business with pedagogy. The market is subdivided into elementary, high school (often referred to as El-Hi), college, and professional. In El-Hi publishing, a well-defined set of criteria is developed for a textbook series, based on analyses of the competition, market surveys, and curriculum guidelines. The El-Hi market typically uses author teams under work-for-hire arrangements; copyright law allows commissioned "instructional texts" to be considered works for hire.

Educational publishers of reading materials in California competed for an $88,613,000 appropriation in one year alone. Twelve publishers, some large and some small, were approved for these monies. California's adoption influences other states (*Publishers Weekly,* October 28, 1982).

The following paragraphs from a letter to me indicate some of the critical problems in educational publishing.

The most common question I am asked is, "who owns what rights?" After that would be, "How do I register ownership?" This is from artists who express concern that their illustrations are being copied by another illustrator for a particular publisher (who even supplies the illustrations to be copied); and from photographers and writers who desire to be published but want to retain certain rights.

Now, virtually all the school districts are into curriculum and materials development, with teachers producing most of these materials. They "borrow" freely from published work (a great deal from _____ Press), and adapt it to whatever school level they represent. (Eventually, all these materials are sold). When these materials are finally "published," teachers claim credit and copyright too; sometimes, though, these materials are also produced with school or federal funds. Again ownership is at issue.

_____ School has similar difficulties. Faculty do research or writing for eventual publication (by a School department, or a publisher not affiliated with _____ School). _____ School provides funds for these efforts either through the School budget, or through grant programs. At the publication phase, a tug-of-war develops over ownership, copyright, and royalties. Thus, the notion of work for hire needs to be addressed.

Samples

One publishing agreement with an educational publisher incorporated the following provisions. For this college reader, a flat fee is given; the author provides narrative ties in the anthology, and for revisions, receives a low or flat fee:

The Work

"Work" as used in this Agreement means all or any part of the Work including, but not limited to, the initial volume and any and all new editions . . . . The Work shall consist of articles, studies, reports, and other published material; an introduction to the book; lead-ins to individual chapters; a bibliography of published materials and sources of information; and a table of contents. The Author shall compile the bibliography, obtain copies of the published materials, select material to be included in the Work, and prepare the introduction, chapter lead-ins, and table of contents.

I like the specificity of the project and the detail on author's duties.

Grant of Rights

For purposes of determining ownership of rights, the Publisher's relationship with the Author shall be one under which the Publisher has engaged the Author to write and prepare the Work.

The Author grants and assigns exclusively to the Publisher, its successors and assigns, during the entire term of the Work's copyright, all rights in and to any and all portions of the Work that are written or developed by the Author. This exclusive grant of rights includes, but is not limited to, the following:

(a) the right to reproduce, publish and sell the Work in any form or media now known or hereafter developed and to license and authorize others to do so;

(b) ownership of the copyright and all copyright rights in the Work

everywhere in the world and the right to apply for, obtain and renew copyright protection in the Work in the Publisher's name or as the Publisher may direct;

(c) the right to prepare supplements to and revisions, adaptations and translations of the Work and to have the same rights in the supplements, revisions, adaptations, and translations as in the original Work; and

(d) the right to use the Author's name in and on the Work and in connection with the advertising and marketing of the Work.

The language of this provision makes this a work for hire under the copyright law, because the publisher developed the idea and "hired" the author to execute it; it is an instructional text (permissible category for a work for hire); and the agreement's in writing. To emphasize the publisher as copyright holder, the language sets forth the bundle of rights to which a copyright holder is entitled.

Perfecting the Rights

The Author, upon the Publisher's written request, shall promptly sign, acknowledge and deliver to the Publisher any documents requested by the Publisher to confirm or enforce any of the rights granted to the Publisher in the Work or in any supplement, revision or translation in the Publisher's name or as the Publisher may direct anywhere in the world. Solely for purposes of carrying out this provision, the Author constitutes and appoints the Publisher as the Author's irrevocable attorney in fact, with full power of substitution, to take any act and to sign, acknowledge and deliver any document in the Author's name and stead for the Publisher's benefit.

The Author's Representations and Warranties (see the Generic contract, plus the following):

(a) be original except for material in the public domain, but may include (1) material for which the Publisher already holds the copyright, (2) excerpts from other works as may be included with the written permission of the copyright owner, and (3) subject to the Publisher's prior approval, limited amounts of sample material (for example, sample forms) created by others who grant and assign to the Publisher the rights to reprint such material;

The Author shall obtain, without expense to the Publisher, written permission to include in the Work any copyrighted material that is not in the public domain as well as any other material for which permission is necessary in connection with the Author's warranty outlined above. These permissions shall be consistent with the rights granted to the Publisher in this Agreement and shall be obtained using the Publisher's Copyright Release Form described herein in Paragraph _____ , a copy of which form is attached hereto. The Author shall deliver to the Publisher a copy of all the permissions with the final installment of the manuscript.

This additional provision recognizes the unique nature of an anthology and its use of previously copyrighted works (I don't think the publisher provided the author with any guidelines to determine if the selections were in the public domain, however).

Submission of the Work

The Work shall be a general reference tool and shall be a comprehensive treatment of the subject matter as defined in Paragraph 1 of this Agreement.

The Author shall deliver complete, acceptable and, in the Publisher's sole discretion, publishable manuscript for the Work on or before the deadline dates specified below. It is understood and agreed by the parties that time is of the essence.

The manuscript for the Work shall contain sufficient material for a book of _____ printed pages. Such manuscript shall be prepared and delivered in three stages.

Stage I: the Author shall prepare a table of contents and draft introduction, both of which shall be delivered to the Publisher on or before _____.

Stage II: the Author shall:

- identify, obtain, review, and prepare a bibliography of key articles, studies, reports, and other published materials on major issues related to _____;
- select and categorize the key articles, studies, reports, and other published materials on major issues related to _____ to be used in the Work as described in Paragraph 1;
- use the form letter provided by the Publisher (a Copyright Release Form) to obtain permission from the author, publisher, or other copyright holder of the selected material for the Publisher to use the selected material in the Work; and
- provide to the Publisher with all materials obtained for use in the Work.

The selected and categorized key articles, studies, reports, and other published materials on major issues related to _____ shall be delivered on or before _____ and shall constitute acceptable manuscript for this stage of the preparation of the Work, provided that:

- previously published material is clean and legible, which is to say, all materials that add to, delete from, or otherwise modify such previously published material must be in typewritten form, double-spaced, on one side of an 8.5 x 11-inch white paper, using one inch margins, and clearly marked, as must the manuscript to indicate where such changes are being made; and
- the Author returns to the Publisher with the selected and categorized

articles, studies, reports, etc., a _____ copyright release form, executed by the author, publisher, or other holder of the copyright of the article, study, report, and other published materials on _____ .

Stage III: complete an acceptable manuscript for the introduction, chapter lead-ins, and any other portions of the Work that are developed or written by the Author as described in Paragraph 1, shall be delivered to the Publisher on or before _____ and shall:

- be submitted as a single integrated document;
- be submitted in typewritten form, double-spaced, on one side of an 8.5 x 11-inch white page, using one-inch margins;
- be submitted, upon mutual agreement of the parties, on disk, in a computer-readable form approved by the Publisher, that is an exact copy of and in addition to the required typewritten manuscript;
- be clean and legible, meaning all materials that add to, delete from, or otherwise modify the typewritten manuscript must be typed in the manner described above and clearly marked, as must the manuscript to indicate where such changes are being made; and
- in all other respects, in the Publisher's opinion, be complete, final and publishable.

If the Author has not delivered the complete and final manuscript to the Publisher by the delivery date(s) herein agreed to, or within a reasonable time thereafter, the Publisher may either return all the manuscript submitted to the Publisher by the Author and terminate this Agreement, by notice in writing to the Author, without liability on the Publisher's part or arrange for the manuscript to be written by other person(s) deemed qualified, including in-house personnel.

In the event the manuscript is prepared by others because of the Author's failure to supply acceptable manuscript on or before the deadline dates specified above, the Publisher shall charge all reasonable costs for the preparation of the manuscript by others against sums accruing to the Author under this Agreement.

Here, the publisher has conceptualized the steps in preparing the anthology and made those practical steps part of a timeline. Although the theory is reasonable, the actual times inserted in the blanks of this contract were unreasonably short, given the length of time it takes to get permissions.

Editing of the Work

The Publisher shall have the right to make such editorial revisions and changes in the manuscript of the Work, either for substantive or format reasons, as it deems appropriate.

When, in the Publisher's sole discretion, submitted manuscript does not

meet the substantive and/or format requirements outlined in Paragraph
_____ of this Agreement, in that the manuscript requires heavy rewriting,
retyping, revision or other excessive editorial intervention, the Publisher
may rewrite, retype, revise or otherwise editorially intervene and charge
the reasonable costs of such editorial work against sums accruing to the
Author under this Agreement. In no case shall the Author be charged for
any retyping necessary due to manuscript markings made by the Publisher's staff once the Publisher has accepted the manuscript.

The publisher should be responsible only for editing of the author's text,
because any editing of the selections would exceed the scope of the permissions.
Changes should be recommended to the author, who would then consider any
alterations to the material he or she selected. This may mean the author will need to
revise the permission.

Subsequent Editions

It is the Publisher's current intent to issue new editions of the Work on
an annual or other periodic basis. Such new editions shall be considered
part of the Work and, as such, are covered by the terms of this Agreement.
The new editions shall consist of entirely new material and shall cover
and/or update the materials described in Paragraph 1.

The Publisher shall notify the Author of its intent to publish a new
edition and set a deadline date for new edition manuscript at least one
hundred eighty (180) days prior to the deadline date for the new edition.
The Author shall, within thirty (30) days of receipt of said schedule, notify
the Publisher of her intention to develop manuscript for the subsequent
edition. In the event the Author does not elect to prepare manuscript for the
subsequent edition, or fails to notify the Publisher that he/she intends to
develop the manuscript, this Agreement shall terminate for cause, without
liability on the Publisher's part except for the obligation to account for and
pay any outstanding compensation due to the Author under this Agreement.

If the manuscript for any new edition(s) shall not have been delivered by
the deadline date(s) specified by the Publisher, the Publisher may, at its sole
option, either terminate this Agreement for cause, by notice in writing to
the Author, without liability on its part, except for the obligation to account
for and pay any outstanding compensation due to the Author, or arrange
for the new edition manuscript(s) to be written by any person(s) deemed
qualified, including in-house personnel, giving such person(s) author's
credit as it deems appropriate.

In the event any new edition is prepared by others because of the
Author's failure to supply acceptable manuscript on or before the deadline
date, the Publisher shall charge all reasonable costs for the preparation of
new edition manuscript against sums accruing to the Author under this
Agreement. It is understood and agreed between the parties that the
Publisher's waiver of its right to terminate this Agreement for the Author's

failure to deliver manuscript under this paragraph shall not constitute a waiver or termination for any subsequent failure to deliver new edition manuscript.

Compensation

As sole and complete compensation for all of the Author's efforts on behalf of the Work, the Publisher shall compensate the Author as follows: A flat fee of six thousand five hundred dollars ($6,500), to be paid as follows:

(a) five hundred dollars ($500) upon execution of this Agreement and, in subsequent years, upon the Author's acceptance of the schedule as provided herein in Paragraph _____ ;

(b) five hundred dollars ($500) upon the Publisher's acceptance of the table of contents and outline as described in stage one of Paragraph _____ of this Agreement;

(c) two thousand dollars ($2,000) upon the Publisher's acceptance of the articles, studies, reports, etc., as described in stage two of Paragraph _____ of this Agreement; and

(d) three thousand five hundred dollars ($3,500) upon the Publisher's acceptance of complete and final manuscript as described in stage three of Paragraph _____ of this Agreement.

Other Publications

The Author may give speeches, publish articles in journals that deal with the subject matter of the Work and, subject to the Publisher's prior approval, use portions of the Work in a professional context.

Here the publisher recognizes that the author's professional work in this area enhances the value of the anthology.

Termination

In the event this Agreement is terminated for cause pursuant to Paragraph _____ , _____ , and/or _____ , the Publisher shall retain all rights of any kind granted herein to the Work. The Publisher may continue publication of the Work and the Author shall receive compensation as specified in Paragraph _____ of this Agreement until the beginning of the next publication cycle at which time the Author's right to compensation under Paragraph _____ of this Agreement shall terminate.

This Agreement may be terminated without cause at any time by either party to this Agreement by notification in writing to the other party one hundred and eighty (180) days prior to the date of termination. During such one hundred and eighty (180) day period this Agreement shall remain in full force and effect and both parties shall remain fully obligated to perform under this Agreement. Upon such termination without cause, all rights and obligations under this Agreement shall cease, except for the

Publisher's obligation to account for and pay outstanding compensation due to the Author.

In the event the Author terminates this Agreement without cause, the Publisher shall retain all rights of any kind granted in this Agreement to the Work, the Publisher may continue publication of the Work and the Author shall receive compensation as specified in Paragraph _____ of this Agreement for one (1) publication cycle following the date of termination.

In the event the Publisher terminates this Agreement without cause, the Publisher shall retain all rights of any kind granted in this Agreement to the Work, the Publisher may continue publication of the Work and the Author shall receive compensation as specified in Paragraph _____ of this Agreement for two (2) publication cycles following the date of termination.

A publication cycle, as used in this Agreement, begins any and every time a new edition or update is published.

Royalties

Royalty advances in El-Hi publishing are rare, and the royalties themselves (figured on net receipts) are often between four percent to six percent for elementary and four percent to eight percent for high school textbooks. Advances for college texts can run in the five figures, with an average royalty of fifteen percent. John B. McHugh, McHugh Publishing Reports, gave a royalty scale for categories of college books in COSMEP's November 1987 issue, after reminding publishers that most of these royalties are paid on net receipts: for hardbound textbooks $29.95 and over, ten percent to fifteen percent; for a reading book/anthology $14.95 and up, five percent to ten percent; and quality paperbacks $15.95 and up, five percent to ten percent. (I know several professors who receive royalties that match their annual university salary.) He opined that trade publishers treat the college market as an additional source of sales rather than becoming embroiled in free instructional items and other negative aspects of college publishing.

Educational Publishing Eccentricities

There are many terms bandied about in educational publishing—the adoption process, giveaways, most-favored-nation statutes, copy-shop copies of materials, Robinson-Patman Act, creationism and secular humanism, affirmative action purchasing procedures, manufacturing standards, specifications for textbooks, and NASTA.

You're very optimistic if you think that your new series, "Esmeralda and Alfonso," will replace Dick and Jane. The procedure for getting texts into the classroom is complicated.

Adoption states, about half of the fifty, purchase with state funds only those books approved by the state. This complex procedure includes:

- administration by an agency of the state educational system.
- a cycle of adoption (four years or more).
- an invitation or call to bid.

- varying approval processes, including committee/teacher reviews and sometimes public comment.
- placement on list from which schools can order.
- giveaways, which are required based on numbers of copies purchased.

The most-favored-nation (MFN) requirements of many states and some cities means that a publisher must offer its textbooks at the lowest price at which the texts are offered elsewhere, and must automatically lower its price to all schools, if it reduces prices for any one institution.

Both these concepts—adoption and MFN—bog down in interpretation and application. (Refer to discussions of educational publishing in PLI's various book publishing texts.)

Arizona's adoption and statutory MFN requirements are reproduced here:

§ 15-725. Contract for purchase of textbooks and instructional computer software

A. The state board of education shall enter into contracts with publishers for the purchase by the school districts of the textbooks and instructional computer software desired from the suggested lists of the state board for each grade and each course taught in the common schools. Publishers shall give a cash or corporate surety bond payable to this state and approved by the state board indemnifying the school districts in the purchase of textbooks and instructional computer software in an amount not less than five hundred nor more than ten thousand dollars as may be determined by the state board, conditioned that:

1. The publisher will faithfully comply with the conditions of the contract and will furnish to this state the textbooks and instructional computer software provided for in the contract at prices not exceeding the lowest prices then granted to any buyer.

2. If there is a decrease in the prices given to a person purchasing the textbooks or instructional computer software provided for in the contract from the publisher, the state shall have the benefit of the decrease in price.

B. The publisher shall file with the state board a statement sworn to before some officer in the state stating the lowest prices for which the publisher's series of textbooks or instructional computer software is sold anywhere in the United States. If the publisher of a textbook or instructional computer software adopted by a school district issues a special edition of the textbook, or essentially the same textbook or instructional computer software, the school district may substitute the textbook or instructional computer software at the net price at which it is sold elsewhere.

C. Every contractor who enters into any contract with the state board for furnishing textbooks or instructional computer software shall, upon request of a member of the board, mail to the board a sworn price list of the textbooks or instructional computer software which the contractor fur-

nishes or desires to furnish to this state.

D. If a contractor becomes a party either directly or indirectly to a combination or trust to control the prices of school textbooks or instructional computer software, any contract entered into with the contractor is void.

E. If a contractor violates a condition of the contract entered into, the attorney general shall, upon request of the school district, the governor or the state board of education, institute an action for damages on the bond of the contractor.

F. The state board of education may determine that it is in the best interests of this state to have the department of administration assume responsibility for contracting with publishers of highly rated instructional computer software for bulk discounts. If this determination is made, the state board of education is exempt from the instructional computer software requirements in subsections A through D.

Here are some snippets of case law that affect educational publishing:

- Nine publishers successfully sued New York University to stop university professors from sales of copy-shop copies of copyrighted materials, and reached a consent decree halting this illegal copying.
- The United States Supreme Court crippled creationism when it disallowed a statute that forbade the teaching of the theory of evolution unless accompanied by instruction in the theory of "creation science."
- Likewise, the Court determined that fundamentalist families' religious beliefs were not unconstitutionally burdened when a basal reading program conflicted with their religious beliefs.

The Manufacturing Standards and Specifications for Textbooks (MSST), issued by a committee of the National Association of State Textbook Administrators (NASTA), are included in adoption contracts. MSST concerns itself with every aspect of manufacturing a textbook—from paper weight and color to binding.

If you plan to enter educational publishing, be sure that you retain a knowledgable lawyer at the conception stage of your project.

Periodical Publications

If you publish periodical material (magazines, newsletters, catalogues, brochures, weeklies, newspapers) you are most likely to use in-house employees, freelancers, multiple contributors, and, it is to be hoped, a number of carefully constructed contracts. There is no difference between for-profit and not-for-profit periodical publications. Choose one of these for your publishing arrangements with non-staff employees:

- A periodical-author contract.
- A letter agreement.
- An on-the-check agreement.

Avoid oral agreements, as they may leave you out on the limb when the freelance writer sells the same article for publication in the same month to your competitor, or you discover that the article was originally a chapter in one of the freelancer's old books.

Dan Poynter's contracts include a writer-magazine agreement. A simple sample "on-the-check" agreement follows:

> **Endorser received from XYZ Press, Inc., as full payment for all rights and interests, including copyright, in the article titled "_____." The endorser warrants the article is unpublished and original and authored and owned by him; and that the article will not infringe any copyright, proprietary right or other right, nor will it defame or invade the privacy of anyone.**

Pretty short, huh? It covers a lot.

Here's a longer one created by a non-profit organization that issues a quarterly publication:

> **I want to thank you for agreeing to work on our project. It is always exciting to see a manuscript come in. To ensure that our records are complete prior to press time, please sign the original of this letter and return it to me as soon as possible. It constitutes the agreement between _____ and you (as author) on the project.**
>
> **[ ]   As an employee of _____, you have completed this manuscript as a "work for hire." The museum retains copyright of the material for this project and later uses. You will receive no fee other than your regular salary. You are entitled, however, to 25 copies of the _____ (and any other publication) in which your material appears. *Please note:* only those sections with an "x" in the [ ] apply.**
>
> **[x]   As an outside contributor to _____ Press, you will retain your residual rights to the _____ Press publication in which your work appears. _____ Press retains rights for the "Life of Publication." This means that the Press can reprint or revise the work in which your material appears as long as it stays in print, here defined as out-of-print for no more than one year. _____ Press agrees to make no other use of this material with the sole exception of advertising that is directly related to the publication. For the life of publication, the museum also retains the right to grant permission to quote passages of the work included in the publication.**
>
> **[x]   As an outside contributor, you will be given an honorarium of $100.00. If you wish to waive this honorarium, please sign on the line immediately after this section.**
>
> **Signature _____**

If you have any questions, please give me a call. And thank you, again, for your participation—and hard work.
Cordially,

Information above is correct and agreed to:

Signature _____   **Date** _____

Publishers of periodicals seek a variety of rights and provisions, including:

- the right to use the work after its publication.
- all magazine rights, including reprint and anthology rights in the contribution, in all languages worldwide.
- restriction on a competitive contribution or book for a period of months.
- sole discretion as to revisions of the contribution.
- use of the contributor's likeness.
- copyright to publication.
- payment on acceptance or on publication, with a kill-fee if not published.
- warranties (set forth earlier).
- first or second serialization—along with a time schedule and the number of words or specific excerpt from the book serialized.
- exclusive rights.
- a schedule for the contribution or serialization.

The more rights you buy, the more you pay, and few contributors will contract away their rights to the material in book, film, or movie form.

Minimally, you need to provide contributor's guidelines for your publication. It is possible to include these guidelines in your agreement by reference. If you are unsure of what the guidelines should encompass, collect some from other publishers by requesting them via letter and an SASE. Reproduced are guidelines provided to writers for two specialty periodicals:

Editorial Policy Regarding Article Proposals
1. Submissions should be in the form of an outline *and* a prose synopsis of the proposed article. All proposals must be accompanied by good quality slides or black & white photos, representative of the subject of the article.
2. If you are not confident about your writing skills, we recommend that you work with a professional writer. We will be happy to put you in touch with a writer in your area, if you do not know one.
3. All articles must be cleanly typed or computer printed, double spaced, with one-inch margins and 25 lines per page (in this format, there are approximately 250 words per page). An additional photocopy would be

helpful, but is not mandatory. Please keep one copy of your submitted manuscript, in case we need to confer about it on the phone.

4. Writers are responsible for accuracy of fact and correct spelling of names, places, and titles of works. We do not have the resources to check all of this information, so we must be able to depend on the writer's accuracy.

5. Unless other arrangements are made with the editor, authors are responsible for collecting all visual material to illustrate their article, and for providing all caption information. Complete caption information includes artist's name, title of work, dimensions, materials and techniques used, year of execution, in whose collection and where, name of photographer, and designation for top of work shown. Authors must also provide appropriate names and addresses, for correct return of visuals.

6. The editor may request necessary revisions of the article, and final editing of the material is at the editor's discretion. Writers are responsible for abiding by the word limit established for the article; manuscripts that substantially exceed the word count will be returned to the writer for shortening.

7. Deadlines are serious. All manuscripts, illustrations, and caption information are due by the date indicated, unless specifically discussed with the editor prior to that time. The editor reserves the right to kill any piece that is not submitted on time.

8. No kill-fee will be paid if the material is not acceptable and if, in the editor's opinion, revisions will not make it so.

9. Payment for articles is usually made upon publication. The signed author's agreement is confirmation of amount due. Additional expenses must be discussed with the editor, prior to submission of the completed manuscript.

We will be happy to send a complimentary copy of _____ to you, and additional copies for you to give the subject(s) of your article. We look forward to receiving your proposals.

Writers' Guidelines

We use only factual, authenticated material concerning events which took place before 19____. We will, however, allow stories to spill over into a later period.

We will not accept fiction based on fact nor do we want a story based on legends or rumors. We do not want dialogue unless it can be documented and we do not accept poetry except as part of a story. All stories must be factual, but they still should be colorful, humorous, adventurous, and exciting. They must be well-written, with drama and tragedy, action and suspense. Mystery, secrets, unusual events are all good.

Sources should be submitted with each story. Follow the bibliographic format outlined in *The Chicago Manual of Style*, or Kate Turabian's *Guide for Writers of Term Papers, Theses, and Dissertations*. We are more interested in ORIGINAL source material than we are in stories based on published resources. So it helps to sell a story to us if it is based on courthouse records, church archives, family bibles, and/or other original sources.

Manuscripts must be typewritten and double-spaced with the word count provided by the author. The author's name and address should be on the first page.

Maximum length is 4,500 words. Ideal length to break in is 2,000–2,500 words. We like shorter stories and will take them from 100 to 1,000 words.

First person accounts have built-in hazards. We must be sure the person has the correct name for lakes, rivers, mountains, etc. Dates should be in the story whenever needed and must be checked by the author.

Photos are crucial. We seldom buy a story without sharply focused, large format black-and-white photos. We like a combination of old and new photos showing how it was originally and what it is like today. Photos really help sell a story to us.

A feature of 3,000 words or more needs at least six and preferably eight or ten photos. A 1,000 word story needs at least four photos. Usually the more good photos the better.

When submitting queries, enclose photostats of the photos you intend to submit or list the photos available for the story. Enclose a stamped, self-addressed envelope. When sending manuscripts on speculation, include photos or send photostats and enclose a large, stamped, self-addressed envelope.

Manuscripts are processed in order of their arrival and a decision is usually made within six weeks. We buy a year or more ahead of publication so be patient if your story is purchased; it may not be published for quite some time.

WHAT WE PAY... We pay 3 cents to 5 cents per word for manuscripts and $10 per photo for one-time publishing rights. Photos are returned after publication. If you want to sell us permanent rights to the photos, we will negotiate a higher fee for any we want to buy.

Maps and illustrations are good, but in most cases, we prefer to have you submit a hand drawn map and have one of our illustrators redo it for publication. If illustrations are needed we prefer to obtain them from our illustrators also. Maps are essential with ghost towns, historic sites, abandoned mining camps, old forts, western trails, and similar stories.

We never accept a story which does not name the actual participants in the story.

A common complaint of freelancers is that editing is done at the last minute on their work and they are given no opportunity to review the final text. *Be sure you have permission to do that* or that your contract specifies that that is your company's normal procedure. Also, make a good-faith analysis of whether it's needed. In a work for hire, the article belongs to the buyer who, within the constraints of content restrictions, should be able to edit the article. Since the United States voted to adhere to Berne, this may be questionable, as under Berne the moral rights of an author are not transferable (see discussion of Berne, pages 209-210).

The same consideration on restrictions in content apply to periodicals, that is, libel, invasion of privacy, commercial appropriation of a likeness, obscenity, and ownership. The usual privacy considerations also apply. Even employees have privacy rights, so don't force your mailroom employee (as one publisher did), to pose as a photographic model for a rape article unless it's in his job description or you get a photography release and pay some consideration.

Once you develop a standard writer-publication contract, letter of agreement, and/or check endorsement contract, let your lawyer review it. Don't be penny-wise and pound-foolish.

Too, if you've purchased exclusive first-serial rights to a book exposing the secrets of a famous personage, or to a bestselling author's new novel, you need to have your lawyer customize that license agreement.

Here's an agreement for first serialization actually used for the first edition of *Making It Legal.*

AGREEMENT TO
PURCHASE PORTION OF THE FIRST SERIALIZATION RIGHTS OF
MAKING IT LEGAL:
A Law Primer for the Craftmaker, Visual Artist and Writer

This agreement is made between Martha Blue and Marion Davidson, hereinafter called Writers whose book *MAKING IT LEGAL: A Law Primer for the Craftmaker, Visual Artist and Writer,* is scheduled for publication by McGraw-Hill in August of 1979, and _____, hereinafter called Magazine.

1. Writers grant Magazine the right to publish a selection from their book prior to publication in book form. The selection shall be entitled __

_____

and shall not exceed _____ words. Because of the technical nature of the material, Magazine agrees that any changes made by it in the text of the selection must be approved by Writers prior to publication.

2. Writers retain all copyrights in the selection. Further, Mazagine agrees to place Writers' copyright notice—© 1979 by Marion Davidson and Martha Blue—in prominent fashion on any of the pages where the selection appears.

3. Publication of the selection shall occur no later than the July issue of the Magazine. Magazine acknowledges that this deadline is of the essence, as a later publication of the selection may interfere with _____ rights.

4. In consideration of the grant of rights made by Writers, Magazine agrees to pay the sum of __NA__ .

5. Writers warrant that *MAKING IT LEGAL* does not infringe on any copyrights: that it does not contain any libelous material or violate the rights of any person or corporation.

6. Writers' authorship will be acknowledged in the customary fashion for Magazine. Further, the following credit line will appear contiguous to the selection: "This exerpt is from *MAKING IT LEGAL: A Law Primer for the Craftmaker, Visual Artist and Writer*, by Marion Davidson and Martha Blue, to be published by _____ in August. Individual copies available from Legalcraft, _____ .

Legal Right to Periodical Titles

Because periodicals appear so often, the title of the work becomes important for customer identification. If a periodical title is determined to be generic rather than descriptive, no infringement can be charged.

- *Software News* versus *Computer & Software News.*
- *Consumer Electronics Product News* versus *Consumer Electronics Monthly.*

Trademark registration is refused for descriptive titles like:

- *Air Cargo*
- *Pocket Book*
- *The Playground*
- *Credit Card Marketing*
- *Motor Trend*

If a descriptive title acquires a secondary meaning, however, it can have trademark protection such as:

- *TV Guide*
- *Science*

For a complete and detailed discussion of application of trademark infringement criteria to magazine titles, and the likelihood of confusion, see PLI's 1984 *Magazine Industry* publication (page 223 et seq.) You know the names in these cases: *Woman's Day, Penthouse, People, Us, True Confessions, Playboy, Seventeen, Life,* and *American Heritage.*

Journals

The number of journals is staggering. This form of periodical publishing deserves special mention because of its rigid publishing specifications. *Herpetologica* and *Physiological Zoology*, for example, are both very serious and formal journals with precise requirements.

Both place copyright notices on the inside page, in the name of the publisher (the Herpetologist's League, Inc., and the University of Chicago, respectively), and on each article. One contains three pages (in small print) on "Instructions to Contributors," which provide in part:

INSTRUCTIONS FOR CONTRIBUTORS

General Information

Herpetologica publishes original papers dealing largely or exclusively with the biology of amphibians and reptiles; theoretical and primarily quantitative manuscripts are particularly encouraged. Contributors need not be members of The Herpetologists' League, but they should realize that publication costs are paid in part by membership dues. Payment of printing costs is voluntary and is not a condition for publication in *Herpetologica*. Authors having access to funds for payment of printing costs are encouraged to contribute to the publication fund, and authors of articles exceeding 15 printed pages are expected to make some contribution to the fund.*Authors are expected to pay for any special handling that may be required for their illustrations, such as color photographs and rubylith overlays.

Manuscripts should be sent, in **triplicate,** to the **Editor,** who will assign them to appropriate Associate Editors, who in turn will seek two or three reviews of each paper. Manuscripts will be judged on the basis of their scientific merit. Authors should retain the original typescript and figures until the manuscript is accepted for publication; photocopies of both typescript and figures are adequate for purposes of review.

The Manuscript

All manuscripts are to be in English, although a Resumen (in Spanish) can follow the discussion section of appropriate papers. The active voice is preferred. Manuscripts should be typewritten on one side only of good quality bond of standard size (21.5 x 28 cm). The entire typescript should be double-spaced and should have wide margins, including literature citations, tables, and captions to figures. Words should not be divided at the right-hand margin. For information on style of the manuscript, contributors should examine the most recent issue of *Herpetologica* and the fourth edition of the *Council of Biology Editors Style Manual.*

Manuscripts should be arranged in the following order: title, author's name, author's address, abstract, key words, text, acknowledgments, literature cited, appendices, tables, legends to figures, figures. All pages should be numbered, including tables, and labeled with the author's name in the upper right-hand corner.

---

*Note the reference to subsidized publishing.

It goes on to detail the requirements for titles, abstracts, key words, text heading, references, appendices, table, figures, footnotes, numerals, and abbreviations. The provision on reprints, proofs, and revisions is worth including here:

Reprints, Proofs, and Revisions
Reprints of articles may be purchased from Allen Press, using the forms provided, at the time page proofs are received. Each author should check proofs carefully against the edited manuscript. Printer's errors are best detected when two persons read proof together—one reading aloud from the proofs, the other following on the typescript. The editorial staff of *Herpetologica* does not read proof on articles, so authors must assume full responsibility for detecting errors.

Revisions should not be made in proofs; changes in proofs other than correction of printer's and editor's errors will be charged to authors at the rate of $2.00/line. **Both the edited manuscript and corrected proofs should be returned to the *Editor* as soon as possible to prevent a delay in publication.**

There's no negotiation here; the journal contributor pays for each correction he or she requests, period.

The other journal condensed its contributor guidelines to less than two pages:

Preparation of Manuscripts
The following suggestions are intended to help contributors to *Physiological Zoology* by answering questions which frequently arise during the publication process.

I. Typescript
All manuscripts should be submitted in triplicate and should be typed double-space (text, literature cited, footnotes, figure legends, and tables). Xeroxes of text and figures are acceptable for the duplicate copies. Please allow right- and left-hand margins of at least 1¼ inches. Each manuscript must be accompanied by (1) an abstract suitable for *Biological Abstracts*. This should state authors, title, and a summary paragraph not to exceed 200 words. (2) A running page head not to exceed 60 characters (including spaces).

II. Title page
A. The title page should be the first page of manuscript, with the title typed at least 2 inches from the top edge of the paper.

B. Please allow 1 inch of space below the title and type the name(s) of the author(s) on a separate line.

C. Affiliations should be typed on a separate line 1 inch below the name(s).

III. Citations
"Literature Cited" follows the text. These listings should be typed on a separate page or pages in alphabetical order by authors' last names. Each

line after the first of each reference should be indented ½ inch. All literature cited should be referred to in the text by author's name and year of publication. The following examples illustrate various citations:

A. Journal article

Authors' names (senior author, name inverted; other authors, names not inverted). Year of publication. Article title (no quotes; capitalize only the first letter of the first word and proper nouns; underline genus and species). Journal title in full (the copyeditor will make any necessary abbreviations); volume number: full page numbers. Examples:

Gilbert, J. J. 1967. Control of sexuality in the rotifer *Asplanchna brightwelli* by dietary lipids of plant origin. Proceedings of the National Academy of Science 57:1218–1225.

Hamby, R. J., and G. Fraenkel, 1965. Effects of high temperatures on the prosobranch snail, *Littorina littorea*. Biological Bulletin 129:406–407.

Snyder, R. L., D. E. Davis, and J. J. Christian. 1961. Seasonal changes in the weights of woodchucks. Journal of Mammalogy 42(3):297–312.

B. Book

Authors' names. Year of publication. Book title. Publisher, city of publication. Number of pages. Example:

Carleton, H. M., and R. A. B. Drury. 1957. Histological technique for normal and pathological tissue and the identification of parasites. Oxford University Press, London. 343pp.

C. Other types of references

1. Chapter in an edited book:

Foxon, G. E. H. 1964. Blood and respiration. Pages 151–209 *in* John A. Moore, ed.Physiology of the amphibia. 2d ed. Academic, New York.

2. Dissertation or thesis:

Whitley, L. S. 1963. Studies on the biology of the Tubificidae. Ph.D. thesis. Purdue University, Lafayette, Indiana. 108 pp.

3. Two separate references to different works by the same author in the same year: Alphabetize by article title and put *a* after the first reference and *b* after the second reference. Text references include these letters: Burger (1963a).

IV. Footnotes

A. Acknowledgments and address

A footnote of acknowledgment or information on grants received by the author should be marked with a superscript "1" after the title of the paper. A footnote giving the author's present address (when it differs from his affiliation as published) will then become footnote 2, with a superscript "2" appearing after the author's name.

B. Text footnotes

All footnotes should be typed together (paragraph style) on sheets following the literature cited. They should be numbered in order and should correspond with the numbers in the text. Footnote numbers in both places should be shown as superscripts. Examples: (text) . . . in the study. [4]

(footnote)　　　[4]J. P. Jones, . . .

C. Citation

Footnotes are not necessary if only to refer to a work cited. In this case, the information should be placed in the text in parentheses. Example: . . . in that study (Jones 1956, p. 8) . . . Footnotes are only necessary for further explanation of something within the text.

V. Tabular material

Each table should be typed on a separate sheet of paper following the footnotes. Each table should be numbered and referred to *in order* in the text.

VI. Illustrations

Each illustration (figure) should be separate (5″x7″ originals or glossy photographs, not Xerox® copies), with uniform lettering, and should follow the tabular material. Legends for the illustrations should be typed in order on a sheet of paper which should accompany the illustrations. All illustrations should be referred to *in order* in the text as figure 1, figure 2, and so on.

VII. Miscellaneous

Any unusual symbols or abbreviations in the text should be identified in the margin in pencil to aid the copyeditor and compositor.

Additional help may be found by consulting current issues of *Physiological Zoology, Council of Biology Editors Style Manual* (American Institute of Biological Sciences), and *The Chicago Manual of Style* (University of Chicago Press).

Why reproduce these particular criteria? Because both set forth specific manuscript requirements for journal contributors to achieve "satisfactory" status. For certain publications, such an explanation could objectify the satisfactory manuscript clause.

From another journal: "*The Journal of Arizona History* assumes no liability for statements or opinions of contributors." A neat disclaimer.

The title page for a University of Chicago publication clearly sets forth its responsibilities for a missed issue:

Claims for missing numbers should be made within the month following the regular month of publication. The publishers expect to supply missing numbers free only when losses have been sustained in transit and when the reserve stock will permit.

Finally, add to your instructions an indication that all contributors, by submitting a manuscript, warrant their work (see sample warranty clause, page 166) and indemnify the journal against any liability arising out of the work. (A diet fanatic could, for example, apply research on the physiology of salamanders to his overeating, die, and his estate could sue the journal).

Be prepared to reassign the copyright to the author; many academic authors use their journal articles as starting points for books.

Basics of Copyright

10

T**he copyright law protects expression: the content of literary works, the form and aesthetics of art, photography, and sculpture. Trademark laws (a species of unfair competition) protects the words and symbols that are individual and specific to you, the publisher, or to other manufacturers of products offered in the marketplace. General unfair competition laws plug the gaps between specific trademark laws and copyright.

Overview

The United States Copyright Act governs the property rights of authors. The *ownership* of this property derives from the act of *creation,* except for "works-made-for-hire," where the creativity, and thus ownership, belong to the employing party. Thus, articles, books, or artwork created by in-house or staff members on company time belong to the publishing house. Initial property rights to all other manuscripts are vested in the writer or artist, and the publisher negotiates permission to produce and market same. Thus, the copyright law gives rights to writers and artists, or copyright owners, rights enforceable by copyright infringement actions. An action can be proved by direct *or* circumstantial evidence, once the plaintiff shows copyright ownership and copying by the defendant. Remedies include damages and injunctive relief.

The mere sale of a manuscript, a photograph, or other graphic art to you, the publisher, *does not* transfer the copyright in the work to you. Object and copyright ownership are two distinct entities.

Fundamental copyright questions publishers need to consider are: How can you acquire the necessary rights to publish an author's work? How can you (and your writers) protect the content of the literary works that you publish? How can you use someone else's work? This chapter and the three following answer these questions.

Copyright Circulars

Copyright Office publications are available on a variety of topics, Circular RL, *Publications of the Copyright Office* (available from the Information and Publications Sections LM-455, Copyright Office, Library of Congress, Washington D.C. 20559) briefly describes the information available. (This information is detailed *and clear* and generally free). Here's a publication list:

COPYRIGHT OFFICE APPLICATION FORMS,
CIRCULARS, AND REGULATIONS
(Revised July 14, 1988)

APPLICATIONS FORMS

FORM CA:	For supplementary registration to correct or amplify information given in the copyright record of an earlier registration
FORM SE:	For registration of each individual issue of a serial
FORM GR/CP:	An adjunct application to be used for registration of a group of contributions to periodicals
FORM PA:	For published and unpublished works of the performing arts (musical and dramatic works, pantomimes and works, motion pictures, and other audiovisual works)
FORM RE:	For claims to renewal of copyright in works copyright under the law in effect through December 31, 1977 (1909 Copyright Act)
FORM SR:	For published and unpublished sound recordings
FORM TX:	For published and unpublished nondramatic literary works
FORM VA:	For published and unpublished works of the visual arts (pictorial, graphic, and sculptural works)

Circulars

1	Copyright Basics
1b	Limitations on the Information Furnished by the Copyright Office
1e	The Certification Space of the Application Form
2	Publications on Copyright
2b	Selected Bibliographies on Copyright
3	Copyright Notice
4	Copyright Fees
5	How to Open and Maintain a Deposit Account in the Copyright Office
6	Obtaining Copies of Copyright Office Records and Deposits

Circulars of particular importance are: Circular 2b (selected bibliographies on copyright), which provides additional material for you to consider for your publishing library. Circular 5, which describes requirements for maintaining a deposit account at the copyright office; a deposit account is for the copyright registrant's convenience, so that separate remittances need not be sent with each application or other requests for services. The deposits must be at least $250, a minimum of twelve transactions must take place per year, and the exact name and account number must appear on all registration applications or requests for services. Circular 6 covers investigation of a given work's copyright status. Circular 7c describes what happens if you don't reply promptly to Copyright Office correspondence: closing of your file, non-refund of certain fees, and so forth. Circular 12 spells out recordation of transfers and other documents, recording fees, and submission documents. (When I submitted the copyright transfer from my co-author to me for recording, I discovered that the assignment document was not sufficient in itself if it contained a reference to another document. That assignment included a contract, which I had to attach.)

Circular 22 contains a search request form. According to the circular, in such a search you:

- examine a copy of the work for such elements as copyright notice, place and date of publication, author and publisher.
- make a search of the Copyright Office catalogs and other records, such as the *Catalog of Copyright Entries* (CCE), which is maintained in some libraries.
- have the Copyright Office make a search for you.

Before I jump into detailed copyright issues, let's consider copyright history and copyright basics.

Historical Overview

Copying is an old practice. St. Benedict's rules treated copying as a virtuous activity. In an early reference, St. Columbo copied Abbot Finnian's Psalter, whereupon the abbot demanded the copy and was refused. The problem was referred to the Irish King Diarmid in his palace at Tars, A.D. 567. The king, in settling the disputed property rights, ruled in favor of the abbot, saying, "To every cow her calf," and accordingly, to every book its copy.

The first recorded instance of copyright occurred in Venice in 1469, when John of Spira received an exclusive five-year right to print the Epistles of Cicero and Pliny.

The necessity of copyright protection arose with technology—just as now the copyright laws struggle to encompass new electronic technology. In 1476, Caxton established a press in Westminster, England; this invention advanced the art of copying, and scribes vigorously opposed it. By mid-sixteenth century, the leading printers in London had formed the Stationer's Company, and in 1556, Catholic Queen Mary gave them a printing monopoly in an effort to control the spread of Protestantism, intertwining the printed word, copyright, and censorship forever. After two hundred seventy-four years of confusion, Parliament adopted the first copyright statute in 1710 and called it "An Act for the Encouragement of Learning."

Summarized, the Statute of Anne provides:

> Whereas printers... have of late frequently taken the liberty of printing ... books ... without the consent of the authors ... to their very great detriment and too often to the ruin of them and their families... the author of a book shall have the term of fourteen years. . . . [E]very such offender ... shall forfeit one penny for every sheet which shall be found in his ... custody. . . .

Just as ancient poets and dramatists refused to sing unless they were paid in food and lodging, authors wanted to control the use of their work and to share in its profits. A large and complex body of copyright laws evolved to protect literary works, beginning with this statute.

In the United States, Noah Webster, eager to protect his *Blue-backed Speller,* first published in 1783, journeyed to several state capitals to lobby for the passage of state copyright acts. He was successful in this effort, and gradually, Americans adopted state copyright laws. In 1790, a United States Constitutional provision gave Congress the authority to enact national copyright (and patent) laws. Article I, section 8, clause 8, provides:

> The Congress shall have the power ... to promote the Progress of Science and useful Arts, by securing for limited Times to Authors and

Inventors the exclusive Right to their respective Writings and Discoveries.

A few days later, the first copyright was issued for the *Philadelphia Spelling Book*.

This federal copyright act was amended at fairly regular intervals until the Copyright Act of 1909, which remained the basic law (referred to as the "old law") until January 1, 1978, the effective date of the "new" law, formally dubbed the Copyright Revision Act of 1976.

The evolution of federal copyright law can be charted thus:

- 1790 maps, charts, and books.
- added 1802: historical or other print or prints.
- added 1831: musical compositions.
- added 1865: photographs and photographic negatives (because Mathew Brady's photos of the Civil War were attaining fame).
- added 1870: paintings, drawings, chromos, statuettes, statuary, models, or designs of fine art.
- rewritten 1909: a major consolidation of the above statutes. All the above, plus composite and encyclopedic work, directories, gazetteers, periodicals, newspapers, lectures, sermons, addresses, dramatic or dramatico-musical compositions, works of art, reproductions of works of art, drawings or plastic works of a scientific or technical character, and pictorial illustrations.
- added 1912: motion pictures.
- added 1971: sound recordings.
- changed 1976: Copyright Revision Act. Original fixed work which can be perceived including: literary works, musical works (including accompanying words), dramatic works (including accompanying music), pantomime and choreographic works, pictoral, graphic, and sculptural works, motion pictures, and other audiovisual works and sound recordings.

The 1909 law, rooted in old English common-law principles regarding literary property, failed to keep pace with modern technology and new communication techniques—satellites, cable television, computers, video-tape, records, photocopying machines, etc. The revision process started in 1955 with numerous studies, drafts, and negotiations. The Register of Copyrights, speaking on the new law, commented that "Practically everything in the bill is the product of at least one compromise, and many provisions have evolved from a long series of compromises reflecting constantly changing technology, commercial and financial interests, political and social conditions, judicial and administrative development, and—not least by any means—individual personalities. . . ."

The following bare-bones outline overview of the new act is adapted from a *General Guide to the Copyright Act of 1976,* September 1977, an uncopyrighted guide used for internal training of Copyright Office staff. Copyright is a subject that mandates an overview before delving into its details; for further study, order a copy of the text of the copyright law from the Copyright Office. (Any citations in the chapter refer to Title 17 of the United States Code, "Copyright.")

Introduction and Background
- Copyright—U.S. copyright laws stem from Article I, Section 8 of the Constitution. A copyright is a statutory grant of certain rights for limited times.
- Need for a new copyright law
  - last major revision of the Copyright Law, the Act of 1909, was based on the printing press as the prime disseminator.
  - development of new technologies—wide range of new techniques for communicating, e.g., cable television, communications satellites, computers, etc.
  - the "copyright revision program" culminated with the signing of the new law on October 19, 1976; with fundamental change in the very philosophy of copyright itself; plus compromise of all provisions.
- Legislative History
  - Senate Report 94-473, House Report 94-1476 and House Report 94-1733.

Major Provisions
- Preemption of state and common law copyright protection.
  - single national system for all works within the subject matter of copyright, fixed in a copy or phonorecord.
  - Protection begins on the date of creation.
- Duration
  - for works created after the effective date of the new law.
    - basic term: life of the author plus fifty years.
    - joint work: life of the last surviving author, plus fifty years.
    - anonymous, pseudonymous, and works made for hire: 75 years from first publication or 100 years from creation, whichever is shorter.
    - copyright office to keep records.
    - presumptions established to govern the situation where a user cannot determine the date of the author's death.
  - for preexisting works under common law protection, on the effective date of the new law.
    - same terms as above.
    - to assure that all works are given a "reasonable" term, guarantee of 25 years of protection. If work published before 2002, term of protection extended another 25 years.
  - duration of *subsisting* copyrights—(maximum of 75 years)
    - for works in their first term on January 1, 1978, 28 years for the first term and provision for a renewal term of 47 years.
    - for works already in their second, renewal terms, including copyrights whose renewal terms have been extended, the renewal term is automatically extended to make a total of 75 years.
  - all terms expire on December 31st.

- Ownership
  - copyright ownership in the first instance belongs to the author.
  - works made for hire.
  - divisibility: first statutory recognition. Any of the exclusive rights that go to make up a copyright can be transferred and owned separately. The definition of "transfer of ownership" makes it clear that the principle of divisibility applies whether or not the transfer is "limited in time or place of effect."
  - transfers of copyright ownership must be in writing and signed by the owner of the rights conveyed, or by such owner's duly authorized agent.
  - documents to be recorded in the copyright office.
- Termination of Transfers and Licenses
  - grants by the author (other than by will) made on or after January 1, 1978, of exclusive or non-exclusive rights arising under the new law (but not including works made for hire) may be terminated during a five year period beginning at the end of 35 years from the date of the grant. If, however, the grant covers the right of publication, the termination period begins 35 years from the date of publication or 40 years from the date of the grant, whichever is shorter.
- Scope of Exclusive Rights—Section 106 sets forth five basic rights, which are cumulative and to some extent overlap.
- Limitations on the rights of copyright owners
  - doctrine of fair use—generally speaking, copying without permission from, or payment to, the copyright owner is allowed where the use is reasonable and not harmful to the rights of the copyright owner.
    - four factors to be considered are included.
    - restates present judicial doctrine; it is not intended to change, narrow, or enlarge it in any way.
    - guidelines for educational use of print material and music.
  - reproduction by libraries and archives—Section 108.
  - computer and data base uses. Recognizes computer programs and data bases as copyrightable subject matter but freezes protection respecting use in automatic storage and retrieval systems.
  - compulsory licenses (A compulsory license is a device allowing use of the copyrighted work without the owner's permission but guaranteeing remuneration for the owner)—new law has four.
    - compulsory license for making and distributing phonorecords embodying nondramatic musical compositions.
    - public performance by means of coin-operated phonorecord players.
    - secondary transmissions.
    - use of published nondramatic musical works and pictorial, sculptural and graphic works by noncommercial broadcasters.
    - creation of a Copyright Royalty Tribunal to determine the reasonable terms and rates of royalty payments, to distribute the royalties collected and to resolve certain disputes.

- Formalities: notice, deposit and registration. Relaxed, and more amenable to international standards.
  - notice: preserves the requirement for a notice on copies that are publicly distributed anywhere but lessens the effects of accidental or even deliberate errors or omissions. Subject to certain safeguards for innocent infringers, protection would not be lost by the complete omission of the notice from large numbers of copies or from a whole edition, if registration for the work is made before or within 5 years after such publication and a reasonable effort is made to add notice to copies or phonorecords publicly distributed in the U.S. after the omission is discovered.
  - deposit and registration
    - registration and deposit are now separate formalities which could and would usually be combined.
    - deposit for the Library of Congress of copies or phonorecords published with a notice of copyright in the United States. Failure to deposit after written demand makes the copyright owner liable for the cost of the copies and fines.
    - registration permissive, but is a prerequisite to an infringement suit.
- Remedies
  - definition of an infringement.
  - injunctions.
  - impounding and disposition of infringing articles.
  - damages and profits.
    - actual damages.
    - statutory damages.
    - must elect between actual and statutory damages.
  - attorneys' fees.
  - criminal provisions.
  - alternation of programming by cable systems.

Before I dwell on the further intricacies of copyright, let's talk about the value of the law to the copyright owner.

What Does the Copyright Owner Get?
The new law's heart is the grant of certain exclusive rights to the copyright owner. These exclusive rights are:

- to reproduce the copyrighted work in copies or phonorecords.
- to prepare derivative works.
- to distribute to the public.
- to perform publicly.
- to display publicly certain works.

Assume that a work of fiction entitled *Trading Cass,* a novel about a woman trader's adventures, is self-published. There's no transfer of copyright, no grant of rights or subsidiary rights to a publisher. The author–copyright owner kept all the rights: to distribute or license the work world-wide (such as to Penguin Books in England) in varying editions; to allow translation rights and foreign rights (in Botswana, perhaps); to abridge the work (possibly for a Reader's Digest condensed book); license it to a book club (Book of the Month); license first (to *Cosmopolitan*) and second (to the *New York Times*) serialization rights, which are magazine and newspaper rights before and after book publication; syndicate it (*Ms* magazine); use it in advertising Navajo rugs; and adapt it for public radio, television, theater or film (starring Meryl Streep and Robert Redford?).

If this book had been contracted for and released by a second party—a trade publisher—the author may well have retained the copyright, but would have had to transfer some or all rights, under the grant of rights, to the publisher.

Recent Changes in the Copyright Law: The Berne Convention

The United States joined the Berne Convention effective March 1, 1989. See "One Hundred and Two Years Later, the U.S. Joins the Berne Convention" by Jan C. Ginsburg and John M. Keinochn (Columbia VLA Journal of Law and the Arts, Volume 13, No. 1, Fall 1988). Berne adherence was sought to enhance international protection of U.S. copyrighted works; the changes in U.S. law to achieve compatability were minimal.

A Summary of Changes

The significant changes in the United States copyright law center around registration, recordation, and deposit. The proponents and opponents of moral rights continue to push for modification and supplementation of the Implementation Act on moral rights. During the legislative process, some proponents argued that existing U.S. law provides equivalent moral right protection, while others insisted that the U.S., in its Implementation Act, adhere to specific moral right provisions of the Berne Convention. The U.S. Berne Implementation Act, as adopted, does not explicitly recognize moral rights.

Notice Under Berne

Under the Berne Convention, copyright protection may not be conditioned on the observance of any formalities.

Under the old U.S. act, publication without notice was fatal (see discussion, pages 233–34); under the 1976 act, the copyright owner could correct the omission of notice during a five-year grace period; now, under Berne, the concept of mandatory notice has been abandoned. Notice of copyright, therefore, is optional.

Ignore the option and include an appropriate notice of copyright because:

- certain members of the Universal Copyright Convention (UCC) impose notice formalities (some of these are not members of Berne)
- the presence of a notice of copyright defeats the innocent infringer test

By omitting the notice, U.S. copyright owners risk subjecting the protection of their material to various court interpretations.

Registration and Deposit

Under the Berne implementation legislation, non-U.S. works from countries adhering to the Berne Convention no longer need to be registered prior to filing an action alleging copyright infringement. Registration-prior-to-suit is still required for works of U.S. origin. Those who do not register promptly, even non-U.S. works, run the risk of losing these benefits:

- works registered within three months of first publication keep statutory damages and attorneys' fees.
- registration within five years of publication gives certain presumptive proofs regarding the registration certificate:
  - the author's identity
  - creation and publication dates
  - copyright validity

Whether material is of U.S. or non-U.S. origin, the Berne Implementation Act abandons the requirement to record transfer contracts prior to suit. However, in any suit involving infringement, the ownership of the copyright must still be proved and, often, the first recorded copyright transfer can settle disputes between conflicting claimants to a copyright interest.

Conclusion

After Berne, publishers can expect court decisions interpreting the Berne Implementation Act as well as further legislation in this area. Practically speaking, publishers should protect their work as provided for under the 1976 copyright act. True, the formalities of notice and registration have diminished, but failure to comply with those formalities may result in the loss of critical benefits.

Let's look at the how, what, when, where, and why of copyright in the publishing world.

Ownership and Subject Matter of Copyright

11

If *you wish to be a writer, write [and copyright]."* (Epictetus: *Discourses II*) This quote reflects the basics of creativity for an author, that is, to develop a body of work. The remarks are mine and reflect the business aspects of writing.

What is Copyright?

Copyright is a legal remedy available to the "authors" of literary, dramatic, musical, artistic, and other intellectual works that can be copied. "Author" is a technical term referring to the creator (whether it be a writer, musician, artist or craftmaker) of intellectual property. The author can also be the purchaser, heir, employer, or other individual who acquires the creator's rights.

If you check the constitutional provision regarding copyright against the foregoing definition of statutory copyright, you'll notice an apparent contradiction. Statutory copyright law gives the author exclusive control over the created product, which diminishes the federal statutory purpose of encouragement of creative endeavors and their dissemination through society.

Common Law Copyright

Under the old law, there was dual protection: "common-law copyright" and statutory copyright. Common-law copyright existed from the moment of creation and continued to "publication." This protected any work, such as old letters or unpublished manuscripts, from unauthorized copying before publication or disclosure. Under the old law, if the work was made public without a copyright notice on it, it passed into public domain and could be freely copied by anyone. A work in the public domain is fair game for anyone who wants to use the work for any purpose. If the work bore a notice, it was protected by federal law and the author had a mechanism through which to remedy infringement.

Here's a memorandum of law to a client concerned about a pre–1978 copyright legal problem.

Memorandum of Law
FROM: Attorney
RE: Acrylic renderings of cartoon character Ginny the Giraffe

Client wants to know if cartoon drawings that she exhibited in 1975 without any copyright notice at several art festivals in metropolitan shopping center malls can now be copyrighted if she has not sold them.

Under the facts of this case, client's situation would be covered by the old law.

Under *Letters Edged in Black Press, Inc. v. Public Building Commission of Chicago,* 320 F.Supp. 1303 (N.D. Ill. 1970), the answer is no. In that case, Picasso designed a monumental sculpture for the plaza of the Chicago Civic Center. After Picasso donated the design for the sculpture, the commission began a publicity campaign to publicize the Chicago Picasso. This included press shows, distribution of photos to the public, and display of the model at the Tate Museum. Neither the model nor the photographs had the copyright notice attached.

Later, the sculpture itself was dedicated with a copyright notice and registered with the copyright office. The court held that as a result of the publicity the Chicago Picasso was in the public domain *prior* to the attachment of a copyright notice on the monumental sculpture and anyone could copy the work without paying the owner of the work.

The dual system of common-law copyright protection before publication and federal law protection after publication has *now* been replaced by a single federal system for all fixed work, published or unpublished. The new system makes federal protection available from the moment of creation.

A group of court cases provide extra protection for unpublished works. In *Salinger v. Random House, Inc.,* a U.S. Court of Appeals held that J.D. Salinger "has a right to protect the expressive content of his unpublished writings for a term of his copyright, and that right prevails over a claim of fair use under 'ordinary circumstances.'" In that case, there was a special emphasis on the unpublished nature of the letters.

Who Can Obtain Copyright?
The ownership of the copyright initially belongs to the person who creates the

work, *except* in the case of employees. Traditionally, common-law copyright passed with the sale of the creation, *unless* a written agreement provided for the author retaining the copyright. The new law provides the opposite: the creator retains the copyright *unless it is conveyed in a signed written agreement.*

What if more than one person contributes to a single work? The creators are co-authors and co-owners if the work is indivisible. This is called a joint work. The court-made law provides that co-owners shall have free use of jointly owned property, subject to the duty to account for profits. Since you can't infringe your own copyright, unresolved problems between co-owners of a copyright are handled by filing a lawsuit for an accounting (i.e., a remedy also available for other types of oral and written partnerships).

In a divisible work, a series of photographs by different photographers, or text by one person and illustrations by another, the copyright could be held these ways:

- Each creator can obtain individual copyright for each part.
- One can obtain copyright in the name of all.
- One can obtain the copyright in trust for the rest.

Recently, I reviewed the warranty-indemnification provisions of a contract proposed to an author. The work consisted of a photographic rendering of the daily life of a New Mexico pueblo. Of course there were permission issues, but of more pressing concern were copyright-ownership issues. Only a few photos were taken by the author, others were taken by a friend when she was at the pueblo for a celebration, and the rest were taken by a collaborator under the terms of an oral agreement. To further complicate the issue, a Pueblo man wrote one of the chapters. I recommended that the author reduce the collaboration agreement to writing; have the friend assign the copyright in her photos to him; and have the copyright in the text assigned to him, with a written grant of rights for same. A letter agreement that the chapter was commissioned and was a work for hire could also have been used.

An important *exception* to the general rule that the creator owns the copyright concerns works created by an employee for an employer. In these instances, the employer is presumed to own the copyright to the employee's work. The "work-made-for-hire" doctrine (first court-recognized under the 1909 Copyright Act, still in force under the new act) gives the copyright *not* to the hired or creating party, but to the *hiring* party. It's a simple test to apply to a salaried employee, but bogs down in freelance or independent contractor situations.

Clearly, Congress intended to narrow the scope of work for hire, but instead of treating "employee" to mean a full-time salaried worker, various federal courts have construed the term to mean one merely *hired* by another, thus sometimes giving the copyright to the publisher or "employer." Conflict in court decisions abound and predictions about ownership rights are unreliable, a real concern for publishers.

The new law continues the general rule that, where the work is made by an employee within the scope of employment, a "work for hire" belongs to the employer. The copyright of certain works created by employees outside the scope of their jobs, or by independent contractors, belong to the creator, unless the parties agree in writing that the piece shall be a work for hire. A specially commissioned or ordered work is presumed to be a work for hire in a number of situations or categories:

- a contribution to a collective work.
- part of a motion picture or work for other audiovisual use.
- translations.
- supplementary works.
- compilations.
- instructional texts.
- atlases.

The work-for-hire issue raises its ugly head so often that it's useful to explain it from another point of view: Works for hire are born when an employee creates a copyrightable work during employment, or if the work (one of several types) was commissioned or ordered *and* both parties agree in writing the piece is a work for hire.

Case Incident:
A client, a freelancer, was paid to prepare textual material for a multipaged brochure, only to discover a few months later that the customer's advertising company was using parts of the brochure in ads. The customer thought she had bought all rights, even though there was no written agreement. What an uproar it caused when the author-freelancer insisted he owned the copyright. The freelancer was right legally, but lost a good customer.

Here's part of my opinion, in which I concluded it was not a work for hire, and advised the freelancer to use a written agreement to clarify, for the client's sake and goodwill, that the freelancer has two rates, one for which he keeps the copyright and one for which the client buys it. This opinion was prepared before the United States joined the Berne Convention.

Under the provision of the Copyright Act of 1976 (17 U.S.C. §101–810), only the author or his/her heirs or assigns can assert copyright ownership or control, i.e., copyright vests initially in the author or authors of the work. Under §201(b), the author of a "work made for hire" is not the creator who actually creates the work, but the creator's *employer*.

While this is artificial, the doctrine is longstanding. The practical effect is to give the employer control in a creative work beyond the needs that pertain to the employer's business.

The new act limits some of the harshness of the work-made-for-hire rule for those creative persons working as *independent contractors* rather than employees.

There are two provisions of the new act that are critical to this discussion. Section 201(b) and §101 of the Act read as follows:

(b) *Works made for hire.* In the case of a work made for hire, the employer or other person for whom the work was prepared is considered the author for purposes of this title [17 USCS §§ 101 et seq.], and, unless the parties have expressly agreed otherwise in a written instrument signed by them, owns all of the rights comprised in the copyright.

§101

A "work made for hire" is:

(1) a work prepared by an employee within the scope of his or her employment; or,

(2) A work specially ordered or commissioned for use as a contribution to a collective work as a part of a motion picture or other audiovisual work, as a translation, as a supplementary work, as a compilation, as an instructional text, as a test, as answer material for a test, or as an atlas, if the parties expressly agree in a written instrument signed by them that the work shall be considered a work made for hire. For the purpose of the foregoing sentence, a "supplementary work" is a work prepared for publication as a secondary adjunct to a work by another author for the purpose of introducing, concluding, illustrating, explaining, revising, commenting upon, or assisting in the use of the other work, such as forewords, afterwords, pictorial illustrations, maps, charts, tables, editorial notes, musical arrangements, answer material for tests, bibliographies, appendixes, and indexes, and an "instructional text" is a literary, pictorial or graphic work prepared for publication and with the purpose of use in systematic instructional activities."

The right to a work's integrity is that moral right which is most dependent on the clear and explicit recognition of the intimate relationship between the artist and his creation (DuBoff, *Textbook of Art Law,* p. 831). A few summary background remarks should clarify the problem faced with editorial changes of work.

The artist-writer has a personal interest in seeing his/her creation retain its given form and insuring credit as the creator—these rights are referred to as moral rights (*les droits moreaux* or *le droit morale*). European countries, particularly in France, afford protection to artists-writers by this doctrine (including the right to create, to disclose and complete the work, to withdraw the work, to name attribution, and to control alterations and modifications), while moral rights of artists-writers in the United States have not developed as far. The Berne Convention for the Protection of Literary and Artistic works recognizes the rights of disclosure, paternity, and integrity, as well as copyright. (The United States has recently joined the Berne Convention.)

While it's the opinion of some that the 1976 Copyright Revision Act has made United States Copyright law more consistent with the Berne Convention provisions (HR 94-1476 at 135), there are still no blanket artist-writters' moral right provisions.

It is best to handle editing questions contractually; however, there is some case law that is helpful, as well as a statutory construction of new copyright law. In *Chesler v. Avon Book Division,* 352 N.Y.S. 2d 552 (1973), plaintiff, author of *Women and Madness,* sought to enjoin the defendant from publishing a paperback edition of Doubleday's hardcover edition due to omissions, alterations, and rearrangements in the text. The court summarized the agreement between the author and Doubleday as not reserving to the author editing and/or other rights in the final hardcover or reprint editions. The court stated the contract, unfortunately for the author, did not forbid alterations or omissions in her work without her consent, but even where the author transfers her work, the author has a property right that the work shall not be used for a purpose not intended or in a manner which doesn't fairly represent the creation of the author. The court refused to be a literary critic, noted the provocative, revolutionary thesis of the work, but did conclude that there were omissions and editorial changes. The court's holding was that while Avon may have the right contractually to condense or abridge the work, the readers must be so advised.

The new Copyright Act (17 U.S.C.S. §106) gives the copyright holder, among his/her exclusive rights, the right to "prepare derivative works based upon the copyrighted works." Section 101 of the Act defines a derivative work as "a work consisting of editorial revisions, annotations, elaborations, or other modifications which, as a whole, represent an original work of authorship. . . ." Arguably (in the absence of a contractual provision), the licensee given the right to use certain material doesn't have the right to edit or adapt the copyright owner's work. There's a dearth of case law interpreting the 1976 Copyright Act, but see *Midway Mftg. Co. v. Arctic International Inc.,* 547 F. Supp. 999, 216 U.S.P.Q. 413 (1983), where a speed-up kit in the form of a circuit board and ROM for increasing the pace of a video game infringed the copyright by altering the game as a derivative work.

The later section, §101, brought three major changes in the work-for-hire schemes. First, only works prepared in "the scope of . . . employment" can qualify. Second, only nine specific types of works (usually requiring collaboration), created on special order or commission can be works for hire. And third, even these works must have an express written agreement to have that status. The first is an employer, while the second and third apply to independent contractors. These definitional changes, then, have curtailed the work-for-hire doctrine in its application to independent contractors and their works, so commissioned works not included in the nine categories of §101, as well as work of independent contractors who do not agree to the for-hire treatment of their work, aren't works for hire and the sponsor receives only an implicit license to own the work for the commissioned purposes.

Some of the case law under the new act on this point has turned on whether the commissioning party made a meaningful contribution to the work. Some cases have said there is a co-ownership of copyright in a joint work by an independent contractor and his sponsor: *Mr. B. Textiles v. Woodcrest Fabrics,* 523 F. Supp. 21 (S.D.N.Y. 1981) involving a fabric design, and *BPI v. Leith,* 532 F. Supp. 208 (W.D.Tex. 1981) involving a commission by a computer software manufacturer. In cases where there was no contribution to the work by the commissioning party, an independent contractor was considered the sole owner of the copyright.

A significant interpretation of the work-for-hire provision of the law came in the recently ajudicated *Reid v. Community for Creative Non-Violence* (109 S.Ct. 2166 [1989]). Since Congress did not define "employment" in the new Copyright Act, the Supreme Court determined in the Reid case (which involved copyright ownership of a sculpture created by an artist at the request of an organization) that a court, in trying a copyright dispute of this nature, must determine "using principles of general common law of agency, whether work was prepared by an employee or an independent contractor." If the latter, then the court must further decide (in order for the work to be a work for hire) that it was ordered or commissioned for use in one of nine categories and the parties agreed in writing to treat it as a work for hire.

Not only did the Court emphasize the hiring party's rights of control, but added another set of criteria:

- hired party's skill?
- source of hired party's tools and equipment?
- length of relationship between the parties?
- hiring party's right to assign additional work to the hired party?
- hired party's ability to decide when and how long to work?
- payment method?
- hiring and paying of hired party's assistants?
- work part of hired party's regular business?
- hiring party's business status?
- tax treatment and employee benefits of hired party?

In *Reid,* the Court concluded that the sculptor was not an employee, and therefore, the sculpture was not a work for hire. The case was, however, sent back to the lower court to determine if the parties were *joint authors.*

So it's still a case-by-case situation. A creator cannot be turned into an employee simply by virture of declaration or argument. The publisher *can* negotiate an agreement in which the creator assigns his or her copyright to the publisher, or one in which the creator keeps the copyright and grants the publisher a license to use it for specific purposes. Once again, the issue seems to turn on the necessity of an explicit statement signed by both parties in advance.

Publishers and Work For Hire

At a 1982 hearing in the United States Senate, testimony attested to the take-it-or-leave-it attitude of mass-market publishers. With sixty-five percent of the twenty-five largest mass-market magazines created on a work-for-hire basis, this attitude has power. New legislative proposals are continually being introduced to reform or refine this part of the law, however.

Some publishers insist that their authors agree in writing that *any* work is a work for hire. The higher rate is charged for work-for-hire work because the author loses rights. (California law requires employers who use this tactic to give the freelancer certain employment percs!) In response, some freelancers charge two different rates. Under the copyright law, a periodical publisher has a right to its employee's literary and artistic work product in "work prepared by an employee within the scope of his or her employment." Once work is assigned, it doesn't matter how it's put in fixed form—handwritten, typed, taped, drawn, placed on a diskette. The employer can use the work in any form. Any reassignment of rights or copyright to the employee must be in writing.

Let's see how some publishers use the work for hire.

I queried *Coins* magazine about their interest in an article on Indian trader's tokens, or tin money . *Coins* accepted the article (a chapter of a book in progress) on first North American rights terms. The next form I received said that Krause Publications, of which *Coins* is a part, would keep the copyright.

> Your story on "Tin Money" has been accepted for publication in *Coins* magazine. Payment will be released upon publication; tentative publication date is not determined.
>
> Krause Publications purchases "works for hire" within the terminology of the Copyright Act of 1976 and Krause Publications shall own the rights to the manuscripts in the name of Krause Publications or otherwise for the full copyright term and any copyright renewal and the right of publishing and republishing in any of our periodicals or other publications unless specific exceptions are noted thereon.
>
> 2,108 words at 3 cents/word, plus 5 photos at five dollars each.

The editor answered my letter about the copyright issue and said that regardless of the *form communications* I might receive, this would not alter the arrangements for North American rights. A fair man.

The check received had this notation on the back:

> By acceptance of this check in payment for the submissions documented on the statement of manuscript purchase payments #_____ which accompanies it, you understand and agree that they were offered to Krause Publications as "works for hire" within the terminology of the Copyright Act of 1976 and that Krause Publications shall own all the rights to the manuscripts in the name of Krause Publications or otherwise for the full copyright term and any copyright renewed and the right of publishing and republishing in

any of our periodicals or other publications, unless specific exceptions are noted thereon.

It was accompanied by this statement of Manuscript Purchase Payments:

DATE	8/25/88
MONTH	AUGUST
STATEMENT#	14275
CHECK#	0113187
S.S.#	000–00–0000§
PAGE#	1

Enclosed please find our check in payment for the manuscript submissions listed following:

Name of Manuscript	Number of Words‡	Rate	Payment	Date Recorded
CM-TIN MONEY	2108	.0300	63.24	5/18/89
CM-PHOTO FOR ABOVE ARTICLE	5	5.0000	25.00	5/18/89
R5-PERPETUAL BUT				
NON-EXCLUSIVE RIGHTS				

‡ or Other Basis of Payment   *Not Subject to 1099–NEC Reporting
TOTAL PAYMENT ENCLOSED 88.24

Thank you for keeping Krause Publications in mind when you have material available for consideration which you feel may interest our readers.

By acceptance of the above indicated check in payment for the submissions documented on this statement, you understand and agree that they were offered to Krause Publications as "works for hire" within the terminology of the Copyright Act of 1976, and that Krause Publications shall own all the rights to the manuscripts in the name of Krause Publications or otherwise for the full copyright term and any copyright renewal and the right of publishing and republishing in any of our periodicals or other publications, unless specific exceptions are noted hereon.

You further warrant that each contribution is an original work that has not been in the public domain or previously published, that each article has not been registered as an unpublished work, except as may be specifically noted hereon, and that each is free of unauthorized extractions from other sources, copyrighted or otherwise. You further understand that Krause Publications shall have the privilege of referring to you in promotional and advertising material as one of its valued contributors.

§Social Security numbers must be on file for all editorial contributors. This information is required for the filing of year end 1099–NEC reports with the Internal Revenue Service, and is mandatory for those contributors whose total payments amount to $600 or more. If your Social Security number is not on record with us, should your total payments reach the $600 figure, additional payments may not be made.

—Krause Publications, Inc.

The publisher also included an information return form that needed completion to satisfy Internal Revenue Service requirements:

August 25, 1988

Dear Ms. Blue:

As part of the Tax Equity and Fiscal Responsibility Act of 1982, we are required to report to the Internal Revenue Service payments to an individual or organization for services rendered.

To assist us in complying with this legislation we ask that you complete the information below and return it to us.

IMPORTANT NOTICE: Failure to complete and return this notice may result in a 20% withholding of all payments to you.

Complete and Return

Check the appropriate box and fill in your employer identification number or social security number.

I.D.# or S.S.#

( ) Corporation   _____

( ) Partnership   _____

( ) Individual/Proprietorship   _____

( ) Other–Please Explain   _____

Signature _____   Title _____

Date _____

Be flexible in your relations with authors, artists, etc. Make sure they aren't a marginal part of your publication cost; give them equitable remuneration. If you acquire the right to use an article, and profit from its use for the next fifty years or so (occasionally a movie results from magazine feature articles, foreign sales, anthologies and books), pay a fair price for same.

In the Krause situation, my article only fit into their *Coins* publication, not the others (collector car, comic books, sports memorabilia, record and postcard publications). That, *plus* the amount of compensation, didn't warrant giving the copyright to the publisher.

Freelance magazine pieces do not always neatly slip into the second category of work for hire. The deciding point is whether the piece is "specially ordered or commissioned." Melvin Nimmer, a copyright authority, identified the key factor as whether the publication conceives the story idea and contacts a writer to execute it. Publishers who didn't conceive of the idea but force authors into work-for-hire agreements could be acting both illegally and unfairly.

Let me restate the general rule: When you buy a work from an author, the author retains the copyright to it when the author has not transferred the copyright in writing and the work was not a work for hire.

What Can Be Copyrighted?

Under the new law, you can copyright any "original work of authorship fixed in any tangible medium of expression" that can be perceived and communicated directly or through any mechanical means or device. Any minimal expression of originality is okay so long as it's reduced to tangible form. The seven broad categories of "original works of authorship" fixed in tangible form that can be copyrighted are:

- literary works.
- musical works (plus accompanying words).
- dramatic works (plus accompanying music).
- pantomimes and choreographic works.
- pictorial, graphic, and sculptural works.
- motion pictures, other audiovisual works.
- sound recordings.

The definition of literary works makes clear the distinction between "works" and "material objects." Thus, under the new law, a "book" is not a work of authorship but a particular kind of "copy." Instead, the author may write a "literary work," which in turn can be embodied in a wide range of "copies" and "phonorecords," including books, periodicals, computer punch cards, microfilm, tape recordings, et cetera. How's that for fine-tuning the concept.

Literary works include books, leaflets, catalogs, directories, anthologies, compilations and pamphlets (whether fiction or non-fiction), poetry, essays; plus periodicals such as bulletins, magazines, newsletters, newspapers, services; and contributions to periodicals such as ads, articles, cartoons, and drawings. Even scripts delivered orally—lectures, speeches, monologues, sermons—can sometimes be included in the copyrightability of literary works. "Literary" doesn't mean Shakesperean-quality work. The definition of "literary works" refers to works expressed in "words, numbers, or other verbal or numerical symbols or indicia."

The category of "pictorial, graphic and sculptural works" includes "two-dimensional and three-dimensional works of fine, graphic, and applied art, photographs, prints and art reproductions, maps, globes, charts, technical drawings, diagrams and models." This translates into art reproductions, advertising artwork, cartoons, dolls, drawings, names, glassware, greeting cards, labels, filmstrips, paintings, photographs, prints, postcards, sculpture, slides, tapestries, wallpaper and fabric designs, and scientific and technical works, such as astronomical charts and maps.

Although computer programs are not mentioned as copyrightable subject matter in section 102(a) and are not referred to explicitly in the definition of "literary works," a careful reading of the new law, along with the legislative reports, makes it clear that computer programs, or "software," are copyrightable subject matter. Although a programmer's "literary" expression, as embodied in a program, would be copyrightable, his or her ideas, system, and methodology would not.

No Copyright for Certain Matters

Another fundamental legal principle is that copyright protection does not extend to ideas, systems, or methods, processes, principles, procedures, etc., no matter how unique, if not in fixed form.

For this reason the copyrightability of recipes becomes difficult to determine. Some cases allow it, but copyright office regulations say recipes are a "mere listing of ingredients or contents," although the law *may* prevent the word-for-word reproduction of a recipe.

Can copyright protect characters? Sometimes, sometimes not. Utilizing a copyright-infringement theory, United Feature Syndicate, Inc., sued University of Wisconsin after a student publication showed a pregnant Peppermint Patty, a Peanuts comic strip character.

In "A Picture is Worth a Thousand Words: The Basis for Copyrightability of Characters in Public Domain Works," by Adele L. Gentin, *Law & the Arts* (vol. 12, no. 1, Autumn 1987), the author traces the history and the present confusion in this area and concludes:

> As attractive as one all-encompassing principle of character copyrightability may be, . . . the very diversity of character infringement problems—cartoon, literary, impersonation, voice, name . . . mandates a diversity of solutions . . . .
>
> The distinguishing features of copyright, trademark, misappropriation and unfair competition make these theories more or less appropriate for the protection of the many different elements of a character. . . . The solution to the complex problem of the protector of characters is . . . the utilization of the

theories of intellectual property that the law has already developed.

Creativity and Originality

Creativity refers to the work's nature, and originality refers to the author's creation, using his or her own skill, labor, and judgment. Such unoriginal objects as butterflies, cocker spaniels, and flowers made into original art creations have been held to be copyrightable, as have the artistic arrangement of panels on gift wrap. On the other hand, an arrangement of plastic flowers and a scaled-down reproduction of an Uncle Sam bank that had passed into the public domain did not have the necessary creativity and originality to qualify for copyright protection. Originality is a necessary ingredient to copyright art reproductions, but creativity is not; the original work had the necessary creativity.

Creation of the same work by two persons, independent of each other, gives protection if *others* copy the copyrighted works, but does not exclude either of the two individuals from copyrighting his or her particular expression.

Summarized, copyright does not protect the following:

- ideas, methods, systems, principles.
- works in the public domain.
- common or standard works (contains common property if no original authorship—height and weight charts or tables from public documents).
- obscene works.
- devices and blank forms (blank forms record rather than convey information).
- *deminimus* works (works where creativity is too slight such as names, title, slogans, coloring, etc.).
- works of the United States government (works produced by officers and employees as part of official duties).

Works prepared under a government grant may be copyrightable by an independent contractor or grantee. The government can hold copyrights transferred to it by assignment, bequest, or otherwise. Sometimes, the government requires contractors to copyright the work in their name and then assign these rights to the government.

If your publishing house wants to protect an idea, don't disclose it without a contract. If your company came up with the idea of "scratch-scent" books, but didn't have the funds to develop it, you might offer to disclose the idea to Hot Shot World Book Distributors, provided they consent not to make use of the idea until, and if, a mutually agreeable price is reached.

A work that falls into the public domain cannot by copyrighted, and is available to everyone for use without payment or permission. A copyrighted work enters the public domain under the old act when the first twenty eight-year term of copyright expires without renewal.

Once a work has gone into the public domain, copyright is lost permanently. The new law does not allow restoration of copyright.

Case Incident:

An attempt to enjoin publication of a daily horse-racing newsletter, admittedly copied from plaintiff's, failed because plaintiff's work was simply a compilation of facts in the public domain. The defendant took the horse-racing data from plaintiff, but presented it in a visually and factually different manner. *Triangle Publications, Inc. v. Sports Eye,* 415 F.Supp. 682 (E.D. Pa. 1976).

On the other hand, another court found that a defendant who admitted copying a third of names and addresses of garden product suppliers from plaintiff's work was infringing copyright even though the names and addresses were public-domain information. The defendant saved time by not engaging in independent efforts. *Schroeder v. William Morrow and Co.,* 566 F.2d 3 (7th Cir. 1977).

Obscene Works

As a matter of practice, the Copyright Office registers "lewd" works, since it will not make decisions on what is obscene. But if someone infringes your "lewd" work and you sue the infringer, the alleged infringer can raise the defense that there is not a valid copyright because the work is obscene.

Compilations and Derivative Work

A compilation or derivative work is copyrightable if it represents an "original work of authorship" and falls within certain categories.

Remember, there's a correlation between protection of pre-existing material and of new material in a particular work. The most important point is that copyright covers only the material added by the later author, and has no effect on the pre-existing material's copyright or public domain status.

A compilation results from the process of selecting, bringing together, organizing, and arranging previously existing material of all kinds, regardless of whether the individual items in the material have been or ever could have been subject to copyright. Thus, it would be possible to have a copyright in a compilation of blank forms, or a compilation of all the speeches given by Arizona's ousted governor, Evan Mecham.

A derivative work requires a process of recasting, transforming, or adapting "one or more pre-existing works." The pre-existing work must come within the general subject matter of copyright, regardless of whether it is currently, or was ever, copyrighted.

Copyright is conditioned upon the copyright owner's consent to the use of pre-existing material. The new law provides that protection does not extend to "any part of the work in which such material has been used unlawfully." An unauthorized translation of *The Color Purple* could not be copyrighted at all. However, a copyright owner of a poetry anthology could sue someone who infringed the entire anthology, even though the infringer proves that publication of a poem was unauthorized. Anthologies often contain narrative works and dissertations, and it is the arrangement of the selections that's critical. Legislative reports on copyright indicate that this concept serves to prevent an infringer from benefiting, through copyright protection, from his unlawful act, while still preserving protection for those parts of the work that do not *employ* the pre-existing work.

Timing—When To Copyright

Material should be copyrighted on or shortly before publication, evidencing your intent to copyright through placement of an appropriate copyright notice in the work.

The term "publication" is a technical term in the world of copyright. And confusing, too. Under the old law, "publication" generally occurred if the work was sold or distributed to the general public, or displayed in a public place with no restrictions. The new definition of publication is ambiguous. The new law states that "public performance or display of a work does not of itself constitute publication" but "the offering to distribute copies . . . to a group of persons for the purposes of . . . public display, constitutes publication." Treat the term as meaning public distribution. Too, distribution occurs when you sell, rent, lease, lend, or transfer the work or copies to people not restricted from disclosing the work's content to others.

Under the new law, the date of publication becomes less important; it simply serves to establish time-limits for remedies following registration. If a work is not registered within three months of publication, and there is a subsequent lawsuit for infringement, the infringer would not be liable to reimburse the plaintiff's attorney's fees and to pay statutory damages but could still have to pay actual damages, penalties, or fines.

The date of publication determines the five-year period to cure the omission dictated by the copyright act.

After I've explained the concept of copyright as a matter of intent, a client says:

    C: "Well, I can't copyright because I can't afford to send in the ten bucks and the copyright form with two copies of each magazine I've got an article in."

  MB: "That's not what I said."

      The client then pays attention. I repeat myself.

  MB: "You give *yourself* copyright. You show your intent to copyright by placing a proper notice in the right place on the work."

    C: "I don't have to register?"

  MB: "You don't have to, to get copyright," I pause, "but you have to to sue for infringement." There's a glimmer of light and I go on. "If I sell you my house but don't record the sales paper, I've still sold you my house. By not recording the deed, however, there's not as much protection from other persons or claims."

    C: "Okay. So I can choose which pieces to register. I just lose the right to go after attorneys' fees, costs and . . . ?"

  MB: "Statutory damages," I offer. "So although that may affect whether you sue for copyright infringement, you still hold the copyright."

C: "So I'll just put the notice on the works I create."
MB: "Right."

Delivery of a manuscript for consideration for publication is not publication (same word, two different meanings) and the author need not put a copyright notice on the manuscript.

Remember the Salinger case I mentioned earlier—it deals with protection of unpublished works. A biographer's attempt to portray a living subject, J.D. Salinger, author of *The Catcher in the Rye* and *Franny and Zooey,* failed when the subject objected, first, to the author's use of some quotations from Salinger letters in library collections, and then to paraphrasing his unpublished letters. The third version, written in accordance with all these restrictions (Ian Hamilton, *In Search of J.D. Salinger: A Writing Life* [Random House]), was critically panned.

This principle was repeated. *Publishers Weekly* (June 3, 1988) reported that a New York District Court halted the distribution of Holt & Company's L. Ron Hubbard biography with a temporary restraining order, because the book used important unpublished works without the authorization of the owner of the copyright. The plaintiff (New Era Publishing, which holds some Hubbard copyrights), however, had to place $125,000 in an escrow account to "make Holt whole," to cover its losses if later, the court determines the book should have been released.

Protect the work. Don't exhibit, display, or sell it without properly affixing a copyright notice.

How Long Does It Last?

Copyright protection under the new law lasts for:

- a basic term of life of the author plus fifty years after death.
- fifty years from the death of last author of a joint work.
- the shorter of seventy-five years from publication or one hundred years from creation for works for hire or anonymous and pseudonymous works.
- life plus 50 or 75/100 terms for unpublished or uncopyrighted works in existence before 1978.

Under the old law, the first term of copyright was twenty-eight years, renewable for an additional twenty-eight years. Now, those pre–1950 works, with copyrights renewed prior to 1978, will be protected for seventy-five years from the date of the original copyright; protection for works copyrighted between 1950 and 1977 is extended forty-seven years, *if* a valid renewal registration is made by December 31 of the twenty-eighth year.

Even if works are in the public domain because the copyright term has expired, beware of how you promote them. Author Louis L'Amour achieved a qualified victory with a publisher who reprinted L'Amour short stories, even though copyright to those pieces had expired. L'Amour forced changes in the promotional material, advertising, and cover art of the reprints to clarify to the public that he was unconnected with the publications.

Copyright, Not Wrong

12

Is the notice requirement as complicated as it sounds? No.

Requirements of Copyright Notice

Copyright notices are like three-ring circuses—both require three elements to be valid:

- the copyright symbol ©, or the word "copyright," or the abbreviation, "copr."
- the year of first publication of the work.
- the name of the copyright owner.

If you want international protection, use the copyright symbol © , the name of the owner, and the year of first publication. For protection in the Western Hemisphere, you must add the words "All Rights Reserved."

© 1990 Martha Blue
All Rights Reserved

The Copyright Act does not explicitly state the order of those three elements, but the order above is most commonly used.

As previously stated, the year of publication of your work is generally the year the work is presented to the public for sale, rental, or lease. In compilations, derivations, or works using previously published material, the year of the first publication of the compilation or derivation work is sufficient.

You can omit the date when art work is reproduced on greeting cards, postcards, stationery, jewelry, dolls, toys, or any other functional article. If you want to include it, but the exact date is not known, simply put the year of completion of your particular work on the copyright notice. Even if the wrong date or name is put in the copyright notice, it is likely all the protections of the Copyright Act will be in force.

Put both the owner's first and last name on the notice (Hortense Mittenfingers). It's also acceptable to put the owner's professional name (Cher, Little Richard) or symbol (HM), if he or she is very well known by it.

Look at the copyright notice in publications that you pick up. You'll learn a lot, including:

- whether the publisher has a policy of retaining copyright.
- if the work was co-authored.
- if a pen name was used.

Here's a selection of portions of copyright notices:

CAREFULLY SELECTED, EDITED, AND PRINTED,
SIGNET CLASSICS PROVIDE A TREASURY OF THE WORLD'S GREAT
WRITINGS IN HANDSOMELY DESIGNED VOLUMES.

THE RED BADGE OF COURAGE

and Selected Stories

STEPHEN CRANE

Edited, and with an Introduction and
Notes by R. W. STALLMAN

COPYRIGHT 1952 BY ALFRED A. KNOPF, INC.
© 1960 BY R. W. STALLMAN

First Printing, March, 1960
Seventh Printing, May, 1964

SIGNET TRADEMARK REG. U.S. PAT. OFF. AND FOREIGN COUNTRIES
REGISTERED TRADEMARK—MARCA REGISTRADA
HECHO EN CHICAGO, U.S.A.

SIGNET CLASSICS *are published by*
The New American Library of World Literature, Inc.
501 Madison Avenue, New York, New York 10022

PRINTED IN THE UNITED STATES OF AMERICA

Notice that:

- Saul Bellow is incorporated (*The Dean's December*).
- The Didion essays probably first appeared in periodicals in different years (*Slouching Towards Bethlehem*).
- The introduction and notes to a piece in public domain can be copyrighted (*The Red Badge of Courage*).
- The copyrights of deceased authors are managed by trust companies (*The Maharajah & Other Stories*).

Location of Copyright Notice

Don't Hide the Notice: It must be placed on the work so that it's not concealed from view upon reasonable inspection. On a three-dimensional work, place it on the front, back, base, or frame or mounting. For jewelry and other works too small to hold all the information required, a tag with the information can be firmly attached to the piece. To protect the designs on yard goods or decorative papers, place the notice every so often on the selvage, or in the design itself. If this is not possible, put the notice on a tag which must be attached both to the material and the spool. On paired items, such as earrings, it is sufficient that the notice be placed on or attached to only one of the two.

Don't go overboard with the size of notice, as did one of my clients. She gave me, in trade for legal work, a bronze sculpture of a Mexican child; the piece was about the size of a large softball. Blazened into the bronze was her copyright notice, complete, but as big as a pocket comb; she could have had a more aesthetically appealing work if she had put the notice on the base. (I gave up trying to position the sculpture on my desk so as not to see the notice.)

For literary works, affix the notice to give reasonable notice of the claim of copyright. The regulations describe acceptable placement:

- reverse of the title page (all the notices reproduced earlier were found on the reverse of title page).
- either side of the front cover, and if none, either side of front page (same for back) for softcover books.
- first page of work's main body.
- last page of work's main body.
- between the front page and first page of main body, as long as the pages between don't exceed ten and the notice is prominent and separated from other material (same for back).

In a collective work, such as a magazine, any of the above are reasonable. In addition, place the notice by the masthead or near the front of the issue, with the issue number, date, and title. The notice in *Writer's Digest* appears near the end of the masthead and in my REI catalogue, on the inside front page.

The elements of the copyright notice needn't "accompany" each other. Under this provision, a name or date that could reasonably be read with the other elements may satisfy the notice requirements, even if they are somewhat separated from them. "Direct contiguity or juxtaposition of the elements is no longer necessary; but if the elements are too widely separated for their relation to be apparent, or if uncertainty is created by the presence of other names or dates, the case would have to be treated as if the name or date, and hence the notice itself had been omitted altogether."

Case Incident:
A cartographer did a series of maps for a production company and distributor. One map contained the copyright symbol and the year, with the names of the cartographer, producer, and distributor on the same page but widely separated from the symbol and date. Whether considered under the old law or the new, the notice was defective.

Position of an Individual Notice in a Collective Work

In order for a separate contribution to a collective work to bear its own notice of copyright, position the notice thus:

- for contribution of one page or less, the notice must appear clearly under the title, adjacent to the contribution, or somewhere else on the page.
- for a contribution of more than one page, the notice must appear under the title or near the beginning of the contribution, on the first page of the main body, or at the immediate end of the contribution.
- in a separate list of contributions by full titles and authors, table of contents, or acknowledgements, in the front or back of the collective work.

A serious problem under the 1909 law was the notice requirements applicable to contributions published in periodicals and other collective works. In the new copyright law, the basic approach is to permit a separate contribution to contain its own notice, or use a single notice that covers the whole work, sufficient to satisfy the requirement for each separate contribution. The rights to an individual contribution aren't affected by the lack of a separate notice as long as the collective work bears a notice.

One exception is advertisements, which do not bear their own notice. If they are published in a collective work with only a general notice, the effect is as though they have been published with the wrong name in the notice. This means that the innocent infringer who, in good faith, was granted a license from the person named in the general notice, would be shielded from the bulk of liability from the advertising contributor.

Before letting work out of their sight, some authors include the following notice to their manuscript:

Copyright © 1990 Martha Blue

An express condition of any authorization to use this work is that the copyright notice in Martha Blue's name appear on all publicly distributed copies of this work in the format indicated above.

Don't ignore this author-dictated condition.

Caveat. When the work consists "preponderantly of one or more works of the United States Government," the notice must identify those parts of the work in which copyright is claimed—that is, the "new matter" added to the uncopyrightable

United States Government work. A failure to do so has the same legal effect as omission of the notice.

Case Incident:
A client wished to know what kind of notice should be used in reprinting an uncopyrighted government work about pack animals, gear, and equipment. The new material consisted of an introduction plus photographs and drawings. The copyright in that case read © 1989 XYZ Press as to acknowledgements, graphic art, and jacket cover.

Omission of Copyright Notice

Don't panic if you omit the notice. Unlike the 1909 law, the outright omission of a copyright notice does not automatically forfeit protection and place the work in public domain. A work published without a notice will still be eligible for statutory protection for at least five years, whether the omission was partial or total, unintentional or deliberate, provided either of two conditions is met:

- if "no more than a relatively small number" of copies or phonorecords have been publicly distributed without notice; or
- if registration for the work has previously been made, or is made within five years after publication without notice, and a reasonable effort is made to add notice to copies or phonorecords publicly distributed in the U.S. after the omission is discovered.

In other words, all is not lost if the notice is omitted from more than a "relatively small number" of copies or phonorecords, but the work will fall into the public domain if you don't correct the error and register it within five years after publication without notice.

Both the House and Senate Reports state that the phrase, "relatively small number," is intended to be less restrictive than the phrase, "a particular copy or copies," used in the old law.

Note that the omission provision applies only to "copies or phonorecords publicly distributed by authority of the copyright owner." If the copyright owner authorized publication only on the express condition that all copies or phonorecords bear a prescribed notice, the notice provisions would not apply, since the publication itself would not be authorized.

This section further provides that an innocent infringer who acts "in reliance upon an authorized copy or phonorecord from which the copyright notice has been omitted," and who proves that he or she was misled by the omission, is protected from liability for actual or statutory damages with respect to "any infringing acts committed before receiving actual notice" or registration. This is considered to be a major inducement to use of the notice.

The removal, destruction, or obliteration of the notice without the authorization of the copyright owner does not affect the copyright protection in the work.

Case Incident:
One of my clients sold several cartoons featuring a certain character, which she'd copyrighted, to a regional establishment. When the establishment amassed a collection of cartoons with the cartoon character in different positions, they fired the cartoonist, snipped off the copyright notice, and revised the cartoon character. The cartoonist stopped them with a copyright infringement lawsuit.

Remember, if someone removes or destroys the copyright notice without your approval, you're still protected by the copyright law. In a case involving yardage, the copyright notice had been printed on the selvage edge of patterned cloth; the selvage is cut off in making garments. If the yardage is copied, the Court has said that the removal of the copyright notice did not eliminate the owner's rights, and copyright protection was not lost.

Restated under the new law, the omission of copyright notice from works publicly distributed does not invalidate the work's copyright if:

- the omission is from a small number of works.
- the registration is made within five years of publication, and a reasonable effort is made to add notices to copies distributed.
- the omission of notice violated a specific written provision that the work distributed bear notice (as in a publishing contract, where there was a requirement for notice that was not fulfilled).
- the notice is removed, obliterated, or destroyed without the copyright owner's permission.

Under the old law, if the copyright notice was omitted from the work, you could not go back and cure the omission. The labor in curing an omission, however, is tedious and gives cold comfort.

Error with Respect to Name or Date in Notice

Under the 1909 law, the omission of a name or date in a copyright notice made it fatally defective. The new law avoids technical forfeiture but encourages use of the correct name and date by protecting users who rely on erroneous information.

What if you use the wrong date, or the notice is ante-dated or post-dated? Where the year is earlier than the year of first publication, any statutory term measured from the year of first publication will be computed from the year given in the notice. Where the year in the notice is more than one year later than the year of first publication, the case is treated as if the notice had been omitted and is therefore governed by that section of the copyright act.

Publishers frequently postdate notices to the next year in works published at *year-end,* and it would be unnecessarily strict to equate cases of this sort with works published without a notice. So long as the post-dated notice is no more than one year subsequent to the actual year of first publication, the notice is considered to be correct.

If copies or phonorecords "contain no name or no date that could reasonably be considered a part of the notice," the result is the same as though the notice had been omitted entirely.

Deliberate Omission

Some may not wish to copyright their work. J. Frank Dobie declined to copyright his work, *Guide to Life and Literature of the Southwest,* with the following delightful non-notice:

> Not copyright in 1942
> Again not copyright in 1952
> Anybody is welcome to help himself
> to any of it in any way

A *Publisher's Guide to Printing in Asia,* published annually by Travel Publishing Asia Limited, states "any part of this guide may be reproduced. Please give proper credit."

Registration

Publication with the complete notice gives the owner a valid copyright in the work *without* registration and deposit of copies.

However, if you pick up *Cheap Stories Anthology* and see an exact copy of your periodical's article, titled "Bargain Basement Romance," reprinted word for word (and you own the copyright), you cannot file a suit for infringement until you have a Certificate of Registration, and you may lose some benefits if you didn't already register.

Deposit two copies* of the work and the application and fee with the Copyright Office within three months of publication. This procedure meets the copy deposit required for the Library of Congress collection, is simple, and gives you greater legal relief. Why a three-month grace period within which to register the first publication with no loss of rights? It's directed to the situation where newsworthy or suddenly popular works might be infringed immediately on publication, before the publisher or the copyright owner has had a reasonable opportunity to register the claim.

Deposit for Library of Congress Combined with Registration

Under the old law, a single deposit could be made for the collection of the Library of Congress and for purposes of copyright registration. Under the new act, the deposit of copies for the Library of Congress may be required when the work is published in the United States with a notice of copyright, even thought the copyright owner does not register the work with the Copyright Office, and the copyright

---

*See discussion of the deposit requirements, including "acceptable copies." Some categories of material are exempt from the deposit-of-copies requirement, and identifying material may be deposited instead.

owner may be subject to certain penalties for failure to deposit, following written demand by the Registrar of Copyrights. While deposit for the Library of Congress can still be combined with registration, you can use the deposit accompanying an application for registration with the Copyright Office (Section 408) to satisfy the Library of Congress deposit provision (Section 407). You only have to register with the Copyright Office:

- if you want to take advantage of the five-year savings clause, that is, you have omitted the copyright notice and after curing the omission you must register.
- if the Copyright Office demands it.
- as a prerequisite to an infringement suit.
- if you want statutory attorneys' fees and damages (file within three months of publication) awarded in an infringement suit.
- if you want presumptive proof that you have a copyright, and the facts stated in the application are true.

Be professional; protect yourself and your author: always register your publishing house's work.

Effective Date of Registration

The effective date of copyright registration is the day the Copyright Office receives an *acceptable* application, deposit, and fee. A delay in the effective date of registration produces serious consequences—for example, loss of statutory damages and attorneys' fees if work is not registered within three months of publication, the copyright is infringed, and suit is brought.

The application form consists of a single sheet to be completed on the front and back. Detachable instructions are part of the form. There is a continuation sheet for use when more space is necessary. Save the instructions, as the Copyright Office only sends one with a set of forms.

Types of Forms

Most applications will be submitted on one of these forms:

- Form TX: for published and unpublished nondramatic literary works.
- Form PA: for published and unpublished works of the performing arts (musical and dramatic works, pantomimes and choreographic works, motion pictures and other audio-visual works).
- Form VA: for published and unpublished works of the visual arts (pictorial, graphic, and sculptural works).
- Form SR: for published and unpublished sound recordings.
- Form RE: for claims to renew copyright in works copyrighted under the old law.

Two other forms are provided for special situations:

- Form CA: for supplementary registration to correct or amplify information given in the Copyright Office record of an earlier registration.
- Form GR/CP: an adjunct application to be used for registration of a group of contributions to periodicals.

Write to the Copyright Office, Library of Congress (Washington D.C. 20559) for free copies of the forms. Information specialists will answer your questions from 8:00 a.m. to 7:00 p.m. (Eastern Standard/Daylight Savings Time). *How to Register a Copyright and Protect Your Creative Work*, by Robert B. Chickering and Susan Hartman (Charles Scribner's Sons, 1980), contains explanatory text on filling out the forms.

Here's the registration form for my revised book, *Making It Legal*, based on a pre-existing work.

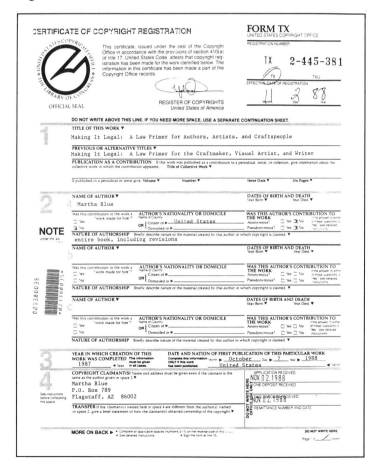

DO NOT WRITE ABOVE THIS LINE. IF YOU NEED MORE SPACE, USE A SEPARATE CONTINUATION SHEET.

PREVIOUS REGISTRATION Has registration for this work, or for an earlier version of this work, already been made in the Copyright Office?
☑ Yes ☐ No If your answer is "Yes," why is another registration being sought? (Check appropriate box) ▼
☐ This is the first published edition of a work previously registered in unpublished form.
☐ This is the first application submitted by this author as copyright claimant.
☑ This is a changed version of the work, as shown by space 6 on this application.
If your answer is "Yes," give: **Previous Registration Number** ▼ 1979 **Year of Registration** ▼

DERIVATIVE WORK OR COMPILATION Complete both space 6a & 6b for a derivative work; complete only 6b for a compilation.
a. **Preexisting Material** Identify any preexisting work or works that this work is based on or incorporates. ▼
Making It Legal: A Law Primer for the Craftmaker, Visual Artist, and Writer was coauthored with Marion Davidson and published by McGraw-Hill. Material has been revised & updated.
b. **Material Added to This Work** Give a brief, general statement of the material that has been added to this work and in which copyright is claimed. ▼
Material updated to include changes in tax law and copyright.

MANUFACTURERS AND LOCATIONS If this is a published work consisting preponderantly of nondramatic literary material in English, the law may require that the copies be manufactured in the United States or Canada for full protection. If so, the names of the manufacturers who performed certain processes, and the places where these processes were performed must be given. See instructions for details.
Names of Manufacturers ▼   **Places of Manufacture** ▼
Krueger W. A.   Olathe, Kansas

REPRODUCTION FOR USE OF BLIND OR PHYSICALLY HANDICAPPED INDIVIDUALS A signature on this form at space 10, and a check in one of the boxes here in space 8, constitutes a non-exclusive grant of permission to the Library of Congress to reproduce and distribute solely for the blind and physically handicapped and under the conditions and limitations prescribed by the regulations of the Copyright Office: (1) copies of the work identified in space 1 of this application in Braille (or similar tactile symbols); or (2) phonorecords embodying a fixation of a reading of that work; or (3) both.
a ☒ Copies and Phonorecords   b ☐ Copies Only   c ☐ Phonorecords Only

DEPOSIT ACCOUNT If the registration fee is to be charged to a Deposit Account established in the Copyright Office, give name and number of Account.
Name ▼   **Account Number** ▼

CORRESPONDENCE Give name and address to which correspondence about this application should be sent. Name-Address-Apt/City-State-Zip ▼
Betti Arnold Albrecht/Northland Publishing
P.O. Box N
Flagstaff, AZ 86002
                   Area Code & Telephone Number ▶ (602) 774-5251

CERTIFICATION* I, the undersigned, hereby certify that I am the
Check one ▶ ☐ author
             ☐ other copyright claimant
             ☐ owner of exclusive right(s)
             ☒ authorized agent of Martha Blue
                                     Name of author or other copyright claimant, or owner of exclusive right(s) ▲
of the work identified in this application and that the statements made by me in this application are correct to the best of my knowledge.

Typed or printed name and date ▼ If this is a published work, this date must be the same as or later than the date of publication given in space 3.
Betti Arnold Albrecht   **date** ▶ 10/10/88

Handwritten signature (X) ▼

MAIL CERTIFICATE TO
Name ▼
Northland Publishing
Number/Street/Apartment Number ▼
P.O. Box N
City/State/ZIP ▼
Flagstaff, AZ 86002

Certificate will be mailed in window envelope

Have you:
• Completed all necessary spaces?
• Signed your application in space 10?
• Enclosed check or money order for $10 payable to Register of Copyrights?
• Enclosed your deposit material with the application and fee?
MAIL TO: Register of Copyrights, Library of Congress, Washington, D.C. 20559

Deposit Requirement

In general, the material to be deposited is one complete copy of an unpublished work, and two complete copies of a published work. (I can't read that phrase without visualizing some copyright clerk opening a wooden crate containing two abstract but near-life-size terra cotta elephant sculptures.)

Fortunately, there are exceptions. One copy of greeting cards, postcards, stationery, labels, ads, scientific drawings, and globes may be deposited. Since actual copies of certain two- and three-dimensional works (jewelry, ceramics, sculptures, and so forth) would be impractical, a substitute for an actual copy, called identifying material, is allowed. Generally, the substitute can be a photograph, slide, or drawing.

If the work is published as a reproduction, you'll have to send two actual reproductions, or one if an unpublished production. For works published in five copies or less, or in limited, numbered editions, you also may deposit one copy (outside the numbered series, but identical) or identifying reproductions. For unpublished pictorial and graphic works, you can also use identifying materials. The photographs, transparencies, or slides should meet the following requirements:

- They should be in the actual colors of the pictorial or graphic work.
- They should be complete, that is, clearly show the work.
- Slides must be at least 35 mm, and mounted if 3 by 3 inches or less.
- Photographs should be not less than 5 by 7 inches or more than 9 by 12 inches (preferably 8 by 10 inches).
- The title and one or more dimensions of the work should be indicated on one copy.
- The image must be life-size or if less, must be large enough to show clearly the entire copyrightable content of the work.
- The position of the copyright notice must be shown on one copy.

I suggest that you write to the Copyright Office for their updated regulations before you send in a registration. When ready, send everything in one package with the proper postage: application, deposit, and required fees. It takes two to three months to get a registration back from the Copyright Office even if it is filled out properly.

If this process seems confusing to you, you are not alone. As a result of the 1976 revisions, new forms and new procedures became mandatory, and complications have ensued. In the summer of 1978, the Copyright Office sent out a public notice that explained that less than twenty percent of all the applications the Office had received could be acted on without correspondence to correct errors or get missing information. The deposit requirements are always in a state of flux, as I said before, so watch for changes.

Claims for registration protection have been made in novel ways. Recently, Crown Publishers released a controversial biography on the Bingham family (Macmillan had dropped it); in the book, Robert W. Bingham, who established a newspaper empire, purportedly drugged his wealthy wife, after she signed a codicil that left him millions. Bingham's son, after he saw Macmillan's galley proofs, registered a copyright to his father's letters and his own written answers to the author's queries. This was presumably done to stop writers from using this material. One lawyer groused that that use of copyright registration was to avoid or circumvent the author's First Amendment rights; the author was a Pulitzer Prize-winning investigative reporter.

Group Registration

You can register "a group of related works" under a single registration.* The legislative report on the new law included, as examples, a group of related jewelry designs, a group of photographs by one photographer, and a series of related

---

*Check with the Copyright Office for a copy of their current regulations on registration for a group of related works and their deposit requirements, which change.

greeting cards. Registration of a group of works under a single registration saves time, money, and paperwork.

Even if a contribution to a periodical does not have its own notice, the author can receive copyright protection based upon the magazine's copyright. However, the author cannot use the registration form for group registration unless each contribution bears the author's own notice. Use Form TX (for registering non-dramatic literary works, or Form VA if it's art) for making a single registration for a group of contributions to various periodicals, then list the titles and publication dates on Form GRKP (an adjunct form). This way, all of your contributions printed in a twelve-month period can be registered for a single fee of ten dollars. At the same time, if you use the adjunct form, deposit one complete copy of each magazine, anthology, or periodical containing the works in question.

Better yet, register these contributions quarterly so that no more than three months pass between publication and registration—the annual copyright fees total forty dollars rather than ten dollars, but the author would not lose his/her statutory damages and attorney's fees in the event of infringement. If it happens that your author's contributions are covered by a single copyright notice in the name of the publishers, the publisher should register the work; your author may ask you, the publisher, to assign it back to him or her.

Because the new act allows divisibility, a magazine's copyright notice covers all the works but does not imply ownership. The author may want you to confirm his/her ownership of the copyright in the piece even though notice was in your name (the name of the magazine or its publisher). The following covers most situations.

CONFIRMATION OF COPYRIGHT

We, (*name of magazine*), of the State of _____ , (*address*), confirm that (*writer*) is the true owner of copyright in the work(s) entitled _____ which appeared in the _____ issue of _____ , which was registered in the U.S. Copyright Office under the registration number TX _____.

DATE: _____   Signed: _____

                                   Capacity: _____

                                   For: _____
                                              (*Name of Magazine*)

(Notary)

Since the new copyright law requires that any conveyance of ownership of copyright be written and signed by the owner of rights conveyed, you might adapt this form to your needs:

COPYRIGHT ASSIGNMENT

That _____ with its principal place of business at _____ and called Assignor, grants to _____ his/her successors and assigns the following:

    a. The sole and exclusive license under the copyright set forth below and the right to use or authorize the use of the following rights in the work described below:

       [List whether magazine, reprint rights, etc.]

or:

    a. Under the copyrights set forth below, the Assignor assigns, transfers, sets over and conveys to _____ all the right, title and interest in the copyrights registered in the Copyright Office in and to the following work created by _____ and (*name of magazine, list title of pieces, and issue*), which work titled _____ was registered for copyright under the following number: _____.

DATE: _____   Signed: _____

                                        Capacity: _____

                                        For: _____

                                              (*Name of Magazine*)

(Always have this notarized)

Copyright with Contributor to Collective Work

The new copyright law provides special treatment for contributions to collective works.

Absent an agreement to the contrary, the copyright of each contribution remains with the author, even though the only copyright notice appearing on the collective work is the publisher's. Further, unless otherwise agreed, the publisher receives not only the right to use the contribution in the collective work *but also* gets the right to use the contribution as part of any revision of the collective work, or as part of a later collective work in the same series.

An article "How to Make Fried Bread," contributed to *Ol' Cooking* magazine, may be used again in your annual publication, *100 Best Recipes of Ol' Cooking,* or be run again three years later, unless the author states in the contract that he/she gives one-time-use rights *only.* The new copyright law implies these two rights.

Renewal of First-Term Copyrights

For pre-1978 copyrights (originally registered between January 1, 1950, and December 31, 1977), renew on or before December 31 on Form RE of the year of the term's end. This extends protection for a second term of forty-seven years. For example, a 1962 copyright must be registered for renewal during the 1990 calendar year.

Use the same form to renew a group of works first published as contributions to periodicals in the same year—for example, in 1990, a renewal registration can be made for all the author's contributions to collective works first published in 1962. If you're missing any important information needed to complete the renewal form, the Copyright Office will do research for you, for a fee.

For those pre-1978 situations where the publisher copyrighted the contribution, you may be asked to reassign the copyright for that piece to the author, who, in turn, will record the assignment.

Widows and Orphans Exemption

A skeleton in the copyright closet permits authors and certain heirs to terminate contracts before the end of their book's copyright term. This popularly termed "Widows and Orphans Exemption" applies to all published works in which grants were made through the end of 1977. For grants made after that date, termination is allowed by the author and certain heirs thirty-five years after a book is published or forty years after a contract is signed, whichever comes first.

This little-known wrinkle in the copyright law benefits authors' heirs, and sometimes authors. As you know, under the old law there were fifty-six years of protection, which was then changed to the author's lifetime plus fifty years. Congress added an additional nineteen years to the renewal term, bringing the total term to seventy-five years for works copyrighted prior to 1978. While Congress gave the author, or certain of the author's heirs, benefit of the nineteen-year extension (note that authors such as Gertrude Stein, with no widow, children, or grandchildren, are left out), the whole termination process requires the precision of a watch repairman. The heirs of Edgar Rice Burroughs, author of *Tarzan*, lost in court when they challenged MGM's remake of *Tarzan*; a contributing factor to their loss was erroneous termination notices.

Too, under the new act, any transfer of rights under copyright may be terminated by the author or certain of the author's heirs thirty-five years after publication of a book (for example), or forty years after execution of the contract, whichever is earlier.

This provision is a result of the unequal bargaining position of authors vis-a-vis publishers, and the difficulty of determining the value of a work until it is marketed. If your publishing house's policy requires transfer of copyright to you, the author or his or her heirs can terminate it after thirty-five years. Believe me, this is watertight; it can't be contracted away. Thus, a book published in 1979 could have the copyright terminated in 2014, if the author or the author's heirs follows the complicated procedure.

Some publishing houses specialize in reprints, or retrospective publishing, and these terminations could be significant. Practically speaking, when you, a publisher, receive a termination notice, *renew negotiations*—you may be successful. (Please see Carrol E. Rinzler's article, "A New Lease on Life for Old Books," [*Publishers Weekly,* July 10, 1987] for an excellent discussion of all the other pitfalls, for both authors and publishers, in these complex provisions of the copyright law.)

Remember these basic principles:

- Termination may be effected by serving a written notice no less than two nor more than ten years before termination is to take effect. Notice must comply with Copyright Office regulations and a copy of the notice must be recorded in the Copyright Office before the effective date of termination.
- All rights revert to those with a right to terminate, except that derivative works prepared before termination may continue "to be utilized" under the terms of the grant.
- Rights vest on the date that the notice is served.
- Termination of the grant may be effected notwithstanding any agreement to the contrary, including any agreement to make a will or to make any further grant.

Some Further Amplifications of Copyright Registration

Copyright Office regulations provide a procedure to correct or amplify information given in a prior registration, or to correct applicant errors the Copyright Office didn't catch in its examination. Use Form CA; this supplementary registration requires a separate fee and is maintained as an independent record, separate and apart from the record of earlier registration. The earlier registration is identified so that the two registrations are tied together in Copyright Office records. The original record cannot be expunged or cancelled, otherwise a complete public record would not exist.

A copyright certificate constitutes only "prima facie evidence of the validity of the copyright and of the facts stated in the certificate." This means that the plaintiff does not need to prove all the facts that underlie a valid copyright unless the defendant-infringer challenges those, and thereby shifts the burden of proof to the plaintiff-copyright holder.

A Baker's Dozen on Copyright

Approach the issue of copyright in your publishing concern by:

- devouring all articles and information that come your way on copyright.
- developing consistent policies for certain situations:
  - payment differential for publisher-held copyrights.
  - acquisition of articles, if you're a periodical publisher.
  - extension of grant of rights to you, so that your bundle of rights comes close to what a copyright owner who hasn't licensed work holds.
  - determination of the status of graphic art work.
  - reduction of policies and procedures to writing for inclusion in your in-house manual.
- being aware of state laws that treat work-for-hire situations as requiring the payment of employee-type benefits.
- educating your staff to place the appropriate copyright notice on all material eligible for copyright.
- keeping a well-stocked copyright larder—forms, circulars, and so forth.

- stopping the project wheels when a claim of copyright infringement is raised.
- keeping copies of all permissions or photographic releases that your writer obtains.
- being sure to cover who owns the copyright in any relationship where someone produces work for you.

Fair Use and Infringement

13

It may not be in words of one syllable, but the new law spells out that "anyone who violates any of the exclusive rights of the copyright owner . . . is an infringer of copyright."

The copyright owner has three years from the date of infringement to file an infringement action in federal court against the infringer. The names of parties to infringement actions are surprising:

- Alex Haley
- Book of the Month Club, Inc.
- Broadcast Music, Inc.
- Home Box Office, Inc.
- J. C. Penney Co., Inc.
- Metro-Goldwyn Pictures Corp.
- National Broadcasting Co.
- Orth-O-Vision, Inc.
- Peter Pan Fabrics, Inc.
- Universal City Studio
- Warner Bros. Records, Inc.
- William Morrow Co.

My two personal favorite copyright infringement cases, based on name alone, are the *Dallas Cowboys Cheerleaders v. Pussy Cat Cinema* and *Walt Disney Productions v. The Air Pirates*.

There is a fine line between infringement and fair use. First I'll talk about infringement from the plaintiff-copyright claimant's perspective, and then move to the defendant's most frequent defense—fair use.

The classic case of copying involved a history book that had typographical, printing, and spelling errors, which reappeared verbatim in the infringing text. Several cases illustrate fact-patterns of successful infringement actions:

- A copyrighted wall-covering design consisting of a grid of bamboo poles superimposed on three stripes was infringed upon by another wallpaper with a similar design, medium, and colors, even though it had variations in size, spacing, and detail of the bamboo.
- A copyrighted rubber doll was protected against an infringer's doll. Even though the dolls were not identical in sculptural detail, it was still apparent that the infringer's doll was derived from the creator's.
- *Adventures in Good Eating*, a guidebook for restaurants and hotels, infringed another guide where there was similarity of expression and organization.
- Classified Geographic, Inc.'s compilation of cut-up copies of *National Geographic* magazine was an infringement.
- A fictional biography of Clara Barton, in the form of a screenplay, was found infringed by a so-called factual biographical book that used some of the fictionalized episodes.
- The successful play *White Cargo* was held to infringe Ida Vera Simington's novel *Hell's Playground*; the locales in both were the African tropics, the central character in both was a male who lived with a native woman, and both were full of similar incidents and episodes.

A simple test for infringement is whether an ordinary observer, looking at the two works, would believe one is copied from the other. Thus, size does not matter, nor does a change in media, such as making a painting of a photograph or a short story into a screenplay; altering trivial amounts of the original work that is copied also does not forestall infringement charges.

Case Incident:

A client, Adam, was about to publish a study guide, written by Xero, to complement a text written by Yoga for which Yoga also prepared a study guide-book published by Price-Brace; Adam asked if there was a copyright infringement problem. The two guides differed in length, format (one used sentences and the other key words), one was dry, the other enlivened with puzzles, and exams were totally different.

Applying the criteria to determine if there is copyright infringement leads me to conclude that there'd be no finding of infringement. However,

to avoid confusion between the two guides, I recommended that a different term than "guide" be used (like nutshell, topic outline); designate the exact title of the book and guide by Yoga published by Price-Brace; and encourage the purchase of same. Spell out that Xero's text is in no way to be attributed to Yoga and Price-Brace.

Forget, too, the comment artists and authors often make that three changes in a work will beat the infringement rap! If a collage is made up of many copyrighted works, there could still be an infringement if the original work is recognizable. An anthology of selected stanzas from poetry about female "cowboys" could infringe the numerous underlying selections.

Sometimes infringement actions occur because permissions are exceeded. When ABC edited certain Monty Python television films under a license, and the licensee exceeded time or media restrictions, copyright infringement was claimed (*Gilliam v. American Broadcasting Co.*, 538 F.2d 14 [1976]).

An independent creation of an identical work is not an infringement. A court held that there was no infringement by the author of an article *independently researched and written* on the same subject as an unsatisfactory article submitted to the defendant publisher; the published piece, on a Bas Mitzvah for a girl with Down's Syndrome, was dissimilar in both format and written expression from the rejected submission.

The use of the same fundamental plot is not an infringement if there is a difference in the leading characters, action, dialogue, episodes, and locale. In a case involving a movie, *The Seven Per Cent Solution*, the court failed to find that a scholarly writing concerning cocaine addiction at the turn of the century was infringed upon by the movie. Even though plaintiff speculated in his scholarly work that Holmes's fear of Professor Moriarity was a drug-induced paranoid delusion cured by Freud—the basic plot of the movie *The Seven Per Cent Solution*—no infringement was found.

Copying must be proved, as copyright protection does not extend to the expression of an idea. The copyright owner must show in an infringement action that the infringer somehow had access to the work, and, indeed, copied it. In a copyright infringement case involving *Abie's Irish Rose* and *The Cohens and the Kellys*, in both of which Jewish and Catholic young adults fall in love, the court compared the plots to Romeo and Juliet. The court concluded no author could step on another's toes vis-a-vis copyright infringement in developing that Romeo and Juliet concept or idea, unless the expression was identical.

Because of the principle of copyright divisibility, the law enables the owner of a particular right to bring an infringement action in that owner's name alone, while at the same time ensuring (to the extent possible) that the other owners whose rights may be affected are notified and given a chance to join the action. Specifically, the law empowers the "legal or beneficial owner" of an exclusive right to institute a suit for "any infringement of that particular right committed while he is the owner of it." A "beneficial owner" is defined in legislative reports as one who has parted with his legal title in exchange for percentage royalties based on sales or license fees.

Once a copyright infringement complaint is filed, court rules take over. An Arizona company's motion to dismiss a copyright infringement action against them in Wisconsin—for allegedly violating the plaintiff's copyright for men's ties that resembled trout or walleyes—was denied because the Arizona company advertised nationally in a Wisconsin magazine and sold ties in that state.

Be prepared if you file an infringement action to show that:

- the work originated with the author; if some parts don't, the protection goes to the original material.
- you complied with copyright formalities, i.e., the proper copyright notice in place and registration with the Copyright Office.
- you can prove actual copying, i.e., by circumstantial evidence as telltale clues of copying.
- the defendant had access to your work.
- the amount of copying, similarity, and damage to you are significant.
- the defendant had sales and profits.

If you're sued for copyright infringement, you may counter by:

- denying the infringement.
- alleging that the plaintiff's work is in the public domain.
- arguing that the plaintiff's work is not a subject that can be copyrighted, i.e., obscene or the like.
- stating that the plaintiff based his/her work on a work in the public domain, or didn't author it.
- proving your use was fair.
- establishing the statute of limitations (three years) or laches (delay) bars the action.
- showing that you made educational use of the work.
- proving that you had permission, license, or consent.
- arguing First Amendment defense.

(A later chapter discusses steps in litigation.)

Courts may grant injunctions and restraining orders, whether "preliminary" or "temporary," to prevent or stop infringements. Paramount was granted an injunction against another film company's posters that showed a giant ape astride some buildings, which copied King Kong astride the World Trade Center, even though *Ape*, the film, disclaimed association with *King Kong*.

Courts can also impound allegedly infringing articles and order the destruction or other disposition of articles found to be infringing. The articles affected include "all copies or phonorecords" and also "all plates, molds, matrices, masters, tapes, film negatives, or other articles by means of which such copies or phonorecords may be reproduced." In one case, the court seized tape-recording machines of a company that sold blank tapes, rented high speed tape-recording machines to customers, and kept a library of tapes to be used by customers. In another case, they didn't (*Dutchess Music Corp. v. Sterm*, 458 F.2d 1305 [1972] and *Elektra Records v. Gen. Electronics*, 360 F. Supp 821 [1973]). Recalls of infringing books have been court ordered (*Jovan v. A.R. Winarick, Inc.*, 207 U.S.P.Q. 75 [1978]).

Once infringement is found, the infringer is liable for either "the copyright owner's actual damages and any additional profits of the infringer," or statutory damages. Recovery of actual damages and profits or of statutory damages are alternatives between which the copyright owner chooses. The plaintiff's election to recover statutory damages may take place at any time during the trial, before the court has rendered its final judgment.

Since copyright infringement is a tort, the remedy is available against all persons involved in infringement: author, publisher, printer, retailer, and corporate employees (officers and shareholders), if personally involved in the direction of the infringement. The corporate shield may dissolve once liability is sought for breach of tort, not contract.

The award of damages serves a purpose different from an award of profits. The statute provides:

The copyright owner is entitled to recover the actual damages suffered by him or her as a result of the infringement, and any profits of the infringer that are attributable to the infringement and are not taken into account in computing the actual damages.

Damages are paid to compensate the copyright owner for financial losses caused by the infringement, while an award of profits is intended to prevent the infringer from unjustly benefiting from his wrongful act. If profits alone are used as a measure of the plaintiff's damages, however, only one or the other can be awarded. Where the copyright owner has suffered damages not reflected in the infringer's profits, or where there have been profits attributable to the copyrighted work but not used as a measure of damages, *both* may be awarded.

Detailed, the basic provisions are:

- Generally, where the plaintiff elects to recover statutory damages, the court is obliged to award between $500 and $20,000. The court may exercise its discretion within that range, but unless certain exceptions apply, it cannot make an award of less than $500 or more than $20,000.
- An award of minimum statutory damages may be multiplied if separate works and separately liable infringers are involved in the suit; however, a single award in the $500–$20,000 range is to be made "for all infringements involved in the action."
- A single infringer of a single work is liable for a single amount, no matter how many acts of infringement are involved and regardless of whether the acts were separate, isolated, or occurred in a related series.
- Where the suit involves infringement of more than one separate and independent work, minimum statutory damages must be awarded for each work. An example is given in the legislative reports: if one defendant

has infringed three copyrighted works, the copyright owner is entitled to statutory damages of at least $1,500 and may be awarded up to $60,000. All parts of a compilation or derivative work constitute "one work" for the purpose of assessing damages. Moreover, although minimum and maximum amounts are to be multiplied where multiple "works" are involved, the same is not true with respect to multiple copyrights, multiple owners, multiple registrations, or multiple exclusive rights. This is important, since under a divisible copyright, it is possible to have the rights of a number of owners of separate "copyrights" in a single "work" infringed by one act of a defendant.

In exceptional cases, the maximum award can be raised to $100,000 and the minimum can be reduced to $200. Courts are given discretion to increase statutory damages in cases of willful infringement and to lower the minimum where the infringer is innocent. Like a ferris wheel that rises from the ground to the sky, damages awarded in infringement cases can vary.

In a recent lawsuit against the University of Virginia, the recovery of statutory damages and attorney's fees was barred for infringement of photographs used before the copyright to them was registered. The continued use of photographs after registration did not re-establish the right to recover statutory damages and attorney's fees.

A specific clause deals with the special situation of teachers, librarians, archivists, and public broadcasters, and their non-profit institutions. Where such person or institution infringes copyrighted material in the honest belief that what they were doing constituted fair use, the court is precluded from awarding any statutory damages. In these cases, the burden of proof with respect to the defendant's good faith—or lack of it—is said to rest on the plaintiff.

An innocent infringer, like a broadcaster or newspaper publisher, is one "not aware and had no reason to believe that his or her acts constituted an infringement of copyright."

Costs and Attorney's Fees

The award of costs and attorney's fees (as part of the costs) is entirely in the court's discretion. Attorney's fees may be awarded to the prevailing party; an exception to this section is where "the United States or an officer thereof" is the prevailing party.

Criminal Offenses

Four specific types of activities constitute a criminal offense:

- criminal infringement: infringement of "a copyright willfully and for purposes of commercial advantage or private financial gain";
- fraudulent use of copyright notice: with fraudulent intent, to place on an article a notice that the defendant "knows to be false" or to publicly distribute or import any article bearing such a notice;

- fraudulent removal of copyright notice: also requires fraudulent intent in removing or altering a notice;
- false representation: knowingly making a false representation in connection with an application for copyright registration.

Under the terms of that section, the court can fine and/or imprison anyone convicted of this criminal offense.

There is a special provision applied to any person who infringes the copyright in a sound recording or a motion picture willfully and for purposes of commercial advantage. First offense: fine of not more than $25,000 or imprisonment for not more than one year, or both. For each subsequent offense, fine of not more than $50,000 or imprisonment for not more than two years, or both.

Notification

The clerks of the federal courts are to notify the Copyright Office of the filing of any copyright actions, of the final disposition, and the written opinion, if there is one. The Copyright Office is to make these notifications a part of its public record.

State Immunity from Copyright Infringement Action

Those who make a living from intellectual property worry about court decisions that they say grant states license to steal their work—in fact, the *Artist's Magazine* (Spring 1988) reported that, after two hundred years, "the Constitution's guarantee of copyright is not worth the parchment that it is written on," which comment was prompted by the United States Supreme Court refusal to review decisions that bar private citizens from claiming damages against state entities for copyright infringement. States argue that the copyright act has never specifically applied to states; plus, the Eleventh Amendment bars federal courts from hearing private citizen's suits against states, unless the states agree or Congress passes a specific law eliminating state's immunity.

Overseas Infringers

The Golden Arcade in Hong Kong specializes in computer software—illegal copies of American and European software are sold there daily. The four publishing tigers of Asia—Hong Kong, Singapore, Korea, and Taiwan—have copyright laws in place, the last three with recent amendments, but piracy abounds due to small fines and backing of some pirates by organized criminal organizations with important government contacts ("A Pirate's Haven in Hong Kong," *National Law Journal*, August 29, 1988). The picture's changing as the U.S. government pressures these countries to enforce their intellectual property laws. The article suggests several steps that U.S. software companies can take—none cheap—to protect themselves, such as hiring a private investigator in the foreign country.

Some at-home advice might help you:

- Provide certified copies of copyright registrations to the U.S. Customs Service so they can seize any counterfeit copies they find.

- The International Trade Commission in Washington, D.C., can proceed against infringing software, and I assume against other infringing goods, by getting exclusion orders against the goods (usually relief is sought against parties, and therefore you need to know who they are).

According to the International Intellectual Property Alliance for 1985, English-language publishers lost $1 billion in American dollars to book piracy, nearly half in Asia. Taiwan, and until recently, Korea, afforded no legal protection to U.S. works, and still, neither belong to the Berne or the Universal Copyright Convention. South Korea finally reached an agreement with the United States, which appears to be unenforceable prior to July 1, 1987, because in Korea, prosecution cannot occur for violation of an administrative guidance rule. For those works proven to be pirated after July 1, 1987, the fine is only sixty dollars per title. American publishers who licensed foreign publishers in the past found that sometimes they would exceed the license by over-printing the run and under-reporting on royalty statements.

Fair Use of Copyrighted Work

Authors and publishers seek to protect their own work, and yet often copy from others. Fair use allows others to use your copyrighted work without your permission. Since the fair use of a copyrighted work is not an infringement of copyright, what is it? There are two sides to the fair use coin: a defense against a copyright infringement claim and a privilege to use copyrighted material without securing permission.

It's fine to copy a small part of a work for criticism and comment, scholarship, research, news reporting, and teaching (including multiple copies for classroom use). This obscure doctrine's been tabbed as the most troublesome in all the copyright law. The new law doesn't define it, but merely lists some factors to use in determining if use is indeed fair; it doesn't weight the factors, however. If you're unsure whether your proposed use is fair, or if you want to do a substantial amount of copying, you should get permission from the copyright owner.

Although there is no handy-dandy chart that tells how much is fair use and how much isn't, the four most critical factors are:

- the amount of copyrighted work used.
- the nature of the copyrighted material; for instance, if it is heavily factual (an index), or originally creative (a poem).
- the purpose; to contribute to scholarship or to advertise the user's products.
- the financial damage to the copyright owner.

If the copier is competing with the originator in the same market for same customers, claiming fair use won't save the infringer. If the copier is a critic or reviewer discussing the literary merit of the work, it's fair.

Is the nature of the copyrighted work informational as opposed to creative? A wider latitude is allowed for the former.

The commercial factor "is undoubtedly the single most important element of fair use." Or, put another way, a use would not be fair if a subsequent work fulfills the market demand for the copyrighted work (see *Harper & Row Publishers, Inc. v. Nation Enterprises*, 471 U.S. 531 [1985].)

The purpose and character of educational, scientific, or historical use would be considered to be for the public benefit rather than for private commercial gain; this is usually construed as fair use because of motive.

The amount or substantiality of the portions used becomes not only a quantitative but a qualitative substantiality test. Obviously, where the entire work is reproduced, it is not fair use; substantial similarity between the two works is an essential indication of copying. Yet, to determine what extent of similarity would be sufficiently substantial to be an "infringing similarity" is difficult. The two extremes of very little or wholesale borrowing are easy to determine, however.

A line has to be drawn somewhere between no similarity and complete and literal similarity. Here's part of a claim letter on behalf of a self-published author to a periodical publisher who did minimal literal copying:

> The copyright owner, under the new copyright law, is granted exclusive rights, which include the right to reproduce the copyrighted work and copies, to prepare derivative works, and to distribute the work to the public. Under the law, anyone who violates any of the exclusive rights of the copyright owner has three years to file an action for infringement in federal court. It is my understanding that _____ is distributed in New Mexico, as that is where my client purchased a copy. Since the book is for sale in New Mexico, we have met the requirement of showing the infringer's access to the work.
>
> In analyzing this case, I have examined the fair-use doctrine as it applies to this situation. The fair-use defense, as it is called by the courts and by statutory law under the new act, provides that the court examine each case to determine if the use is fair, based on whether the purpose and character of the use is commercial or non-commercial, the nature of the copyrighted work, the amount of work used, and the effect of use on the potential market value for the copyrighted work. It is clear that both ventures are commercial; that both are of the same nature (printed words, not a change from one medium to the other); three pages of your 38-page magazine have infringing text; and that article in your magazine is such as to denigrate the market for the copyrighted text. Over half of my client's publication is pictorial and, therefore, the proportionate amount of your three pages of text is substantial.
>
> There have been numerous court cases recently determining that a nominal percentage of infringing text is enough to support a claim of copyright infringement. A court can, if they find infringement, halt your activities, impound and destroy copies and plates, award damages, and award costs and attorney's fees.
>
> It is our position in this case that the remaining inventory of the pictorial book of _____ copies, retail price $_____, will be unsaleable and, at the very

least, the amount of time to dispose of same has been greatly lengthened due to your infringing activities. (The book was, by the way, favorably reviewed in _____.) Our claim, then, is for the remainder of the books at the retail price for a total of $_____.

Since your copying is literally identical, we do not have to deal with the issues of determining extent of similarity, which will constitute a substantial and, hence, infringing similarity, or whether there is comprehensive, non-literal similarity (see Nimmer, *Law of Copyright*, section 13.03, et. seq.).

Instead, this is a case of literal similarity; even if the similar material is quantitatively small, if it is qualitatively important, there can be a finding of substantial similarity. As you know, since your issue of the magazine was directed to New Mexico, that portion of the book is qualitatively more important for the general purchaser than the remainder of the book.

In *Higgens v. Baker*, 309 S. Supp. 635 (1969), liability existed even though the copying was .8% of plaintiff's work; in *Meredith Corp. v. Harper & Row Publishers, Inc.*, 378 F. Supp. 686 (1974), the Court said "...even a small usage may be unfair if it is of critical importance to the work as a whole and taken by the infringer in order to save the time and expense incurred by the copyright owner"; the copying of one paragraph, consisting of three sentences, was held to infringe, see *Amana Refrigeration Inc. v. Consumer's Union of the United States, Inc.*, 431 F. Supp. 324 (1977); see *Hedeman Products Corp. v. Tape-rite*, 228 F. Supp. 630 (1934), where the Court held the material infringed the plaintiff's work when it constituted less than one percent of the total page area of plaintiff's work. Other cases have found infringement where there is a small usage: a twelve-second segment of a two-and-one-half-minute segment of plaintiff's film was held infringed in another case, and copying of one minute and fifteen seconds from a motion picture was held to infringe.

Fair Use for Educational Purposes
A report on the new law adds guidelines for the educational fair use of copyrighted works that set limits on the length of works that can be copied, require that the copyright notice be placed on each copied work, and limit the number of times works can be copied. These guidelines are important to summarize, since some of your works may be used in the educational field. Acceptable educational fair use includes:

- use of a single copy in teaching a class or in scholarly research of:
  - a book chapter.
  - an article from a periodical.
  - a short story, essay, poem.
  - a cartoon, chart, diagram drawing, graph, or picture from a periodical.
- use of multiple classroom copies (one copy per student in class) of:
  - a complete poem of less than 250 words and not longer than two pages.

- a poem, excerpt of less than 250 words.
- a story, article, or essay of less than 2,500 words.
- an excerpt from a prose work of the lesser of 1,000 words or ten percent of the work.
- one cartoon, chart, etc., per book or periodical.

A teacher *may not*:
- make multiple copies for classroom use if the work has been copied already for a class at the same institution.
- make multiple copies of a work from the same author more than once a term or more than three times a term from the same collective work or periodical.
- make multiple copies of works more than nine times in a term.
- make an overrun of copies for others.
- make a copy of works in place of an anthology.
- make a copy of materials, such as workbooks, that can be consumed.
- repeat copies from term to term.

The Association of American Publishers has brought several actions for illegal photocopying, including one against New York University.

Libraries and Fair Use

For guidelines for fair use by libraries under the new law, obtain a copy of Circular R21, "Reproduction of Copyrighted Works by Educators and Libraries," from the Copyright Office.

Parody and Fair Use

Jack Benny performed a humorous sketch, "Autolight," which burlesqued a motion picture, *Gaslight*, and the court held that the use was unfair. Parody and burlesque necessarily involve the use of an original work, but there is a hazy line between fair use and infringement.

Parodies are artistic compositions that mimic and ridicule the thought and style of an original work to amuse and enlighten the audience; the original work's author could, however, be upset by a disparaging reproduction of his or her work. Some parody cases look at the substantiality of the taking, rather than the economic and commercial interests; otherwise, the original artist could use the copyright law to censor a parody.

Two recent cases apply this standard. In the first, Irving Berlin, the owner of copyrights to hundreds of popular songs, sued *Mad* magazine for publishing a volume that parodied twenty-five of Berlin's copyrighted lyrics—"Lovena Schwartz Describes Her Malady" parodying "A Pretty Girl Is Like a Melody"—and lost, because the court used the economic effect as a major criteria. But Original Applachian Artworks, Inc., manufacturer of the "Cabbage Patch Kids," won against Topps Chewing Gum, who marketed cards and stickers using the "Garbage Pail Kids." This effort was judged "not . . . to make a social comment but an attempt to make money."

Certain Performing and Display Rights

The new law grants another fair-use right for the performance or display of certain copyrighted works. This exception to the general rule of "no use without permission" is fairly specific. In summary, it applies to:

- works displayed in face-to-face teaching at a non-profit educational institution.
- performance or display of works at a religious function, assembly, or church.
- performance of non-dramatic literary works, if there is no admission, no commercial advantage, and no one (promoter, organizer, or performer) receives a fee.

Under the third exception, if an admission fee is charged, all proceeds must go to an educational, religious, or charitable purpose. If this is the case, though, the copyright owner can prevent the performance under most circumstances, as it may be construed to be supporting causes that the owners personally oppose.

Miscellaneous Fair Use

Under the fair-use doctrine, you can quote directly from a work in a dramatic or literary criticism. Also, those working in the fields of sciences and art can use existing copyrighted works, including comments, discussions, and long quotes from earlier work, to write new works. Since the former work is usually a jumping-off place for the latter, this is an important fair use, and is considered necessary to the advancement of science and art. The Copyright Act protects the right of a subsequent author to use material from a prior author's works to serve the fundamental constitutional purpose of encouraging contributions to understanding and knowledge, but the first author is entitled to protection against others who borrow too much.

This is true in instances involving *scene a faire*, an obligatory scene, which would be included in writing a standard treatment of a topic, such as a writer's coming of age. Facts, historical and biographical, are not protected. It is often difficult to prove copyright infringement in historical works, for instance, as the same facts can be used by many, and the conclusions are often similar.

Obtaining Permission for the Use of Copyrighted Material

If you'll check some of the books on your shelf, you'll see a permission list in the book, sometimes catalogued as copyright notices.

For instance, look at Jane Brody's *Good Food Book* (Bantam Books). The copyright is in Jane E. Brody's name, but "author photograph copyright © by Thomas Victor."

The Bantam reprint indicates that the copyright page cannot "legibly accommodate all the copyright notices; page 659 constitutes an extension of the copyright page." The two pages of copyright notices are actually acknowledgments of permission to use various recipes and texts. It's a good way to indicate permissions;

you may want to consider it.

What length should quotations be before you get permission? Publishers have different word limits, depending on the nature of the work: for scholarly works, fifty to two hundred words; poetry, three to four lines (for poetry, if the use is for commercial purposes, don't use a line or the author's name without permission).

The copyright-page statement in some books, which warns that the "unauthorized use of [so many] words is forbidden" does not prevent the fair use of the work. A better practice is to authorize, except for reviews, the use of up to a certain number of words without permission as long as the use is not for advertising or publicity.

The Association of American Publishers has designed a rapid and efficient permission system; contact them to get a copy of their permission request form (220 East 23rd Street, New York, New York 10010). The Copyright Clearance Center (CCC) (27 Congress Street, Salem, Massachusetts 01970) established a central royalty-paying clearinghouse, in which payment terms for photocopying magazine articles are set in advance and coded on each contribution's title page. An extra copy of the title page, indicating the number of copies made and the payment, is sent to CCC, who forwards it to the publisher; the publisher forwards it to the author.

As mentioned in an earlier chapter on contracts, tell your author to keep a record of permissions and follow up if he/she doesn't hear from the company or person. Request full rights, which include translation rights, world-wide distribution, future editions, and subsidiary rights; otherwise, you will have to omit the material or get another permission later. Negotiate to reduce any permission fees quoted. Be realistic about sharing these expenses with your authors and co-publishers. Be sure your author provides executed copies of all permissions, as he or she could vanish or die, and leave you with the defense of a lawsuit.

If you develop permission guidelines, emphasize that it is just that, a guideline, and that circumstances vary. In short, disclaim legal responsibility for the author's activities and efforts in this area.

Permission Guidelines Disclaimer:
We provide these guidelines as merely threshold information about when and how to secure permissions. [List minimum standards.] These are not definitive, and the Supreme Court trend is away from fair use. You could follow these guidelines and still be sued for infringement and bear the cost for same under the indemnity provision of our contract with you. For example, you could overlook a substantial use, or a copyright claimant who gives you permission may not be the owner.

Lynn Wenzel and Carol Blinkowski, co-authors of *I Hear America Singing: A Collector's Guide to American Popular Sheet Music* (Crown) reported in *Publishers Weekly* (August 19, 1988) in "Permissions or Perish: A Preposterous Tale" that their contract required them to get their own rights and permissions, a duty that turned out to be a nightmare. They found not one publisher whose name appeared on sheet music after 1913 (which was the music they wanted to use) existed under the original name. Four months later, they found they had to give up "wonderful illustrative possibilities" because they found no one to say "yes."

I reprint most of that article (opposite, by permission).

Plagiarism

An interesting, modestly priced publication, *Legal Aspects of Plagiarism*, by Ralph Mawdsley (National Organization on Legal Problems of Education, Southwest Plaza, Suite 223, 3601 S.W. 29th, Topeka, Kansas 66614), defines plagiarism as the "conscious and deliberate stealing of another's words and ideas, generally with the motive of earning undeserved rewards." This monograph ties into educational issues, formulates, rules on unacceptable conduct, and prescribes penalties for violation of that conduct. For instance, academic penalties include reduction in grade, loss of course credit, withholding or denial of a diploma, or adverse personnel action for a professional employee engaging in same. Mawdsley states that, to avoid plagiarism charges, student writers should be expected to document the sources whenever the writer:

- uses a direct quotation.
- copies a table, chart or other diagram.
- paraphrases a passage.
- presents specific examples, figures, or factual information taken from a specific source and used to explain or support.

He goes on to distinguish plagiarism as a form of academic dishonesty broader than copyright considerations, since plagiarism of material no longer copyrighted, not copyrightable, or exempted from copyright under fair use can occur. Educational publishers should order the monograph.

Avoiding Copyright Infringement

The Authors League 1982 Symposium on Copyright gave the following tips to avoid infringement. You, as publisher, should suggest that your authors heed these, as should those who create your catalogues, promotional pieces, and the like.

- Do your own independent research from many sources.
- Use public domain sources and older works (never competing, recent works).
- Don't paraphrase or quote.
- Credit others' work.
- Don't appropriate expression.
- For requested permission, state that you think the use you propose is fair use and the request is merely a courtesy.
- And lastly, avoid tracking the other work (order, arrangement, and reference).

MY SAY

EDITED BY DAISY MARYLES

Permissions or Perish: A Preposterous Tale

**BY LYNN WENZEL
AND CAROL BINKOWSKI**

The thrill of getting that first book contract completely overshadowed a brief aside from our agent. "You know you have to get your own rights and permissions?" "No problem," we said. Ha!

The book, a fully illustrated history of American popular sheet music, contained sheet music covers from the early 1800s to the present. Of course, every cover after the early 1900s needed a signed permission from its publisher to allow us reproduction rights.

"As the months went by, our checkbooks began to resemble cornfields after the crows get to them. As it was, almost half of the advance floated into permissions"

Sounds simple, doesn't it? All we had to do was contact the music publisher printed on the cover of the music and . . . forget it. Of the more than 40 music publishers' names appearing on the covers of sheet music after 1913, *not one* that we wanted to include in the book still existed under its original name. Organizations like the American Society for Composers, Authors and Publishers were helpful, but many of their files were woefully out of date. The Library of Congress would have agreed—for a sizable fee—to help, but not in time for our editor's deadline.

We were lost in a morass of conglomerate confusion, in the vast wasteland of technological empires whose very own mazes required us to contact a soft-drink empire in order to be directed to a huge entertainment conglomerate in order to be sent to a movie studio in order, in one instance, to hear, finally, from a harassed assistant, "Look, I don't know who owns this. It could be anybody. Why don't you try contacting the photographer who took the picture 15 years ago?" "Okay, who was that?" we asked. "I really have no idea," she replied.

Often, when we found the proper person, we were then introduced to the fabulous world of fees and the "most favored nations" clause. Once we settled upon our maximum fee per cover, several megacorporations calmly demanded from two to six times this amount. After the first few times, we were able to resist choking from shock. We merely conveyed our "thanks, but no thanks" and cut the picture. But, as the months went by, our checkbooks began to resemble cornfields after the crows get to them. As it was, almost half of the advance floated into permissions.

We also helped support Ma Bell with scores of phone calls throughout the country, spending hours in frustrating conversations with eccentric song writers, bored assistants to the v-p of entertainment rights and 80-year-old family members who were still handling royalties for a long-dead publisher.

Through them, we learned many useful skills and tasty tidbits of information—perhaps handy for chitchat at cocktail parties. Among these findings were: that 15 songs can have the same title; that there is no such thing as a "normal" permissions request; how to locate a famous star; how to unlock doors by using the phrase "name and likeness" instead of just asking for permission to reproduce a star's picture; that certain stars have no right to their own names and likenesses; and that nothing makes sense with copyright.

Yes, we did come into contact with some wonderful people who called us back many times and put out extra effort to send us to the right places. We thank them more than they'll ever know. (And, lest anyone think differently, we are *not* against copyright laws. We are, after all, glad that our own work is protected.)

Very few publishers actually signed our permission form because covers, we found, differ so drastically from printed words or music. Some covers weren't actually copyrighted or ownership was dubious. Worse was when someone didn't own up to not knowing all of this, and a wild goose chase ensued. We were forced to come to the reluctant conclusion that we truly have become not one world, but one conglomerate. Tin Pan Alley had room for hundreds of small music publishers, all making a healthy profit and forced to excellence by their noisy, competitive neighbors. Today, as with soap powder, stereo equipment, soft drinks and, yes, much of book publishing, two or three huge syndicates own *all* the music publishing. No wonder it took us almost four months to accomplish what should have taken two weeks. Saddest of all, for us, were the wonderful illustrative possibilities we had to give up because, though no one had said no . . . we could find no one to say yes, either.

Wenzel and Binkowski are co-authors of I Hear America Singing: A Collector's Guide to American Popular Sheet Music, *to be published by Crown in fall 1989.*

Especially for Periodicals

Don't make your magazine cover confusingly similar to that of another. Commercial parroting is okay, but not commercial pirating. The court wouldn't stop the use of *Daytime TV Stars* against *Daytime TV* as a title, but the former was prohibited from using a cover resembling the latter in size and color of type and arrangement of photographs so that the public would not be confused.

Manufacturing

14

Now you've coaxed, wheedled, or threatened a satisfactory manuscript out of your author, one that has no legal problems or has passed a legal manuscript review with flying colors. You're home free. Right?

Wrong.

Now you've got to take that manuscript and wrestle it through the book-making process.

Publishers Weekly (June 3, 1988) reported that Canadian printers received inquiries from U.S. publishers requesting quotations that were of the "can-we-find-a-lower-price?" type. Quality workmanship, such as that necessitated by high-quality, four-color publications, was less often mentioned. The unit cost (cost to manufacture) on the first printing of a trade book should be, I'm told, one-fifth or one-sixth of the retail, or list, price.

The term "printer" can be *as narrow* as to apply to those who run a printing plant and turn out a printed sheet, which is then manipulated/processed by others, to *as broad* as those who provide all typesetting, design, printing, and binding services.

Before you can knowledgably deal with the printers in a business-like fashion, you must understand the production process. (It's an area that escapes my non-mechanical mind each and every time.)

References
For a very basic discussion of "printer English" and getting print estimates, I

refer you *Bring Out Your Own Book: Low Cost Self-Publishing*, by Barbara McFayden and Marilyn Gayle (Godiva Press, Portland, Oregon 97208).

Another basic book is *How to Plan Printing*, by S.D. Warren Co. (Scott Paper Company, 1978). Warren outlines some nice rules:

- Get more than one quote on printing, but do not overquote (a half-dozen printers would be overquoting).
- If you can live with a resetting, reprinting, or rebinding mistake, do, and the printer will reciprocate.
- Be thorough in determining costs.
- Work with a handful of printers, so that you can choose the right one for the job; try a new one occasionally.
- Know printing trade customs and practices.

As with any other undertaking (yes, I am repeating myself), look at the work the printer has done for others, and check with them. Consider, then, additional requirements, both pre- and post-delivery:

- Shipping costs should be included in the estimate.
- The units should be shipped in sturdy cartons and may need to be shrink-wrapped as well.
- The estimate should be signed.
- The camera-ready copy must be appropriately boxed, insured, and registered.
- Payment should be scheduled to allow some of the payment to be made after delivery and acceptance of the product.
- After delivery, count the work (by counting the boxes and multiplying by number of units per box).
- Spot-check the publication's external appearance: clean covers, even trim, and secure binding.
- Check the inside for paper quality and printing quality.

Your publishing house needs some kind of a work-in-progress chart, but tailored to your particular situation. (There are forms in *Book Design: Systematic Aspects*, by Stanley Rui [R.R. Bowker Co. 1978] for a "books-in-work" checklist.) That same text has several forms that simplify and codify the process: standard instructions for handling pictures and mechanicals; checklists for offset dummies; illustrations to offset camera; art/photo transmittal; illustrations information sheet; title, map specifications; and chart notes.

Bookmaking: The Illustrated Guide to Design/Production/Editing, by Marshall Lee (R.R. Bowker Co. 1979), bills itself, quite accurately, as "an outline of practical information and procedure for those engaged in planning and producing books." Its chapter on schedules and records discusses the time required to manufacture trade books (with various charts), which you might recommend to the anxious author. Its production schedule format per book and the short chapter on "Ordering Printing" are both well done.

One Book/Five Ways: The Publishing Procedures of Five University Presses (William Kaufmann, Inc.) contains completed printing production forms, which are educational. (It includes five book contracts, too.)

Trade Custom

The backbone of the printing industry is trade custom, which has been worked out over the last fifty years or more.

Some printers print general standards, while others prepare their own version. You should be familiar with both. Many publishers get by in printing arrangements with the quotation and the printer's conditions, which are often on the back of the quotation. Let's go a step further than getting by. The same clauses are found again and again, regardless of the nature of the agreement: terms of payment, liability, waiver, indemnification, and arbitration. I'll reproduce varying clauses in each subject area and discuss them briefly. Keep in mind that there are a wide range of charges for the same printing job, due both to the printer's work load and the quality of product you desire. Of course, preferential treatment is often given to loyal customers.

Quotation (Shorthand for soliciting a price for printing)
(From Printer Trade Customs, referred to as A)

1. *Quotation:* **A quotation not accepted within thirty (30) days is subject to review.**
2. *Orders:* **Orders regularly entered, verbal or written, cannot be cancelled except upon terms that will compensate printer against loss.**

(From medium-size printer-bindery, referred to as B. The contract is designated as a bookbinding contract.)

1. **All quotations are based upon regular hourly rates of wages and cost of material prevailing at date of quotation and are subject to amendment or withdrawal at any time prior to _____'s receipt and acknowledgement of customer acceptance.**
2. **Orders placed by the customer, and regularly entered by _____ cannot be cancelled except upon terms that will compensate the latter against loss.**

(From an overseas print broker, referred to as C)

Quotation and Orders: **Prices are based on rates prevailing at time of quotation. No contract will be binding on _____ until quotation is signed by customer and satisfactory credit terms and conditions satisfactory to _____ are met. No cancellation will be accepted without reimbursement to _____ for work performed or materials ordered. Charges for mate-**

rials will reflect prices prevailing at the time of production. **Charges for manufacturing may be changed if order is not completed within 30 days of date of quotation. Any increase or decrease in manufacturing or material prices at time of production will be documented and added to or subtracted from the quoted price.**

Here's a form that was part of a Thomson-Shore, Inc. (P. O. Box 305, Dexter, Michigan 48130) newsletter. This newsletter is available free to publishers. Get on the mailing list.

THIS IS A REQUEST FOR A BOOK PRINTING QUOTATION

TITLE: _____

TRIM SIZE: _____ X _____

QUANTITY: _____

PAGE COUNT: _____

■ **BINDING:**

Case ☐   Perfect ☐

Saddle Stitch ☐

Other _____

■ **MISCELLANEOUS:**

Blues _____

Halftones _____

Other _____

■ **TEXT PAPER:**

50 lb. ☐   White ☐

55 lb. ☐   Natural ☐

60 lb. ☐   Other _____

■ **COVER STOCK:**

10 pt. CIS ☐   65 lb. White ☐

Other _____

■ **COVER INK:**

1 color ☐   2 colors ☐

Other _____

■ **COVER COATING:**   UV Coating ☐

Varnish ☐   Film Lamination ☐

■ **JACKET INK:**

1 color ☐   2 colors ☐

Other _____

■ **JACKET COATING:**

Varnish   ☐

Film Lamination ☐

Please Send Quotation To:

NAME _____

COMPANY _____

ADDRESS_____

CITY _____

STATE _____ ZIP_____

TELEPHONE(   ) _____

Experimental Work and Preparatory Work

These provisions protect the printer from the publisher who encourages the printer to do initial work on the project, and then cancels the order.

The dimensions of your printing job must be clear:

- trim size.
- basic margins.
- page totals.
- layout.
- binding (can affect imposition).
- paper (name, size, weight, quantity).
- kind of plate and blueprint requirements for offset printing.
- placement of wraps and inserts.
- mechanicals and dummies for lithographic or gravure printing.
- dummy with front matter, several pages of text with margins, etc.
- color of ink plus standard ink, with manufacturer, number or swatch, on solid tone.
- transparent or opaque ink.
- sequence of colors.

Variants, listed as earlier described:

A. *Experimental Work.* Experimental work performed at customer's request, such as sketches, drawings, composition, plates, presswork,

and materials, will be charged for at current rates and may not be used without consent of the printer.

Preparatory Work. Sketches, copy, dummies, and all preparatory work created or furnished by the printer, shall remain his exclusive property and no use of same shall be made, nor any ideas obtained therefrom be used, except upon compensation to be determined by the printer.

Preparatory Materials. Art work, type, plates, negatives, positives, and other items, when supplied by the printer, shall remain his exclusive property unless otherwise agreed in writing.

B. Experimental work performed at the customer's request, such as dummies, working samples, etc., including materials, shall be charged for at current rates.

C. *Preparatory Work and Materials:* Sketches, copy, dummies, and all preparatory work created or furnished by us shall remain our property and no use of same shall be made, except upon proper compensation. Art work, negatives, positives, plates, and other items, when supplied by us, will be used only for your work, but shall remain our exclusive property, unless otherwise agreed in writing. Standing negatives or positives will be retained on file for a period of three years after which they will be destroyed unless a special agreement is made in writing. Production printing plates will not be held after completion of this order.

If the publisher pays for the experimental or preparatory work at the current rates (not a price to be determined by the printer or upon payment of proper compensation), and/or for the production materials, the publisher should get the property and be able to use it. Agree in writing that art work, film, etc., supplied by the printer belongs to the publisher once payment is made under the contract.

Copy, Alterations, and Paper

Like the car salesman who quotes a price for a car without options, and the customer who keeps adding gadgets to it, the printer wants protection if you want more than you originally ordered. The problem, from the publisher's perspective, occurs when the original specifications were not specific enough and later specificity ends up as a charge for extra work.

A. *Condition of Copy.* Estimates for typesetting are based on the receipt of original copy or manuscript clearly typed, double-spaced on 8½″ x 11″ uncoated stock, one side only. Condition of copy which deviates from this standard is subject to re-estimating and pricing review by printer at time of submission of copy, unless otherwise specified in estimate.

Alterations. Alterations represent work performed in addition to the original specifications. Such additional work shall be charged at current rates and be supported with documentation upon request.

B. **Proposals are only for work according to the original specifications. Additional work done, or time consumed, by reason of author's or customer's alteration of specifications, changes made in work or materials, holding of equipment for customer okay, or other delays caused by the customer, will be charged for at current rates.**
Following the acceptance of quotation, but before commencement of actual production by customer, customer shall obtain approval of imposition, end-sheet stock, body stock, cover material if furnished by customer, from _____ , _____ reserves the right to reject or revise quotation prior to binding if _____ approved specifications for printing, imposition, and stock are not followed.

C. *Alterations.* **This quotation is for work as we understand your original specifications. Alterations represent work performed in addition to these specifications. Such alterations or additional work shall be charged for at current rates and be supported with documentation upon request.**
Paper. **The paper price included in this quotation is based on the best cost information we have as of this date. The paper industry practice is to invoice with pricing as of the date of their shipment; therefore our final billing can change to reflect any increase in the cost of paper incurred subsequent to the date of our quotation. During paper shortages, we will offer substitute papers for your approval before proceeding with manufacture.**

The publisher should establish in advance what the current rates are, require documentation, and (nag, nag, nag!) be thorough and meticulous in original specifications. (Review any written paper industry practices.)

Proofs

The purpose of these provisions is to establish who is responsible for what. Once you mark "O.K." or "O.K. with corrections," and sign the page proofs, the responsibility is yours.

A. *Proofs.* **Proofs shall be submitted with original copy. Corrections are to be made on "master set," returned marked "O.K." or "O.K. with corrections" and signed by customer. If revised proofs are desired, request must be made when proofs are returned. Printer regrets any undetected errors that may occur through production, but cannot be held responsible for errors if the work is printed per customer's O.K. or if changes are communicated verbally. Printer shall not be responsible for errors if the customer has not ordered or has refused to accept** proofs or has failed to return proofs with indication of changes or has instructed printer to proceed without submission of proofs.

Press Proofs. Unless specifically provided in printer's quotation, press proofs will be charged for at current rates. An inspection sheet of any form can be submitted for customer approval, at no charge, provided customer is available at the press during the time of make ready. Any changes, corrections or lost press time due to customer's change of mind or delay will be charged for at current rates.

Color Proofing. Because of differences in equipment, paper, inks, and other conditions between color proofing and production press-room operations, a reasonable variation in color between color proofs and the completed job shall constitute acceptable delivery. Special inks and proofing stocks will be forwarded to customer's suppliers upon request at current rates.

B. [no provision on proofs in the book binding contract]

C. *Proofs:* Proofs will be submitted with original copy. Corrections, if any, are to be clearly marked on a "Master Set" and returned marked "O.K." or "O.K. with corrections" and signed with the name or initial of the person duly authorized to pass on same. If revised proofs are desired, the request must be made when the proofs are returned. We regret any undetected error that may occur, but cannot be responsible for errors if the work is printed per your O.K. or if any changes are communicated verbally.

Ink Matches: Because of differences in equipment, paper, inks, and other conditions between color proofing systems and production press-room operations, a reasonable variation in color between the color proofing system used and the completed job shall constitute acceptable performance. Special ink matches will be supplied by us if you supply a swatch of your desired color.

Require the printer to use the same inks and paper in proofing and printing stages to achieve color parity. If your project is an art book, you should define "reasonable variation," i.e., register, ink density, color sequence, and color balance tolerances.

One of my clients had a photographer-friend proof a poster for an exhibit. The photographer failed to notice transposed letters in the text, and signed the proof. My client had to pay the printer to get a corrected, saleable poster.

Unless it's your regular printer, or the printer has the same concern for quality that you've had over the years, be present when the work is on press. If it's unacceptable, stop the run until the error is corrected. Look for:

- even ink density.
- clean pages (no stray ink).

- precise registration (no blurring of images).
- accurate color.

Over/Underruns, Production Schedules, and Overtime

Just as lawyers don't sit around twiddling their thumbs, waiting for legal work to pop in the door, printers are usually busy, and set up production schedules to order their workload. Any lost, extra, wasted, or redundant time required by the customer means money. However, due to the nature of press operation, there is make-ready time and sheets that are no good, which sometimes results in "overs" and "unders."

A. *Overruns or Underruns.* **Overruns or underruns not to exceed 10% on quantities ordered, up to 10,000 copies and/or the percentage agreed upon; over or under quantities ordered above 10,000 copies shall constitute acceptable delivery. Printer will bill for actual quantity delivered within this tolerance. If customer requires guaranteed "no less than" delivery, percentage tolerance of overage must be doubled.**
Production Schedules. **Production schedules will be established and adhered to by customer and printer, provided that neither shall incur any liability or penalty for delays due to state of war, riot, civil disorder, fire, strikes, accidents, action of Government or civil authority, and acts of God or other causes beyond the control of customer or printer.**

B. **Jobs requiring close-aligned crossover should be printed on stock squared prior to printing, together with cutting layout or workable dummy made from printed sheets or Dylux of litho flats. Guide and gripper sides shall be marked. Failure on these items relieves _____ of responsibility for errors.**
Production schedules will be established and adhered to by customer and _____ provided that neither shall incur any liability or penalty for delays due to state of war, riot, civil disorder, fire, strikes, accidents, energy failure or shortage, action of Government or Civil Authority, and Acts of God or other causes beyond the control of customer or _____ .

Quotation is for specified quantity to be bound or completed as an initial order. Should, however, customer call for a partial delivery, _____ may add any increase in the cost of labor or material to the quoted price to compensate for additional cost.

_____ makes no hand count on receipt of sheets or material unless separate agreement is made authorizing extra charges. The basis of count shall be the folded and/or gathered record made as soon after receipt of sheets or signatures as convenient. _____ not responsible for shortages if printing overrun is inadequate for binding operations.

Customer will be informed if folding or gathering counts indicate the job will be short. If shortage imminent, job will be stopped until

approval is obtained in writing from customer for short delivery. Cases, skids, boxes, etc., will not be returned to customer unless customer requests return when the material is sent to _____ .

Overruns and underruns, not to exceed 5% of the quantities ordered up to 10,000 copies, and 3% on quantities over 10,000, shall constitute an acceptable delivery, and any excess or deficiency shall be charged or credited to the customer proportionately. Loads and customer's order to be plainly marked in the event excess is not to be processed.

All quotations based on work being performed on a straight-time basis. Any deliveries requiring overtime, due to customer-caused delay, shall be billed at overtime rates. Unless otherwise specified, the price quoted is f.o.b. _____ plant in _____ .

All proposals are based on immediate delivery of the order when completed, or upon immediate delivery of completed units of the order, as may be most convenient to _____ . An additional charge will be made for special packaging, handling, shipping, or storage.

C. *Production Schedules:* This work will be completed in accordance with an agreed-upon production schedule, provided neither party shall be liable for delays or non-performance due to causes beyond either party's control.

Overtime: Overtime incurred because of your delay in furnishing material, holding up the progress of the work, or your request for extremely short delivery time requirements are subject to overtime rates. All quotations are based on our work being performed on a straight-time basis.

Overruns or underruns: Overruns or underruns not to exceed 10% on quantities ordered up to 10,000 copies and/or the percentage agreed upon; over or under quantities ordered above 10,000 copies shall constitute acceptable delivery. We will bill for the actual quantity delivered within this tolerance. If you require a guaranteed "no less than" delivery, our percentage tolerance of overage must be increased.

Customer-caused delays frequently occur with small publishers, because of their understaffing and lack of experience. Overtime rates increase the per-unit cost of the book, newspaper, magazine, or journal. Your most important cost-saver is to make sure that you do not cause any delays and hold up the presses.

Customer's Property and Furnished Materials

Any time you get into a bailment situation (where one party has the legal right to possession, even temporary, of another's property) the problem bell clangs. Where does the responsibility lie if the property is:

- stolen?
- burned?

- damaged?
- lost?
- stored for an unreasonable period of time?
- furnished sloppily?

A. *Customer's Property*. **The printer will maintain fire, extended coverage, vandalism, malicious mischief, and sprinkler-leakage insurance on all property belonging to the customer, while such property is in the printer's possession; printer's liability for such property shall not exceed the amount recoverable from such insurance.**
Customer-Furnished Materials. **Paper stock, camera copy, film, color separations, and other customer-furnished materials shall be manufactured, packed, and delivered to printer's specifications. Additional cost due to delays or impaired production caused by specification deficiencies shall be charged to the customer.**

B. **Customer-furnished goods will not be held after completion of the order except by special agreement, such as fulfillment and shipping of books. _____ shall charge the customer at current rates for the handling and storage of customer's property held more than 30 days. All customer's property and finished goods held in storage is at customer's risk. _____ is not liable for any loss or damage thereto caused by fire, water leakage, theft, negligence, insects, rodents, Acts of God, or any other cause beyond _____ control.**
All jobs shall be furnished to _____ jogged, securely wrapped or skidded, and dry, or otherwise protected from damage. Variations or discrepancies caused by faulty packing, skidding, paper, printing, or customer folding, will result in stoppage or rejection of the job by _____ unless customer acknowledges, in writing, approval of additional costs due to causes beyond _____ control.

C. *Customer-Furnished Materials and Property:* **Paper stock, camera copy, film, color separations, and other furnished materials shall be manufactured, packaged, and delivered in accordance with printing trade customs and our specifications. Any delays or impairment of production that we might incur caused by your failure to do so can cause additional cost and be so charged. Materials delivered from you or your supplier are verified without the cost of a physical count and therefore we cannot accept the liability for shortages based on supplier's tickets. We shall be entitled to charge you for the handling and storage of any materials you supply, or of finished goods after completion. We will maintain insurance coverage to protect your property against fire, water damage, or malicious mischief while in our possession, however, this protection is limited by the amount recoverable from our insurance. You are expected to maintain your own insurance for your property's replacement value.**

Set a date at which storage charges kick in. Try to establish an exception for the printer's gross negligence, in which case the printer will pay the sum between the insurance coverage and replacement value. (See the earlier discussion of transparencies lost by publishers and printers.) Be sure to list the materials you send to the printer in writing; it is not uncommon for disputes to arise as to whether the printer got or already returned materials. Have someone double-check goods both ways.

A. *Delivery.* **Unless otherwise specified, the price quoted is for single shipment, without storage. F.O.B. local customer's place of business or F.O.B. printer's platform for out-of-town customers. Proposals are based on continuous and uninterrupted delivery of complete order, unless specifications distinctly state otherwise. Charges related to delivery from customer to printer, or from customer's supplier to printer are not included in any quotations unless specified. Special priority pickup or delivery service will be provided at current rates upon customer's request. Materials delivered from customer or his suppliers are verified with delivery ticket as to cartons, packages or items shown only. The accuracy of quantities indicated on such tickets cannot be verified and printer cannot accept liability for shortage based on supplier's tickets. Title for finished work shall pass to the customer upon delivery, to carrier at shipping point or upon mailing of invoices for finished work, whichever occurs first.**

B. **[no provision]**

C. *Delivery.* **Unless otherwise specified, the price quoted is for a single shipment, without storage, C.I.F. Port of Los Angeles and is based on carrier at the shipping point or upon mailing of our invoice for finished work, whichever occurs first. We do not control common carriers and cannot be held financially responsible for delays incurred by independent transportation companies. Charges related to delivery service from you to our plant or from your supplier to our plant are not included in our quotation unless specified. Special priority pick-up or delivery service will be provided at current rates upon your request. Prices net f.o.b. unless otherwise specified. This quotation is based on current prices and availability of material and is subject to change and to all terms and conditions outlined on this proposal.**

Terms, Guarantees, Liability Limits, and Indemnification

The printer's payment conditions appear near the end of most standard agreements (often on the back of a quotation). Most printers want payment in thirty days. Just as an auto mechanic has a lien on your car until it's paid for, the printer holds a lien on your property until the bill is settled.

Things do go wrong in projects, and the printer limits your time to complain; you must reject or accept within a given number of days. If the mishap is the printer's

271

fault, the printer will also want to cap its liability.

Some printers argue that liability is limited to each aspect of the contract, for instance, the limitation of liability for rebinding is limited to the cost of rebinding, which follows from the damaged party's duty to mitigate damages under the law.

These provisions are lengthy. (It's unfortunate that the printers' contracts don't go into as much detail about the product you get from them.) The beefy section is what the printer will do to you if you don't pay.

A. ***Terms.*** **Payment shall be net cash thirty (30) days from date of invoice unless otherwise provided in writing. Claims for defects, damages or shortages must be made by the customer in writing within a period of thirty (30) days after delivery. Failure to make such claim within the stated period shall constitute irrevocable acceptance and an admission that they fully comply with terms, conditions and specifications. Printer's liability shall be limited to stated selling price of any defective goods, and shall in no event include special or consequential damages, including profits (or profits lost). As security for payment of any sum due or to become due under terms of any Agreement, printer shall have the right, if necessary, to retain possession of and shall have a lien on all customer property in printer's possession including work in process and finished work. The extension of credit or the acceptance of notes, trade acceptances or guarantee of payment shall not affect such security interest and lien.**

   Indemnification. **The customer shall indemnify and hold harmless the printer from any and all loss, cost, expense and damages on account of any and all manner of claims, demands, actions and proceedings that may be instituted against the printer on grounds alleging that the said printing violates any copyright or any proprietary right of any person, or that it contains any matter that is libelous or scandalous, or invades any person's right to privacy or other personal rights, except to the extent that the printer has contributed to the matter. The customer agrees to, at the customer's own expense, promptly defend and continue the defense of any such claim, demand, action or proceeding that may be brought against the printer, provided that the printer shall promptly notify the customer with respect thereto, and provided further that the printer shall give to the customer such reasonable time as the exigencies of the situation may permit in which to undertake and continue the defense thereof.**

B. **In no event shall customer be entitled to recover any consequential or incidental damages caused, in whole or in part, by any delay, failure or non-performance of _____ . Liability of _____ shall not exceed any sums paid to _____ by customer and the costs of any necessary repairs to or replacement of materials of customer.**

   Terms are net 30 days from date of invoice. _____ may request

advance payment and cease work at any time it has cause to feel uncertain about payment. All claims must be made within 30 days of receipt of goods. Interest will be charged at 1½% per month (18% annual rate) on past due balance.

C. *Guarantee, Liability Limitations, Indemnification:* We will produce this work in a good workmanlike manner and in accordance with the agreed-upon specifications and production schedule. In the event the work is defective or delayed due to our fault, our liability to you shall be limited to reimbursement of amounts paid by you and we shall not be responsible for special or consequential damages, including but not limited to, lost profits or business. Any applicable Federal, State, County, or Local taxes imposed on us on account of this transaction shall be added as an extra charge to this order. If sales tax does not apply to this order, please include your tax exemption number on your letter of credit or purchase order, otherwise sales tax will be charged. _____ may subcontract work to domestic or foreign printers without the prior consent of customer. The terms and conditions of this agreement shall accrue to the benefit of such subcontractor. Customer agrees that if _____ subcontracts any work of Customer to any particular printer, Customer shall not conduct any business with the printer for five years from the date of this quotation. In the event that Customer breaches this paragraph, Customer shall be liable to _____ for lost profits with standard non-discounted rates for a comparable transaction, plus costs of collection including reasonable attorney's fees. Any claims made by you must be in writing and given to us within 15 days after shipment of work. You warrant that the use of materials furnished by you will not infringe or violate any laws or regulations or any rights of others and you will indemnify and save us harmless from any and all damage, cost and expense based on any claims of such infringement or violation, including court costs and attorney's fees.

Terms: Payment shall be by separate irrevocable domestic Letter of Credit from a bank acceptable to us in favor of _____ opened not later than the "Artwork due date" as agreed in the production schedule. The Letter of Credit shall remain open until the time of delivery. Special terms, including deposits and partial payments will be arranged based on individual circumstances. As security for payments of any sum due or to become due under the terms of this agreement, we shall have the right to retain possession of and shall have a security interest in all property owned by you and in our possession.

Be sure the standard provision or contract provides that: "the work will be produced in a good, workmanlike manner and in accordance with the agreed-upon specifications and production schedule." Sometimes, you may not discover defects, damages or shortages until later than thirty days, i.e., the last books shipped aren't sold until eight or ten months after delivery; on opening the remaining boxes, you discover that the books are missing the index, or that the signatures are bound upside down or in a random fashion. Consider adding a provision that you, the customer, will "use reasonable diligence to discover defects, damages, or shortages," but in the event of later discovery of serious flaws, you have a mutually agreed-upon recourse. Randomly check all shipments when they are delivered.

Try to get at least thirty days in which to make a claim. If the delivery date is tied to a special event that makes both time and quality essential to successfully release the book, extend the liability to lost profits. For example, if a book is to be released at a movie premiere or as part of a special event held only once a year, there may be a limited, or non-existent, market if the delivery date and quality standards aren't met.

Provision C is essentially an anti-competition clause. Courts often do not favor such clauses (they usually will not uphold clauses that restrict legal professionals, for instance, from employment for several years by another law office in the same town), and would look long and hard at the five-year restriction specified in this provision.

Resolution of Disputes

The Printing Trade Customs form previously included does not make any provision for resolving disputes, but the bookbinding contract and the broker's contract do, although the provisions differ widely. An area of commonality is that *both* give themselves (not you) the option of suing instead of arbitrating.

A. [no provision]

B. **All disputes between customer and _____ not otherwise resolved will be submitted to binding arbitration in _____ ; pursuant to the rules of the American Arbitration Association, except _____ may proceed against customer in any court of competent jurisdiction to recover monies due _____ from customer.**

C. **Governing Law: This agreement shall be deemed as to have been executed and performed in the State of _____ and shall be governed by the laws thereof. This agreement and any matters not set forth herein shall be governed by the customs and practices prevailing in the printing industry as codified by the Printing Industry of America, Inc. All controversies between customer and _____ will be submitted to binding arbitration in _____ , pursuant to the rules of the American Arbitration Association; except _____ may proceed in any court of competent jurisdiction to recover monies due to _____ from customer. Judgment on arbitration awards may be entered in any court of competent jurisdiction. In the event of any litigation or arbitration, the prevailing party shall be entitled to its costs, including rea-**

sonable attorney's fees. _____ shall not be liable for delays caused due to state of war, riot, civil disorder, fire, labor trouble, strikes, accidents, energy failure, equipment breakdown, action of government or civil authority and Acts of God.

Put both parties on the same footing as to courts or arbitration. Try to have the contract deemed to have been executed and performed in your state, since that will determine the laws of any dispute proceeding, and perhaps where court would be held; a small publisher in Vermont may not be able to resolve a dispute through California arbitration or courts because of the cost of travel and legal representation.

Alternatives

Consider a letter of agreement that incorporates the quotations and conditions with the proviso that any variances between the former and the latter would be covered by the letter of agreement. You could also use a short- or long-form contract. Clearly, a contract should be utilized for long-run periodicals as well as expensive book printing jobs. Think "forms." A lawyer can draft a form contract that's like vanilla ice cream: options, like toppings, can be side-drafted into it.

The contract should cover, minimally:

- the work, divided into the printer's components.
- quantity (over- and underruns).
- terms, including interest on default and price escalation due to printer's increased costs, overtime, and taxes.
- paper requirements and allocation if the supply is short.
- storage of back issues if for a periodical.
- disposition and ownership of press plates and other reproductive material.
- production schedules and specifications (could be generally mentioned in the form contract and be fine-tuned in exhibits).
- hindrances to performance.
- printer indemnification.
- insurance.
- printer confidentiality (periodical publications, especially).
- boilerplate.
- assignments.
- notices.
- written modifications.
- waiver.
- claims and arbitration.

PLI's *Legal and Business Aspects of the Magazine Industry 1979* (page 63, et seq.) sets forth the 1973 CBS printing specifications for several of its publications, including *Popular Library, World Tennis,* and *Field & Stream.* CBS wanted to improve the production operation and economize by producing all the magazines in one or two plants. The specifications covered separations, compositions, and printing. You might consider a similar approach if you publish one or more periodicals, newsletters, or the like.

One of my clients became involved in a dispute with a printer because of a binding error: instead of trimming to 12″ horizontal, the publication was trimmed a half-inch narrower. The parties negotiated a resolution, and the publisher drew up a letter of agreement for the printer to sign. The publisher asked for the lawyer's comments on the agreement. Here's the draft agreement:

**Proposed Settlement Agreement Between
Publisher and Printer**

Memorandum of Agreement Between _____ **(Publisher) and** _____ **(Printer) Regarding** _____
Dated _____ **.**

It is agreed by all parties that the above-referenced book was trimmed to the wrong horizontal size. To settle the dispute involving this situation, the parties mutually agree that the book shall be reprinted by printer at printer's expense.

The publisher agrees that it shall hold the printer harmless and shall not pursue any suit for lost sales through litigation or other means.

The publisher shall accept the reprinted material in a timely manner, and shall pay for it upon acceptance.

The printer may dispose of the extant stock of mistrimmed books in any manner it sees fit, with the explicit exception of sale of the book. The printer is expressly prohibited from distributing the above-referenced book except as sample materials, given, not sold.

This constitutes the complete understanding and agreement between the parties, and shall be binding upon signature of all concerned.

_____	_____
Publisher	**Printer**
_____	_____
Date	**Date**

The lawyer's comments were:

- if printer was incorporated, designate the authority of the individual signing the agreement.
- specify that reprinting is to publisher's specifications, and include those as an exhibit.
- change to a mutual release.
- change the acceptance to meet specifications, and set time for same.

Because of the number of years the printer and the publisher had worked together, resolution was possible. Too, the parties put their dispute resolution in writing (what if the second print run was cropped *two* inches off?) and got a quick legal review. That's a cheap way to get a lawyer's opinion.

Here's another resolution between a publisher of a quarterly price guide, who complained about the quality of the printing job, the extreme delay, and the printer:

Promissory Agreement

WHEREAS, _____ (hereinafter _____) and _____ have engaged in certain business transactions wherein _____ claims that certain sums are due, owing, and payable to _____ from _____ , and _____ claims certain offsets should be applied to said accounts, the extent and nature of said offsets and account balances neither party admits to herein, and

WHEREAS, both _____ and _____ wish to amicably resolve this matter, the following agreement is reached by the parties.

_____ agrees to pay _____ the total sum of _____ Dollars and No/100 ($ _____) as herein provided. The sum of _____ Dollars ($ _____), will be paid by certified check on _____ , 19 ____, to _____ . Thereafter, _____ Dollars ($ _____) will be paid by certified check on _____ , 19 ____ , to _____ . Thereafter, _____ Dollars ($ _____) will be paid by certified check on _____ , 19 ____ , to _____ . Thereafter, the sum of _____ Dollars ($ _____) will be paid by certified check on _____ , 19 ____ to _____ . Under the terms of this agreement, a payment is made by _____ depositing its certified check in a properly addressed and stamped envelope in a U.S. Mailbox or Post Office on the payment date.

In exchange for _____'s payments as described herein, _____ agrees that after the final payment on _____ , 19 ____, _____ will through an authorized agent execute and deliver to _____ the mutual release, attached hereto as Exhibit "A." In any event, _____ herein agrees that upon final payment by _____ under the provisions of this agreement, _____ surrenders, releases, and forever disclaims any claim against _____ or _____ , individually, their agents, assigns or employees for any accounts, debts, charges, interest charges, delivery or freight charges allegedly incurred in the business relations between _____ its agents and employees.

Both parties enter into this agreement to buy their peace and neither admits to or acknowledges the validity in the amounts allegedly owed by _____ to _____ or the offsets allegedly owed by _____ to _____ . Should _____ fail to make any payment as scheduled in this agreement, _____ will retain the right to keep any payment or payments made under the agreement and proceed with collection of its account as if this agreement was for naught, except that any payment actually made by _____ will be credited against the accounts allegedly owed by _____ to _____ . By accepting the first $ _____ payment under the terms of this agreement, _____ agrees to the terms of this agreement.

Release of All Claims

THE STATE OF   )
)
COUNTY OF   )

  WHEREAS, _____ PRESS and _____ have engaged in certain business transactions wherein _____ PRESS claims certain sums are due, owing, and payable to _____ PRESS from _____ and _____ claims certain offsets should be applied to said accounts, the extent and nature of said offsets and account balances neither party admits to herein, and

  WHEREAS, both _____ and _____ PRESS wish to amicably resolve this matter, the following release of all claims is reached by the parties.

  IN CONSIDERATION of the sum of $_____ which _____ PRESS acknowledges has been heretofore delivered and paid, _____ PRESS on behalf of itself, its executors, administrators, assigns, and subrogees, fully release, acquit and forever discharge _____ and all persons and entities in privity with it from all claims, actions, causes of action, liens, rights, demands, costs, loss of services, expenses and other damages of whatever nature sustained as a result of the accounts and business relations between _____ its agents and employees and _____ PRESS.

  FOR AND IN CONSIDERATION of the reduction of the alleged account balance owed by _____ to _____ acting _____ individually and on behalf of all its executors, administrators, assigns, and subrogees, fully releases, acquits and forever discharges _____ PRESS and all persons and entities in privity with it from all claims, actions, causes of action, liens, rights, demands, costs, loss of services, expenses, and other damages of whatever nature sustained as a result of the business relation in question.

  Both parties understand that this is a settlement of doubtful and disputed claims, and that such payments are not an admission of liability by any person or entity herein released, by whom any liability is expressly denied, but such payment is intended only to buy peace. This release of all claims is contractual and not mere recital, and contains the entire agreement with those persons and entities released.

Overseas Printing

Since China, Korea, and Japan began using movable type in the eleventh century, four centuries before the Europeans, it is not surprising that Asia supports major printing centers. If you are considering Asia as a source of printing, order *A Publisher's Guide to Printing in Asia,* a yearly edition, from Travel Publishing Asia Limited (1801 World Trade Center, Causeway Bay, Hong Kong).

According to *A Publisher's Guide,* Americans have a reputation for desiring "saturated colour, reds and blacks" while Europeans and Japanese insist on depth of detail in color print. So be aware of which standard you wish and:

- provide samples of print quality expected.
- indicate the inks to be used for both color separator and printer, so you get an exact color balance.
- be aware of color differences among the Japanese, American, and European inks.

- proof color work with inks to be used in printing; request specific inks if you plan to use only Asian color separations, but not printing.

Print Brokers

For off-shore printing sources, an independent broker may be what you need. A broker in this situation assists by his familiarity with off-shore sources, foreign printing customs, discounts for volume, and the like. (Normally, adding a third party, a middleman, complicates any process, but when working off-shore, the benefits may outweigh the complications.)

Before you decide to work through a broker, clarify in writing whether the broker represents you or the printer. A San Diego broker commented to me that, to the extent he was anyone's agent, he was the agent of the printer. This type of relationship works against the publisher in the long run, because although U.S. law provides strict standards and responsibilities in the agent-principal relationship, you can't benefit from these if you aren't the principal.

It is also in your interest to be aware of the geographical area in which the broker intends to place your job. If your warehouse/distribution center is in a very dry climate and the printer/binder is in a tropical area, you are destined for problems unless specific manufacturing considerations are followed.

Some publishers want to work directly with a printer; others prefer an American or U.S.-based representative who can run interference with the overseas printer and can be accountable for problems that arise. Consider being on hand while your work is printed, or have the services of a reliable broker, at least until the printer and your company have worked through some projects together.

Some recommend working with U.S. representatives of the Asian printing houses to save you plane fare. Remember, these representatives are U.S.-based employees of the overseas company.

Case Incident:

In response to my client's claims for damages due to severely warped hardcover books, the off-shore printer argued that there was no warping and that only the end sheets were slightly wrinkled. In fact, the books, printed in Asia and destined for the arid American Southwest (a fact well-known to the broker), looked like potato chips. At my request, our office cleaning staff stacked other heavy volumes on top of my warped sample copy. The compression had no effect—once the weight was removed, the book reverted to its potato-chip curve within a couple of hours.

The printer accused the publishers of mishandling the books and further denied responsibility for the damage by saying that the atmospheric conditions differed greatly between the two places. You bet they do, but, we argued, that did not excuse them from their responsibility to take that difference into account when binding and supplying my client with a saleable product.

The matter was finally resolved, after many months, when the printer's

representative travelled to the publisher's facility and saw rows and rows of warped books spread out on a table in the publisher's office. The representative was sufficiently embarrassed to suggest a settlement.

Further, when these warped books were sent to a U.S. rebinder, the binder noted that:

- all covers warped due to excessive moisture and/or poor curing.
- wrinkled and puckered end sheets in front and back were caused by inadequate gluing and excessive moisture, coupled with inadequate building-in of the spine binding.
- the too-tight reinforcing gauge for spines extended only ¼" into the front and back covers, rather than the 1½" industry standard.
- the trim was non-uniform.

Remember, these problems can occur with any printer, domestic or foreign, but the farther away the printer, the greater the language barrier, and the more disparate the legal system, the harder it will be to solve manufacturing problems. Pay attention to details and *be specific* with either the printer or broker about your requirements and expectations.

There are a number of potential problem areas. If you have typesetting done by a foreign printer, beware of typographical errors; if the person keyboarding the manuscript material is not well-educated and well-versed in English, you can expect to do plenty of meticulous proofreading, which will extend the time involved in this process.

While expensive binding operations (hardcover, case-bound books) are often more inexpensively performed by off-shore printers, there can be problems with warping, glue, or direction of the binding-board grain. Provide samples of the type binding you want and mention potential atmospheric problems for which the printer/binder must compensate.

Paper weights, grades, finishes, and terms differ throughout the world, so again, request paper samples on your printing bid, and ask the printer to send a bound and trimmed dummy of the project with his paper choice. Also, ask the printer to suggest cost-effective trim sizes; it may save you money based on sheet size (page 55 of *A Publisher's Guide* has a chart with the common paper and book trim sizes in inches, with metric equivalents).

Be aware of various printers' busy seasons and national holidays. In Asia, for example, Chinese New Year (early to mid-February) is often celebrated with a two-week closing. Find out when business is slow, because prices and scheduling may be more favorable to you. Always give yourself an extra four weeks for any printing deadline; delays and complications (usually in trans-oceanic shipping) often occur. Also, take into account cultural differences; as one writer put it "Asian printers do not like to say 'no.' 'Yes' in Asia doesn't mean, 'O.K., I'll do it'; it means 'O.K., I think I understand the question.'"

Payment is usually requested in U.S. currency rather than the currency of the place of manufacture. Most off-shore printers require that you provide them with an international letter of credit, which the printer draws on as portions of the job are completed and exchanges at his currency rate.

There are other costs. Off-shore printers are sometimes reluctant to extend credit to publishers with whom they are unfamiliar, and may require payment before shipping, or a third of the printing estimate on contracting, another third when the proofs are approved, and the last third on receipt of books in your warehouse. Once credit is established, an open account arrangement, payable in up to one hundred twenty days, can usually be worked out. If you delay in sending payment, be aware that the printer may attach the shipping documents on the goods sent, effectively prohibiting you from taking possession until the invoice is paid.

Of course, working with the U.S. representative of the printer, or with a broker, can short-circuit some of these difficulties (it can also create other problems).

However you elect to proceed, study this checklist, reprinted from *Printing in Asia:*

1. Make sure you have set yourself a reasonable time frame for overseas production.

2. Send a quotation request to the advertisers you find here that sound appropriate to your needs.

3. Include samples of the quality and format you want produced, including colour, paper and binding, just the way you want them.

4. Propose a specific production timetable which will comfortably fit your marketing schedule. Allow plenty of room for delays on the first job.

5. Consider investing in a Telex machine.

6. Establish your company with a bank that will arrange a Letter of Credit and foreign currency drafts.

7. Find a shipping broker for each port of entry you expect to use.

8. Establish a consignee for shipments to destinations other than your home base. He must watch for arrival of the goods at Customs, co-ordinate with the shipping broker, pay the delivery charges and guarantee safe storage of your books.

9. Arrange to send your artwork via an air courier service convenient to you and get costs projections.

10. When you've selected a print broker, colour-separator or printer, plan a visit to their office or plant to make personal contact. Start with one or two "trial" projects.

11. Send a formal Print Order, separately from the artwork.

12. Keep a production schedule and make copies of all your correspondence. Send everything by registered mail.

13. Make sure your overseas contractor has all your delivery contacts, addresses and telephone numbers. That information should go on each box shipped.

14. Have the printing invoice and Bill of Lading, as well as samples of the job, sent airmail to each consignee as soon as the books are shipped.

15. Advise your shipping broker, your local delivery service, and your warehouse of the anticipated delivery date, as soon as you can.

16. Start hounding the Customs office if the anticipated arrival date passes without notice.

Conclusion

Whether you publish books, periodicals, or catalogues, the manufacturing process, from a legal-business standard, is parallel. Work with printers who are highly recommended. Use appropriate documents to assure that you receive a satisfactory product, and if you do not, that you can recover your full loss. And again, be specific in your needs and expectations.

Reaching Your Customers 15

Marketing is a two-part affair. One is the actual distribution and sale of the work you contracted for and the other is the marketing of subsidiary or associated rights. Books sometimes sell slowly; as Don Marquis (creator of Archie and mehitabel) quipped, releasing a new book is like "dropping a rose-petal down the Grand Canyon and waiting for the echo."

Don't feel discouraged about marketing when you're trying to do everything yourself. There are myriads of methods and services out there to get your house's products into the hands of hungry readers. This chapter concerns itself with sales and distribution, and the next, with rights.

Distribution

A businesslike and legally sound editorial and production effort must be followed by effective marketing and distribution. These two concerns are the two sides of a Chinese fan; to be functional, the fan must remain open. Customers—individual, direct mail, institutions, government, libraries, and schools—and distribution channels—retail stores, alternative or non-traditional outlets, wholesalers, independent distributors, and book clubs—are supported by the fan's ribs: the marketing tools of catalogs, publicity, sales representation, and advertising.

Consider these permutations of selling and distributing:

- publisher produces, then warehouses, fulfills, accounts for on-site.

- publisher produces, warehouses and fulfills from warehouse in a different region (chosen for its low tax, central location, etc.).
- publisher produces, turns over to a distributor—usually a larger publisher (publishers of many sizes of "small" do this—David Godine, for example).

There are advantages and disadvantages to each, depending on the circumstances of your publishing concern. At times publishing's distribution system seems archaic (see *Publishers Weekly,* November 27, 1987), but there *is* an established procedure.

I'm assuming that you have worked your way through this maze at least once. If you haven't (or have not often), research the subject. Also, see the American Bookseller's Association *A Manual on Book Selling: How to Open and Run Your Own Bookstore* (Haumont Books), which looks at the process from the customers' side, and includes chapters on the use of representatives and wholesalers to a bookstore, receiving and returns, and the mechanics of ordering, including STOP orders.

Publishers Marketing Association (PMA), as mentioned before, is a trade association for entrepreneurial book publishers that offers cooperative marketing and promotion through numerous programs. Membership terms vary based on the number of employees, and includes a monthly newsletter (send for a sample).

Since approximately 40,000 new titles are published each year, and since most of them compete for shelf space in the stores belonging to the two or three chains that own more than 2,000 of the bookstores in existence, you'll need to work to get any degree of market share.

Distributors

Distributors may store or warehouse your books, as well as sell them; they often have a sales staff who carry a number of publisher's titles. They ship the books, bill the customer, collect, and send you some of the money, thus allowing you to spend more time on book production. This type of centralization may meet your needs, particularly if you're not in a position to employ the necessary support staff.

Poynter's contracts on diskette include one for book distribution (number 21) to be utilized between a publisher and dealer-distributor-wholesaler in the book trade.* He refers you to the *Self-Publishing Manual* and PMA's publishing fact sheet, "Using Book Distributors." Here's part of Poynter's Book Distribution Agreement (reprinted with permission).

Contract Number Twenty-one
(Use this agreement when contracting with a dealer or distributor or wholesaler in the book trade.)

---

*Remember, his diskettes save an enormous amount of typing time, and can be adapted to meet your legal needs.

Book Distribution Agreement

AGREEMENT made by and between _____ , a company or corporation of the state of _____ with its principal offices at _____ (hereinafter referred to as "Distributor"), its successors and assigns; and _____ , a company or corporation of the state of _____ with its principal offices at _____ (hereinafter referred to as "Publisher"), its successors and assigns;

Concerning work(s) presently titled:

by

by

by

by

(hereinafter referred to as the "Work").

WITNESSETH:

In consideration of the mutual covenants herein contained, the parties agree as follows:

1. *Services*

Distributor agrees to promote and sell the Work offered by Publisher to the accounts and in the territories identified in this agreement. Distributor agrees to maintain an inventory of each of these books, offer them for sale through catalogs, displays, and sales representatives and to use its best efforts to sell each title offered.

Distributor shall not obligate Publisher to any catalog advertising or other promotional expenses without Publisher's authorization in writing.

2. *Territory*

Distributor shall provide representation in the fifty (50) states of the United States.

Distributor shall service the wholesale and retail book trade consisting of hardcover and softcover (trade paper) retail bookstores, chain bookstores and hardcover and softcover wholesale accounts.

3. *Referrals*

The Distributor and the Publisher shall each refer to the other, mutually, referrals for all sales and markets reserved to the other, respectively.

4. *Exclusivity*

This contract is non-exclusive. Publisher may contract with other distributors and wholesalers.

5. *Discount and terms*

Publisher shall provide the books (Work) to Distributor on a consignment basis at a fifty-five percent 55% discount from list (cover) price.

6. *Title*

Publisher shall retain title to the Work until it is sold and shipped by the Distributor, at which time title shifts to the Distributor. However, Distributor shall be responsible for the Work.

7. *Shipping*

Distributor shall order in even-carton increments. Publisher shall ship in uniform cartons with the title and quantity clearly marked on the outside. Publisher shall pay shipping charges to Distributor's warehouse. That is, shipping terms are F.O.B destination.

8. *Reports*

Distributor shall report sales to the Publisher monthly. This report shall record the number of books of each title received from and returned to Publisher, the number shipped to or returned from Distributor's customers, the net price of each book sold and returned, and the net amount due the Publisher for the month. The report shall include the store name and a location identifier such as the city and state and/or zip code. Reports shall be compiled and mailed to Publisher not later than ten (10) days after the end of each month.

On each 31st of December, Distributor shall take an actual physical inventory of Publisher's books (Work) in Distributor's stock and forward that inventory report to Publisher within ten days. If the beginning inventory for the year plus additions to inventory less sales and returns to the Publisher do not equal the December 31 inventory, Distributor agrees to reimburse Publisher at the rate of 15% of list price for any book that cannot be accounted for.

9. *Payment terms*

Distributor shall pay monies due to Publisher on a net ninety (90) day basis from the end of the month in which the books (Work) are sold by Distributor.

10. *Publisher's samples*

Publisher shall provide thirty (30) covers, jackets or complete books and catalogs for sales representative use.

11. *Insurance*

Distributor shall provide broad form fire insurance sufficient to cover the full value of Distributor's inventory of Publisher's books (Work) and identify Publisher as an additional insured with loss payable clause as respects Publisher's interest. Distributor agrees to provide Publisher on Publisher's request a certificate of insurance from Distributor's insurance carrier. This coverage shall be maintained while books are in Distributor's warehouse or under shipment from Distributor.

12. *Returns*

Distributor may return books considered to be "overstock," shelf-worn or defective to the Publisher for credit. Distributor shall pay freight charges on all returns.

13. *Cancellation*

This agreement may be cancelled by either party by giving one hundred-twenty (120) days written notice. This Agreement may be terminated at the option of Publisher within ten (10) days after any one of the following acts or omissions occur:

A. Failure of Distributor to submit to Publisher any report required by this agreement within thirty (30) days of the date due.

B. Failure of Distributor to make any payment due Publisher within thirty (30) days of the date due.

C. The filing by or against Distributor of any petition or motion under the Bankruptcy Act.

14. *Termination*

Upon termination of this agreement, Distributor agrees to make available to Publisher all of Publisher's books (Work) then held in Distributor's inventory. If Publisher does not remove all books in inventory from Distributor's premises within thirty (30) days of termination, Distributor agrees to ship to Publisher all of Publisher's books then held in inventory.

15. *Audit*

The Publisher or his or her duly authorized representative (for example, an accountant) shall have the right upon written request to examine the books of account of the Distributor insofar as they relate to the Work; such examination shall be at the cost of the Publisher unless errors of accounting amounting to five percent (5%) or more of the total sum paid to the Publisher shall be found to Publisher's disadvantage in which case the costs shall be borne by the Distributor.

16. *Arbitration*

If any difference shall arise between the Distributor and the Publisher touching the meaning of this Agreement or the rights and liabilities of the parties thereto, the same shall be referred to the arbitration of two persons (one to be named by each party) or their mutually agreed umpire, in accordance with the Rules of the American Arbitration Association; judgment on the award rendered may be entered in any court having jurisdiction thereof.

17. *Modification or waiver*

This agreement represents the entire contract made by the parties. Its terms cannot be modified except by a written document signed by the parties. A waiver of any breach of any form will not be construed as a continuing waiver of other breaches of the same or other provisions of the contract. If any part of this agreement is held to be illegal, void or unenforceable, this shall not affect the validity of any other part of this contract.

18. *Interpretation*

This Agreement shall be governed by and interpreted in all respects in accordance with the Laws of the United States of America, state of: _____. This contract is executed in, and any disputes shall be decided in, the state and county where the Publisher is located.

19. *Disputes-attorneys' fees*

In any action upon this agreement, including litigation and arbitration, the party which prevails will have all attorneys' fees and costs paid by the losing party.

IN WITNESS WHEREOF the parties hereto have executed and duly

witnessed this Agreement as of the day and year written below.

Poynter's comments:

Book publishers usually encounter three types of accounts:

1. Bookstores, which order a single copy or very few copies of a title. Some orders are Single Title Order Plan or "STOP" orders, and are accompanied by a check. Some of these bookstore shipments must be billed.

2. Wholesaler and distributors, which order selected titles in large numbers for distribution to retail accounts in the book trade such as bookstores and libraries.

3. Wholesalers and retailers outside the book trade, who order in larger amounts for sale to their customers. An example might be a speaker who talks on aviation subjects and sells aviation books in the back of the room. Another example might be a catalog that carries a few selected, relative books. Publishers have labeled these sales "Special Sales."

For more information on book wholesalers and distributors, see The Self-Publishing Manual and the Publishing Fact Sheet entitled "Using Book Distributors" issued by the Publisher's Marketing Association and drafted by publisher/attorney Gary Moselle.

The *services* you want the distributor to provide will determine the conditions and costs of the arrangement. For some types of titles, one distributor may be better than others. A non-exclusive arrangement leaves you free to deal with other distributors and wholesalers. Certainly consider limiting the territory to the United States, and be sure to have a clear idea of the type of sales and markets you wish to reserve for yourself.

The *limitations of publisher's promotional expenses* in the distributor's catalog benefits the publishers, although you could agree on an amount beforehand, provided you approve in writing and in advance any advertising or promotion of your books. One of your authors may be a recluse and you don't want a distributor violating any of your author-contract provisions. Any covers, text, or graphics reproduced should include an appropriate copyright notice.

The provision on *referrals* represents common business etiquette. The passing of *title* ties into numerous legal matters, such as risk of loss from theft or fire. The provision on *shipping* is designed to regularize records, plus assure that the goods arrive in saleable condition; the paperwork involved in uneven shipments or damaged goods represents lost time and expense for both parties.

There are two immediate problems with the *report* clause. First, there is no provision through which the publisher may check the distributor's inventory. Second, the fifteen-percent compensation seems too low for unaccounted-for units if production costs were high.

The *payment terms* are simple, and are ninety days, not thirty days, to address the distributor's problem of delayed payment terms given to its customers as well as returns, which can equal the amount billed out. Some contracts opt for payments to be due over a several-month period, with different percentages, starting one month after the billings for the books, i.e., fifteen percent one month, twenty-five percent two months, fifty percent three months (figuring most have been returned) and the fourth month, ten percent of the monies due from sales.

Some other variables to consider:

- an outright purchase by distributor.
- some distributors may print from camera-ready copy or film negatives and treat that cost as an advance to the Publisher.
- a license to the distributor of certain subsidiary rights.

I feel a little uncomfortable about *insurance* when the provision does not require the insurance company to notify all insured parties of a lapse in coverage. If the obligated party gets itself in financial straits, it probably won't notify you, the publisher, of its insurance problems on its own.

The *cancellation* provision favors the publisher by reducing the times require for the publisher to get out of the agreement, should any of the three circumstances cited occur. Once a bankruptcy petition (sub-item c) has been filed, however, and the title passes to the distributor on sale and shipment, you've probably lost the stock.

The *termination* clause does not indicate who pays freight charges on returns generated by cancellation, and the time period indicated is too long. I wouldn't leave my property in someone's possession for thirty days if I'd just ended my relationship with them. Shorten the time for publisher removal, and require the distributor to immediately return the books at distributor's freight expense. If the publisher picks up the books, the distributor should still pay the normal freight charges. Consider including a provision that specifies that if the returns are shipped C.O.D., publisher's acceptance of same does not operate as a waiver of the publisher's claim for freight. In an extreme situation, get the books back and niggle about the freight later.

The *returns* provision does not address a distributor's reserve for books returned by the bookstore.

The *audit* clause may not be acceptable to the distributor as written. The distributor might propose changes in the number of days notice, a higher percent of variation, and/or a limit on accountant costs. From your perspective, it is in your interest to keep those numbers low. Don't agree to a thirty-day notice; a company could put together a whole new set of books in thirty days. Don't agree to less than half of the audit expense or more than three percent error. Add the requirement for at least one, preferably two, more annual audits by you. State that payments are due from distributor in ten days, so that you can cancel under paragraph 13B, which states that a payment is considered delinquent according to its due date.

Note: Remember, as I make these comments, another lawyer could look at one of my contracts and improve it.

Arbitration may or may not be to your advantage, but this is a philosophical-business judgment to be reached by you *before* you get to a distribution contract.

You might add that you can assign the contract but the distributor cannot; if you sell your publishing house, the buyer might want assurance it is also buying a distribution contract that is favorable, instead of none at all. Although the distributor may not want your obligations assigned to a third party, the considerations from your end are more important, because the distributor is in possession of your books and receives money in your behalf. Additionally, most small publishers service direct-mail sales to individual customers themselves, and want to reserve special sales to book clubs, groups, premiums, and remainders.

Of course, all the old adages of the respective bargaining positions of the parties apply here. Some distributors may insist that you execute their standard contract. You're going to accuse me of sounding like a Dutch uncle, but their standard contract's the worst deal for you.

If a publisher insists on a short term for the contract, there may be problems; since the distributor's salespeople are selling new products, the distributor may not settle for less than a three-year term. Your distributor may also want a warranty-indemnification clause.

The publisher may want the distributor to include its promotional mailers with the distributor's but the publisher may have to pay these costs, unless the cost is included in the distributor's package.

Inventory shortage and returns are covered more completely in Lindey's Publisher-Distributor Contract Form 43-1. On returns, the contract requires the publisher to pay five percent of the credit given to the bookstore to cover administrative and shipping costs.

The distributor may insist that you follow its credit terms and policies, since the distributor also, in effect, operates as a collection agency. Of course, if your pricing and discount schedules vary from the distributor's *and* you require the distributor to use yours, you will have to pay for that extra accounting expense. The risk of collection rests squarely on the distributor's shoulders, and if payments aren't collected on the books shipped and billed, the distributor theoretically still pays the publisher.

This outline summarizes and contrasts the alternatives available in certain situations.

Outline of Distribution Agreements
- Appointment of Distributor
  - exclusive or non-exclusive
  - territories
- Type of arrangement
  - agency
  - buy/sell
  - sale of Publisher's titles at Distributor's discounts
  - distributor prints from camera-ready copy or film negatives and

charges cost as advance.
- consultation between parties regarding print quantities
- Delivery of books
  - publisher delivers books to Distributor
- Distributor's distribution services may include some or all of the following:
  - selling
  - billing
  - warehousing
  - collecting
  - advertising/promotion/publicity
- Distributor's sales efforts for Publisher's work
- Publisher's grant to Distributor of right to license – rare
  - book clubs
  - periodical rights
  - foreign rights
- Accountings
  - quarterly or semi-annual
  - distribution fee to cover overhead and selling costs
    - a percentage of gross or net billings
    - a percentage of return credits, sometimes included in the fee
  - Distributor's right to maintain reserve for returns
    - reasonable reserve or ceiling on reserve as percentage of either cumulative or current accounting period's gross billings
    - period within which reserve must be liquidated and/or a new reserve established
- Deductions by Distributor from gross billings
  - credits for actual returns
  - reserve for returns
  - distribution fee
  - freight costs
  - manufacturing costs if advanced by Distributor
- Negative net proceeds
  - publisher repays Distributor
  - distributor may carry forward against future positive net proceeds
- Publisher's right to audit the distributor's books of account
- Publisher's warranties and indemnities
- Termination procedures
  - publisher's obligations to remove inventory and administer returns
  - distributor's right to dispose of or destroy inventory if Publisher fails to make timely removal thereof

Changing Distributors
This notice appeared in *Publishers Weekly* (October 7, 1988).

You should notify the trade the best way you can about a distributor change, otherwise you run the risk of alienating booksellers. Obviously, *Publishers Weekly* is an appropriate trade organ to effectuate any legal public notice; still, the publisher would want to notify the major booksellers in writing as well.

Publishers Weekly (September 23, 1988) reported that volume discounter Dan Mendenhall closed twenty Giant Book Warehouses after a $5 million loss; $600,000 was owed to Warner Books, although he paid other creditors, including newspapers with advertising accounts, fifty cents on the dollar. At the same time, he was involved in a multi-million dollar anti-trust suit against Random House, Southeast Booksellers Association, and a Nashville bookstore.

In another case, retailers and distributors were stripping mass-market paperbacks of their covers, collecting on returns, and then reselling the coverless books; a six-year legal battle ensued between them and the Association of American Publishers (AAP). AAP ended its litigation successfully; the defendants agreed to stop the sales, inform AAP of others who were doing this, and pay a fine if the agreement was violated.

Fulfillment

Book-fulfillment services store and ship books—but only for orders you solicit.

Order fulfillment, and its various components, can be contracted out. These services normally include:

- warehousing fee.
- order processing.
- shipping.
- inventorying.

Others may add these services:

- invoicing non-prepaying customers.
- maintaining a bank account in your name for deposit of payments.

- dunning delinquent accounts.
- providing mailing labels.
- providing a monthly accounting, using a computer printout that shows:
  - monthly receipts.
  - storage costs.
  - freight charges.
  - orders processed.
  - customer list.
  - aging accounts list.

A subscription-fulfillment-service-for-publications form contract appears on page 139 of PLI's 1979 *Magazine Industry*.

Sales Representatives

Some factors to consider in any sales representative agreements:

- affirmation of independent contractor status.
- exclusion or inclusion of ledger business.
- competitive titles from other companies.
- geographic area.
- term.
- termination.
- percentage rate of commission and cycle of payment.
- notification of customer service problems.
- publisher-provided material.
  - sales materials.
  - catalogs and order forms.
  - discount schedules.
  - list of what is handled by a distributor.

One way to do business is to organize another structure for part of the process. For instance, Graywolf Press, Lapis Press, and McPherson & Company combined to form Consortium Booksales and Distributors. The three share a common warehouse, discount schedule, order form, billing, fulfillment, and sales representative system. Each publisher, however, is responsible for acquisition, production, printing, and its own catalogue. See Pat Sabiston's articles in *Small Press* (1986 issues) on sales representatives.

Newspaper, Magazine, and Periodical Distribution

If your publishing enterprise requires newsstand distribution, often called single-copy distribution, I refer you to *Legal & Business Aspects of the Magazine Industry 1984* (Practising Law Institute) for sample distribution contracts. A periodical distribution cycle breaks down into subscription sales (either home-delivered as with newspapers, or mail-delivered directly from the publishers) and single copy sales, which can also go to the customer directly from the publisher, with one intervening stop, the retailer. For instance, *Woman's Day* goes from the printing plant to the supermarket to the end consumer. The most common steps for single copy sales, other than the above, is:

publisher → national distributor → wholesalers → retailer → customer.

There's a plague of litigation in the single-copy distribution field, and if your wholesaler goes defunct, that financial failure could make or break your company.

The services of distributors in this field parallel that of books: sales, freighting, promotion, and financial/accounting. The same areas need to be covered, such as exclusive/non-exclusive, returns, and term; the publisher's delivery dates become critical, as most of these pieces have a very finite life on the newsstand.

Subscription

In periodical publication, even if you publish a newsletter, certain distribution and subscription decisions need to be made as part of the organizational structure.

Subscription periodicals are a big part of the average literate person's reading life. In the last few weeks, I've received the following magazines, journals, and newsletters that are technically free, but really come to me as part of my various membership benefits:

- *The Arizona Bar Journal,* a slick paper multi-page monthly magazine with articles and ads of interest to Arizona lawyers.
- The *Columbia-VLA Art and the Law Journal,* published quarterly in a paperbound journal format with a spine.
- The *Arizona History Journal* and the *Ethnohistory Journal,* also perfect-bound softcover journals.
- Newsletters from the Museum of Northern Arizona, the Arizona Historical Society, Southwest Parks and Monuments (annual report), Grand Canyon Natural History Association, PMA newsletter, COSMEP's newsletter, Griffen's Signature, Native American Rights Fund newsletter, Arizona Wildlife Federation newsletter, as well as others.
- Catalogues from Spiegels, REI, L.L. Bean; and catalogues for kitchenware; cheese; fruit; music; books; toys; household products; and what I call "I wonder why" catalogues—the products you wonder why someone didn't invent sooner, such as small traction skids to attach to smooth-soled shoes.

I also subscribe to numerous magazines and periodicals:

- newspapers—the *Arizona Republic* (Phoenix), the *Arizona Daily Sun* (Flagstaff), the *Nava-Hopi Observer* (for the Navajo-Hopi Indian reservations) and the *Navajo Times* (Window Rock).
- magazines—*Small Press, Publishers Weekly, Arizona Highways, Ms, Newsweek, The Writer, Sunset Magazine,* and so forth.

As this specific listing indicates, the consumer subscribes directly with the publisher, or in a looser sense, to the principles of the organization. In the latter instance, one gives financial support and receives an update on activities. The only "free" publications I pick up are Northern Arizona University's newspaper (Flagstaff) and *New Times* (metropolitan Phoenix), which lists and describes events and happenings in Arizona. All of these periodicals and publications have legal-business factors in common.

Subscription Prices

Subscription prices—the amounts of and rationale for—vary as much as the glazes used by a potter:

- discount over a year's newsstand prices.
- further discounts for multi-year subscriptions.
- higher prices for out-of-county, out-of-state, out-of-country because of additional mailing costs.
- multiple gift subscriptions.
- nine-month subscriptions for students.
- discounts for the elderly or members of a specific organization.

The decision on subscription price depends on the market price minus (or plus) cost savings through guaranteed sales, plus the advertising revenues.

Mail Order

If your periodical isn't sold as single copies delivered by hand to homes and bookstores, but rather, is delivered through the mail, you will be concerned with the United States Postal Service (and other transportation services), plus the regulations of the Federal Trade Commission that apply to subscriptions. Among these are the Magnuson-Moss Act and FTC regulations (15 U.S.C. Sec. 2301(1)) "consumer products" which include reference to:

- tangible personal property.
- items distributed in commerce.
- items normally used for personal, family, or household purposes.

Remember, ambiguities are always resolved in favor of compliance.

USPS regulations and charges change as fast as a chameleon's coat so I suggest you order federal publications relative to the operation of a mail-order subscription business (contact the Superintendent of Documents, U.S. Government Printing Office, Washington D.C. 20402). These publications range from the simple *Domestic Mail Manual* (mail class descriptions) and *Postal Operator's Manual* (customer services, delivery, and transportation) to the complex weekly *Postal Bulletin*, which previews changes. Each has a hefty price tag but includes periodic updates. Another publication of interest is *International Mail*. A free monthly newsletter for mail operations, *Memo to Mailers* (P.O. Box 1, Linwood, New Jersey 08201) is also available to assist users in keeping up with this area.

In order to most efficiently use the USPS as your distributor, a staff member must become knowledgable about mailing rates, procedures for regular and promotional mailings, and when first, second, or third class rates apply.

First-class mail is the most expensive, but if undeliverable, it is returned to you or forwarded at no extra charge. Most commercial magazines and newspapers, however, are mailed second-class. For instance, my recent issue of *Publishers Weekly* came via second-class mail. Eligibility for second-class mail privileges depends on the type of product; a paid-for publication, pre-sorting, and certain advertising restrictions qualify. Third-class rates include the bulk-mail category. First class is, of course, the fastest method. Second-class rates favor small, local publications, but costs vary with the distance to be covered. Third class is probably the slowest way to send things. Promotional mail is usually sent third-class, "bulk mail." A fourth-class book-post rate also exists and the rate is different depending upon the sender's status: for-profit or non-profit; a permit is required to utilize either.

Publishers often use mailing houses for promotional mailings. Contract for this so that you get the services you need without the hassle of filling out appropriate postal forms.

You might also consider business reply permits. Study the fees for those to see which deal is best for you. As with all other government functions, certain mailings or services are heavily regulated. For instance, "business reply cards" must be a certain size, or a penalty is attached to each piece; this could be hefty for a massive mailing.

The Domestic Mail Manual (Section 123.4) governs solicitations, which include renewal invoices. Be sure to check current regulations on forwarding of mail, how long address changes last, and combining post office boxes and street addresses in one address.

Postal regulations also govern:

- qualifications for fourth-class mail.
- any special rates for catalogues meeting certain specifications.
- merchandise packaging.
- special handling fees.
- book-rate conditions.
- registered mail.
- insuring mail.
- C.O.D. requirements.

Since using the postal service is necessary in subscription service, you don't want to run afoul of the postal regulations. As Mae West said: "It ain't no sin if you crack a few laws now and then, just so long as you don't break any."

Here's a reproduction of the Postal Service bibliography and prices. This should give an idea of what's available and relative costs.

UNITED STATES GOVERNMENT PRINTING OFFICE
SUPERINTENDENT OF DOCUMENTS
WASHINGTON, D.C. 20402

SUBJECT BIBLIOGRAPHY (SB)

SB-169
FEBRUARY 26, 1988

NOTICE

Prices shown were in effect on the above date. Government documents' prices are subject to change without prior notice. Therefore, prices in effect when your order is filled may differ from prices on this list. Since it is not feasible to change prices shown in Government documents in print, the price printed in a document may differ from the price in effect when your order is processed.

POSTAL SERVICE

Administrative Support Manual *Subscription service consists of a basic manual and supplementary material for an indeterminate period. Describes matters of internal administration in the Postal Service. It includes functional statements as well as policies and requirements regarding security, communications (printing, directives, forms, records, newsletters), government relations, procurement and supply, data processing systems, maintenance, and engineering. Subscription price: Domestic - $22.00; Foreign - $27.50. (ADSM) (File Code 1P)*
P 1.12/10:

S/N 939-001-00000-0

Code of Federal Regulations, Title 39, Postal Service, Revised July 1, 1987 1987: 466 p.
AE 2.106/3:39/987

S/N 869-001-00127-5 $13.00

Microfiche of the above 1987:
AE 2.106/3:39/987 MF

S/N 869-002-00127-1 $3.75

Domestic Mail Manual *(Irregularly.) Subscription service includes four cumulative issues a year. Designed to assist customers in obtaining maximum benefits from domestic postal services. It includes applicable regulations and information about rates and postage, classes of mail, special services, wrapping and mailing requirements, and collection and delivery services. Subscription price: Domestic - $17.00; Foreign - $21.25. (PDMM) (File Code 2S)*
P 1.12/11:

S/N 839-001-00000-2

Employee and Labor Relations Manual *1984, Consolidated reprint. Subscription service consists of a basic manual and updated transmittal letters for an indeterminate period. In looseleaf form, punched for 3-ring binder. This manual sets forth the personnel policies and regulations governing employment with the Postal Service. Topics covered include organization management, job evaluation, employment and placement, pay administration, employee benefits, employee relations, training, safety and health, and labor relations. Subscription price: Domestic - $29.00; Foreign - $36.25. (ELRM) (File Code 1P)*
P 1.12/7:

S/N 939-003-00000-2

Financial Management Manual *1987, Consolidated reprint. Subscription service consists of a basic manual and supplementary material for an indeterminate period. This manual presents an overview of the financial activities of the Postal Service. It summarizes the following topics: general accounting, post office accounting, accounts receivable and accounts payable, budget and planning, payroll accounting and control of assets. Subscription price: Domestic - $27.00; Foreign - $33.75. (FML) (File Code 1P)*
P 1.12/9:

S/N 939-004-00000-9

International Mail Manual *(Irregularly.) Subscription service includes three cumulative issues. Subscription price: Domestic - $14.00; Foreign - $17.50. (PINTM) (File Code 2S)*
P 1.10/5:

S/N 839-002-00000-9

Misleading and Deceptive Mailings to Social Security Beneficiaries, Hearing Before the Subcommittee on Social Security of the Committee on Ways and Means, House, 100th Congress, 1st Session, March 10, 1987 1987: 501 p.; ill.
Y 4.W 36:100-2

S/N 052-070-06346-7 $14.00

National Five-Digit ZIP Code and Post Office Directory, 1988 *Contains complete information relating to the five digit ZIP Code System and information on United States Postal Service facilities and organizations.* 1988: 2460 p.

S/N 039-000-00274-4 $13.00

Postal Bulletin *(Weekly.) Contains current orders, instructions and information relating to the United States Postal Service, and Commemorative Stamp Posters, formerly sold as a separate subscription. Subscription price: Domestic - $64.00 a year; Foreign - $80.00 a year. Single copy price: Domestic - $1.25 a copy; Foreign - $1.56 a copy. (POB) (File Code 2E)*
P 1.3:

S/N 739-001-00000-5

Postal Life, The Magazine for Postal Employees *(Quarterly.) This periodical contains articles, with illustrations, about new methods, techniques, and programs of the United States Postal Service. Its purpose is to keep postal employees informed and abreast of developments in the United States Postal Service. Subscription price: Domestic - $5.50 a year; Foreign - $6.90 a year. Single copy price: Domestic - $1.75 a copy; Foreign - $2.19 a copy. (POLI) (File Code 2N)* P 1.43:	S/N 739-002-00000-1	
Postal Operations Manual *Subscription service consists of a basic manual and updated transmittal letters for an indeterminate period. In looseleaf form, punched for 3-ring binder. This manual sets forth policies for the internal operations of post offices. It includes retail services, mail processing, transportation, delivery services, and fleet management. Subscription price: Domestic - $37.00; Foreign - $46.25. (PORM) (File Code 1P)* P 1.12/8:	S/N 939-007-00000-8	
Title 39, United States Code, United States Postal Service, April 15, 1987 *Includes amendments through end of 99th Congress.* 1987: 105 p. Y 4.P 84/10:Un 3/5/987	S/N 052-070-06310-6	$3.00
Title 39, United States Code, United States Postal Service, Public Law 100-90 *An Act to Amend Title 39, United States Code, to Extend to Certain Officers and Employers of the United States Postal Service the Same Procedural and Appeal Rights With Respect to Certain Adverse Personnel Actions as are Afforded Under Title 5, United States Code, to Federal Employees in the Competitive Service. Approved August 19, 1987.* 1987: 1 p. AE 2.110:100-90	S/N 869-003-00090-5	$1.00
United States Code, 1982 Edition, Containing the General and Permanent Laws of the United States, in Force on January 14, 1983, Volume 14, Title 36, Patriotic Societies and Observances, to Title 41, Public Contracts *Includes Title 39, Postal Service.* 1984: 1138 p. Clothbound Y 1.2/5:982/v.14	S/N 052-001-00221-1	$30.00
United States Postage Stamps: An Illustrated Description of All United States Postage Stamps and Special Service Stamps *This official United States Postal Service guidebook and its supplements offer an illustrated description of all United States postage and special service stamps issued from July 1, 1847 through 1982. Tables containing detailed statistics on postage stamps issued from 1933 to the present are appendixed. Transmittals are looseleaf.*		
Transmittal Letter Number 1 *Gives information on all United States postage stamps from July 1, 1847 to June 30, 1970.* 1970: 287 p.; ill. P 4.10:970/trans.1	S/N 039-000-00224-8	$8.50
Transmittal Letter Number 2 *Gives information on all United States postage stamps from July 1970 to February 1972.* 1973: 52 p.; ill. P 4.10:970/trans.2	S/N 039-000-00243-4	$5.00
Transmittal Letter Number 3 *Gives information on all United States postage stamps from February 1972 to December 1973.* 1974: 62 p.; ill. - P 4.10:970/trans.3	S/N 039-000-00251-5	$5.00
Transmittal Letter Number 4 *Gives information on all United States postage stamps issued during 1974.* 1975: 42 p.; ill. P 4.10:970/trans.4	S/N 039-000-00255-8	$4.75
Transmittal Letter Number 5 *Gives information on all United States postage stamps issued during 1975.* 1976: 34 p.; ill. P 4.10:970/trans.5	S/N 039-000-00256-6	$4.75
Transmittal Letter Number 6 *Gives information on all United States postage stamps issued during 1976 and 1977.* 1979: 40 p.; ill. P 4.10:970/trans.6	S/N 039-000-00262-1	$4.75
Transmittal Letter Number 7 *Gives information on United States postage stamps issued during 1978, 1979, and 1980.* 1981: 53 p.; ill. P 4.10:970/trans.7	S/N 039-000-00266-3	$4.00
Transmittal Letter Number 8 *Includes minor revisions to material submitted under previous transmittal letters and new material for stamps issued during 1981 and 1982.* 1985: 58 p. P 4.10:970/trans.8	S/N 039-000-00271-0	$3.25
Set of the above, Transmittal Letters, Numbers 1 Through 8 1974-1985: 664 p.; ill. looseleaf.	S/N 639-000-00267-5	$24.00
United States Postal Service Procurement Manual *1987. (Formerly Postal Contracting Manual.) Subscription service consists of a basic manual and supplementary material for an indeterminate period. In looseleaf form, punched for 3-ring binder. This manual establishes uniform policies and procedures relating to procuring facilities, equipment, supplies and services under the authority of Chapter 4, Title 39, of the United States Code, and mail transportation services by contract under Part 5, Title 39, United States Code. Subscription price: Domestic - $103.00; Foreign - $128.75. (POCM) (File Code 1P)* P 1.12/6:	S/N 939-006-00000-1	

Federal Trade Commission

Likewise, you want to steer clear of Federal Trade Commission problems. The Federal Trade Commission Act declares unlawful certain unfair or deceptive acts or practices (15 U.S.C. Section 45(a)(1)). The activities prohibited under this section are various, including:

- falsely representing products as prepared to government specifications.
- making use of another's registered tradename and giving products misleading names.
- falsely or misleadingly using the word "free" in advertising.

The 30-day Rule

Delayed delivery is a critical issue under the Federal Trade Commission regulations. In 1975, the Federal Trade Commission promulgated a rule, commonly called the "30-Day Rule," that tells the mail marketer what it must do when it cannot properly fill an order. Stated another way, unless a publisher reasonably believes that the first copy of a subscription will be sent within thirty days of receipt of an order, the promotional material must state the time within which the subscriber can expect the first copy. If there is no disclaimer, you have to send the copy in thirty days. There's a heavy penalty for each infraction of the rule.

Various organizations, such as the Direct Marketing Association, have put together packets of information regarding the rule. These packets include text, summaries, articles, and memos on the subject.

So that you can get an idea of the complexity of this area, the Code of Federal Regulations for mail order is reproduced below:

---

§ 435.1

PART 435—MAIL ORDER MERCHANDISE

Sec.
435.1   The Rule.
435.2   Definitions.

§ 435.1   The Rule.

In connection with mail order sales in commerce, as "commerce" is defined in the Federal Trade Commission Act, it constitutes an unfair method of competition, and an unfair or deceptive act and practice for a seller:

(a)(1) To solicit any order for the sale of merchandise to be ordered by the buyer through the mails unless, at the time of the solicitation, the seller has a reasonable basis to expect that he will be able to ship any ordered merchandise to the buyer: (i) Within that time clearly and conspicuously stated in any such solicitation, or (ii) if no time is clearly and conspicuously stated, within thirty (30) days after receipt of a properly completed order from the buyer.

(2) To provide any buyer with any revised shipping date, as provided in paragraph (b) of this section, unless, at the time any such revised shipping date is provided, the seller has a reasonable basis for making such representation regarding a definite revised shipping date.

(3) To inform any buyer that he is unable to make any representation regarding the length of any delay unless (i) the seller has a reasonable basis for so informing the buyer and (ii) the seller informs the buyer of the reason or reasons for the delay.

(4) In any action brought by the Federal Trade Commission, alleging a violation of this part, the failure of a respondent-seller to have records or other documentary proof establishing his use of systems and procedures which assure the shipment of merchandise in the ordinary course of business within any applicable time set forth in this part will create a rebuttable presumption that the seller lacked a reasonable basis for any expectation of shipment within said applicable time.

(b)(1) Where a seller is unable to ship merchandise within the applicable time set forth in paragraph (a)(1) of this section, to fail to offer to the buyer, clearly and conspicuously and without prior demand, an option either to consent to a delay in shipping or to cancel his order and receive a prompt refund. Said offer shall be made within a reasonable time after the seller first becomes aware of his inability to ship within the applicable time set forth in paragraph (a)(1) of this section, but in no event later than said applicable time.

(i) Any offer to the buyer of such an option shall fully inform the buyer regarding his right to cancel the order and to obtain a prompt refund and shall provide a definite revised shipping date, but where the seller lacks a reasonable basis for providing a definite revised shipping date the notice shall inform the buyer that the seller is unable to make any representation regarding the length of the delay.

(ii) Where the seller has provided a definite revised shipping date which is thirty (30) days or less later than the applicable time set forth in paragraph (a)(1) of this section, the offer of said option shall expressly inform the buyer that, unless the seller receives, prior to shipment and prior to the expiration of the definite revised shipping date, a response from the buyer rejecting the delay and cancelling the order, the buyer will be deemed to have consented to a delayed shipment on or before the definite revised shipping date.

(iii) Where the seller has provided a definite revised shipping date which is more than thirty (30) days later than the applicable time set forth in paragraph (a)(1) of this section or where the seller is unable to provide a definite revised shipping date and therefore informs the buyer that he is unable to make any representation regarding the length of the delay, the offer of said option shall also expressly inform the buyer that his order will automatically be deemed to have been cancelled unless (A) the seller has shipped the merchandise within thirty (30) days of the applicable time set forth in paragraph (a)(1) of this section, and has received no cancellation prior to shipment, or (B) the seller has received from the buyer within thirty (30) days of said applicable time, a response specifically consenting to said shipping delay. Where the seller informs the buyer that he is unable to make any representation regarding the length of the delay, the buyer shall be expressly informed that, should he consent to an indefinite

delay, he will have a continuing right to cancel his order at any time after the applicable time set forth in paragraph (a)(1) of this section by so notifying the seller prior to actual shipment.

(iv) Nothing in this paragraph shall prohibit a seller who furnishes a definite revised shipping date pursuant to paragraph (b)(1)(i) of this section, from requesting, simultaneously with or at any time subsequent to the offer of an option pursuant to paragraph (b)(1) of this section, the buyer's express consent to a further unanticipated delay beyond the definite revised shipping date in the form of a response from the buyer specifically consenting to said further delay. *Provided, however,* That where the seller solicits consent to an unanticipated indefinite delay the solicitation shall expressly inform the buyer that, should he so consent to an indefinite delay, he shall have a continuing right to cancel his order at any time after the definite revised shipping date by so notifying the seller prior to actual shipment.

(2) Where a seller is unable to ship merchandise on or before the definite revised shipping date provided under paragraph (b)(1)(i) of this section and consented to by the buyer pursuant to paragraph (b)(1)(ii) or (iii) of this section, to fail to offer to the buyer, clearly and conspicuously and without prior demand, a renewed option either to consent to a further delay or to cancel the order and to receive a prompt refund. Said offer shall be made within a reasonable time after the seller first becomes aware of his inability to ship before the said definite revised date, but in no event later than the expiration of the definite revised shipping date:

Provided, however, That where the seller previously has obtained the buyer's express consent to an unanticipated delay until a specific date beyond the definite revised shipping date, pursuant to paragraph (b)(1)(iv) of this section or to a further delay until a specific date beyond the definite revised shipping date pursuant to paragraph (b)(2) of this section, that date to which the buyer has expressly consented shall supersede the definite revised shipping date for purposes of paragraph (b)(2) of this section.

(i) Any offer to the buyer of said renewed option shall provide the buyer with a new definite revised shipping date, but where the seller lacks a reasonable basis for providing a new definite revised shipping date, the notice shall inform the buyer that the seller is unable to make any representation regarding the length of the further delay.

(ii) The offer of a renewed option shall expressly inform the buyer that, unless the seller receives, prior to the expiration of the old definite revised shipping date or any date superseding the old definite revised shipping date, notification from the buyer specifically consenting to the further delay, the buyer will be deemed to have rejected any further delay, and to have cancelled the order if the seller is in fact unable to ship prior to the expiration of the old definite revised shipping date or any date superseding the old definite revised shipping date: *Provided, however,* That where the seller offers the buyer the option to consent to an indefinite delay the offer shall expressly inform the buyer that, should he so consent to an indefinite delay, he shall have a continuing right to cancel his order at any time after the old definite revised shipping date or any date superseding the old definite revised shipping date.

(iii) Paragraph (b)(2) of this section shall not apply to any situation where a seller, pursuant to the provisions of paragraph (b)(1)(iv) of this section, has previously obtained consent from the buyer to an indefinite extension beyond the first revised shipping date.

(3) Wherever a buyer has the right to exercise any option under this part or to cancel an order by so notifying the seller prior to shipment, to fail to furnish the buyer with adequate means, at the seller's expense, to exercise such option or to notify the seller regarding cancellation. In any action brought by the Federal Trade Commission alleging a violation of this part, the failure of a respondent-seller:

(i) To provide any offer, notice or option required by this part in writing and by first class mail will create a rebuttable presumption that the respondent-seller failed to offer a clear and conspicuous offer, notice or option;

(ii) To provide the buyer with the means in writing (by business reply mail or with postage prepaid by the seller) to exercise any option or to notify the seller regarding a decision to cancel, will create a rebuttable presumption that the respondent-seller did not provide the buyer with adequate means pursuant to paragraph (b)(3) of this section.

Nothing in paragraph (b) of this section shall prevent a seller, where he is unable to make shipment within the time set forth in paragraph (a)(1) of this section or within a delay period consented to by the buyer, from deciding to consider the order cancelled and providing the buyer with notice of said decision within a reasonable time after he becomes aware of said inability to ship, together with a prompt refund.

(c) To fail to deem an order cancelled and to make a prompt refund to the buyer whenever:

(1) The seller receives, prior to the time of shipment, notification from the buyer cancelling the order pursuant to any option, renewed option or continuing option under this part;

(2) The seller has, pursuant to paragraph (b)(1)(iii) of this section, provided the buyer with a definite revised shipping date which is more than thirty (30) days later than the applicable time set forth in paragraph (a)(1) of this section or has notified the buyer that he is unable to make any representation regarding the length of the delay and the seller (i) has not shipped the merchandise within thirty (30) days of the applicable time set forth in paragraph (a) (1) of this section, and (ii) has not received the buyer's express consent to said shipping delay within said thirty (30) days;

§ 435.2

(3) The seller is unable to ship within the applicable time set forth in paragraph (b)(2) of this section, and has not received, within the said applicable time, the buyer's consent to any further delay;

(4) The seller has notified the buyer of his inability to make shipment and has indicated his decision not to ship the merchandise;

(5) The seller fails to offer the option prescribed in paragraph (b)(1) of this section and has not shipped the merchandise within the applicable time set forth in paragraph (a)(1) of this section.

(d) In any action brought by the Federal Trade Commission, alleging a violation of this part, the failure of a respondent-seller to have records or other documentary proof establishing his use of systems and procedures which assure compliance, in the ordinary course of business, with any requirement of paragraph (b) or (c) of this section will create a rebuttable presumption that the seller failed to comply with said requirements.

NOTE 1: This part shall not apply to subscriptions, such as magazine sales, ordered for serial delivery, after the initial shipment is made in compliance with this part.

NOTE 2: This part shall not apply to orders of seeds and growing plants.

NOTE 3: This part shall not apply to orders made on a collect-on-delivery (C.O.D.) basis.

NOTE 4: This part shall not apply to transactions governed by the Federal Trade Commission's Trade Regulation Rule entitled "Use of Negative Option Plans by Sellers in Commerce", 16 CFR Part 425.

NOTE 5: By taking action in this area, the Federal Trade Commission does not intend to preempt action in the same area, which is not inconsistent with this part, by any State, municipal, or other local government. This part does not annul or diminish any rights or remedies provided to consumers by any State law, municipal ordinance, or other local regulation, insofar as those rights or remedies are equal to or greater than those provided by this part. In addition, this part does not supersede those provisions of any State law, municipal ordinance, or other local regulation which impose obligations or liabilities upon sellers, when sellers subject to this part are not in compliance therewith. This part does supersede those provisions of any State law, municipal ordinance, or other local regulation which are inconsistent with this part to the extent that those provisions do not provide a buyer with rights which are equal to or

16 CFR Ch. I (1-1-88 Edition)

greater than those rights granted a buyer by this part. This part also supersedes those provisions of any State law, municipal ordinance, or other local regulation requiring that a buyer be notified of a right which is the same as a right provided by this part but requiring that a buyer be given notice of this right in a language, form, or manner which is different in any way from that required by this part.

In those instances where any State law, municipal ordinance, or other local regulation contains provisions, some but not all of which are partially or completely superseded by this part, the provisions or portions of those provisions which have not been superseded retain their full force and effect.

NOTE 6: If any provision of this part or its application to any person, partnership, corporation, act or practice is held invalid, the remainder of this part or the application of the provision to any other person, partnership, corporation, act or practice shall not be affected thereby.

NOTE 7: Section 435.1(a)(1) of this part governs all solicitations where the time of solicitation is more than 100 days after promulgation of this part. The remainder of this part governs all transactions where receipt of a properly completed order occurs more than 100 days after promulgation of this part.

(38 Stat. 717, as amended; 15 U.S.C. 41, *et seq.*)

[40 FR 49492, Oct. 22, 1975]

§ 435.2 **Definitions.**

For purposes of this part:

(a) "Shipment" shall mean the act by which the merchandise is physically placed in the possession of the carrier.

(b) "Receipt of a properly completed order" shall mean:

(1) Where there is a credit sale and the buyer has not previously tendered partial payment, the time at which the seller charges the buyer's account;

(2) Where the buyer tenders full or partial payment in the proper amount in the form of cash, check or money order, the time at which the seller has received both said payment and an order from the buyer containing all the information needed by the seller to process and ship the order.

Provided, however, That where the seller receives notice that the check or money order tendered by the buyer has been dishonored or that the buyer does not qualify for a credit sale, "receipt of a properly completed order" shall mean the time at which (i) the seller receives notice that a check or money order for the proper amount tendered by the buyer has been honored, (ii) the buyer tenders cash in the proper amount or (iii) the seller receives notice that the buyer qualifies for a credit sale.

(c) "Refund" shall mean:

(1) Where the buyer tendered full payment for the unshipped merchandise in the form of cash, check or money order, a return of the amount tendered in the form of cash, check or money order;

(2) Where there is a credit sale:

(i) And the seller is a creditor, a copy of a credit memorandum or the like or an account statement reflecting the removal or absence of any remaining charge incurred as a result of the sale from the buyer's account;

(ii) And a third party is the creditor, a copy of an appropriate credit memorandum or the like to the third party creditor which will remove the charge from the buyer's account or a statement from the seller acknowledging the cancellation of the order and representing that he has not taken any action regarding the order which will result in a charge to the buyer's account with the third party;

(iii) And the buyer tendered partial payment for the unshipped merchandise in the form of cash, check or money order, a return of the amount tendered in the form of cash, check or money order.

(d) "Prompt refund" shall mean:

(1) Where a refund is made pursuant to paragraph (c)(1) or (2)(iii) of this section a refund sent to the buyer by first class mail within seven (7) working days of the date on which the buyer's right to refund vests under the provisions of this part;

(2) Where a refund is made pursuant to paragraph (c)(2) (i) or (ii) of this section, a refund sent to the buyer by first class mail within one (1) billing cycle from the date on which the buyer's right to refund vests under the provisions of this part.

(e) The "time of solicitation" of an order shall mean that time when the seller has:

(1) Mailed or otherwise disseminated the solicitation to a prospective purchaser,

(2) Made arrangements for an advertisement containing the solicitation to appear in a newspaper, magazine or the like or on radio or television which cannot be changed or cancelled without incurring substantial expense, or

(3) Made arrangements for the printing of a catalog, brochure or the like which cannot be changed without incurring substantial expense, in which the solicitation in question forms an insubstantial part.

(38 Stat. 717, as amended; 15 U.S.C. 41, *et seq.*)

[40 FR 49492, Oct. 22, 1975]

Periodicals have other legal concerns, including:

- subscription expiration laws.
- direct-mail promotion.
- rental of customer lists.
- advertising restrictions.
- government regulations of subscription offers.
- plus all the problems on restrictions in material like libel, obscenity, invasion of privacy.

You'll need to follow subscription-expiration laws, which require two things:

- renewal invitations must alert the subscriber to his/her subscription expiration date—the month and year.
- any renewal must commence after the subscription expires.

Sweepstakes

Be wary of state laws.

From the customer's viewpoint, it is heartening to know that sweepstakes are regulated. This regulation can be a pain if your publishing company wants to run a game-of-chance subscription promotion, however. Florida courts have held that mere mailing of sweepstakes into that state gives the Florida legal system authority to act, as Reader's Digest Association's sweepstakes found out. Some states require that the rules of a sweepstakes be filed before promotion and the lists of certain categories of winners be available. Sweepstakes are also governed by federal law.

Public Notices

Reproduced below are statements regarding ownership, management, and circulation required by law (39 U.S.C. 3685).

<table>
<tr><td colspan="4" align="center">U.S. Postal Service
STATEMENT OF OWNERSHIP, MANAGEMENT AND CIRCULATION
Required by 39 U.S.C. 3685)</td></tr>
</table>

1A. TITLE OF PUBLICATION	1B. PUBLICATION NO.	2. DATE OF FILING
Arizona AAA Highroads	2 4 4 8 6 0 0 0	9/26/88

3. FREQUENCY OF ISSUE	3A. NO. OF ISSUES PUBLISHED ANNUALLY	3B. ANNUAL SUBSCRIPTION PRICE
Bimonthly	6	$2.00

4. COMPLETE MAILING ADDRESS OF KNOWN OFFICE OF PUBLICATION *(Street, City, County, State and ZIP Code) (Not printers)*

3144 N. 7th Avenue, P.O. Box 33119, Phoenix, Maricopa, Arizona 85067

5. COMPLETE MAILING ADDRESS OF THE HEADQUARTERS OF GENERAL BUSINESS OFFICES OF THE PUBLISHER *(Not printer)*

3144 N. 7th Avenue, P.O. Box 33119, Phoenix, Maricopa, Arizona 85067

6. FULL NAMES AND COMPLETE MAILING ADDRESS OF PUBLISHER, EDITOR, AND MANAGING EDITOR *(This item MUST NOT be blank)*

PUBLISHER *(Name and Complete Mailing Address)*

Phoenix, Maricopa, Arizona 85067

Arizona Automobile Association, 3144 N. 7th Ave., P.O. Box 33119,

EDITOR *(Name and Complete Mailing Address)*

85067

Rebecca Ross, AAA, 3144 N. 7th Ave., P.O. Box 33119, Phoenix, Maricopa, AZ

MANAGING EDITOR *(Name and Complete Mailing Address)*

85067

Harold Lehrer, AAA, 3144 N. 7th Ave., P.O. Box 33119, Phoenix, Maricopa, AZ

7. OWNER *(If owned by a corporation, its name and address must be stated and also immediately thereunder the names and addresses of stockholders owning or holding 1 percent or more of total amount of stock. If not owned by a corporation, the names and addresses of the individual owners must be given. If owned by a partnership or other unincorporated firm, its name and address, as well as that of each individual must be given. If the publication is published by a nonprofit organization, its name and address must be stated.) (Item must be completed.)*

FULL NAME	COMPLETE MAILING ADDRESS
Arizona Automobile Association	P.O. Box 33119, Phoenix, Maricopa, Arizona 85067
(a not-for-profit, non-stock corporation)	

8. KNOWN BONDHOLDERS, MORTGAGEES, AND OTHER SECURITY HOLDERS OWNING OR HOLDING 1 PERCENT OR MORE OF TOTAL AMOUNT OF BONDS, MORTGAGES OR OTHER SECURITIES *(If there are none, so state)*

FULL NAME	COMPLETE MAILING ADDRESS
NONE	NONE

9. FOR COMPLETION BY NONPROFIT ORGANIZATIONS AUTHORIZED TO MAIL AT SPECIAL RATES *(Section 423.12 DMM only)*
The purpose, function, and nonprofit status of this organization and the exempt status for Federal income tax purposes *(Check one)*

(1) ☐ HAS NOT CHANGED DURING PRECEDING 12 MONTHS	(2) ☐ HAS CHANGED DURING PRECEDING 12 MONTHS	*(If changed, publisher must submit explanation of change with this statement.)*

10. EXTENT AND NATURE OF CIRCULATION	AVERAGE NO. COPIES EACH ISSUE DURING PRECEDING 12 MONTHS	ACTUAL NO. COPIES OF SINGLE ISSUE PUBLISHED NEAREST TO FILING DATE
A. TOTAL NO. COPIES *(Net Press Run)*	181,845	185,400
B. PAID CIRCULATION 1. Sales through dealers and carriers, street vendors and counter sales	-0-	-0-
2. Mail Subscription	172,920	173,143.
C. TOTAL PAID CIRCULATION *(Sum of 10B1 and 10B2)*	172,920	173,143
D. FREE DISTRIBUTION BY MAIL, CARRIER OR OTHER MEANS SAMPLES, COMPLIMENTARY, AND OTHER FREE COPIES	358	380
E. TOTAL DISTRIBUTION *(Sum of C and D)*	173,278	173,523
F. COPIES NOT DISTRIBUTED 1. Office use, left over, unaccounted, spoiled after printing	8,567	11,877
2. Return from News Agents	-0-	-0-
G. TOTAL *(Sum of E, F1 and 2—should equal net press run shown in A)*	181,845	185,400

11. I certify that the statements made by me above are correct and complete

SIGNATURE AND TITLE OF EDITOR, PUBLISHER, BUSINESS MANAGER, OR OWNER

Rebecca L. Ross, Editor

PS Form 3526
July 1982

(See instruction on reverse)

U.S. Postal Service

STATEMENT OF OWNERSHIP, MANAGEMENT AND CIRCULATION
Required by 39 U.S.C. 3685)

1A. TITLE OF PUBLICATION	1B. PUBLICATION NO.	2. DATE OF FILING
The Indian Trader		Oct. 23, 1989

3. FREQUENCY OF ISSUE	3A. NO. OF ISSUES PUBLISHED ANNUALLY	3B. ANNUAL SUBSCRIPTION PRICE
monthly	twelve	$18.00

4. COMPLETE MAILING ADDRESS OF KNOWN OFFICE OF PUBLICATION *(Street, City, County, State and ZIP+4 Code) (Not printers)*

603 So. Second St., Gallup, McKinley, New Mexico 87301

5. COMPLETE MAILING ADDRESS OF THE HEADQUARTERS OF GENERAL BUSINESS OFFICES OF THE PUBLISHER *(Not printer)*

603 So. Second St., Gallup, McKinley, New Mexico 87301

6. FULL NAMES AND COMPLETE MAILING ADDRESS OF PUBLISHER, EDITOR, AND MANAGING EDITOR *(This item MUST NOT be blank)*

PUBLISHER *(Name and Complete Mailing Address)*

Martin Link, 2302 Mariyana Dr., Gallup, New Mexico 87301

EDITOR *(Name and Complete Mailing Address)*

Bill Donovan, 104 Valley View Dr., Gallup, New Mexico 87301

MANAGING EDITOR *(Name and Complete Mailing Address)*

Bill Donovan, 104 Valley View Dr., Gallup, New Mexico 87301

7. OWNER *(If owned by a corporation, its name and address must be stated and also immediately thereunder the names and addresses of stockholders owning or holding 1 percent or more of total amount of stock. If not owned by a corporation, the names and addresses of the individual owners must be given. If owned by a partnership or other unincorporated firm, its name and address, as well as that of each individual must be given. If the publication is published by a nonprofit organization, its name and address must be stated.) (Item must be completed.)*

FULL NAME	COMPLETE MAILING ADDRESS
The Indian Trader, Inc.	603 So. 2nd St., Gallup, NM 87301
Martin Link	2302 Mariyana, Gallup, NM 87301
Bill Donovan	104 Valley View, Gallup, NM 87301

8. KNOWN BONDHOLDERS, MORTGAGEES, AND OTHER SECURITY HOLDERS OWNING OR HOLDING 1 PERCENT OR MORE OF TOTAL AMOUNT OF BONDS, MORTGAGES OR OTHER SECURITIES *(If there are none, so state)*

FULL NAME	COMPLETE MAILING ADDRESS
none	

9. FOR COMPLETION BY NONPROFIT ORGANIZATIONS AUTHORIZED TO MAIL AT SPECIAL RATES *(Section 423.12 DMM only)*
The purpose, function, and nonprofit status of this organization and the exempt status for Federal income tax purposes *(Check one)*

(1) HAS NOT CHANGED DURING PRECEDING 12 MONTHS	(2) HAS CHANGED DURING PRECEDING 12 MONTHS	*(If changed, publisher must submit explanation of change with this statement.)*

10. EXTENT AND NATURE OF CIRCULATION *(See Instructions on reverse side)*	AVERAGE NO. COPIES EACH ISSUE DURING PRECEDING 12 MONTHS	ACTUAL NO. COPIES OF SINGLE ISSUE PUBLISHED NEAREST TO FILING DATE
A. TOTAL NO. COPIES *(Net Press Run)*	4,000	4,000
B. PAID AND/OR REQUESTED CIRCULATION 1. Sales through dealers and carriers, street vendors and counter sales	300	300
2. Mail Subscription *(Paid and/or requested)*	3,100	3,100
C. TOTAL PAID AND/OR REQUESTED CIRCULATION *(Sum of 10B1 and 10B2)*	3,400	3,400
D. FREE DISTRIBUTION BY MAIL, CARRIER OR OTHER MEANS SAMPLES, COMPLIMENTARY, AND OTHER FREE COPIES	300	300
E. TOTAL DISTRIBUTION *(Sum of C and D)*	3,700	3,700
F. COPIES NOT DISTRIBUTED 1. Office use, left over, unaccounted, spoiled after printing	250	250
2. Return from News Agents	50	50
G. TOTAL *(Sum of E, F1 and 2—should equal net press run shown in A)*	4,000	4,000

11. I certify that the statements made by me above are correct and complete

SIGNATURE AND TITLE OF EDITOR, PUBLISHER, BUSINESS MANAGER, OR OWNER

Martin Link, Publisher

Junk Mail

State laws sometimes prohibit the sale or rental of a customer list to another who will use it for advertising purposes. These laws are primarily directed to the sale of motor vehicle registration lists, public utility lists, and so forth.

Ever wonder what the courts could do about junk mail? Junk or unwanted mail is not an unconstitutional invasion of privacy, opined a federal judge, who also said, "The mail box, however noxious its advertising contents seem to judges as well as other people, is hardly the kind of enclave that requires constitutional defense to protect 'the privacies of life.' The short, though regular, journey from mail box to trash can . . . is an acceptable burden, at least so far as the Constitution is concerned " (*Lamont v. Canons of Motor Vehicles,* 269 F.Supp 880, aff. 386 F.2d 449 at 339 [Wy. ct] cert. denied).

Purely commercial advertising is not protected from government regulation. If a customer does not order merchandise, the customer can't be required to pay for it (39 USC Sec. 3009). Thus, in promotional material for periodical subscription, you must explain clearly to the potential subscriber that by returning the coupon, he or she is ordering a periodical for a fixed term. Be very clear in your promotions that if the order blank is returned, subscription begins.

Mail Order References

There are several excellent texts on mail-order business (which is what you'll be doing if you sell books through a catalogue). See Lawson Traphagen Hill's *How to Build a Multi-Million Dollar Catalogue Mail Order Business by Someone Who Did.* Also, *Success in Newsletter Publishing, A Practical Guide*, by Frederick D. Goss (The Newsletter Association, Colorado Building, #700, Washington D.C. 20005), is an excellent reference for newsletter publishers. It covers some technical areas, particularly postal regulations, extremely well. A newer publication is *Publishing Newsletters*, by Hound Penn Herdson (Charles Scribner's Sons) promoted by the Newsletter Clearinghouse (44 West Market Street, P.O. Box 311, Rhinebeck, New York 12572); they also publish the Hudson Newsletter Directory, which is in its seventh edition and includes journals, reporting services, publication information, and subject categories.

Standard Rates & Data Service (Skokie, Illinois) publishes useful books for newspapers, magazines, and catalogues in advertising; information is also provided on list-rental rates, mechanical requirements, and other areas of concern.

Robert J. Posch, Jr., secretary and counsel for Doubleday Book & Music Clubs, Inc., authored two McGraw-Hill books: *The Direct Marketer's Legal Advisor* and *What Every Manager Needs to Know About Marketing and the Law.* A more recent text of his seems to be more technical and therefore costs more: *The Complete Guide to Marketing and the Law* (Prentice-Hall).

Anti-trust Matters Affecting Publishers

You've seen the term "anti-trust" bandied about in the news. Anti-trust laws are directed to elimination of monopolies. In your world, it rears its ugly head on issues regarding the legal requirements of copyright, mergers and acquisitions, price discrimination, and promotional assistance.

Since copyright is a monopoly, it automatically conflicts with the anti-trust laws. In a line of old cases, the Supreme Court restrained the copyright law's "exclusive rights," granted to the holder of the copyright, by subjecting it to anti-trust law. The copyright act, said the court, was not intended to authorize agreements in unlawful restraint of trade and tending to monopoly. There is nothing in the copyright law that allows the copyright holder to approve a minimum resale price of the product at a retail level. A different result accrues when a copyright is licensed, because price maintenance provisions become merely attempts to secure the monies the copyright holder would be entitled to under the holder's copyright monopoly.

Sometimes territorial restrictions become involved in copyright licensing; licensor and licensee agree to territorial restriction to protect tradenames and copyrights. Territorial restraints among existing competitors may not be valid, though. Book publishers have been stopped from participating in agreements to establish non-competing territories or customers for sale and distribution.

The Robinson-Patman Act (15 U.S.C. Sec. 13a-f) controls and prohibits certain price discrimination by suppliers to competing customers and requires that promotional assistance be offered equally.

Section 2(a) provides:

It shall be unlawful for any person engaged in commerce, in the course of such commerce, either directly or indirectly, to discriminate in price between different purchasers of commodities of like grade and quality, where either or any of the purchases involved in such discrimination are in commerce where such commodities are sold for use, consumption, or resale within the United States . . . and where the effect of such discrimination may be substantially to lessen competition or tend to create a monopoly in any line of commerce, or to injure, destroy, or prevent competition with any person who either grants or knowingly receives the benefit of such discrimination, or with customers of either of them . . .

The act says for price discrimination to exist, there must be the following:

- the seller must:
  - engage in commerce.
  - discriminate in the course of it.
  - one or more of the transactions must cross state lines.
- must be a price difference:
  - not one price for all customers.
  - price means sale price.
  - two sales to two purchasers.
- don't count:
  - sales to non-profit institutions.
  - to subsidiary.

Some of these principles pop up in book-publishing-related cases, such as *Students Book Co. v. Washington Law Book Co.* (232 F.2d 49 [1955]), which involved the sales of student law books to competitors at preferential prices and terms. In the larger marketplace, the names of the companies involved in price discrimination cases are household words—Gulf Oil, Sun Oil, Zenith Radio, Anheuser-Busch, Record Club of America, Ford Motor Co., Bruce's Juices Inc., and Sony. Treble damages are at stake if the plaintiff can prove illegal price discrimination and actual injury.

Where publishers participate in retail book catalogues, be aware that the Robinson-Patman Act hammer can strike. If you, as a publisher, provide money, services, or goods in the catalogue, they must be equally available to competing companies, and that availability must be known.

This *proportionally equal standard* applies to promotional assistance. These provisions are:

Section 2(d):
It shall be unlawful for any person . . . to pay or contract for the payment of anything of value to or for the benefit of a customer of such person . . . for any services or facilities furnished . . . in connection with the processing, handling, sale, or offering for sale of any products . . . unless such payment or consideration is available on proportionally equal terms to all other customers competing in the distribution of such products or commodities.

Section 2(e):
It shall be unlawful for any person to discriminate in favor of one purchaser against another purchaser . . . by contracting to furnish or furnishing . . . services or facilities connected with the processing, handling, sale, or offering for sale of such commodity so purchased upon terms not accorded to all purchasers on proportionally equal terms.

Summarized, it is unlawful for a seller to supply one customer with money or facilities for promotional services without doing it for another. Thus, the Polish Publishing House could not favor Polish-ancestry booksellers with special advertising, handbills, window and floor displays, and so forth, in selling their book list without making the same things available to all booksellers.

Of course, as with all laws, there are defenses:

- cost justification.
- lower price (or services or facilities) necessary to meet the low price offered by a competitor.
- lower price made available to all the competing entities.
- changing conditions.

Merger deals are reported weekly, it seems, in *Publishers Weekly*. Both the Clayton Act (Sec. 7 [15 U.S.C. Sec. 18]):

No person engaged in commerce or in any activity affecting commerce shall acquire, directly or indirectly, the whole or any part of the stock ... or any part of the assets of another person engaged also in commerce or in any activity affecting commerce, wherein any line of commerce or in any activity affecting commerce in any section of the country, the effect of such acquisition may be substantially to lessen competition, or tend to create a monopoly.

and the FTC Act apply to mergers. (FTC Sec. 5(a)(1) (15 U.S.C. Sec. 45(a)(1)):

Unfair methods of competition in or affecting commerce, and unfair or deceptive acts or practices in or affecting commerce, are declared unlawful.

The legal thrust is that acquisitions or mergers that substantially increase market concentration are unlawful. The most common type of merger challenged is the horizontal one, i.e., mergers between competitors. Challenges to conglomerate acquisitions succeed where the acquiring firm's attributes (dollars or business lines) confer competitive advantages in the acquired firm, which must, prior to the merger, have dominance in a concentrated market, or one in which a few companies account for over half of the sales.

There is an excellent introduction to this entire area in *PLI's Book Publishing 1984*, "Current Anti-trust Issues in Book Publishing," by Peter D. Standish.

The highly publicized *Northern California Bookseller's Association v. Hearst Corp. and Bantam Books* (No. C-82-1468 [N.D. Cal.]) concerned small retail bookseller's complaints that publishers granted larger discounts to the national chain bookstores. The publishers posited the "cost justification" defense.

Publishers Weekly (October 13, 1987) reported the dismissal of some suits by NCBA and the status of the Bantam suit referred to above. I reprint the article (with permission) so that you can see the following litigation points applied to a business problem:

- a counterclaim by the defendant.
- the expense of litigating against a big company.
- the terms of settlement.
- each parties' views of the settlement.
- judicial rulings on pricing policies.

A good way to see the complications in this area is to read part of a Competitive Impact Statement filed by the government in connection with a proposed Final

Judgment in an anti-trust suit against CBS; the challenge was to CBS's acquisition of Fawcett Publications:

UNITED STATES DISTRICT COURT
SOUTHERN DISTRICT OF NEW YORK

UNITED STATES OF AMERICA,	)	
	)	
Plaintiff,	)	
	)	78 Civ. 2491 (P.N.L.)
v.	)	
	)	
CBS INC.,	)	
	)	
Defendant.	)	
	)	

COMPETITIVE IMPACT STATEMENT

The United States pursuant to Section 2(b) of the Antitrust Procedures and Penalties Act, 15 U.S.C. §16(b)–(h), files this Competitive Impact Statement in connection with the proposed Final Judgment submitted for entry in this civil antitrust proceeding.

I
NATURE AND PURPOSE OF THE PROCEEDING

On June 1, 1978, the United States filed a civil anti-trust complaint under Section 15 of the Clayton Act, 15 U.S.C. §25, challenging the acquisition of Fawcett Publications Inc. (Fawcett) by CBS Inc. (CBS) as a violation of Section 7 of the Clayton Act, 15 U.S.C. §18. The complaint alleges that the effect of the acquisition may be substantially to lessen competition or to tend to create a monopoly in mass market paperback publishing. The complaint charges that competition between CBS and Fawcett was eliminated, competition in the mass market paperback industry in general may be lessened, and concentration had been increased in that industry to the detriment of actual and potential competition. The complaint sought to have CBS divest Fawcett and restore it to its pre-acquisition posture and to enjoin CBS, its directors, agents, and all other persons acting on its behalf, from acquiring the stock or assets of any firm engaged in the publishing, distribution or sale of mass market paperback books.

Entry of the proposed Final Judgment will terminate this litigation. The Court will retain jurisdiction to construe, modify, or enforce the proposed Final Judgment.

II
THE ACQUISITION AND THE ALLEGED VIOLATION

On January 7, 1977, JAC Inc., a wholly-owned subsidiary of CBS acquired Fawcett for $50 million in cash. At the time of the acquisition, Fawcett published mass market paperback books under the Gold Medal and Crest imprints; trade paperback books under the Premier, Fawcett, and Fawcett Special imprints; three monthly special interest magazines; and a number of annual and "one shot" publications in magazine format. Fawcett also operated a printing plant not utilized in the production of paperback books, a magazine subscription service, and a distribution service which sold Fawcett's magazines and mass market paperback books to the more than 500 independent wholesalers in the United States and Canada. Since the acquisition, CBS has sold the Fawcett printing plant.

Prior to the Fawcett acquisition, CBS was engaged in mass market paperback publishing through its Popular Library Books Division (Popular Library), which it acquired in 1971. The United States alleged that Popular Library and Fawcett were competitors in two lines of commerce: the purchase of the rights to publish mass market paperback books and the sale of mass market paperback books.

Mass market paperback books were described in the complaint as paperbound books, usually of standard rack size (4¼″ x 7″), which are distributed predominantly to mass market outlets such as newsstands, drugstores, and variety stores by local wholesale distributors, who in turn receive the books from national distributors. The complaint alleged that mass market paperback books differ from all other books in their method of distribution, price, size, physical components, production facilities, and marketing methods.

The complaint stated that Fawcett and Popular Library accounted for approximately 9.4% and 2.6%, respectively, of 1976 mass market paperback sales, with the top four companies accounting for approximately 53% of 1976 sales and the top eight for approximately 81%. The complaint additionally alleged that the industry was experiencing a trend towards further concentration.

III
THE PROPOSED CONSENT JUDGMENT
AND ITS ANTICIPATED EFFECTS ON COMPETITION

The proposed Final Judgment contains two principal forms of relief. First, the defendant is required to sell Popular Library. Second, the defendant is enjoined from acquiring any other mass market paperback publisher, except with the prior written consent of the United States, for ten years from the date the proposed Final Judgment is entered, or until it ceases owning a mass market paperback publisher, whichever occurs first.

A. *CBS Has A Duty To Divest Popular Library*

Under the proposed Final Judgment, CBS is ordered to sell Popular Library within two years from the date of entry of the proposed Final Judgment. Popular Library is defined in the proposed Judgment as "the Popular Library paperback book imprint of the Fawcett Books Group of the Consumer Publishing Division of CBS."

The proposed Final Judgment specifically delineates the assets to be divested. CBS must sell the exclusive right to use the Popular Library name in the paperback book publishing business. CBS must also sell the rights to books previously published under the Popular Library imprint, the rights to books purchased for the Popular Library imprint which have not been published at the time of divestiture, the assignable rights to contracts with Popular Library authors, and all inventories of books published under the Popular Library imprint. If the buyer agrees, CBS may, with the consent of the plaintiff, sell less than all of these assets. If such consent is refused, CBS may do so with the Court's approval. CBS must sell or grant to the purchaser of Popular Library all rights owned by CBS for the trademarks or colophons (*i.e.,* the publisher's distinctive emblems) used for Popular Library on or after January 7, 1977, except for any trademark or colophon which includes the words "CBS" or "Fawcett."

If the purchaser so desires, CBS must provide the purchaser of Popular Library with distribution services. The services are to be provided for up to three years following divestiture, or for as long as CBS remains in the business of distributing books to magazine wholesalers, whichever is shorter, and at a reasonable price and upon reasonable terms and conditions, including those concerning the quantity of titles to be distributed by CBS. CBS is not obligated to distribute any book inconsistent with the standards it in fact applies to other books it distributes to magazine wholesalers. The United States insisted that a distribution contract be made available to the purchaser of Popular Library to ensure that the purchaser's opportunity to become a more substantial competitor in mass market paperback publishing not be hindered by any bottleneck in the distribution system.

CBS is to make known the availability of Popular Library for sale by means customary in the publishing industry. Among the means currently being considered by CBS are the following: counsel for CBS stated that CBS plans to contact all firms which it believes may be interested in purchasing Popular Library and CBS is planning to prepare an offering circular which will be sent to those who may be interested.

If Popular Library has not been divested at the end of one year, CBS must employ one or more investment banking firms or business finders to sell Popular Library. The compensation for any such firm or firms is to be based in significant part on a commission arrangement contingent upon the firm bringing about the sale of the business.

Any divestiture will be complete and final, except that CBS may retain a security interest to secure performance of any unpaid portion of the purchase price or to secure performance of the contract of sale. If CBS reacquires control of Popular Library pursuant to the exercise of such a security interest, its control must be divested within one year thereafter.

The CBS obligation to divest Popular Library or to resell any interest in Popular Library reacquired through the exercise of a security interest terminates at the end of the two-year and one-year time periods, respectively, unless the Court orders otherwise. At any time during either time period specified above, the United States has the right to petition the Court for an order requiring additional CBS efforts to sell Popular Library. Such an order shall be issued upon a showing that divestiture has not been accomplished either because of an inadequate effort to sell or upon any rejection of a reasonable offer to buy. Such an order should require CBS to accept a specific reasonable offer to buy. The United States may also, within 45 days of the end of either time period specified above, secure an order extending the time for CBS to divest Popular Library and requiring additional efforts by CBS.

B. *Prohibited Conduct*

For ten years from the date of entry of the proposed Final Judgment or until it ceases owning a mass market paperback publisher, whichever occurs first, CBS is forbidden from acquiring all or any part of the stock or book publishing assets, other than books or publication rights in the normal course of business, of any mass market paperback publisher, except with the prior written consent of the United States, or if such approval is refused, then upon approval of the Court.

C. *Scope Of The Proposed Final Judgment*

The provisions of the proposed Final Judgment apply to CBS and each of its directors, officers, employees, agents, subsidiaries, affiliates, successors, and assignees, and to all other persons in active concert or participation with any of them who receive actual notice of the proposed Final Judgment by personal service or otherwise.

D. *Effect Of The Proposed Final Judgment On Competition*

The assets to be divested plus the distribution contract should either enable someone not already in mass market paperback publishing to enter, or permit an existing small publisher to become a more significant competitor. The United States believes, therefore, that the disposition of this proceeding by the proposed Final Judgment is appropriate and in the public interest.

IV
REMEDIES AVAILABLE TO POTENTIAL PRIVATE LITIGANTS

Section 4 of the Clayton Act (15 U.S.C. §15) provides that any person who has been injured as a result of conduct prohibited by the anti-trust laws may bring suit in federal court to recover three times the damages the person has suffered, as well as costs and reasonable attorney fees. Entry of the proposed Final Judgment will neither impair nor assist private antitrust damage actions. Under the provisions of Section 5(a) of the Clayton Act (15 U.S.C. §16(a)), the proposed Final Judgment has no *prima facie* effect in any subsequent private lawsuit that may be brought against the defendant.

V
PROCEDURES AVAILABLE FOR MODIFICATION
OF THE PROPOSED CONSENT JUDGMENT

As provided by the Antitrust Procedures and Penalties Act, 15 U.S.C. §16(b)–(h), any person wishing to comment upon the proposed Judgment may, for a sixty-day statutory period submit written comments to the United States Department of Justice, Attention: Alan L. Marx, Acting Chief, General Litigation Section, Antitrust Division, Department of Justice, Washington, D.C. 20530. Such comments and the Government's response to them will be filed with the Court and published in the Federal Register. The Government will evaluate all such comments to determine whether there is any reason for withdrawal of its consent to the proposed Final Judgment.

VI
ALTERNATIVES TO THE PROPOSED FINAL JUDGMENT

The alternative to the proposed Final Judgment considered by the United States was a trial on the merits and on relief. While the complaint sought divestiture of Fawcett to restore the competition lost due to the merger, the United States considers the proposed Final Judgment to be an acceptable alternative to seeking divestiture of Fawcett via a trial on the merits.

The proposed Judgment would achieve the objectives of the lawsuit, and also save the Government the expense of litigation. The principal anticompetitive effect alleged in the complaint was the loss of competition in the mass market paperback industry. The divestiture of either Fawcett or Popular Library would tend to restore the competition lost due to this merger.

Under the circumstances, the United States believes that entry of the proposed Final Judgment is in the public interest.

VII
DETERMINATIVE MATERIALS AND DOCUMENTS

No materials or documents of the type described in Section 2(b) of the Antitrust Procedures and Penalties Act were considered in formulating this proposed Final Judgment.

Respectfully submitted,

Attorneys
Antitrust Division
Department of Justice
Washington, D.C. 20530

Judge Dismisses Suits Between NCBA, Chains

The Northern California Booksellers Association has dropped its antitrust suit against the major chains over alleged "discount prices" of books in order to focus on its pending litigation against publishers, according to counsel for the independent booksellers. At the same time, Crown has dismissed its counterclaim against the NCBA, charging price fixing and other anticompetitive acts.

Both actions were dismissed with prejudice—the suits cannot be refiled—on October 1 before Federal Judge William H. Orrick in San Francisco. The NCBA agreed to drop its suit against Waldenbooks (and its parent company K mart), B. Dalton Booksellers, Barnes & Noble and Crown Books, and Crown agreed to drop its countersuit on the following conditions:

Each party will pay its own costs, expenses and attorneys' fees. The NCBA and defendants release each other from any claim made in their respective complaints. And each of the defendants releases the NCBA and its counsel from any claim made by Crown in a motion filed September 10 to recover attorneys' fees and expenses.

The NCBA filed suit against the chains on January 26 and Crown immediately countersued. At a pretrial conference on September 10, Judge Orrick set a January 4, 1989 trial date and ordered both parties to go forward with discovery, which had been stayed for the preceding five months.

According to NCBA counsel William Petrocelli the suits' dismissal left no winners or losers in a legal battle pitting the independent bookstore Davids against the chain-store Goliaths. "It's a mutual dismissal of the case," he said. "Our primary reason in dismissing the suit was to enable us to concentrate on the litigation with publishers."

The new Bantam/Doubleday/Dell incentive plan was a secondary impetus for the dismissal, Petrocelli said. "If we had concentrated our money and effort on this case against the chains, by the time we got to trial the whole thing may be moot because discount policies would have changed by then, and the litigation issues wouldn't have been current."

But attorneys for three of the defendants say that the NCBA "surrendered" because the independent bookseller "David" ran out of shards to fling.

"We went along with the resolution because it was a total victory of our position and a surrender by the NCBA," said Howard B. Possick, the Washington, D.C.–based lead counsel for Crown. "In our view the NCBA's raising the possibility that one of the publishers may change its pricing policy was a pretext for the NCBA to ask us to agree to a dismissal of the suit so that the NCBA could save face. It came on the heels of a request for a stay that was denied, our motion to recover fees and the upcoming hearing on that motion."

"I believe what's happened here is that the plaintiffs decided it wasn't a meritorious case and decided to dismiss it," said George Weickhardt, the San Francisco attorney for B. Dalton and Barnes & Noble. "Clearly the plaintiffs had done nothing in the case since filing it. It's a complete defeat for the NCBA."

Petrocelli said Possick and Weickhardt's comments were "ridiculous." "I wouldn't call this action a defeat. It allows us to concentrate on other litigation. It's a shift in tactics, and one that I'm very confident in."

In a motion filed on September 10, Crown charged that it was entitled to recover attorney fees and expenses in opposing the NCBA's preliminary injunction because Petrocelli had filed the injunction in "bad faith . . . for only tactical reasons; to harass defendants, to force them to incur unnecessary burden and expense and to generate publicity and funds for NCBA."

Petrocelli claims that he "had no alternative" but to withdraw the motion for enjoinment four days following the defendants' March 23 filing of opposition to the injunction because during that period of time he was responding to a number of motions. "I'm a solo practitioner and they had at least six law firms turning out paperwork. It was a ploy on their part," he said.

Possick said that Petrocelli approached him immediately after the September 10 hearing to ask for dismissal of the case contingent upon dropping its motion. "It was something we were contemplating anyway—a dismissal or settlement of the case," said Petrocelli. Litigation is still pending in the Bantam and Avon suits charging "secret preferential price discounts" to the chains, Petrocelli said. In the action against Bantam, there are no motions pending; however, he said that he is in contact with Bantam attorneys. "We are waiting to see how the program [the BDD price incentive plan] is implemented." Petrocelli said the NCBA is in active negotiations with attorneys for Avon. A status conference is planned for November 5 before Federal Judge Thelton E. Henderson. Avon is appealing Judge Henderson's findings of fact in 1986, which concluded that pricing policies of paperback firms contributed to the growth of chains. The court must still rule on two other elements: whether the unequal discounts had an impact on competition among booksellers and whether the discounts were necessary for Avon to meet the competition.

—Molly Colin

Advertising within a Publication

Magazine publishers make money through advertising. A rate card should be part of any document acknowledging the advertising order. Incorporate through reference the terms and conditions of advertisement.

Here's a simple rate insert that appears in a local weekly.

NAME _____   _____

ADDRESS _____

PHONE _____

I understand that there are no cash refunds and that the CANYON SHOPPER has the right to correct and edit my ad if necessary. If ad runs without being paid in advance, I agree to pay all attorney and collection fees. I further understand that there is a $5.00 charge for returned checks.

Signed _____ Date _____

Simply print your ad clearly in the spaces below, using one word per box. Please include a phone number and/or address in your copy. (Information above is for our office use only.) Any series of numbers counts as one word.

Ads must be accompanied by payment (check or money order) payable to CANYON SHOPPER. All ads must be received by Tuesday Noon at our office, **2608 N. Steves Boulevard 86004** to appear in Wednesday's issue. Ads arriving or paid after this deadline will appear in the following issue.

MINIMUM CHARGE - $4.00 for 10 words or less. Bold capitals 25¢ per word. Centering 25¢ per line. Prices shown include applicable sales tax.

Please read your ad for errors the first day it appears. The CANYON SHOPPER assumes no responsibility after the first insertion. Credit will be issued in the event of an error. Credit memo held for 6 months only. NO CASH REFUNDS. We can not guarantee specific page placement.

No changes, corrections or cancellations of ads after Monday 5pm.

IMPORTANT Please do not submit any ad that in any way falls short of our policy on family reading. If such an ad is mistakenly accepted, the amount of the ad will be credited, not refunded.

THE CANYON SHOPPER reserves the right to properly classify all ads.

☐ **MISCELLANEOUS**

☐ **REALTY**

☐ **AUTOMOTIVE**

☐ **WHO'S WHO**
  IN SERVICES

AD OPTIONS
PLEASE CIRCLE

BOLD CAPS
25¢ extra per word

CENTERING
25¢ extra per line

DATES TO APPEAR

_____ _____

_____ _____

_____ _____

TOTAL COST
$_____

4.04	4.04	4.04	4.04
4.04	4.04	4.04	4.04
4.04	4.04	4.14	4.24
4.34	4.44	4.54	4.65
4.75	4.85	4.95	5.05
5.15	5.25	5.35	5.45
5.55	5.66	5.76	5.86

Beware of picking up liability for the content of advertisements. Add some indemnity language coupled with a warranty for advertisers, i.e., "The advertiser represents that it is authorized to use any testimonials, the names and/or likenesses of persons, and any copyrighted or trademarked material contained in the advertising authorized for publication, and that the material is not libelous or invasive of the privacy of a person, firm or corporation." (Take the indemnity clause from the earlier contract provisions.) Generally, you have the First Amendment right to reject advertising.

Be sure your rate card gives you the authority to position the advertising in your publication. You can also run into difficulties with your advertisers by failing to mention them in a common device used in periodicals, that is, the Index to Advertisers. *Publishers Weekly* nips that problem in the bud by stating:

This index is provided as a service. The Publisher does not assume any liability for errors or omissions.

And, of course, laws vary from country to country. *Shape* magazine, obviously distributed in Canada, includes this notice about advertisements under Canadian law:

ATTENTION CANADIAN
READERS

The laws that govern the manufacture and sale of health foods in Canada sometimes differ from those in the U.S. This requires, in some products, a modification of the trade name, ingredients and claims. While the products you order in Canada can sometimes be slightly different form those sold in the U.S., they, in fact, contain similar ingredients which will fulfill the purpose of the product as advertised.

Be assured that by purchasing your food supplement requirements from Weider Institute (Canada), you are receiving a fine formula, made form the finest ingredients, under the strict control and laws of the Department of National Health and Welfare of the Canadian government. You can buy Weider products with great confidence in Canada.

WEIDER HEALTH FOOD SUPPLEMENTS AND WEIDER EQUIPMENT ARE AVAILABLE IN BETTER HEALTH FOOD AND SPORTING GOODS STORES THROUGHOUT CANADA.

Prices, design, composition and construction on some products advertised in this magazine may vary in Canada. For a Canadian catalogue, please write to: WEIDER INSTITUTE, 2875 Bates Road, Montreal P.Q., Canada H3S 1B7.

Marketing Rights

16

If you're subscribing to *Publishers Weekly,* you've read Paul Nathan's "Rights" column. Have you noticed the number of major publishers who acquired reprint rights from small presses? Nathan reports an increase in the number of auctions for books from small or specialized presses. If your book sales pay manufacturing and developmental costs and leave you profit, a rights sale is pure gravy. Someone on your staff, or an agent, needs to take over the sale of subsidiary rights to book clubs, reprint publishers, magazines, and other media that might use part or all of the work.*

A "smallish outfit," as Paul Nathan labeled Yankee Books (publishers of *The Old Farmers Almanac*), undertook to publish *Winter Wolves,* a first novel by Earle Wescott. At that time, the manuscript had been turned down by ten mainstream publishers. Yankee Books' first novel in ten years went to auction with a $37,500 floor, and Bantam's bid of $55,000 got it. California's Presidio Press auctioned one of the few novels produced in its fourteen-year history; *Fire Arrow,* by Franklin Allan Leib, was bought by New American Library (NAL), which paid $600,000 for the reprint rights.

For a discussion of first serial rights, see the article by Howard Junker (editor of *ZYZZYVA* a literary quarterly), entitled "Subsidiary Rights" (*Small Press Market,*

---

*If you need to, review the earlier discussion of subsidiary rights.

March/April 1987). He used excerpts from thirty West Coast publishers' works in the quarterly's first seven issues. The money, at most a $100 honorarium, was token, but the publicity and promotion of the books was invaluable.

Publishers sometimes hold options on foreign rights. The annual Frankfurt Book Fair (an October event held in West Germany) is the most important international trade book show. If your company has products that are of interest to those in other countries, or if you want to buy rights to foreign publications to reprint and sell in the U.S., Frankfurt is the fair to attend. There are also other specialized international fairs in Bologna, London, and Madrid.

Often, first and second serialization rights are retained by authors, because of the nominal sums given by buyers. However, if your small press has contacts with mass-media firms, you should utilize those for your authors; the publicity can be valuable in marketing the work.

Did you keep some subsidiary rights? Do you need an agent? The answer depends on what an agent can and will do for you.

Agents

Subsidiary rights agents sell your publishing house's marketable book rights to others. Their contacts with editors, subsidiary rights buyers, and foreign agents are critical, particularly if your publishing house is located in Cerola, New Mexico, or Key West, Florida.

An agent is an independent contractor who uses your material, for which licenses are sold. An agent only gets paid if he/she makes you money. If your publishing concern is a newsletter, magazine, journal, or newspaper, an agent is probably not necessary; if books are your business, though, an agent can be a definite asset.

My feeling is that most small presses are a day late and a dollar short on marketing subsidiary rights. How many have you marketed the past six months? It's something that can be done yourself; I spoke with an author-self-publisher who studied the Huenefeld agent guides to marketing subsidiary rights and then sold book club rights to her self-help legal book. Yet, if you have a number of books, the time, energy, and contacts required to sell rights can diminish the time you have to create your product.

Most authors contracting with small presses are agentless. Thus, the subsidiary rights, along with book rights, go from author to publisher; they may then go to a rights agent.

While agents understand contracts better than most, you must know your particular contracts well enough to at least be aware of what rights your company has available. An agent operates as your effective and prepared negotiator, aware of the going rate for the sale of a right, angles on sales potential, and who's looking for, or interested in, the type of material you publish. A subsidiary rights agent can keep your publishing concern's motor revved—there's nothing like outside interest, and potential high-dollar rights sales, to keep your attention. (For more information on agent duties, see "What Does An Agent Do," by Edward K. Sachs, *Small Press*

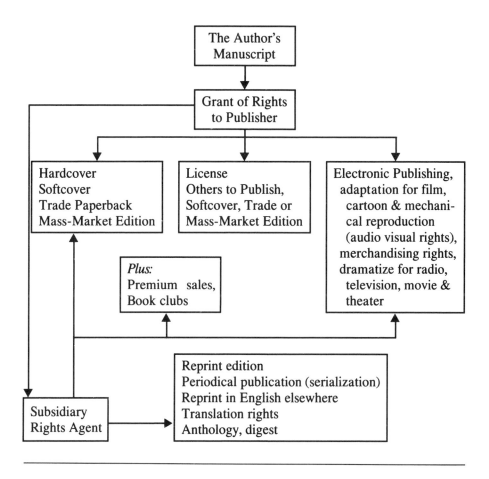

```
                    ┌─────────────────┐
                    │  The Author's   │
                    │   Manuscript    │
                    └─────────────────┘
                             │
                    ┌─────────────────┐
                    │ Grant of Rights │
                    │  to Publisher   │
                    └─────────────────┘
```

| Hardcover
Softcover
Trade Paperback
Mass-Market Edition | License
Others to Publish,
Softcover, Trade or
Mass-Market Edition | Electronic Publishing,
adaptation for film,
cartoon & mechani-
cal reproduction
(audio visual rights),
merchandising rights,
dramatize for radio,
television, movie &
theater |

Plus:
Premium sales,
Book clubs

Subsidiary
Rights Agent

Reprint edition
Periodical publication (serialization)
Reprint in English elsewhere
Translation rights
Anthology, digest

September-October 1986.) The Practising Law Institute's *Legal and Business Aspects of Book Publishing 1988*, outlines the duties of an agent as seen through the eyes of a lawyer-agent, Eugene H. Winick.

As with publishers and editors, there's a tremendous range of age, training, experience, and competence among literary agents. Finding and selecting the right agent for your publishing house requires some work if you cannot get a name through networking. Watch Nathan's "Rights" column in *Publishers Weekly*. Several agents featured there seem to regularly handle small press rights. Try *Literary Market Place*'s section devoted to agents; contact the two agents' organizations: the Society of Author's Representatives (SAR) and the Independent Literary Agents Association (ILAA). Also, there's *Literary Agents of North America,* Third Edition (Research Associates International, 340 East 52nd Street, New York, NY 10022).

Membership in these organizations is predicated on demonstration of the sale of a certain number of properties. However, non-membership, according to Richard Curtis, agent-author of *How to Be Your Own Literary Agent* (Houghton-Mifflin

Co.) does not mean an agent will perform poorly, or be dishonest or incompetent.

If you've found a literary agent, the agent will propose a written agency agreement. Treat it as a starting point for negotiation. From your perspective, the agreement may be incomplete. Here's an actual letter agreement from an agent to a small press, with my comments between its paragraphs:

Dear Publisher:

I agree to use, during the term hereof, due diligence in endeavoring to sell, license, option, or otherwise dispose of certain subsidiary rights to all works published by you whose rights you control.

In consideration of the foregoing, you hereby appoint me as your sole and exclusive agent for those rights designated below to negotiate for such sale, license, option or disposition. However, no such disposition or commitment shall be binding unless you consent thereto.

Sometimes the term "best efforts" is used instead of "due diligence." Neither phrase is exact, but is interpreted to mean that the agent uses commercially viable means common in the publishing world to act on your behalf. The "certain subsidiary rights" are defined later in the agreement, *but* as to those rights, are exclusive. This means that agent is the only person with authority to represent your press in marketing licenses to your press's work—that is, the licenses listed in the letter agreement.

If, prior to this letter agreement, you licensed, optioned, or sold certain of the subsidiary rights, you need to specifically exclude these, i.e., ". . . by you whose rights you control, except for those rights in the works which have been disposed of: all foreign rights in *Bicycle Touring in Europe,* book club sales to QPBC for *A Sexual Guide for Middle-Aged Women.*" Be sure to also exclude works you have out for consideration; allow at least sixty days for licensing those rights. Exclude all works to which the author kept the rights. For contracts capped with a time limit on subsidiary rights sales, indicate these limits.

Require that all offers be submitted to you, i.e., "your written consent thereto; all offers will be submitted to you."

Define the geographic scope of agent's responsibilities: U.S., North America, Europe, etc. Most of the foreign rights in Japan are marketed through a handful of agents, which means that you should reserve these rights for sale through one of these agents.

Notice that there is no actual term to this exclusive agency, just a skimpy termination provision. Add a definitive term, i.e., ". . . your sole and exclusive agent for two years from the date of this agreement for those rights. . . ."

For my services as your agent, you agree to have all monies paid directly to me and I shall deduct sums equal to percentages of the gross proceeds as below specified and forward the remaining percentage to you. Said

sums are payable when received by me during the term hereof, or thereafter, for or in conjunction with the sale, lease, license, or other disposition of or dealings of the below-specified subsidiary rights (and works), when any such contracts or agreements were negotiated for or entered into during the term hereof, even though payments thereon may become due or payable after the expiration of the term hereof, and, upon modifications, extensions, additions, supplements, substitutions, or renewals of such contracts or agreements substituting for or replacing, directly or indirectly, contracts or agreements now in existence or entered into or negotiated during the term hereof, and with respect to those subsidiary rights on which I was to act as your exclusive agent, whether such sales result from my efforts or otherwise.

The last sentence covers your sale of rights during the time the agent operated on an exclusive basis. It can also be written to include sales made after the agreement is terminated; sales made, for example, within sixty days of termination as a result of work done by agent before termination.

Briefly, this clause says that, if your agent sold rights for you, he/she always and forever gets a share of the income, even if you have gone on to another agent. That's an irrevocable financial interest. Add, for clarity's sake, that for any license rights that revert back to publisher after representation ceases, there is no agent interest in same. Also, notice that there is no time period in which the agent is to forward monies. Add one: "forward within ten working days . . ." or the like.

When setting the agency percentage, determine what services this agent can effectively provide. For instance, some agents specialize in marketing foreign rights; some are lawyers who offer legal advice as well; others audit publisher's royalty statements. Some agents specialize in film rights. Most agents ask for, and receive, fifteen percent for the sale of literary rights, up to twenty percent on film and television rights, and up to twenty-five percent in foreign rights.

You recognize that I am in the agency business generally and shall have the right to render to others having creative properties similar to yours, services similar to those I render to you even though the properties may be competitive with yours.

This provision is necessary given the number of works produced by each publisher each season. Most agents handle a number of publishers, and must be able to represent competing works.

I shall keep you fully informed of the progress of all negotiations pertaining to the disposition of the aforesaid subsidiary and foreign rights.

This provision is too general; move the requirement that all offers be submitted to you here. Detail what you consider to be appropriate information, and the timelines for giving you that information.

You represent and warrant to me that you have the power and authority under your agreement with the authors of the works covered by this agreement to enter this agreement with me.

This is just like other warranties and indemnities: you warrant you have the legal right to sell specific rights in the work; you can't sell what you don't own. If the agent sells to another publisher license rights that you do not have, that publisher may come back to your agent for compensation in the event of a legal dispute. The agent will, in turn, seek to recover damages from you.

You agree to list me as your subsidiary rights representative for purposes of negotiating the dispositions covered hereunder in all trade publications such as *Literary Market Place,* and in sales catalogues published or authorized by you.
　　This agreement shall automatically continue from year to year unless either party shall give written notice to the other party of its desire to terminate this agreement at least sixty days prior to the anniversary of this agreement.

See my previous comment. On the one hand, an agent invests time in a house's list and this investment may not pay off right away. You should give the agent two years to produce for you and if he or she does, continue it year to year. Do not tie the termination to the anniversary date. If the latter is February 1, and you have had it with your agent on June 1, under the terms of the agreement, you'll have to wait till December to cut the tie.

You shall pay mailing expenses not to exceed $30.00 per month, upon submission of a bill each month.

Some of the agent's costs directly related to marketing your house's work that are not overhead follow:

- mail costs, including airmailing overseas.
- messenger services (to take a contract across Manhattan).
- book copies (if you do not provide them).
- photocopying.
- long-distance telephone calls.
- cables, telegrams, telex.

Under this provision, only the mailing expenses are deducted. Here, I'd add "actual mailing."

This letter constitutes our entire understanding. There are no representations, warranties or undertakings other than those expressly set forth herein.

If the foregoing correctly sets forth your understanding, please sign both copies of this letter, retaining one fully signed copy for your files and returning the other copy to me for mine.

This provision means that oral changes, additions, etc., are not binding. In this sort of agreement, as in others previously discussed, everything should be reduced to the written word. If changes or modifications are handwritten in, they should be initialled by both parties.

This contract's major flaw is the lack of a clear-cut termination clause. That clause can balance the agent's need to benefit from his/her long-term efforts on your behalf (which may come to fruition ten days after you send a unilateral termination notice) with your need for new or more effective representation. Without such a clause, the agent may be forced into an "I'll sue you" mode. While termination can normally take place at any time upon breach of contract by either party, in most cases, it occurs in the manner dictated by the agreement's terms. If your agreement has no specific direction, you could be caught in a tedious legal problem, as well.

Here's a termination clause from an actual author-agent agreement.

This agreement is effective immediately and continues in effect until either you or I have cancelled it, which either may do by one giving the other thirty (30) days' notice in writing of such cancellation, providing that you will continue to function as agent and to receive your commission on all contracts theretofore negotiated and concluded during the life of this agreement, said commission being hereby assigned and transferred to you as an agency coupled with an interest. In the event within sixty (60) days after effective termination date hereof, I enter into a contract covering any of my aforementioned literary rights with a person or firm with whom you had, prior to such termination, been negotiating for the disposition of said rights, said contract shall be deemed to have been entered into during the term of the within agreement.

There haven't been many cases reported on agents. A federal court reduced the $60,000-plus award to Kitty Kelly to $41,407 because her agent, Luciann S. Goldberg, withheld royalties of $41,407, but cut off further commissions to the agent in Kelly's *Elizabeth Taylor: The Last Star* (*Publishers Weekly*, March 9, 1984 and December 16, 1983). Even before the reduction in damages, Kelly's lawyer, who filed the $2.5 million suit, called it a "sad" victory.

The Independent Literary Agents Association Code of Ethics, and the Society of Authors' Representatives, Inc.'s, Canons of Ethics, set forth general agency principles. These codes follow:

ILAA
Code of Ethics

1. A member shall represent his or her client in a professional manner,

consistent with all applicable law and in accordance with the member's fiduciary responsibility to the client. A member shall deal honorably and in good faith with other agents, publishers, and all others with whom he or she has professional dealings.

2. A member shall take responsible measures to protect the security and integrity of the client's funds. A member shall deposit funds received on behalf of the client promptly upon receipt, and shall make payments of funds due the client promptly, but in no event later than ten business days after clearance. A member's books of account pertaining to the client shall be open to him or her at mutually convenient times.

3. A member shall inform his or her client of significant matters relating to the client's work. A member shall provide all information, including copies of agreements and royalty statements, concerning the client's work that the client shall reasonably request.

4. A member shall discuss and agree with the client at the outset of their relationship the commission and/or other compensation to be retained or received. A member shall discuss in advance those expenses that shall be paid or reimbursed by the client, which may include, among others, expenses for books and galleys, photocopies, legal fees, messenger fees, postage, long distance telephone calls, telex and cable charges.

5. A member shall not be engaged professionally, on a regular or continuing basis, not exceeding twenty per cent (20%) of the member's professional activity, in acquiring authors' services and rights to literary properties, as distinct from representing clients in the sale of such services or granting of such rights. The foregoing shall not apply to a member's scouting activities. A member shall disclose to his or her client the member's professional involvement in acquiring rights to literary properties (including scouting), or engaging author's services, at the outset of any transaction which could create a conflict of interest for the member, or the appearance of such a conflict. Whenever a member proposes to acquire literary property from, or engage the services of a client, the member shall advise the client fully of the member's role in the proposed transaction, and of the client's right to obtain separate representation therein.

Reprinted by permission of Independent Literary Agents Association.

SOCIETY OF AUTHORS' REPRESENTATIVES, Inc.
CANON OF ETHICS
(as promulgated by the Committee on Ethics and Practices)

1. The members of the Society of Authors' Representatives are committed to the highest standard of conduct in the performance of their professional activities. While affirming the necessity and desirability of maintaining their full individuality and freedom of action, the members pledge themselves to loyal service to their clients' business and artistic

needs, and will allow no conflicts of interest which would interfere with such service. They pledge their support to the Society itself and to the principles of honorable coexistence, directness, and honesty in their relationships with their co-members. They undertake never to mislead, deceive, dupe, defraud, or victimize their clients, other members of the Society, the general public, or any person with whom they do business as a member of the Society.

2. Members must maintain separate bank accounts so that monies due authors are not commingled with member's other funds.

3. In addition to such compensation for ordinary agency services as may be agreed upon between the individual members and their individual clients, each member may, subject to the approval of his or its client, pass along to such client charges incurred by the member on the client's behalf, such as copyright fees, manuscript retyping, machine copies, copies of books for use in the sale of other rights, long distance calls, cables, special messenger fees, and travel costs. Such charges shall only be made after first notifying the author to ensure his approval.

4. Members shall keep each client apprised of all matters entrusted to them, and shall promptly furnish such information as the author may reasonably request.

5. Members shall not represent both buyer and seller in the same transaction unless the member notifies both parties before any negotiations proceed and offers the opportunity to either party to arrange for other representation in that transaction. The member shall receive a commission or payment from only the author or the employer, not both.

6. Members may not receive a secret profit in connection with any transaction involving a client. If such profit is received, the member must promptly pay over the entire amount to the client.

7. Members must treat their clients' financial affairs as private and confidential except as required by law.

8. Payments and accounts to clients shall be rendered promptly on receipt by members within ten days unless otherwise instructed by the client. Revenues from translation rights shall be paid to the client within a reasonable time of their receipt. However, on stock and similar rights, statements of royalties and payments shall be made the month following receipt by the member, each statement and payment to cover all royalties received to the 25th day of the previous calendar month. Payments for amateur rights shall be made every six months. Members' books of accounts must be open to the client at all times with respect to transactions concerning him.

9. Where a member has a written contract with an author, it shall not be assignable by the member without the author's prior written consent, except to organizations merging with or acquiring the member, or substantially all its assets.

10. On the death of an author, the member shall continue to remit all net

sums from payments made in accordance with agreements existing to the date of death.

Licenses

A grant of a subsidiary right is accomplished through a "license." A license is merely a property-right-holder's permission to another to use the property in a certain, often very specific and narrow, way. The earlier chart of subsidiary rights (page 321) graphically explains the scope of rights that you may be able to market under your particular contractual arrangements with an author. Many of these can be further subdivided. For instance, foreign translation rights can be separated into sales in many languages, and include audio cassette translations for unwritten languages.

Generally speaking, because you operate a small publishing house does not mean that subsidiary rights are without value. Nathan reported in *Publishers Weekly* (August 14, 1987) that Dana Randt set up a new publishing enterprise in Ketchum, Idaho, and the company's very first title, *Carson: The Unauthorized Biography*, by Paul Corkery, was doing as well "in the subrights market as any New York house. . . ." *Good Housekeeping* picked up the first and second serial rights; the *National Enquirer* and Literary Guild took it as an alternate selection. Nathan concluded "that's not bad for a tenderfooted backwater publisher." Or consider that little Conari Press's (Berkeley, California) first new title in six years, *Coming Apart: Why Relationships End and How to Live Through the Ending of Yours*, by Daphne Rose Kingma, was acquired by the Literary Guild and Doubleday Book Club (Nathan, *Publishers Weekly,* November 20, 1987). In December 1987, Nathan reported that military- or technical-book publishers with first works of fiction concerning the Cold War were finding themselves with best-sellers that often ended in a paperback auction. To wit: Naval Institute Press, *The Hunt for Red October,* by Tom Clancy and *Flight of the Intruder,* by Steven Coonts; Presidio Press, *Team Yankee: A Novel of World War III*, by Harold Coyls; TAB Books of Blue Ridge, *Good Friday,* by Robert Lawrence Holt.

Reprint

This is an arrangement with another publishing house in which your book is reprinted by them in a different form. If, for example, you've published a hardcover fiction work, the right to reprint and release that same work in a quality trade paperback or mass-market paperback can be sold to another publisher. Some categorize the reprint rights as the most valuable; the publisher and author normally share equally in the proceeds. Only very successful, well-known authors get more than fifty percent of the reprint income.

A reprint contract can include bonuses for best-seller lists, prizes, movie sales, and so forth. Reprint sales for a small press book can be crucial to the book's success, either through sales or prize recognition. Nathan reported that TAB's auctioneer, Tammy Ray, ran the auction for *Good Friday* with a floor of $20,000; she worked through five bidding rounds with four publishers. New American Library's bid of $300,000 won. In response to Nathan's question "how does someone miles from New York who has never run an auction do it?" Ms. Ray said, "We read about them . . . and we figured out how to go about it ourselves. We are very proud of the result." Another success story. Mary Quinlan, vice-president of Quinlan Press, simply sent a copy of *A Cop's Cop,* by a Boston police superintendent, and a short note to editors at paperback houses; in an accompanying letter, she inquired about their interest in mass-market rights. Avon Books called her with an offer of $5,000, and Quinlan then called the other publishers she'd queried telling them of Avon's interest and asking about theirs.

If you want to try this yourself, start your research with Lindey's discussion of reprint contracts on the auction method of selling paperback rights. Nathan's "Rights" column frequently describes what happens during paperback auctions, too. Follow that column if you are going to be involved in rights auctions.

As your author cannot grant you what he or she does not have, you cannot grant to a reprint publisher any rights that you aren't given in your author–publisher contract. If you didn't acquire the subsidiary rights, and there's some interest, you'll need to negotiate an addendum prior to negotiating reprint contracts.

Reprint licenses are usually given for five years (sometimes more). As with any other contract, be sure the commencement of the term is given as a specific date. If you run it from the date the reprint publisher publishes the work, you have granted an additional year or so to the term. Beware of two other provisions that can extend the term of your reprint agreement:

- termination cannot occur until the reprint publisher sells a certain quantity of the books, or
- if the reprinter goes back to press within X period of time of the end of the contract, automatic renewal is accomplished.

I suggest that you reread your author–publisher contract and highlight any unusual provisions, such as limits on promotion or using the author's likeness and biographical data, so that the same restraints are reflected in the reprint contract. It's best to avoid automatic renewal and extension clauses, but if you can't, tie them into another advance.

Since you don't want a cheaper edition of the book to cut into the sales of your hardcover edition, delay the reprinting of the cheaper edition until sales of the original book have peaked, usually within eighteen months.

Ten Speed Press's *Ladies' Own Erotica,* by the Kensington Ladies' Erotica Society, became a Pocket Books lead mass-market title for February 1986; the reprint contract included provisions for floor displays, bookmarks, and author appearances. (See "Think Mass Market," by Joseph Barbato, *Small Press,* March/April 1986.) Royalties often start at six percent and go upward to ten percent of list price, depending upon the author's name. Percentages, of course, are sometimes tied to sales points, often referred to as break points, under the theory that, at a certain level, the overhead costs of the reprint publishers have been met.

Advances on reprint sales are important, since sometimes, this edition will reduce your own sales of the book; for small presses, reprints by big houses also serve to get their book into much wider distribution and spur hardcover sales. Sometimes, non-repayable advances, or bonuses, are given for:

- each appearance on a best-seller list.
- position of the book on the list.
- a motion picture production.
- an award of an important literary prize.
- the sale of a large number of editions, or for a great number of books in print.

For sums payable in installments, put a date on the second installment, regardless of whether the paperback edition is printed or not.

Obviously, you've got to stand behind the reprint publisher if they are sued; you must agree to indemnify them. In the usual situation, the reprint publisher may have better or more sophisticated legal talent available, but it would be difficult for the small publisher to control the legal costs and resolution of the suit. Be sure to retain the right to sue third persons who may infringe your or your author's copyright. At least, be able to sue if the reprint publisher doesn't act.

Be wary of option clauses, and if you've got to grant one, limit it to a pretty tight timeline. Also restrict the time on the first refusal clause and add a statement that the reprint publisher must meet any figure that you may be offered by another publisher.

Refer to the discussion of reduced royalties (page 121), as highly discounted books could drop your reprint royalties to less than half of the regular rate. Consider:

- a reduced royalty, at quarter- or half-percent levels, for each percentage point over 50%.
- dropping the discount percentage figure upon which your reduced royalty kicks into effect. Example: copies sold at a discount of 60% or more, rather than 50% or 55%.
- capping the royalty at a figure no lower than one-half of the original royalty.

The PLI *Book Publishing* texts set forth several reprint contracts. Reproduced below are two unusual proposed license agreements regarding works published by small presses. The first work is a proposed licensing agreement for a video production and the second, a self-help manual that a mail-order company wanted to include in its catalogue. Comments about each proposed license follow the license. In each of these situations, the individual small press felt that the marketing capabilities of the larger companies might warrant their distribution of the product, even though it cut into the press's own sales.

Dear Sir:

The following, when signed by both parties, shall constitute our agreement as follows:

1. *Grant of License.* ("Licensor"), as the holder of rights licensed hereunder in certain video recordings (the "Work"), listed in Appendix A hereby grants to _____ worldwide exclusive rights, for fair value received, to manufacture, distribute and sell video recordings derived from the Work ("copies") intended for private home entertainment.

2. *Consideration.* _____ shall have the absolute right to approve the content of all Programs and upon such approval and, as full consideration for all rights herein granted, _____ agrees to pay the Licensor the amount indicated in Appendix A for each title as a non-refundable, fully recoupable advance against 50% of Earnings from Operations of _____'s sales of the aforementioned Program. For purposes of the foregoing, "Earnings from Operations" shall be defined as net revenues after all credits for returns, trade discounts, allowances or other rebates less all actual duplication, printing and other manufacturing costs as well as all sales, advertising, distribution, and administrative ("SADA") expenses. Said SADA expenses will be budgeted by _____ at a level not exceeding 25% of _____'s anticipated net revenues for the Program, provided that no less than ½ of such SADA expenses shall be budgeted for advertising expenses. Notwithstanding the foregoing it is understood that such budgeted expenses shall be a guideline only and that _____ shall have full discretion to provide such discounts and payments and to determine how best to promote, advertise and market the copies and to exploit any additional right granted hereunder. _____ shall not be responsible to Licensor for any particular level of sales or amount of gross proceeds therefrom.

3. *Accounting.*

   (a) _____ shall render statements of account to Licensor, setting forth in reasonable detail the computation of the amounts due Licensor hereunder semi-annually during the term hereof within forty-five (45) days after the close of each six-month period ending June 30 and December 31, together with payment of the full amount due. Copies sold in any such six-month period and returned in a subsequent six-month period may be deducted on _____'s statements up to the total number of copies sold in the previous six-month period. _____'s statement shall show the number of free copies distributed under this Agreement with a maximum of 500 free copies per Work per year.

   (b) Licensor, or a duly authorized representative thereof, shall have the right to inspect and make extracts from _____'s books and records insofar as said books and records pertain to the exercise of any rights granted to _____ hereunder. Such inspection shall be made at the Licensor's expense on ten (10) business days' written notice, during _____'s regular business hours on normal business days at _____'s principal place of business, but not more frequently than two times a year.

4. *Territory.*

   (a) The territory of the license is the World.

   (b) _____ shall release copies of the Works in the United States of America no later than _____ months after receipt of the master tape of the Works, liner and label notes information, all in form and content satisfactory to _____ . _____ may release copies at such later time in such other places within the Territory as _____ in its sole discretion shall determine.

5. *Licensor's Warranties and Representations.* Licensor hereby warrants, represents and agrees that:

   (a) Licensor has the right to enter into this Agreement, to grant _____ the rights licensed hereunder and is under no disability, restriction, or prohibition in respect to the right to execute this Agreement and to perform the terms hereof; the full and free exercise of the rights granted hereunder will not conflict with or infringe upon any right of any party.

   (b) All persons whose performances, names and recognizable likenesses are embodied in the Works and all other persons or entities whose rights may be involved therein have been or will be completely paid by Licensor for the release of such rights or will have given written waiver of such rights or will have given written waiver of any such payment in connection with the Works.

   (c) Licensor has the right to use and to allow _____ to use the names, likenesses and biographical material for all persons whose performances are embodied in the recordings.

6. *Indemnification.* Each of the parties hereto undertakes and agrees to indemnify, save and hold the other, and anyone claiming through the other, free and harmless from any and all liability, loss, damage, cost or expense, including reasonable attorney's fees arising out of, connected with or related to any claim by any third party which is inconsistent with any of the parties' respective agreements, warranties, or representations hereunder; provided that the indemnified party shall give the indemnifying party (a) prompt notice of any such claim, (b) opportunity to defend or settle same solely with counsel of its choice, (c) cooperation in the defense or settlement thereof. The indemnified party shall have the right, if the indemnifying party does not assume the defense, to defend any claim with its own attorney, but no settlement of any claim shall be made without consent of the indemnifying party; provided that as and when it is reasonably required by the indemnified party, the indemnifying party shall post a bond or provide some other security sufficient in value to indemnify the indemnified

party fully against the claim and all related liability, loss or expense. This provision shall survive the termination or expiration hereof.

7. *Label Copy, Mechanical, Music Credits.* Licensor agrees to furnish promptly to _____ the proper label copy regarding any musical composition embodied in the Works to enable _____ to verify that any required mechanical reproduction license has been obtained and to provide appropriate music credits.

8. *Credits.* _____ agrees to give appropriate credit to Licensor in a mutually agreed upon form. If the Work includes any material protected under the United States Copyright Act, _____ agrees to affix to the copies an appropriate copyright notice. _____ shall have the right to add its own trade identifier(s) and any nonduplication announcements to the Works prior to the start of any material provided by Licensor and after the conclusion of any material provided by Licensor, and to modify any title, credit or end frames in accordance herewith. _____ may, in its sole discretion, retitle the copies as it deems appropriate. Except as provided herein, _____ shall not alter the Works and shall use the entire Work, including any and all trade identifiers of Licensor (or his contractors) embodied in the Work.

9. *Remedies.* The rights and remedies of Licensor in the event of any breach of this Agreement, shall be limited to Licensor's right, if any, to recover money damages in an action at law, and in no event shall Licensor be entitled by reason of any such breach to terminate this Agreement or to enjoin, restrain, or interfere with the production, licensing, performance, distribution, advertising, or any other means of exploiting the Work or the copies. _____ shall, in the event of a material breach hereof by Licensor not cured in accordance with Par. 14 *infra,* have the sole option to terminate this Agreement in addition to all other rights and remedies provided at law or equity.

10. *Licensor Copies.* _____ shall promptly upon commercial release of the copies, provide to Licensor at no charge ten (10) finished copies of each Work covered by this Agreement.

11. *Term.* The term of this Agreement shall be for five (5) years from the date of commercial release of the copies. At the expiration of the term of this Agreement, it may be extended on the mutual consent of the parties.

12. *Force Majeure.* If, because of an act of God, inevitable accident, fire, lockout, strike or other labor dispute, riot or civil commotion, act of public enemy, enactment, rule order or act of any government or governmental instrumentality (whether federal, state, local or foreign), failure of technical facilities, failure or delay of transportation facilities, or other cause of a similar or different nature not reasonably within _____'s control, _____ is materially hampered in the manufacture, distribution, or sale of copies hereunder, then, for the

duration of such event or circumstance, _____ may suspend the term hereof by written notice to Licensor to such effect. Nothing contained herein shall affect _____'s obligation under this Agreement to pay royalties due to the Licensor for copies sold after the suspension or termination of this Agreement.

13. *Construction.* This Agreement shall be construed in accordance with the laws of the State of New York governing contracts fully made and to be performed entirely within said State. It is the entire Agreement between the parties and cannot be modified except by a written instrument signed by both Licensor and _____. Invalidity or unenforceability of any part of this Agreement shall not affect the validity or enforceability of the balance thereof.

14. *Waiver and Curing Breach.* Waiver of any provision of this Agreement shall not affect either party's rights thereafter to enforce such provision or to exercise any right or remedy in the event of any other default. Each party must give the other party at least thirty (30) days' notice of any breach or default hereunder and the party receiving such notice shall have thirty (30) days from the receipt thereof within which to cure said breach or default.

15. *Notices.* All notices or demands which either party shall be required or desire to give to the other hereunder shall be in writing at the address indicated, or at such other address as a party shall designate in writing, and shall be given by either personal delivery or by mailing them registered or certified mail, return receipt requested.

16. *Effective Date and Confidentiality.* This Agreement shall become effective upon execution by both parties and shall be deemed confidential by the parties, each of which shall take such reasonable steps with respect to its contents as they normally take to safeguard confidential materials from disclosure to third parties.

Please signify your acceptance of the foregoing by signing in the space provided below.

Very truly yours,

By: _____
Title: _____

The video letter/license agreement did not include the advance and it did not refer to revenue from other sources. Some of my comments to my client about the proposed video license follow:

Grant of License:
• Need to see Appendix A.

- Appendix A or body of agreement needs to accept sales that _____ makes through _____ outlets, its mail order catalog, _____ .
- Worldwide exclusive rights need to be subject to the above.

Consideration:
- Appendix A apparently includes the advance. You might negotiate a higher one or offer _____ a flat fee.
- _____ has approved the content of the video recording _____ .
- COGS is listed in the EFO worksheet but it is not defined in the contract and needs definition.
- Are the terms "non-refundable" and "fully recoupable" mutually exclusive?
- The SADA expenses include duplication, printing, and manufacturing costs, which would also be included in COGS unless SADA includes COGS, selling, administration, and distribution costs, and if so, the exhibit should reflect that.
- Should establish a base so that they do not undersell _____ direct sales in terms of item price.

Accounting:
- If they give more than 500 free copies per work per year, if you apply the consideration paragraph, you still don't get paid.
- Aren't 500 free copies quite a few?
- Ten (10) business days' written notice seems too long but may not be worth hassling about.

Territory:
- "Liner and label notes information"? Who provides that?

Licensor's Warranties and Representations:
- (a) Add "except as disclosed in Exhibit A."
- Under (b), it looks like _____ need to give a written waiver of any payment from _____ to them at the very least and/or waive such rights due to the payment of considerations as set forth in the agreement between _____ and themselves and the letter agreement of such and such a date.
- Are there other persons whose performances are embodied?

Indemnification:
- Doubt if you could get them to change any provision here.

Label Copy, Mechanical Music Credits:
- Isn't the label copy already on the video? Change that _____ accepts that label copy.

Credits:
- Does this mean that they are going to do another box?
- Retitling the copies may not be agreeable to _____ .

Remedies:
- _____'s remedies should be available to the Licensor, which includes remedies at law or equity and termination for material breach.
- This means that if they have been cheating _____, you can't terminate the contract.
- Should be able to terminate it at least after six months or a year, or if there is a material breach.
- Are ten (10) copies enough?

Term:
- Probably okay because of the size of the company.

Force Majeure:
- Limit suspension of the term for not longer than 90 days unless mutually agreed upon in writing for each such event.

Construction, et al. through Paragraph 16:
- Means you've got to sue them in New York State and that you've agreed to be sued in New York State, not good.
- Thirty (30) days' notice and thirty (30) days to cure seem like a helluva long time.

Other comments:
- Suggest "the rights granted hereunder shall be exclusive to _____ except that the rights with respect to home video distribution by _____, by marketing through the _____, and marketing through _____'s normal and usual distribution channels and all preexisting uses and/or licenses shall not be precluded hereunder."
- Some limitation on commercials, see last two sentences under Consideration.
- Define private home entertainment as the exposition of the work by means of a cassette in private living accommodations where no viewing fee is charged to the viewer of such exhibition.
- Sometimes non-theatrical exhibition is added, which covers schools and other educational institutions, libraries, government agencies, military installations, churches, etc.
- Does the provision in Credits allowing them to "modify any title, credit or end frames in accordance herewith" just allow them to modify their own trade identifiers, etc.?
- This modification shall not delete credits that Licensor considers appropriate.
- To clarify the waiver section, perhaps we could add there "that any payments required to be made to any person, group or institution who participated in the production of the program will be made by Licensor and shall not be the responsibility of Licensee."

We could add:
- All work manufactured and distributed by _____ shall be of first-

class technical quality, although that might be insulting, but could be of concern to _____.

- The Licensor has licensed _____ as set forth in paragraph _____, however, Licensor agrees that it will not sell, assign, license, grant or encumber or utilize licensed _____ to other than indicated previously.
- _____ shall have the complete, exclusive control of the distribution, exhibition, exploitation and other disposition of _____ directly except for the limitations on same in paragraph _____.
- Upon the expiration of this agreement, or the termination of the same, _____ shall not manufacture any further copies of the video _____ and the reproduction masters shall be returned to the Licensor. _____ shall have a period of six months in which to dispose of the inventory of video cassettes of the work on hand as of the applicable date of termination of expiration and shall remain liable for the payment of royalties for the sale of the work in its inventory as of such expiration or termination but at the end of six months, shall return to Licensor the unsold inventory.
- This contract shall be binding on the heirs, executors, successors in interest or administrators of the parties, or assigns, but no assignment shall be binding on either party without the written consent of the other.

The second license was for a publication, a self-help manual that a national company wanted to add to its catalogue. It is reproduced in its entirety due to its non-exclusivity, product liability, insurance coverage, quality of merchandise, and distribution provisions.

Dear _____

This letter sets forth the terms and conditions of the license between _____ (LICENSOR) and _____ (LICENSEE):

WHEREAS, LICENSOR is the owner of all rights, including copyright and trademarks in the characters, names and/or designs listed in Schedule "A" of the Annex, or has the power and authority to grant the rights granted hereunder, and;

WHEREAS, LICENSOR has the sole right to license others to use the names of characters and/or designs appearing therein and of their likenesses and visual and audio representations and of any symbols and designs appearing therein or derived therefrom (hereafter referred to, whether separately or collectively, as "the Property");

WHEREAS, Licensee desires to utilize the Property upon and in connection with the manufacture, sale, distribution and promotion of articles hereinafter described;

THEREFORE, in consideration of the mutual promises herein contained, it is hereby agreed:

1. GRANT OF LICENSE

(a) Licensor hereby grants to Licensee the right to utilize the Property on products which Licensee produces and distributes. The items to which this license extends are listed in Schedule "A."

(b) The territory of this license is the United States of America and its Territories.

(c) Articles produced under this license shall be sold via direct mail chains of distribution, and in up to eight (8) LICENSEE-owned retail outlets.

(d) The term of this agreement shall commence on _____ and continue to _____ under the conditions listed below in Paragraph 2 (a). Assuming these conditions are met, this license shall be automatically extended in one year increments, unless either party shall provide written notice to the contrary within sixty (60) days prior to the end of the term.

2. TERMS OF PAYMENT

(a) Royalty Rate shall be _____ on net sales. The term "net sales" shall mean gross sales less trade quantity and cash discounts, returns, and postage allowance. Postage allowance shall be calculated as follows:
Units sold X _____ = Postage allowance. _____ is the percentage of orders received with cash, on which LICENSEE pays postage at the rate of _____ per unit. In the event of a postage increase, this formula shall be adjusted to reflect the actual postage paid.

(b) Advance and Guarantee:
LICENSEE shall pay LICENSOR _____ upon signing, as a non-refundable advance against royalties.

(c) Promptly on the thirtieth (30th) day of the months of April, July, October, and January, LICENSEE shall furnish LICENSOR with complete and accurate statements, showing the number, description and gross sales price, and itemized deductions as described in Paragraph 2 (a), of each product covered by this agreement. Royalty payment shall accompany the statements furnished.

3. EXCLUSIVITY

(a) It is understood that this is a non-exclusive license, since LICENSOR has already established channels of distribution which may include direct-mail catalogs.

(b) LICENSOR agrees, however, to provide notice to LICENSEE prior to granting licenses to manufacturers or distributors who directly compete with LICENSEE at retail or through direct mail.

4. INDEMNIFICATION BY LICENSEE AND PRODUCT LIABILITY INSURANCE

Licensee hereby indemnifies Licensor and undertakes to defend Licensee and/or Licensor against and hold Licensor harmless from any claims, suits, loss and damage arising out of any allegedly unauthorized use of any patent, process, idea, method or device by Licensee in connection with the articles covered by this Agreement or any other alleged action by Licensee and also from any claims, suits, loss and damage arising out of alleged defects in the articles or personal damages or injury resulting from the use of the licensed articles or services by others. Licensee agrees that it will obtain, at its own expense, product liability insurance from a recognized insurance company which has qualified to do business in the State of _____, providing adequate protection (at least in the amount of $500,000) for Licensor and Licensee against any claims, suits, loss or damage arising out of any alleged defects in the articles. As proof of such insurance, a fully paid certificate of insurance naming Licensor as an insured party will be submitted to Licensor by Licensee for Licensor's prior approval before any article is distributed or sold, and at latest within thirty (30) days after the date first written above. Any proposed change in certificates of insurance shall be submitted to Licensor for its prior approval. Licensor shall be entitled to a copy of the then prevailing certificate of insurance, which shall be furnished Licensor by Licensee. As used in the first two sentences of this Paragraph 6, "Licensor" shall also include the officers, directors, agents and employees of the Licensor or Licensor's parent, subsidiaries, or any of its or its parent's subsidiaries or affiliates, any person(s) the use of whose name may be licensed hereunder and the package producer.

5. QUALITY OF MERCHANDISE

(a) Licensee agrees that the articles covered by this Agreement shall be of high standard and of such style, appearance and quality as to be adequate and suited to their exploitation to the best advantage and to the protection and enhancement of the Property and the good will pertaining thereto, that such articles will be manufactured, sold, distributed and promoted in accordance with all applicable Federal, State and local laws, and that the policy of manufacture, sale, distribution and/or promotion by Licensee shall be of high standard and to the best advantage of the Property and that the same shall in no manner reflect adversely upon the good name of Licensor or the Property. To this end Licensee shall, before selling or distributing any of the articles, furnish to the Licensor free of cost, for its written approval, a reasonable number of samples of each article and its cartons, containers and packing and wrapping material. The quality and style of such articles as well as of any carton, container or packing or wrapping material shall be subject to the approval of Licensor. Any item submitted to Licensor shall not be deemed approved unless and until the same shall be approved by Licensor in writing. After samples have been approved pursuant to this paragraph, Licensee shall not depart therefrom in any material respect without Licensor's prior written consent, and Licensor shall not withdraw its approval of the approved samples except on sixty (60) days' prior written notice to Licensee. From time to time after Licensee has commenced selling the articles and upon Licensor's written request, Licensee shall furnish without cost to the Licensor not more than five (5) additional random samples of each article being manufactured and sold by Licensee hereunder, together with any cartons, containers and packaging and wrapping material used in connection therewith.

(b) It is understood that Licensor shall have the right to take samples at random from production runs twice a year but that, if quality problems are encountered as a result of the examination of samples, Licensor shall have the right to take such samples more frequently than that in an effort to assure that proper quality control has been established. Moreover, Licensor shall have the right to have its representatives visit the plant or plants where the articles covered by this license are made and where the containers, packaging material and the like are printed or produced in order to determine whether or not proper quality controls are being exercised.

6. LABELING

(a) LICENSEE agrees to provide proper notices on all product and promotional material developed as a result of this agreement.

(b) Correct form for product shall be: _____.

LICENSOR shall provide reproduction-quality logos for use by LICENSEE.

(c) Correct form for packaging and promotional material shall be: _____.

(d) LICENSEE will not, without written permission of LICENSOR, use or sell the articles licensed hereunder as premiums, either alone or in connection with another product. LICENSEE may, at its discretion, use articles licensed hereunder, as a sample in its catalogs, intended to show quality of the products offered for sale. However, LICENSEE will notify LICENSOR in writing before so doing.

(e) Licensee agrees to cooperate fully and in good faith with Licensor for the purpose of securing and preserving Licensor's (or any grantor of Licensor's) rights in and to the property. In the event there has been no previous registration of the Property and/or articles and/or any material relating thereto, Licensee shall, at Licensor's request and expense, register a copyright and trademark and/or servicemark in the appropriate class in the name of Licensor or, if Licensor so requests, in Licensee's own name. However, it is agreed that nothing contained in this Agreement shall be construed as an assignment or grant to the Licensee of any right, title or interest in or to the Property, it being understood that all rights relating thereto are reserved by Licensor, except for the license hereunder to Licensee of the right to use and utilize the Property only as specifically and expressly provided in this Agreement. Licensee hereby agrees that at the termination or expiration of this Agreement Licensee will be deemed to have assigned, transferred and conveyed to Licensor any trade rights, trademark, servicemark or copyright, equities, good will, titles or other rights in and to the Property which may have been obtained by Licensee or which may have been vested in Licensee in pursuance of any endeavors covered hereby, and that Licensee will execute any instruments requested by Licensor to accomplish or confirm the foregoing. Any such assignment, transfer or conveyance shall be without other consideration than the mutual covenants and considerations of this Agreement.

7. TECHNICAL AND PROMOTIONAL MATERIAL

(a) Upon selection of artwork, LICENSOR shall furnish LICENSEE with original artwork for reproduction. Such artwork remains the property of LICENSOR and shall be returned.

(b) LICENSEE shall not offer for sale or advertise or publicize articles covered hereunder without prior approval of LICENSOR. Such approval will not be unreasonably withheld, and approval will be deemed to have been given if written notification to the contrary is not received by LICENSEE within ten (10) days of receipt of these materials by LICENSOR.

8. DISTRIBUTION

(a) Licensee agrees that during the term of this license it will commence by the date shown in the Annex, Paragraph 4(a) of this Agreement and, thereafter, it will diligently and continuously manufacture, sell, distribute and promote articles covered by this Agreement and that it will make and maintain adequate arrangement for the distribution of the articles. In addition to all other remedies available to it hereunder, Licensor may remove from this Agreement any Property listed on Schedule "A" or any articles or class or category of articles which are not so diligently and continuously used by Licensee in the manufacture, sale, distribution and promotion of such articles for a period of three (3) consecutive months by giving thirty (30) days' notice to Licensee.

9. RECORDS

Licensee agrees to keep accurate books of account and records in a form meeting the generally accepted standards of the profession of certified public accountants covering all transactions relating to the license hereby granted, and Licensor and its duly authorized representative shall have the right at all reasonable hours of the day to an examination of said books of account and records and of all other documents and materials in the possession or under the control of Licensee with respect to the subject matter and terms of this Agreement, and shall have free and full access thereto for said purposes and for the purpose of making extracts therefrom. Upon demand of Licensor, Licensee shall at Licensor's expense furnish to Licensor a detailed statement by an independent certified public accountant showing the number, description, gross sales price, itemized deductions from gross sales price and net sales price of the articles covered by this Agreement distributed and/or sold by Licensee to the date of Licensor's demand. If such examination and audit shall disclose a deficiency in royalty payments of five (5) percent or more, then in addition to making up such deficiency, Licensee shall reimburse the expense of such examination and audit. All books of account and records shall be kept available for at least two (2) years after the termination of this license.

10. DEFAULT AND TERMINATION

(a) If Licensee shall fail to pay when due any and all payment required under this Agreement or fails to perform any of its other obligations under the terms of this Agreement or breaches any covenant contained or referred to in this Agreement, Licensor shall have the right to terminate the license hereby granted upon thirty (30) days' notice in writing, except that with regard to any failure or breach relating to copyright notification, royalty payments or royalty statements, the notification period shall be ten (10) days, such termination shall become effective unless Licensee shall completely remedy the failure or breach within either the ten (10) or thirty (30) day period as appropriate and satisfy Licensor that the failure or breach has been remedied.

(b) Termination of the license under the provisions of Paragraph 12 shall be without prejudice to any rights which Licensor may otherwise have against Licensee. Upon the termination of this license, notwithstanding anything to the contrary herein, all royalties on sales theretofore made shall become immediately due and payable and no minimum royalties shall be repayable.

11. FINAL STATEMENT UPON TERMINATION OR EXPIRATION

(a) Ninety (90) days before the expiration of this license and, in the event of its termination, ten (10) days after receipt of notice of termination or the happening of the event which terminates this Agreement where no notice is required, a statement showing the number and description of articles covered by this Agreement on hand or in process shall be furnished by Licensee to Licensor. Licensor shall have the right to take a physical inventory to ascertain or verify such inventory and statement, and refusal by Licensee to submit to such physical inventory by Licensor shall forfeit Licensee's right to dispose of such inventory, Licensor retaining all other legal and equitable rights Licensor may have in the circumstances. Failure by Licensee to render the final statement as and when required by this provision shall result in a forfeiture by Licensee of Licensee's right to dispose of its stock (as provided by the next paragraph hereof).

12. DISPOSAL OF STOCK UPON TERMINATION OR EXPIRATION

After termination or expiration of the license under the provisions hereof, Licensee, except as otherwise provided in this Agreement, may dispose of articles covered by this Agreement which are on hand or in process at the time notice of termination is received or upon the expiration date, whatever the case may be, for a period of one hundred and twenty (120) days thereafter, on a non-exclusive basis, provided advance and royalty payments are up-to-date for the current period and statements are furnished for that period in accordance with Paragraph 2. During this period, Licensee shall sell licensed articles at established wholesale prices. During the last thirty (30) days of such period, Licensee, upon written approval of Licensor, may dispose of stock-on-hand at a reduced price. Notwithstanding anything to the contrary herein, Licensee shall not manufacture, sell or dispose of any articles covered by this license after its expiration or its termination based on the failure of Licensee to affix notice of copyright, trademark or servicemark registration or any other notice to the articles, cartons, containers or packing or wrapping material or advertising, promotional or display material or because of the departure by Licensee from the quality and style approved by Licensor pursuant to Paragraph 7. All applicable royalties shall be paid on articles sold during the sell-off period within twenty (20) days following the expiration of said sell-off period.

13. EFFECT OF TERMINATION OR EXPIRATION

Upon and after the expiration or termination of this license, all rights granted to Licensee hereunder shall forthwith revert to Licensor, who shall be free to license others to use the property in connection with the manufacture, sale, distribution and promotion of the articles covered hereby, and Licensee will refrain from further use of the Property or any further reference to it, direct or indirect, or anything deemed by Licensor to be similar to the Licensee's products, except as provided in Paragraph 15. It shall not be a violation of any right of Licensee if Licensor should at any time during the term hereof enter into negotiations with another to license use of the Property in respect of the articles described hereof within the Territory, provided that it is contemplated that such prospective license shall commence after termination of this license.

14. LICENSOR'S REMEDIES

(a) Licensee acknowledges that its failure (except as otherwise provided herein) to commence in good faith to manufacture and distribute in substantial quantities any one or more of the articles listed in Paragraph 1 within the period specified and to continue during the term hereof to diligently and continuously manufacture, sell, distribute and promote the articles covered by this Agreement or any class or category thereof will result in immediate damages to Licensor.

(b) Licensee acknowledges that its failure (except as otherwise provided herein) to cease the manufacture, sale, distribution or promotion of the articles covered by this Agreement or any class or category thereof at the termination or expiration of this Agreement or any portion thereof will result in immediate and irremedial damage to Licensor and to the rights of any subsequent licensee. Licensee acknowledges and admits that there is no adequate remedy at law for such failure to cease manufacture, sale, distribution or promotion, and Licensee agrees that in the event of such failure, Licensor shall be entitled to equitable relief by way of temporary and permanent injunctions and such other and further relief as any court with jurisdiction may deem just and proper.

(c) Resort to any remedies referred to herein shall not be construed as a waiver of any other rights and remedies to which Licensor is entitled under this Agreement or otherwise nor shall an election to terminate be deemed an election of remedies or a waiver of any claim for damages or otherwise.

15. EXCUSE FOR NONPERFORMANCE

Licensee shall be released from its obligations hereunder and this license shall terminate in the event that governmental regulations or other causes arising out of a state of national emergency or war or causes beyond the control of the parties render performance impossible and one party so informs the other in writing of such causes and its desire to be so released. In such events, all royalties on sales theretofore made shall become immediately due and payable and no minimum royalties shall be repayable.

16. NOTICES

(a) All notices shall be furnished in writing, and the date of postmark shall be deemed the date notice or statement is given. All notices shall be made to: _____ .

17. NO JOINT VENTURE

This agreement contains the total understanding of the parties, and nothing in this agreement shall be construed to place the parties in the relationship of joint venturers.

In WITNESS WHEREOF, the parties hereto have caused this agreement to be duly executed.

Licensor	Licensee
_____	_____
By _____	By _____
Title _____	Title _____
Date _____	Date _____

SCHEDULE A

This schedule lists the artwork covered by this agreement. The schedule will be added to as required.

Some of my comments on the proposed license follow (compensation terms had been worked out on the telephone).

Grant of License

(d) Does the agreement commence _____ , 19____ and what is your proposal for term?

Exclusivity

Add that Licensee acknowledges that all current arrangements by Licensor for direct mail, retail and wholesale distribution are permissible by Licensee.

Labeling

(d) Want limit on portion of _____ used as a sample in catalogs of say just a page or two, or in addition that licensee will notify licensor in writing of its intent to include a portion of _____ as a sample in its catalogs with the approval of _____ if the sample includes more than one page of _____ .

(e) Omit "if Licensor so requests, in Licensee's own name."

Technical and Promotional Material

(a) Define original artwork as indicated in letter as original artboards with the return in ninety (90) days after receipt undamaged (or longer if you need them for another thirty or sixty days); to be insured by Licensor on sending same to Licensee and to be insured by Licensee while said property is in Licensee's possession, as well as insuring same upon return to Licensor; Licensee assumes all risks of loss or damage to the art work until same is received back by Licensor; and Licensee to provide insurance in the amount of $10,000 or proof of insurance covering same.

Distribution

The terms "diligently and continuously" need some objective classification either by the number of catalogs it appears in or sales quantities or a combination of both.

Default and Termination

(b) Restate to read "all royalties on sales irrespective of returns."

Stock Upon Termination or Expiration

Add a provision that "upon receipt of notice of termination or upon the expiration date whatever the case may be, the Licensor shall have the option of purchasing the licensed articles at the initial costs per unit."

Miscellaneous

_____ proposes a _____ percent (____) royalty in exchange for promotional space, that is on reviewing _____ the pages with _____'s text modifications _____ will end up with an extra page, and _____ could use that page for promotion for _____ and _____ .

License Negotiation

And so, for a quick review, here's a checklist to guide you in negotiating a license arrangement for one of your works or in discussing the license terms with your agent:

- grant of what rights?

- territories to be covered?
  - can't exceed yours under the grant of rights (and if the license is being geographically divided, be clear).
- is the term of the license long enough to allow the licensee to establish the work and to make a return but short enough to enable licensor to get the rights back or renegotiate better terms?
  - fixed period of commencement.
  - warranty and indemnity clauses (don't make broader than your author-publisher contract).
- termination by licensor and licensee specified?
- proofs on the work, approval of translations, and so forth available for review by originating publisher?
- advances and royalties?
  - sliding scale royalty or flat fee?
    - how are advances recouped?
    - amount and how often paid?
    - other sources of income?
  - is reserve percentage limited?
  - currency (in translation rights sales or foreign rights; at least semi-annual, or quarterly accounting)?
  - audits?
  - editorial changes?
- remainders?
- print situation?
- notification of reversion of rights?
- option clauses?
- other termination provisions?
- other provisions usually at end of contracts (boilerplate)?

Book Clubs

Try to sell book club rights to your books. Although the income is often minimal, you don't pay for the advertising in a book club's catalog to its members, and it's great exposure. Quality Paperback reported that in 1987, twelve percent of its offerings originated with small presses, with two titles selling over 30,000 copies each: *Ladies' Own Erotica*, by Kensington Ladies' Erotica Society (Ten Speed Press) and *Writing Down the Bones: Freeing the Writer Within*, by Natalie Goldberg (Shambhala); see Carol T. Anthony's article, "Book Clubs—How They Work," *Small Press,* September/October 1984.

It is estimated there are 140 book clubs, with advances ranging from $2,000 to $10,000; six-figure advances are paid only for big selections. Different royalty schedules (divided into three rates) are used by each of the book clubs. The first rate applies to copies distributed as a main or alternate selection; the second, to copies distributed as premiums or at nominal charge to get new members; and the last, to all other sales. Often a club pays a flat sum-per-copy, not a royalty.

If the selection is used to solicit new members, the royalty rate is often reduced by half; the usual royalty rate is somewhere between eight percent to ten percent of the club member's purchase price. You can occasionally sell book club rights on a non-exclusive basis, but this will probably depend upon the status of the particular club; five years is a reasonable term. Beware of the definitions that change the royalty rate. Book clubs don't remainder in the normal sense. ("Publisher's over-stock" direct mail catalogs aren't book clubs.)

Often, book club income is split 50/50 with your author. You may be asked to provide the printing film so that the book club can save production costs, enabling them to offer the book at a cheaper price. Depending on the club, the book-club version of your book will be printed without frills. It is also common practice for a book club to tie into your print run, which decreases your own unit cost if they buy enough copies.

In 1988, the Literary Guild distributed the books it purchased through the following clubs: American Garden Guild, Book Club Associates, Cook Book Guild, Doubleday Book Club, Fireside Theatre, International Collectors Library, the Literary Guild of America, Military Book Club, the Mystery Guild, Science Fiction Book Club, and Doubleday Romance Library.

If the book club wants to do an abridgement and/or foreign translation, get a warranty–indemnity provision as well as approval (without jeopardizing the warranty–indemnity), plus some provision to arbitrate differences.

Following is a book club license agreement (reprinted with the permission of Doubleday Book & Music Clubs, Inc., courtesy of Robert J. Posch Jr., counsel, an author himself of legal works for lay persons, and PLI).

Standard Contract

TITLE

AGREEMENT made this _____ day of _____ , _____ , by and between **Doubleday Book & Music Clubs, Inc.**, of Garden City, New York (hereinafter referred to as "Licensee")

and   PUBLISHER/LICENSOR
                             ADDRESS
                             CITY, STATE   ZIP

(hereinafter referred to as "Licensor") in the matter of an edition or editions of a book (hereinafter referred to as the "Work") entitled _____
_____ , by _____ ,
designated as the BOOK CLUB (ALTERNATE/DUAL) selection for use beginning with Licensor's publication date or Licensor's distribution date, whichever comes sooner.

1. **Licensee shall have the exclusive book club rights (in any and all formats) in the Work for the United States of America, Canada, (AUST./NEW ZEALAND IF APPLICABLE) and non-exclusive book**

club rights in the Work in the open market for the period of five years from the date Licensee commences distribution of the Book and thereafter until terminated by Licensor upon six months prior written notice to the Licensee. Licensor warrants that in the event a paperback edition of the Work is authorized for publication, copies of such publication shall not appear on the market within one year after Licensor's publication date.

2. Distribution is to be made to members of or in the solicitation of prospective members of the BOOK CLUB as a (DUAL) full selection, an alternate selection, bonus book, gift book or book distributed in solicitation of members, beginning with Licensor's publication date or Licensor's distribution date, whichever comes sooner. Licensee may also distribute the Work in similar manner to members of or in the solicitation of prospective members of any other book clubs, operated by Licensee or Licensee's affiliates, subsidiaries or Licensees during the term of this Agreement.

3. Licensee shall, as it deems necessary, publish in its advertising materials selected portions of the Work (identified as such) for the purposes of promoting the regular sale of the Work to current members and/or using the Work in solicitation of prospective members.

4. In consideration of rights granted, Licensee agrees to pay Licensor a total minimum royalty payment of _____. Payable the first day of _____, _____. Licensee agrees to pay Licensor a royalty of _____ per copy* on each copy distributed (less returns) by the BOOK CLUB pursuant to the rights granted in this agreement to a "bona fide member" as a full or alternate selection and a royalty of _____ per copy* on each copy distributed (less returns) by that club as a gift book or book distributed at nominal charge in solicitation of members. On each copy distributed (less returns) by the other book clubs, Licensee agrees to pay no less than the minimum royalty listed on the attached schedule. Royalties earned in excess of the minimum royalty will be paid within sixty (60) days following the close of the quarterly accounting periods ending July 31, October 31, January 31, and April 30 of each year.

   *If the price charged the member changes, the royalty will change proportionately on those books distributed to bona fide members.

   For purposes of this Agreement, the term "bona fide member" shall mean any person who is a member of Licensee's Club or Licensee's affiliated Book Club that has paid for at least one Club selection or Alternate Selection of the respective Book Club.

5. Licensor warrants that it has not conveyed and agrees that it will not convey book club rights in the Work to anyone other than the Licensee during the period specified in this Agreement.

6. In addition to the rights granted Licensee herein, Licensor agrees that

Licensee may "remainder" (as that term is generally now or hereafter understood in the publishing industry) the Work at any time or times after the earliest of (a) the first anniversary of Licensee's first distribution date as defined in Paragraph 2; (b) the date on which Licensor first remainders the Work (of which event Licensor shall give Licensee at least 30 days' advanced written notice); and (c) the date on which the Work is first sold or otherwise distributed to the public in paperback form. Upon expiration of this Agreement, Licensee shall have a continuing right to dispose of copies of the Work remaining on hand. Licensee shall not be required to make any payments to Licensor pursuant to Paragraph 4 hereof or otherwise, with respect to Works remaindered by Licensee. All the foregoing is contingent on Licensee first offering the quantity to be remaindered to Licensor at Licensee's manufacturing cost and Licensor will not have accepted such offer within 30 days.

7. Licensor warrants to Licensee (a) that it has full power to enter into this Agreement and to grant the rights granted herein; (b) that the Work will be protected by valid copyright; (c) that Licensee's exercise of its rights hereunder will not infringe, violate, nor be subject to any trademark, trade name, copyright, literary, artistic, dramatic property rights or any proprietary right at common law of any person, firm or corporation; (d) that the Work contains no matter that is obscene, libelous, nor contains injurious formulas, recipes or instructions, nor is in violation of any right of privacy, nor otherwise in contravention of law.

8. Licensor shall indemnify and hold Licensee harmless from any claim which if sustained would constitute or involve a breach of any of the foregoing warranties, including all expenses, losses, damages, court costs, attorneys' fees, amounts paid in settlement, and all other liabilities incurred by Licensee in connection therewith. Licensor will at its own expense defend any action instituted against Licensee with counsel of its own choice, satisfactory to Licensee, and Licensee may join in such defense at its own expense. The provisions of this Paragraph shall inure to the benefit of the book clubs operated by Licensee or Licensee's affiliates.

9. Licensor agrees to obtain permission for the entry of the Work into Canada, (AUST./NEW ZEALAND IF APPLICABLE) for distribution to members of book clubs affiliated with Licensee.

10. Licensee shall secure copyright in any condensed or abridged version in the name of Licensee and protect the existing copyright by printing on the copyright page, the copyright notice furnished by the Licensor.

11. In order to enable Licensee to meet its manufacturing schedule, appropriate personnel in Licensor's organization will be available during the term of this agreement to assist the Licensee in meeting the Licensee's

deadline dates and in fulfilling Licensee's requirements as set forth below and as itemized in the specification forms referred to in subparagraph (f) below.

(a) Licensee's edition shall be produced by a manufacturer selected by Licensee or may be printed from Licensor's plates at Licensor's manufacturer without charge for use of said plates. (b) Licensor agrees to deliver to Licensee eight copies of the Work as soon as available, or until said eight copies are ready for delivery, two sets of final page proofs of all copy not later than six months prior to Licensee's month of selection. Licensor shall thereafter advise Licensee immediately of any changes or corrections. (c) If Licensor's edition or a part thereof is printed by letterpress, Licensor agrees to have ready for delivery as designated by Licensee, without charge, all original artwork, photographs, jacket proofs and final reproduction proofs of all copy, all in A-1 condition not later than four months prior to Licensee's month of selection. (d) If Licensor's edition or a portion thereof is printed by offset lithography, Licensor agrees to have ready for delivery as designated by Licensee, without charge, all original artwork, photographs, jacket proofs and final reproduction proofs of all copy in addition to complete duplicate negative or positive lithographic film, if requested, all in A-1 condition, not later than the date specified in subparagraph (c). (e) Licensor agrees to supply, without charge, all artwork or reproduction proofs of binder's stamping dies not later than the date specified in subparagraph (c). (f) Licensee will immediately, on completion of this agreement, supply Licensor with specification forms to be completed by Licensor and returned to Licensee as quickly as possible.

12. The Agreement shall be governed by and construed and enforced in accordance with the laws of the State of New York applicable to agreements made and to be performed entirely in New York.

13. It is understood and agreed that unless this Agreement is fully executed by Licensor by _____ , _____ , _____ , this Agreement will be voidable at the sole option of Licensee.

Doubleday Book & Music Clubs, Inc.

_____   by _____
Witness

_____   by _____
Witness

                                      Date _____

The following are the book clubs through which the Work may be distributed, as provided in the Agreement, as selections, alternate selections,

bonus books, gift books, or books distributed at nominal charge in solicitation of members. Licensor is to receive on each copy so distributed (less returns) a royalty *no less than* the amount set forth opposite each club:

MINIMUM ROYALTY SCHEDULE

Book Club		Book Club	
Book Club Associates	6¢	Doubleday Book Club	15¢
International Collectors		Fireside Theatre	12¢
Library	15¢	Military Book Club	15¢
The Literary Guild of		Science Fiction Book Club	12¢
America	15¢		
The Mystery Guild	15¢		

Doubleday is somewhat unique in that it does print its own editions on its presses. In that regard, it acts almost like a second publisher. Most buy already-printed books or hook into the publisher's print run (with a different title page designation).

If you plan to start a book club, develop a standard contract for acquiring book club rights and be prepared to meet any legal requirements for marketing and distribution (some of these requirements are discussed later). Be aware of the use of mailing lists, postal regulations, the thirty-day requirement, the "free" rule, negative options, and federal trade commission regulations. The fact that there are only 140 or so book clubs in the United States, as compared with the number of small publishers, means the book club market can be a hard one to crack.

Movie, Television, and Dramatic Rights

In "Naiad Press & Film Rights," an article by Janet Marinelli (*Small Press,* September/October 1986), the author traces the sale of movie rights to *Desert of the Heart* (first published in 1968, reissued by Naiad in 1983, and produced by an independent filmmaker). This was a publicity bonanza for that small press, and was followed by the sale of movie rights to *Lesbian Nuns: Breaking Silence* to ABC; the rights went for $75,000, with $25,000 of that up front, much higher than the usual ten percent.

Richard Curtis, in *How to be Your Own Literary Agent,* paints a picture of the psychological rush you'll feel when movie people express an interest in one of your properties, and then he explains why it is unlikely to come to fruition, even though you may get some up-front money (see his discussion on page 149 et seq.). There are numerous books concerning the financing and distribution of movies. A movie, or a television production, is darned hard to put together; first, the financing needs to be found, then it needs to be produced, and finally, it needs to be distributed. While there are a lot of publishers and authors who are parties to movie options, I haven't met many who have had the option exercised. Basically, an option means that the person who acquires it, sometimes a producer, ties up the property exclusively for X period of time, for X sum of money. Options, according to Curtis, range in the neighborhood of $5,000 to $10,000 annually. The problem is, you can't wait to negotiate the terms of the actual movie deal once the option is negotiated, because the deal, even in abbreviated form, must be part of the option.

The following outline is reprinted with the permission of Wayne S. Kabak, General Counsel of Josephson International, Inc. and Senior Vice-President of International Creative Management, Inc. (© 1984 Wayne S. Kabak, and PLI).

Licensing Motion Picture, Television and Dramatic Rights
I. Licensing of Theatrical Motion Picture Rights
  A. Making the Deal — The Basics (the "Deal Memo")
    1. Option versus Outright Sale
      a. Term of option
      b. Applicability of option payments against purchase price
      c. Reversion
        i. Reversion after option
        ii. Reversion after outright grant if no production
    2. Forms of Compensation
      a. Option payment
      b. Fixed compensation
        i. Fixed amount
        ii. Bonuses based on size of budget (See Deal Memo, Items 1-3, in annexed materials)
        (A) Percentage of budget
        (B) Alternative amounts as a function of size of budget
        (C) Incremental increases based on size of budget
        iii. Bonuses based on book's appearance on best-seller list (See Deal Memo, Item 1, in annexed materials)
        iv. Bonuses based on sales of book (See extract, Item 4, in annexed materials)
        v. Production bonus
      c. Contingent compensation
        i. Theatrical Motion Picture Revenue Flow (See Chart, Item 5, in annexed materials)
        (A) Theatre box office receipts
        (B) Distributor's gross receipts
          (1) Distribution fees
          (2) Distribution costs
          (3) Third party gross participations
          (4) Negative cost
          (5) Contingent deferments
        (C) Breakeven
        (D) Net profits
        ii. Forms of contingent compensation
        (A) Participation in sale of rights to third party (See Deal Memo, Item 1, in annexed materials)
        (B) Contingent deferment (See Deal Memo, Item 1, in annexed materials)
        (C) Percentage of gross receipts (before or after breakeven)
        (D) Percentage of adjusted gross receipts (before or after breakeven)
        (E) Percentage of gross receipts after rolling breakeven (See Memo, Item 6, in annexed materials)

  (F) Percentage of 100% of net profits

  (G) Percentage of producer's share of net profits

  (H) The relationship of various forms of contingent compensation (See Chart, Item 7, in annexed materials)

 3. Credit

 4. General Considerations — Studio or Independent Producer

  a. Reversion

  b. Net profit definition

  c. Participation in proceeds of sale to a third party

B. Fleshing Out the Deal — The Details (the "Long Form Contract")

 1. Grant of Rights

  a. Theatrical and television rights

  b. Merchandising and commercial tie-ups

  c. Limited publication rights (7500 words)

  d. Rights to freely adapt and exploit

  e. Geographical scope of grant

 2. Reserved Rights

  a. Author-written sequels

  b. Publication rights

  c. Live stage rights

  d. Live television and radio (limited recording)

  e. Restrictions on reserved rights

   i. Holdback

   ii. Rights of first negotiation and refusal

 3. Compensation

  a. Option payments (See I.A.2.a above)

  b. Fixed (See I.A.2.b. above)

  c. Contingent (See I.A.2.c. above)

  d. Sequel and remake rights

  e. Television movie-of-the-week (m.o.w.), series, specials and pilots

 4. Representations, Warranties and Indemnities

  a. Dealing with special problems: "Real people in quasi-fiction"

   i. Qualification: "to best of knowledge"

   ii. Qualification: identifying real people and shifting burden (See Extract, Item 12, in annexed materials)

  b. Errors and Omissions Insurance

  c. Purchaser's counter-representations

 5. Credit (See I.A.3 above)

 6. Miscellaneous Clauses

  a. Consultation rights

  b. Right to make changes

  c. Audit and accounting rights

  d. No obligation to produce

  e. Use of name

  f. Assignability

II. Licensing of Television Rights — Differences in Compensation

 A. Compensation Based on Length of Program

 B. Bonuses for Theatrical Release

III. Licensing of Dramatic Rights

A. Option versus Outright Sale
B. Compensation — Fixed and Contingent
   1. Advance
   2. Weekly Royalty (percentage of gross weekly box office receipts)
   3. Percentage of Profits
C. "The Formula" — Revolutionizing Theatrical Financing Through Royalty Reduction and Profit Sharing
D. The Merger of Rights in the Book and the Play
E. Credit
IV. Novelizations and Movie Tie-Ins
A. Ownership of Novelization Rights
   1. The Rights of the Screenplay Writer
   2. The Rights of the Film Producer
B. The *Un*availability of Works Made For Hire
C. The Publisher's Right to Use Artwork from the Film
D. The Marketplace
V. Licensing Rights — The Roles of Author, Agent and Publisher

Remember, this area is so complex, and there are so many things to consider, that you need to obtain the services of a knowledgable lawyer, or agent, or both—someone in the entertainment field—to thoroughly and adequately represent your interests.

Periodicals

Periodicals, to a lesser extent, also license rights, such as to a foreign language edition of a magazine or individual articles, a video production, and/or syndication. *Shape* magazine includes in its copyright notice a mention of licenses for foreign translations.

Legal Miscellany

17

This chapter embraces some new subjects—insurance, employers, credit—and amplifies some old ones. Why? Because the body of knowledge you've picked up as you near the end of this text makes these subjects more understandable.

Disclaimers and More Restrictions in Content

As you know, content can give rise to complaints.

The most famous case is *Carter & Bertrand v. Rand McNally & Co.* (1980), a Massachusetts case in which a jury found Rand McNally negligent in publishing a junior-high-school science text. Two experiments, although not printed wrong, were located close to one another; this allegedly caused an explosion. The awards to the plaintiffs were substantial: $800,000 and $300,000, which were reduced by a finding of twenty-five percent comparative negligence.

From the publisher's perspective, an interesting case is *Alm v. Van Nostrand Reinhold Company, Inc.,* (480 N.E.2d 1263 [1985]). There, the plaintiff sued the publisher of a tool-making book for injuries incurred in following the instructions. The court refused to adopt a theory of liability that would effectively require publishers to review and test procedures included in their publications and extend the scope of liability to a "uncalculable number of readers."

There have been a number of personal-injury lawsuits against publishers. So far, the courts have held that, absent a guarantee, warranty, or endorsement of the product advertised, or knowledge that the product is defective, the publisher has no duty and cannot be held responsible for injuries resulting from use. But if the publisher endorsed the product, liability for negligent misrepresentation (if not strict liability and breach of warranty) may be appropriate. In a Texas case, a jury awarded $9.4 million to the relatives of a man shot and killed by a hit-man hired through the "gun-for-hire" advertisements in *Soldier of Fortune* magazine.

Be careful if you publish charts, as you may have a higher standard of duty or care.

For a detailed discussion and case-by-case analysis of legal problems generated by the content of your written works, see Barbara E. Schlain's "Errors and Omissions in Editorial Content and Related Torts and New Technologies" (PLI, 1988).

Claims are made for negligent infliction of emotional distress, such as publishing inaccurate information regarding someone's death. Claims of outrage, intentional infliction of emotional distress, and/or *prima facie* tort have been made. Probably Jerry Falwell's case against *Hustler* magazine for libel and intentional infliction of emotional distress—over a parody depicting him as an alcoholic committing incest with his mother in an outhouse—is the most well-known. The U.S. Supreme Court concluded that "public figures and public officials may not recover for the tort of intentional infliction of emotional distress by reason of publication, such as the one here at issue, without showing in addition that the publication contains a false statement of fact which was made with 'actual malice.' "

Legal disputes based on content cases abound:

- an author's lawsuit against the *New York Times* for failure to include the author's book on the bestseller list, which caused the author to experience emotional distress.
- a suit by a professional soccer player alleging a host of legal complaints, as a result of a broadcast participant's outrageous conduct in removing the soccer player's photo from a mounting, drawing a mustache and beard on it, and spitting and jumping on it.
- a lawsuit concerning a story about the death of the plaintiff's husband, which stated that a body was removed from a fire along with that of another woman, after the two of them had been seen in a bar; this was alleged to have caused the plaintiff intentional, inflictional, emotional distress and invaded her privacy.
- a verdict of $10,000 was entered against a pornographic magazine upon a finding of "malicious misidentification"; the plaintiff was an aspiring actress.

Can you minimize the risk of claims? This is an area where you're damned if you do and you're damned if you don't. The Restatement of Torts provides that "it is only where the actor is under a duty to the other, because of some relation between them, to protect him against such misconduct; or where the actor has undertaken the obligation of doing so; or his conduct has created or increased the risk of harm through the misconduct that he becomes liable." This provision may affect or dictate your standard of care.

Obviously, certain kinds of books and subjects demand extra precautions:

- cookbooks.
- how-to books.
- formulas and measurements.
- financial advice.
- accounting and/or legal advice.
- health books.
- first novels.

Make sure that if your book includes recipes, experiments, or projects, they have been fully tested. Don't let advertising and sales claims exceed the capacity of a particular project. Prepare an appropriate disclaimer.

When you put together a disclaimer, don't forget to review it with your lawyer and, specifically, provide the lawyer with whatever information he or she needs to review the material in question in order to prepare the disclaimer.

You may need to:

- disclaim any warranty as to performance or merchantability.
- disclaim any statements made by sales people as constituting an express warranty (again, if you are selling a very, very limited edition of a book and the salesman insists its real value is four or five times the retail price, you may be liable on misrepresentation).
- disclaim fitness for a particular purpose and advise the user to test it.
- consider admonishing buyers to use the information at their own risk.
- limit damages to a refund of the work or replacement.
- proofread carefully materials where typographical errors could present problems, such as dosages.
- be aware that if you publish a significant number of works in a specific field, such as health, diet, or exercise, a higher standard of care may be implied to you.

As you can see, some of these disclaimers obviously won't apply to certain books, but would apply to, say, computer programs. For certain works, such as software, the Magnuson-Moss Warranty–Federal Trade Commission Improvement Act (15 U.S.C. Section 2301) applies; when you warrant the product in any way, that particular act comes into effect. Certain states limit or preclude limitations on remedies where goods or services are used or bought primarily for personal, family, or household purpose.

Put the disclaimer in a logical place; I always look for a disclaimer near the copyright or title page of a work. Make it readable and prominent.

Here is a sampling of disclaimers that I found in my home library.

Durk Pearson and Sandy Shaw, authors of the *Life Extension Companion* (Warner Books) in their foreword state:

WARNING: Watch for sections marked CAUTION and WARNING: these are meant to be read carefully and taken seriously. In addition, remember that this book is designed to be used in conjunction with *Life Extension, a Practical Scientific Approach*. Before taking anything, you should check all the index entries for that substance in *Life Extension*, or, at the very least, all relevant CAUTIONs and WARNINGs in *Life Extension*.

Let's Get Well, by Adele Davis (Signet) includes a publisher's note:

The ideas, procedures, and suggestions contained in this book are not intended as a substitute for consulting with your psysician [sic]. All matters regarding your health require medical supervision.

The *New Our Bodies, Ourselves: A Book by and for Women*, by the Boston Women's Collective (Simon and Schuster, Inc.) states in the preface/introduction:

While the information contained in *Our Bodies, Ourselves* will hopefully empower you and give you useful tools and ideas, this book is not intended to replace professional health and medical care.

Carolyn J. Niethammer's recent cookbook, *The Tumbleweed Gourmet: Cooking With Wild Southwestern Plants* (University of Arizona Press), includes an excellent disclaimer; the cookbook applies ethnobotanical research and information to gourmet cooking, and this disclaimer reads as follows:

Neither the author nor the University of Arizona Press will accept responsibility for any illness, injury or death resulting from misidentification of desert plants used in this book. Those readers who elect to gather such plants should take special care to check them against a standard guide to regional flora. State and local regulations for gathering plants, seeds and fruits on public lands vary widely; readers are therefore strongly urged to seek guidance from the appropriate authorities before collecting. Of course, any collecting on private property must be done with the permission of the owner of that property.

Your lawyer should check to see whether the proposed disclaimers comply with the Uniform Commercial Code (UCC), the Magnuson-Moss Act, and any state-law variations to the UCC that may exist.

Product Liability

The legal doctrine of product liability often tips the scales in favor of consumer victory. The product-liability theory rests on the concern for consumer injury that grows from the mass-production economy, which unavoidably produces defective products. The theory assumes that manufacturers and retailers are better equipped to bear the loss caused by defective products than is the injured consumer.

The legal rule: a defective product, plus injury arising from customary or foreseen use, equals maker or seller pays. In Canada, defective products also raise the question of tort liability.

Due to what I would call mixed-media products (such as a harmonica and instruction books) this area merits more concern than previously. If you have to recall a book or a book-product combination, work out the recall with your lawyer.

Remember that there is strict liability in tort for a defective product if the injury was from customary or foreseen use; it is not defense to contend that a customer should have known *not* to do something.

You can take several steps to guard against injury and consequent liability. Exercise some quality control to make sure you are not selling defective items. "Idiot proof" your work by figuring out all the possible mishaps that could occur, and guard against them by changing the design, or warn the public of a particular harm. Include specific instructions on the use of the work to avoid possible harm; in the disclaimer for the Neithammer cookbook, the publisher envisioned every way someone could get into trouble by following the recipes in the book, including improper plant identification and illegal collection on federal, state, or private land.

Insurance

If there is concern about possible litigation, you might need to investigate the purchase of product liability insurance coverage for a particular product. Disclaimers and efforts to warn or advise the consumer may not be sufficient. A general liability insurance policy most often is limited to claims for bodily injury and property damage; therefore, a claim for lost profits from use of a tax-advice book would not be covered.

While error-or-omission claims for bodily injury or property damage arising from a book's content often are considered covered under a general liability policy, some carriers have taken the position that such claims are not within their contract.

A significant editorial-products-liability concern is that the insurance carrier chooses counsel and controls litigation; their choice may not be as concerned with First Amendment implications as you are. The nice thing about insurance, however, is that it pays your lawyer fees.

An error-and-omission policy is designed to protect you against claims arising from negligent acts and errors or omissions committed or alleged to have been committed by you. Obviously, this doesn't cover intentional acts, such as libel or criminal or criminal-like acts, punitive damages, or similar problems.

Insurance can be used to limit the risk of financial loss. Business insurance, a catchall term for a variety of plans, is an important consideration when you begin publishing, especially if your business involves an initial investment of time and money. A major loss early in your business life would spell the end. If your small press is a hobby (although everyone strives to make it a business in order to deduct the losses on their income tax), your household insurance may cover certain catastrophes, such as a slip and fall. Homeowner's policies generally exclude coverage for occurrences related to the business, however. Your auto insurance may cover injuries to those injured on their way to a business meeting (but not if you said you never used your car on business).

A comprehensive general liability policy, often called "premise liability," covers persons injured on your business premises. A rider or endorsement (an amendment) may be needed to cover computers and software; these aren't usually included in a homeowner's policy or a business policy.

The first step in obtaining insurance is to find a good insurance broker. An independent agent represents many companies, and a broker represents *you* in dealing with companies. Either one will be able to help you more than a single-company agent, who represents only one carrier. Get estimates; your broker should understand your particular business and personal needs so that he or she can develop an insurance package tailored to suit your situation, and generally assist in all insurance matters. Also, look for insurance from a mutual insurance company that returns profits to the owner/customer in the form of reduced premiums.

Know what types of coverage you're getting. The common types of insurance coverage are for fire, theft, extended coverage (vandalism, malicious mischief, damage caused by aircraft or vehicles, etc.), premises, and auto liability. Your broker can give you information about employee benefit insurance—health, life, and disability; workers' compensation; and unemployment compensation. As soon as you have even one employee, worker's compensation insurance is required by law in most states. It covers on-the-job injuries, pays the injured employee a percentage of wages, pays medical bills; it pays to defend you, as well.

Sometimes the comprehensive policy can include extended coverage to cover other risks, for instance, employee theft. Business-interruption coverage (which may not include floods) helps defray the cost of getting started again when you are visited by a catastrophe. Valuable-papers coverage is for important, original, or valuable photographs and documents. Other types of business insurance include coverage for business interruption and unpaid accounts receivable.

Many times, the policy only pays the fair market value of the item destroyed, not the replacement value. So if you want to get enough money from your insurance company to replace the laser jet printer that blew away when the explosion rocked your town, consider paying a little extra for a rider to the policy that requires the insurer to pay you the *replacement* value of lost items.

For most types of policies, group rates are cheaper. Check out your professional or business organizations. Since purchase of an insurance "package" can result in reduced rates for coverage, all your insurance needs should be examined when purchasing business insurance to ensure the greatest coverage for the least premiums. An umbrella policy extends the coverage limit above your limit. Remember, too, that the higher the deductible, the lower the premium.

When selecting insurance coverage, be sure that it fits your business structure. If you don't have the right business structure, liability claims can risk your personal assets, and unreimbursable losses or high legal fees could break you.

Finally, beware of exclusions. When I read policy exclusions, I'm often left wondering exactly what *is* covered.

Underwriting Media Liability

Companies writing publisher's liability insurance, also called media special-perils policies, change. Check through your broker or agent or the Association of American Publishers to determine which companies offer such coverage when you are ready to make an inquiry.

This insurance covers you, to some extent, against intentional torts such as defamation, copyright infringement, rights of privacy and publicity claims, plagiarism, and misappropriation. Through riders, endorsements, or additional policies, you might be able to get coverage against infliction of emotional distress, certain kinds of product liability, unfair competition, the right of publicity, and a variety of tradename and trademark problems. Often the less common incidents are excluded; criminal, dishonest, and fraudulent acts are always excluded. Make sure coverage extends through to, and includes, the bookseller. If you issue computer software, be sure that it is specifically included. Check for coverage against problems that can arise in advertising—jacket covers, publicity and promotional materials. Most policies cover actual damages, and, depending upon language, punitive damages might be included as well; but you can expect a struggle with the insurance carrier about that. Ideally, you want to cover all liability losses imposed by law or settlement.

In some jurisdictions, there are problems with getting coverage for punitive damages because of state law or policy that bars this type of protection. (See a discussion of this principle in Heather Grant Florence's "Publisher's Liability Insurance," *PLI Book Publishing 1984,* page 130 et seq.).

As with all insurance, distinguish between an *occurrence* and a *claims-made* policy. The former covers works published during the policy coverage, regardless of when made. The latter covers claims made during the policy term. Be cautious about how "occurrence" is defined—you wouldn't want, say, six different claims on your book, *Rats Employed During President Reagan's Term,* to each require a separate deductible.

Don't ignore any claim made against you; most policies require prompt notification. The selection of counsel is up to the insurance company in most policies, but be sure that you have broadly defined defense-expense coverage that includes not just legal fees, but also discovery, court costs, accounting, investigative expenses, bonds, and interest. Some companies will specify that the insured's consent for settlement is sufficient, with mutual agreement necessary for appeals. Beware of provisions that require certain acts, such as a restriction or correction, in order to preserve your coverage.

If authors are covered by the publisher's policy, the publisher's premium will be higher. You can extend your coverage to the author under a variety of terms, and vary the amount of coverage from contract to contract, depending upon the author. Some of these variations concern partial payment of the deductible, and sharing a certain amount of the deductible. Be sure that, if the insurance policy imposes requirements on you, the same requirements are imposed on the author; these should be incorporated in your author-publisher contracts. You may also want to contractually provide for the author's use and payment of a separate lawyer. If you're entrepreneuring, be sure your coverage extends to partners, joint venture participants, etc.

A libel policy often contains a high deductible. You may be able to tack on coverage for financial losses with another policy, rider, or endorsement. Make sure your deductible applies to any combination of publisher's liability, i.e., legal fees, settlements, and judgments.

A self-insurance program can also be established. This means that you take the premiums that you would normally pay on all your various insurance policies, invest them, and keep them as a reserve against claims that are made and sustained. Sometimes, an outside firm is hired to manage the program. I don't recommend this system, though, unless your business can be absolutely devoted to investing that money for self-insurance, and you're able to set up inviolate procedures for this.

People Who Work for You

Owner-operators are both employer and employee, jacks-of-all-trades. But at one time or another, other categories of people may be involved, usually as independent contractors and employees.

Normally, an independent contractor (or freelancer) is paid by the job or piece, and not by the hour; is responsible for providing any equipment required by the job; generally has control over the project; and performs a specialized service.

Imagine that Blue Inc. Press published a special book on reptiles of the Grand Canyon, with calligraphed text on handmade paper. They wanted Betty Book Binder, a reknowned hand-bookbinder, to do the job. Blue Inc. Press did not want Betty to inadvertently become an employee, however. Blue Inc. asked for some information from its lawyer.

MEMORANDUM

To: Blue Inc. Press
From: MB
Re: Independent Contractor: Yes or No

I am glad that you have requested this memorandum on the question of independent contractors. It is an important subject, because should a court or the government decide that your independent contractor is an employee, the consequences may be serious—for example, liability for damage caused by an employee while on the job, as well as payment of back federal and state payroll and withholding taxes.

There is no set answer to the question of who is an independent contractor. Each situation is different. There are many tests that can be applied to the relationship between you and your worker to see if he or she is an independent contractor. The following list of principles should be helpful in establishing an independent-contractor relationship between yourself and Betty Book Binder:

- independent contractors set their own hours. You just agree on the completion date.
- independent contractors keep a regular set of business books and are in business for themselves, with a realistic opportunity for profit or loss.
- independent contractors have the power to choose their own workers.
- independent contractors provide their own equipment and tools.
- independent contractors are paid by the piece or by the job, not by the hour.
- independent contractors usually work at their own place of business.
- independent contractors maintain all required business licenses, permits, et cetera, and pay all other job-related expenses.
- independent contractors are not covered by your liability and health insurance, nor any bonus, vacation, sick-pay program, or training programs that you may have.
- independent contractors cannot be fired if they perform according to your agreement with them.
- independent contractors perform the entire job, including cleaning-up, without supervision.
- since independent contractors are in business for themselves, they provide their services not only to your company but also to the general public.

Write down your agreement with Betty Book Binder, covering as many of the points listed above as are relevant to your contract. You certainly do not have to include every item on the list—a court looks at the overall situation to determine if independent-contractor status exists. Also, clip any of Betty's promotional literature or advertising to the contract. Take a picture of Betty's van showing the business name and address. Attach that to the contract.

Finally, get used to calling Betty Book Binder the independent contractor, for that is who she is.

Review any arrangements you may have with non-employees; be especially vigilant of the factors indicating an independent-contractor status that may be missing, and remedy at the first opportunity.

Employees
Under federal law, all employers must have a federal employer's identification number, which is obtained by filing an application with the Internal Revenue Service.

Form **SS-4**	**Application for Employer Identification Number**	
(Rev. November 1985) Department of the Treasury Internal Revenue Service	(For use by employers and others. Please read the separate instructions before completing this form.) For Paperwork Reduction Act Notice, see separate instructions.	OMB No. 1545-0003 Expires 8-31-88

1 Name (True name. See instructions.)	2 Social security no., if sole proprietor	3 Ending month of accounting year

4 Trade name of business if different from item 1	5 General partner's name, if partnership; principal officer's name, if corporation; or grantor's name, if trust

6 Address of principal place of business (Number and street)	7 Mailing address, if different

8 City, state, and ZIP code	9 City, state, and ZIP code

10 Type of organization	☐ Individual ☐ Trust ☐ Partnership ☐ Plan administrator ☐ Other ☐ Governmental ☐ Nonprofit organization ☐ Corporation (specify)	11 County of principal business location

12 Reason for applying ☐ Started new business ☐ Purchased going business ☐ Other (specify)	13 Acquisition or starting date (Mo., day, year). See instructions.

14 Nature of principal activity (See instructions.)	15 First date wages or annuities were paid or will be paid (Mo., day, year).

16 Peak number of employees expected in the next 12 months (If none, enter "0")	Nonagricultural	Agricultural	Household	17 Does the applicant operate more than one place of business? ☐ Yes ☐ No

18 Most of the products or services are sold to whom? ☐ Business establishments (wholesale) ☐ General public (retail) ☐ Other (specify) ☐ N/A	19 If nature of business is manufacturing, state principal product and raw material used.

20 Has the applicant ever applied for an identification number for this or any other business? ☐ Yes ☐ No
If "Yes," enter name and trade name. Also enter approx. date, city, and state where the application was filed and previous number if known. ▶

Under penalties of perjury, I declare that I have examined this application, and to the best of my knowledge and belief it is true, correct, and complete. | Telephone number (include area code)

Signature and Title ▶ _____ Date ▶ _____

Please leave blank ▶	Geo.	Ind.	Class	Size	Reas. for appl.	**Part I**

You will be required to withhold federal income taxes from the wages of all your employees, and employees must file Form W-4, Exemption from Withholding (an employee who falsely fills out a Form W-4 is subject to a $500 penalty) with you. You will also have to pay Social Security taxes and federal unemployment tax. You will get credit in this federal tax assessment for any state unemployment tax paid. Be sure to file and pay your withholdings. Don't fudge or put off obligations to Uncle Sam. (I can name five defunct businesses that could have been successful, profitable enterprises right now had they been diligent about the issue of withholdings.)

Since each of the above taxes requires setting up special records, filing returns, and making payments, a business about to hire employees should obtain the assistance of an accountant or the local office of the Internal Revenue Service. Publication 15 of the Internal Revenue Service, *Employer's Tax Guide,* discusses withholding, Social Security, and unemployment taxes. *Your Business Tax Kit,* also available from the Internal Revenue Service, contains most of the forms that are required by an employer to file and pay these taxes. If you have any questions, the taxpayer's service of the Internal Revenue Service will provide assistance.

Other federal laws governing employees are the Minimum Wage Law (Fair Labor Standards Act) and the Civil Rights Act, as amended (be especially aware of equal-employment-opportunity provisions). Age discrimination complaints can also surface; a federal court suit was filed against McGraw-Hill for firing an employee, aged fifty-five (*Publishers Weekly,* January 27, 1984).

The state tax standards for employees somewhat parallels the federal system. Most states, and some cities, withhold state income tax. To obtain the necessary forms and information concerning state withholding tax, call the state tax department. State law also generally requires that employers pay an unemployment tax and provide unemployment compensation coverage, which is usually based on the number of employees and employee hours per year for the business. Contact the state agency that normally handles questions about unemployment insurance.

Also required by state law is some form of workers' compensation insurance, to cover any employee injured on the job. States vary in the manner in which workers' compensation is provided. The state office administering this program should be contacted for further information.

In a recent Arizona case, an employer obtained the employee's resignation by promising the employee "a very generous and fair separation agreement"; a committee was to be appointed to recommend the package. The employer rejected the committee's package and the subsequent lawsuit wound its way through *two* appellate courts after trial. The employee finally won *treble* damages.

Case Incident:
A periodical publishing concern fired its only salesman because it planned to take over the sales itself. There was a one-paragraph written employment contract which attempted to address any ongoing commissions the salesman was owed. It was unclear. The parties negotiated a written settlement agreement of the commissions owed, and the respective attorneys drew up an agreement to tie up that as well as other loose ends.

In summary, one way to avoid these additional requirements is to use independent contractors wherever possible rather than hiring employees.

Credit

Time is money in any business. It is critical that you secure payment for your products with a minimum amount of follow-up on your part. The legal rules for extending credit vary from state to state. Have your credit application approved by your attorney, or use one that's been developed by one of your industry's professional organizations and attorney-approved.

Follow the same credit policies, regardless of how delicious a sale looks. Be able to prove that your product was shipped and delivered; for large orders, UPS offers the most easily traceable method.

Case Incident:
A California publisher released a book about a Hispanic topic that tied into a festival being held in New Mexico. An inexperienced staff member filled an order for 1,000 books and gave a huge discount without a credit check. The book buyer had set up business for the festival only, failed to sell all the books, and returned them with shipping due. The book buyer also skipped.

For credit practices, see Bernard Kamoroff's *Small Time Operation: How to Start Your Own Small Business, Keep Your Books, Pay Your Taxes and Stay Out of Trouble* (Bell Springs Publications), and Dan Poynter's *The Self-Publishing Manual* (Para Publishing). Develop a standard collection policy along with forms, and an automatic tickler system; that is, a thirty-day overdue notice, a forty-five-day overdue notice, and so forth. Set up your accounts so that you can bring suit in your county. Develop forms suitable for that with your lawyer.

The Entrepreneur

Please refer to PLI's 1988 *Book Publishing Manual* and the article by Richard Gallen, "The Entrepreneur."

To publish or not to publish—that's a risk-management decision, whether made by a publishing conglomerate, a small press, a self-published author, or an entrepreneur. All the other aspects of publishing—acquisition of a work, manufacturing, and distribution—can be contracted out in one way or another.

If a project comes up that looks good, but you don't have the funds or the expertise to carry it off, do some entrepreneuring.

Case Incident:

Through a series of events, an individual, Mr. Q, became the holder of a partially completed publishing project that involved a concept for sale to institutions. This person contacted a printer who saw the potential for income and franchising from the project and that Q did not understand the printing industry. The printer then offered Mr. Q a royalty agreement, which made the printer the publisher.

The publisher offered to pay a royalty to Q of $1+ per actual printed work sold, for which funds were collected. If less than two-thirds of the works sold, the rights reverted back to Q.

The arrangement was an interesting start, but the parties needed to add details: the term of sale, treatment of samples and damaged goods, and so forth.

One way to do business is to organize another structure to provide part of the services. Earlier, I mentioned the Graywolf Press, Lapis Press, and McPherson & Company's common distribution arrangements.

Two entrepreneurs teamed up to become Euphrosynu, Inc. (the Greek god of joy), which created the Sweet Pickles series. These stories concern an animal in the community getting into a "pickle" and then getting out. In less than ten years, forty million sales of forty titles lead to its inclusion in "My Weekly Reader Book Club," a Xerox® activity package, book club selections, a sixteen-volume dictionary, and record albums sold worldwide.

If Your Author Dies

The questions an author faces regarding his or her will are nicely summed up in a chapter in *The Writing Business: A Poet or Writer's Handbook* (New York: Poet &

Writers, Inc., 1988). If appropriate, ask your author if a will exists, who the literary executor is, and refer the author to this article.

When an author dies, you can be confronted with some unusual problems, depending on the stage of the author's work: a manuscript due under a contract, galleys, revisions, or royalty-producing.

Don't pay out royalties until you've had your lawyer review any court documents presented to you by the executor of the estate. The executor is the person charged with collecting the assets and paying the bills of the deceased person. If there's no executor, exercise even more caution.

Here are some provisions from an author's will; several books had been published and two were under contract.

It is my will and desire that my personal property shall pass and vest as follows:

1. It is my will and desire that all rights of the book "_____" pass and vest in and to _____, together with all copies in paperback that I may have in stock.

2. It is further my will and desire that all rights, including royalties, of the book "_____" which has been published by _____ shall pass and vest in and to said _____ .

3. It is further my will and desire that all rights, including royalties, of the books "_____" and "_____", as covered by the publisher's contract, shall pass and vest in and to _____, these books currently being published by _____ of _____ .

4. It is further my will and desire that all rights, including royalties, of my book entitled "_____" shall pass and vest in and to _____, this book currently being under publisher's contract with _____ .

5. It is my will and desire that all book rights, including royalties, from my book "_____" shall pass and vest in and to _____, whose present address is _____. Any and all other rights, including royalties, monies, television earnings, et cetera, which have to do with said publication, I request and desire and it is my will and desire that same be shared equally by and between _____ and _____ .

6. In the event the book I am currently completing entitled "_____" shall develop value, it is my will and desire that all rights including royalties pass and vest in and to _____ of _____ .

7. Should it be that the _____ currently under contract with _____ having to do with the _____, be completed under whatever title same may finally be published and become productive, it would be my will and desire that all rights and royalties which may come from said publication be divided equally between _____ and _____ .

The executor collects the royalties until the estate closes. The publisher would then pay the royalties pursuant to the will, if such decisions became part of the final court order on the estate. The particular heir(s) of a book property are the legally appropriate persons with whom to negotiate any contract changes or to approve licenses (if so required by your contract). Be sure to notify the executor and/or heirs of any claims against the works.

If the author didn't complete the manuscript before death, you've got to decide whether to drop the project and make a claim against the estate for a refund of the advances or hire another author to finish it. If you pursue the latter course, you would be wise to reach a written agreement with the estate before you pump any more money into the project. Sometimes heirs cause publishers headaches. The recent litigation between John Cheever's wife and Academy Chicago over a collection of Cheever short stories is an example.

Some Miscellaneous Thoughts
- Make sure your publishing goods are:
  - fit for ordinary purposes.
  - fit for a particular purpose.
  - lien-free.
  - meet the warranty of authorship.
- Put time, effort, and thoroughness into disclaimers.
- Be alert to works that require caution, such as "how-to" books.
- Be wary when issuing mixed-product goods.
- For insurance, get a broker.
- Determine your needs and costs, and have the broker assemble an appropriate package.
- Always pay employee withholdings *on time* and *in full.*
- When a contracted author dies, list the potential problems and talk to your lawyer.

Buying/Selling a Publishing Concern

18

You may not be Theodore Cross, publisher-lawyer, who sold Warren, Gorham & Lamont for $80 million in 1980, then invested $800,000 in a periodical, *Investment Dealer's Digest,* which he sold for $40 million in 1986 (*Publishers Weekly,* December 23, 1988), but you can jump on the entrepreneurial bandwagon by starting a business, building it up, and then disposing of it and repeating the process.

A Checklist

The acquisition or disposal of a publishing concern presents some unique problems. What follows is a minimum checklist of provisions to include in an agreement to purchase a publishing concern. This checklist substantially amplifies a general checklist from 16 *AmJur Legal Forms 2d* (Rev) (see 226:24, "Sale of Business"). Your county law library has this set and you can use it at the library.

Checklist for Sale of a Publishing Concern

- Identify the parties.
- Legal status of each:
  - designate imprint of larger house or subsidiary status.
  - other states in which qualified to do business.
- Recitals:
  - nature of publishing concern now.

369

- business subject to sale.
- desire of seller to sell and buyer to buy.
- Assets subject to sale:
  - business building and other real property.
  - cash including deposits:
    - utilities.
    - telephone.
    - others.
  - equipment, furniture, and fixtures:
    - describe by item, age, and identification number.
  - good will, use of firm name or customer lists.
  - book contracts, copyrights, patents, trademarks, and trade names.
  - insurance policies.
  - notes and accounts receivable.
  - inventory (backlist and frontlist).
  - other assets (licenses, merchandising rights, characters).
- Valuation of assets sold.
- Purchase price allocation to assets:
  - analyze products, pricing, sales.
  - furnishing of customer list.
  - furnishing of supplier list.
  - if buildings/land, see appraisals.
  - organizational structure and personnel plus any personnel manuals.
  - review of all contracts with authors, agents, printers, distributors.
  - review corporate records.
  - review financial statements, tax returns, leases.
- Liabilities affecting sale:
  - see elsewhere.
  - deferred subscription obligations.
- Time and manner of payment:
  - professional fees, such as lawyer, broker, and accountant, and how paid.
  - on closing or earlier:
    - cash, debt, stock, or other assets.
  - deposit held until escrow closes.
  - installment payments.
    - buyer consider contingent liabilities re: payments—lawsuits, violations of zoning laws, recapture of taxes, refunds, liability for various taxes (payroll, sales, property) and other post-sale "surprises" re: installment payments.
  - mortgage or other security.
  - forfeiture of deposit for default.
  - other methods of payment:
    - contingent payments on cash flow, earnings, bestseller lists.
  - personal guaranty of payment.

- Closing:
  - inspection of assets.
  - date of closing.
  - conduct of business until closing.
  - file final tax returns and if terms of sale require it, dissolution of corporation.
  - obtain necessary rulings and approvals.
  - deliver transfer instruments.
  - payment.
- Inspection of books, records, and premises.
- Representations by seller:
  - enforceability of contracts.
  - title to property and assets.
  - authority to agree.
  - accuracy and completeness of books and records.
  - accuracy of circulation.
  - discharge of outstanding liens, taxes, contracts, judgments, and other obligations.
  - cover royalties due authors.
  - absence of labor disputes.
  - validity of patents, copyrights, trademarks, and tradenames.
  - compliance with all laws affecting business.
  - survival of representations.
- Representation by buyers:
  - financial assets.
  - experience.
  - full disclaimer.
- Indemnification of buyer.
- Assumption by buyer of lease, if any:
  - obtaining of lessor's consent to assignment of lease.
- Assumption by buyer of outstanding contracts:
  - disavowal of contracts not listed by seller.
- Compliance with UCC Article 6 or other bulk sales provisions.
- Instruction of buyer by seller in operation of business.
- Retention of seller's executives and staff:
  - employment of seller or seller's executives or staff as executive staff of buyer.
    - utilization of employment contracts with benefit, bonus, compensation clauses as well as non-competition and amicable departure provisions.
  - consulting arrangements.
- Covenant not to compete:
  - territory.
  - duration.

- covers officers, executives, editors, and key staff.
- Responsibility for obtaining necessary approvals and making necessary filings:
  - tax rulings.
  - similar approvals.
- Payment of sales or use taxes imposed on transfer of assets.
- Payment of other taxes.
- Transfer of tax identification numbers.
- Insurance.
- Contingencies:
  - on buyer's obtaining license or permit.
  - on buyer's continuation as franchisee.
  - other.
- Risk of loss.
- Closing.
- Execution of bill of sale to transfer personal properties.
- Transfer of titles of motor vehicles.
- Execution of warranty deed to transfer real properties.
- Remedies on default:
  - seller considers limit on warranty protection and absorption if claims up to certain amount by buyer.
- Assignability of rights under agreement.
- Modification of agreement.
- Arbitration of disputes.
- Manner of giving notice.
- Binding effect of agreement on successors and assigns.
- Governing law.
- Date of execution.
- Signatures.

Prior to negotiations, study this list with your attorney, who may suggest deleting or adding items, depending upon the circumstances.

How often have you tried to increase a price you've previously set and been successful? Before you set the price, talk to your accountant and check with Realtors or financial people in your area. If you have real estate, have it appraised. There are rules-of-thumb that seem to indicate that a selling price is set at one-to-three times annual gross revenues. The SBA-published book, *How to Buy or Sell a Business,* by John A. Johansen, talks about a discounted future cash flow, also set forth in an article in *In Business* (November/December 1988).

The bottom line is that any enterprise is worth what you can get for it.

I started with this sales agreement checklist so that you'd keep in mind the number of issues you'll need to cover in the negotiations, whether as buyer or seller. In a big deal, the seller may insist on a confidentiality agreement so that the buyer keeps confidential information learned during the negotiation and review process. Have your lawyer review it.

Too often, the seller takes the verbal deal to his or her lawyer to write up, only to have the lawyer raise half a dozen issues that the parties never discussed. These issues may be essential to the sale of that business, but raising them at the last minute destroys the karma between purchaser and seller.

An example: Lawyers will insist on a detailed list of personal property to be transferred. The seller will mentally retain certain personal property, which retention may have been vaguely discussed with the buyer. The buyer's mental list of property that he or she will get with the sale, however, includes everything in sight. Too, sellers without lawyers often forget to add a contract provision regarding what happens if the buyer sells the business. If the seller is carrying the note, the seller may not want to risk installment payments with a new purchaser.

Another "for instance" is the training provided by seller to buyer. Both parties tend to be overly optimistic, generous, and sometimes foolhardy about the scope and length of training the seller gives to the buyer. Business styles differ; most sellers feel the reason that they have something to sell is because of the way they ran the business. Too often, buyer and seller are at each other's throat before the training ends.

Case Incident:

X, as a salesman for advertising in periodicals, felt that the purchase of a regional publishing house specializing in directories presented an excellent opportunity. X didn't feel she could spend money on a lawyer, so the parties drew up the papers and X paid the seller in full. X said the seller represented that a directory contract with a large educational institution was part of the deal. This was not mentioned in the contract, nor were any supporting documents incorporated in the contract, nor did the buyer examine any of the documents that may have existed to support this claim. X discovered that, in fact, the seller only bid on the directory and immediately following the sale, another publishing company got the bid. X had counted on this revenue to carry her through the first year.

Even if the buyer could get out of the situation, it would cost several times the amount of the original legal fee.

Anything that forms the basis of the deal should be covered in the contract. If it involves transactions with others, the prospective buyer needs to see the supporting documentation so that the buyer can evaluate its true worth. In X's case, she would have quickly determined that the "business asset" was merely a bid; she could have conditioned the sale of the business upon the successful award of the bid.

Sometimes the seller wants to dispose of only part of the business. *Publishers Weekly* (December 23, 1988) reported that Zebra Books planned to acquire the Canadian mass-market paperback house, Paperjacks; that is, its backlist and contracts. The president of Paperjacks did not include her distribution company, Select.

If you're the buyer, you should be entitled to review financial statements, business books, and tax returns. Also review the annual report, a multi-purpose document—it covers the past, present, and future of an incorporated business; investment potential can sometimes be deduced from an annual report. Request written confirmation on the existence, or lack thereof, of any claims, lawsuits, or causes of action of which the publisher has actual or constructive notice. In a book-publishing acquisition, examine the book contracts.

Case Incident:

Y purchased Z Publishing House. Z Publishing, in its thirty-year history, had four publishers of diametrically opposed temperaments and business practices. Y felt she knew what she was getting because she'd studied the backlist and the frontlist, but failed to review the underlying contracts and determine the status of any claims. After purchase, Y discovered that Z's old contracts contained narrow grants of rights along with permissions that extended to only the first two editions of most of the backlist books of the publishing house. This meant that to do a subsequent edition, the contracts had to be renegotiated and new permissions obtained at an additional cost. Not only the out-of-pocket costs, but the staff time, were a serious blow to the efficient operation of the takeover publisher.

Always remember that time is money; this is true even for people who don't charge for their time. If your publishing staff is spending time clearing up a problem that would not have existed had precautionary measures been taken, you're cutting into your profits. Being faced with renegotiating a contract with an author whom you don't know, and who may have resented the sale of the publishing house, is not negotiating from a position of strength.

If, however, as a new publisher, you're forced to renegotiate contract terms, look at all the old contracts and determine all the changes needed. Do a form letter explaining the necessity for the modification of the contracts, indicate why it is in the author's interest to execute same, and what advantages it offers the publisher. Since the common goal is to sell more books, that's the most reasonable rationale. In most situations where that technique is used, authors will agree to the amendment(s). This approach has been used when a publishing house updates or enlarges its marketing and sales outlets (which usually require greater discounts); when royalties need to be computed on net sales, rather than retail price, in order for it to be financially feasible to reprint a book; and when a backlist book has a narrow grant of rights, which prevents the publisher from licensing subsidiary rights.

Don't try to sell something you don't have. If you have a chance to sell rights and you don't have them, you have to see if you can get them by proposing a modification to the contract. Acquisition of another publisher's contracts can be a frustrating experience when the market and financial potential of a property cannot be exploited.

Beware, too, of lingering defamation claims, copyright infringement claims, inadequate permission files, and so forth. I recommend examining the contract and supporting documents for each backlist publication to determine what may be missing or incomplete, and then trying to rectify that situation through the utilization of form letters. After all, if the book has been out a year, the author dies or goes crazy, and someone makes a claim for copyright infringement because of unfair use of permitted material, you may be stuck with defending that matter. You will need a good working file.

Are there any reserves, royalties, advances, or license revenues owed to any of the authors, and if so, how will those be resolved? Possibly, you could use a technique that is utilized in construction contracts, in which ten percent of the contract funds are held back for the warranty period to see what claims are made, with procedures for utilization of that reserved money to settle any claims clearly specified. Be aware also of claims by third persons or the authors themselves.

Perhaps the similarities and diversities of the seller and buyer's interests are best shown through reproducing part of the proposed sales agreement for a group of periodicals. In this instance, the seller drafted an agreement regarding the sale of a periodical, and then the buyer drafted an agreement. The seller's place of business was in New Mexico but the buyer planned to move the business to its corporate headquarters in Oregon. Due to the nature of the periodical publication, that is, regular and tight deadlines, the timing of the closing became very important, as did the seller's involvement in forthcoming issues. Even on the buyer's exhibit list, the assets listed were far too general. How far back do customer lists have to go? Or what happens if there are no back issues available? Will the seller want to keep a set of back issues?

Here are the first few pages of the seller's contract.

Sale of Assets

Sale. **Subject to the terms and conditions of this Agreement, at the time and place of closing, which will be designated as stated herein, Seller shall sell and Buyer shall buy the following assets located in _____, and owned by Seller:**

1. **Any and all furniture, fixtures, equipment, and supplies used in connection with the publishing of the property, listed on Exhibit "A", attached hereto and made a part hereof for all purposes;**
2. **The goodwill of the business;**
3. **All trademarks, trade names, copyrights, customer lists, files, back issues, data files on _____, reference books, trade show displays, and related materials.**

Excluded from Sale. **There are expressly excluded from this sale the following assets and items:**

1. **Cash on hand on the date of closing;**
2. **All account receivables. On the date of closing, Seller and Buyer shall prepare a list of account receivables, and after date of closing, Buyer agrees to collect for and on behalf of Seller all account receivables reflected on the list, and promptly remit all payments on such account receivables to Seller. Payments received by Buyer after date of closing shall be considered to be paid on pre-existing account receivables before being applied to current invoices or receivables.**

3. All office furniture, fixtures, equipment, and other assets not listed on Exhibit "_____".

Purchase Price

Purchase Price. The purchase price of the assets purchased pursuant to Paragraph 1 above, shall be the total sum of $_____. The allocation of said purchase price shall be as follows:

ITEMS:	AMOUNT
Furniture, fixtures, equipment, files, and related materials	$_____
Goodwill, use of the name "_____," copyrights, trademarks, tradenames	$_____
Customer lists, back issues, data files on _____, reference books, trade show displays, related materials	$_____
Consulting fee	$_____
Covenant not to compete	$_____
TOTAL PURCHASE PRICE	$_____

Method of Payment. At the time of closing, Buyer agrees to pay and deliver to Seller the following:

1. The cash sum of $_____ at closing;
2. Buyer agrees to execute and deliver to Seller a promissory note in the original principal sum of $_____, payable to Seller as follows:
   a. A payment in the sum of $_____, shall be due and payable on or before _____; and
   b. Seller shall make payments on the principal in semi-annual installments of $_____, with the first installment due and payable on or before _____, and the others regularly and semi-annually on or before the 1st day of _____ and the 1st day of _____ of each year until the principal has been paid.
   c. The above described Promissory Note shall bear no interest from date until maturity. Matured unpaid principal shall bear interest at the highest legal rate allowed by law from date of maturity until paid.

Security for Note. Buyer agrees to secure the payment of the aforementioned promissory note, as follows:

1. Buyer agrees to execute and deliver to Seller security agreements and UCC Financing Statements, securing the payment of the above described promissory note. Said security agreements and financing statements shall grant Seller a first lien purchase money security interest in and to all of the assets to be transferred hereunder.
2. The Security Agreement shall contain a provision preventing the sale of the assets conveyed to Buyer to a third party without the prior written approval of Seller. If Buyer transfers any part of the property without Seller's prior written approval, Seller may declare the debt secured by the security instruments immediately due and paya-

ble, and invoke any remedies available to Seller pursuant to the security instrument.

Prorations and Adjustments. Payroll, rent, sales taxes, utilities, payments for telephone listing agreements, payroll taxes, and other prepayments or payables shall be prorated as of the date of closing. It is anticipated that Seller may continue in possession of the premises of the business office, therefore, Seller agrees to pay the cost of rent and utilities incurred after date of closing, up until such time as Seller vacates the premises.

Seller and Buyer agree to split and pay the costs of services of _____ from the date of closing until termination (anticipated to be on or about _____) equally, 50% each.

After receiving the seller's contract, the buyer proposed her own. Hers was twice as long; the first material variance was the provision on purchase price, and she increased the seller's warranties from five to fifteen in number. Here's the rest of the seller's draft of the sales agreement:

Representations of Seller

Seller represents, warrants and covenants to Buyer as follows:

1. Seller is the owner of all the assets transferred herein, free and clear of all liens, encumberances, security agreements, pledges, claims, charges and restrictions.

2. Buyer shall receive good and marketable title to such assets sold herein.

3. No litigation, governmental proceeding or investigation is pending or threatened against the business of Seller.

4. Seller has paid all payroll and other taxes incurred by it as of the date of closing, and all tax returns required to be made by Seller have been properly filed as required by law.

5. Seller shall conduct the business of publishing "_____" up to the date of closing in a regular and normal manner.

Transactions at Closing

At the closing:

1. Seller shall deliver to Buyer such bills of sale and such endorsements, assignments and other good and sufficient instruments of transfer and conveyance as shall be effective to vest in Buyer good and marketable title, free and clear of all liens, to the assets.

2. Buyer and Seller shall prepare and deliver all exhibits as contemplated herein.

3. At the time of closing, Seller and Buyer shall complete all prorations.

4. All property to be transferred hereunder shall be delivered to Buyer.

5. Buyer shall deliver to Seller the cash sum of $_____.

6. Buyer shall deliver to Seller a promissory note, executed by Buyer, in the original principal sum of $_____.

377

7. Buyer shall execute and deliver security agreements and UCC Financing Statements.

Seller's Covenant Not To Compete

For and in consideration of the mutual covenants and agreements contained herein and for the further consideration of the sum of TEN AND NO/100 DOLLARS ($10.00) and other good and valuable consideration paid to Seller by the Buyer, the receipt and sufficiency of which is hereby acknowledged by Seller, Seller hereby agrees that Seller shall not, directly or indirectly, render any service, whether as an owner, employee, shareholder, officer, director, agent, consultant, or in any form or manner, engage in any business, commercial or otherwise, that publishes _____ for a period of _____ years from the date of closing hereof, in the United States of America.

Consultation Agreement

Seller agrees to act as a consultant to Buyer, to aid Buyer in the operation of the business, and to generally assist Buyer in the transition of the sale. Seller agrees to assist Buyer in learning all facets of the business, and Seller agrees to use best efforts and reputation in developing the business for and on behalf of Buyer. In addition to generally aiding Buyer, Seller agrees to:

1. Edit _____ with Buyer, through the anticipated finish date of _____ .

2. Seller agrees to assist Buyer in implementing address changes, telephone changes, establishing new bank accounts, and maintaining vendor and customer relations.

The term of this consultation agreement shall commence on the date of closing, and terminate on _____ .

Indemnity

Seller agrees to indemnify and hold Buyer harmless from any and all obligations, liabilities, costs, expenses, charges and attorney's fees with reference to the assets of Seller existing up to the date of closing.

Buyer agrees to indemnify and hold Seller harmless from any and all obligations, liabilities, costs, expenses, attorney's fees and any and all other matters arising from or growing out of the business and assets purchased herein by Buyer from and after the date of closing.

Confidentiality

Seller and Buyer agree that, unless and until closing has been consummated, the parties shall hold the prospect of this Agreement and the purchase and sale in strict confidence, and will not use such information to the detriment of the business, and shall not disseminate such information to the public.

In connection with this sale, Seller agrees that she will not negotiate with any other corporation, company or individual, or entertain or consider inquiries or proposals relating to the possible sale of the assets contemplated herein, or a possible merger or acquisition of the business with or by another entity, prior to _____ , unless this Agreement shall be sooner terminated.

Failure to Close

Buyer's Failure to Close. Buyer has deposited the sum of $_____ as earnest money in this transaction with Seller. In the event Buyer fails or refuses to close this transaction, through no fault of Seller, Seller shall have the right to retain the earnest money as liquidated damages in the event of such breach, or shall have the right to enforce his rights under this Agreement, at law or in equity, including specific performance, and the defaulting party shall be obligated to pay, in addition to all damages that may be assessed, all costs for such breach, including reasonable attorney's fees and court costs.

Seller's Failure to Close. In the event Seller fails or refuses to close this transaction, through no fault of Buyer, Buyer shall have the right to enforce his rights under this Agreement, at law or in equity, including specific performance, and the defaulting party shall be obligated to pay, in addition to all damages that may be assessed, all costs for such breach, including reasonable attorney's fees and court costs.

The buyer countered with these provisions.

Covenants of Seller

Nondisclosure. At all times after the date hereof, Seller shall not, directly or indirectly, communicate, publish or otherwise disclose to any person or company, or use for the benefit of any person or company, any confidential knowledge or information concerning the Publications or the Assets or the conduct and details of Seller's business. Confidential information shall not include any information which is now known by or readily available to the general public, or which becomes known by or readily available to the general public other than as a result of any breach by Seller of this Section.

Consultation and Noncompetition. For and in consideration of that portion of the Purchase Price:

a. Seller agrees to act as a consultant to Buyer, to aid Buyer in the operation of the business, and to generally assist Buyer in the transition of the sale and for a period of _____ years after the Closing Date. Seller agrees to assist Buyer in learning all facets of the business, and Seller agrees to use her best efforts and reputation in further developing the business for and on behalf of Buyer. Seller's consultations with Buyer may take place in person, by telephone or by correspondence. In connection with her consultation services hereunder, Buyer shall reimburse Seller for reasonable expenses incurred by Seller which have been approved in advance in writing by Buyer. In addition to generally aiding Buyer, Seller agrees to:

i. edit _____ with Buyer, through the anticipated finish date of _____ ;

ii. assist Buyer in implementing address changes, telephone changes, establishing new bank accounts, and maintaining vendor and customer relations;

iii. during 19____, provide Buyer with overall and specific advice on publishing the _____ in the _____ 19____; and

iv. consult with Buyer with respect to the _____ Publications from time to time at Buyer's reasonable request.

b. Seller shall not, for a period of ten (10) years after the Closing Date, directly or indirectly, in any capacity, for the benefit of any person or company, establish, own, manage, operate or control, or participate in the establishment, ownership, management, operation or control of, or be a director, officer, employee, agent or representative of, or be a consultant to, any person or company which conducts a business similar to or competitive with the Publication or any similar _____ or _____ at any location within the United States of America.

Enforcement. Seller acknowledges that any breach of the covenants stated in Sections ____ and ____ ("Covenants") will result in irreparable injury to Buyer for which money damages could not adequately compensate. In the event of any such breach, Buyer shall be entitled, in addition to all other rights and remedies which Buyer may have at law or in equity, to have an injunction issued by any competent court enjoining and restraining Seller and any other parties involved therein from continuing such breach.

The nondisclosure and consultation provisions in the buyer's draft covered totally different areas and responsibilities. The buyer's enforcement provisions attempted to establish the groundwork for injunctive relief against the seller, i.e., obtaining a court order, for instance, that would stop the seller from competing with the buyer.

Indemnification

Seller's Obligation to Indemnify. From and after the Closing Date, Seller shall indemnify and hold harmless Buyer from and against any and all actions, suits, claims, demands, debts, liabilities, obligations, losses, damages, costs and expenses (including without limitation reasonable attorney's fees), arising out of or caused by any or all of the following:

a. Any material misrepresentation, breach or failure of any warranty or representation made by Seller in this Agreement or pursuant hereto;

b. Any failure or refusal by Seller to substantially satisfy or perform any term or condition of this Agreement (or any other agreement contemplated hereby) to be satisfied or performed by it;

    c. Any debt, liability or obligation of Seller with respect to the Publication and the Assets;

    d. Any matter involving the operation of the Publication by Seller before the Closing Date;

    e. Any debt, liability or obligation arising from Seller's failure to comply with the Bulk Transfer Provisions of the Uniform Commercial Code;

    f. Any debt, liability or obligation for commissions or finders' fees payable to brokers or other intermediaries in connection with this Agreement and the transactions hereunder; and

    g. Any successful action by Buyer against Seller to enforce this Agreement (or any other agreement contemplated hereby).

Buyer's Obligation to Indemnify. From and after the Closing Date, Buyer shall indemnify and hold harmless Seller from and against any and all actions, suits, claims, demands, debts, liabilities, obligations, losses, damages, costs and expenses (including without limitation reasonable attorney's fees), arising out of or caused by any or all of the following:

    a. Any material misrepresentation, breach or failure of any warranty or representation made by Buyer in this Agreement or pursuant hereto.

    b. Any failure or refusal by Buyer to substantially satisfy or perform any term or condition of this Agreement (or any other agreement or note contemplated hereby) to be satisfied or performed by either or both of them.

    c. Any debt, liability or obligation of Buyer with respect to the Publications and the Assets.

    d. Any matter involving the operation of the Publications by Buyer on or after the Closing Date.

    e. Any successful action by Seller against Buyer to enforce this Agreement (or any other agreement or note contemplated hereby).

By this provision, the buyer indicated her dissatisfaction with the seller's general indemnification relative to obligations.

Defense of Actions. Whenever one party ("Indemnitor") is obligated under this Section 11 to indemnify the other party ("Indemnitee"), the Indemnitor shall be responsible, at her expense, for litigating, defending or otherwise attempting to resolve any action, suit or proceeding against which the Indemnitee is indemnified under this Section 11, except that (a) the Indemnitee may, at her option, participate in such defense or resolution at her expense and through counsel of her choice; (b) the Indemnitee may, at her option, assume control of such defense or resolution if the Indemnitor does not in good faith pursue such defense or resolution, or if the Indemnitee in good faith believes that such defense or resolution will have a material adverse effect on its relations with one of its customers, employees, agents or representatives; and (c) the Indemnitor shall not agree to any settlement without the Indemnitee's prior consent which shall not be unreasonably withheld. In any case, the parties shall fully cooperate with each other in their efforts to litigate, defend or otherwise resolve any such action, suit or proceeding.

The buyer here established a procedure (non-existent in the seller's proposed contract) that enabled her to jump into the problem with her attorney and control, to an extent, defense or resolution. For instance, if the seller procrastinated in defending a copyright infringement claim that the buyer wanted resolved in order to license subsidiary rights, the buyer could step in and take over.

Notices and Payments. **With respect to each separate matter which is subject to indemnification under this Section:**

a. Upon the Indemnitee's receipt of written documents pertaining to such matter, or, if such matter does not involve a third party demand or claim, after the Indemnitee first has knowledge of such matter, the Indemnitee shall promptly give notice to the Indemnitor of the nature of such matter and the amount demanded or claimed in connection therewith ("Indemnification Claim Notice").

b. After a final agreement is reached or a final judgment or order is rendered with respect to such matter, the Indemnitee shall give notice to the Indemnitor of the amount owing by it ("Indemnification Amount") with respect to such matter ("Indemnification Payment Notice").

c. The Indemnitor shall pay the Indemnification Amount to the Indemnitee (or to such person as the Indemnitee instructs) within ten (10) days after the Indemnification Payment Notice was given.

The following buyer's provisions for termination and remedies referenced the theme expressed in her document, i.e., maximum protection for the buyer. She could end the deal for no reason at all, but the seller was tied to contract conditions.

Termination and Remedies
Termination on Default. **"Default" means that any of the representations and warranties made by a party or parties in this Agreement or pursuant hereto is or becomes false or misleading in any material respect, or any obligation to be performed by a party or parties is not substantially performed in a timely manner, for reasons within the reasonable control of such party or parties. If a Default occurs and is not cured within five (5) days after the date written notice is given by the non-Defaulting party to the Defaulting party specifying the nature of such Default (or on or before the Closing Date if sooner), then the non-Defaulting party may terminate this Agreement immediately upon notice to the Defaulting party.**

Termination as a Result of Investigation. **Notwithstanding anything** contained herein to the contrary, Buyer may terminate this Agreement for any reason within the fifteen (15) day investigation period provided in Section _____ .In such event, Section _____ shall not apply, this Agreement shall be null and void and neither party shall have any liability to the other.

Termination at Closing. If any of the conditions stated in Section _____ are not satisfied or waived on or before the Closing Date, then Seller may terminate this Agreement by notifying Buyer on the Closing Date. If any of the conditions stated in Section _____ are not satisfied or waived on or before the Closing Date, then Buyer may terminate this Agreement by notifying Seller on the Closing Date.

Remedies. Each party acknowledges that its obligations hereunder are unique and that it would be extremely difficult to measure the damages that would result from a Default. Accordingly, in the event of a Default, the non-Defaulting party shall be entitled, in addition to all other rights and remedies which she may have, to sue for specific performance and/or injunctive relief, and each party expressly waives the defense that a remedy in damages is adequate.

Application. The foregoing provisions of this Section 13 shall terminate if and when the Closing is held, and shall have no application to the provisions of this Agreement which survive the Closing Date or which govern the obligations of the parties after the Closing Date. Once the Closing is held, each party shall have waived its rights to terminate or rescind this Agreement, but without affecting any other rights and remedies which such party may have.

Both the seller and buyer provided that the agreements, representations, warranties and covenants survived the closing date. Both had provisions regarding:

- benefit.
- time.
- entire agreement and amendments.
- other documents.
- enforceability.

The buyer added provisions that required each to bear her own expenses and that section headings are reference only. Most importantly, the buyer added:

Setoff. Buyer, in addition to all of _____ other rights and remedies, shall have the right to set-off against any monies owed to Seller any sums to which Buyer is entitled to indemnification pursuant to this Agreement. Buyer's right to indemnification hereunder shall not be limited by this right of setoff.

Thus, the buyer wished to preclude any surprises and cover any equipment breakdowns or damaged-inventory costs. The ability to set off monies against installments due the seller was a legitimate concern to the seller, as under a worst-case scenario, the seller could receive only the down payment.

From the seller's perspective, the buyer's draft presented some problems; because of the ongoing nature of periodical publishing, which means something is always at the printers, the language, "to the best of the seller's knowledge," was too vague. The incorporations of the oral transactions and representations also could present serious problems: for example, the publication being sold was a household antique guide—thus, if the seller orally warranted an increase in prices in the antique market and the market collapsed, she could be penalized.

The buyer's draft of the seller's representations, which follows, presented a legal tightrope for the seller.

Representations of Seller

Seller represents, warrants and covenants to Buyer as follows:

1. Seller is the owner of all the Assets free and clear of all claims, liens, encumbrances, security agreements, pledges, claims, charges or restrictions of any nature.

2. Seller has, and is hereby transferring to Buyer, good and marketable title to the Assets, free and clear of all claims, liens, encumbrances, security agreements, pledges, claims, charges or restrictions of any nature.

3. No litigation, governmental proceeding or investigation is pending or threatened against Seller with respect to the Publication.

4. Seller shall conduct the business of publishing up to the Closing in a regular and normal manner, consistent with past practices.

5. Exhibit "_____" is an accurate and complete list of all of the Equipment and Supplies (with serial numbers where applicable) and their dates of purchase, costs and book values. All of the Equipment and Supplies are at Seller's business premises and are in good operating condition, ordinary wear and tear excepted.

6. All of the Inventory is at Seller's business premises and is reasonably salable or usable in the ordinary course of business.

7. Seller has duly filed a fictitious name registration to do business under the name "_____," in the State of _____. Seller has filed no other fictitious name registrations in the State of _____ with respect to the Publication, Seller has filed no fictitious name registrations in any other jurisdiction, and does not do business under any other name.

8. Seller's operations, the conduct of Seller's business with respect to the Publications, and the Assets comply in all material respects with all applicable laws, rules and regulations, including without limitation all laws, rules and regulations concerning minimum wages, worker's compensation, health and safety, and other employment matters. Seller has obtained and maintains all permits and licenses necessary for the conduct of the business of the Publication.

9. Seller has no debts, liabilities or obligations of any nature, known or

unknown, fixed or contingent with respect to the Publication. No tort, breach of contract, discrimination or other claim of any nature has been asserted against Seller, and to the best of Seller's knowledge, there is no basis for any such claim. No litigation, investigation, arbitration or other proceeding is pending, or to the best of Seller's knowledge has been threatened, against Seller or any of the Assets. There are no outstanding judgments or orders against or affecting Seller or any of the Assets.

10. Seller has accurately prepared and properly filed all tax returns, annual reports and other returns and reports required to be filed in connection with the Publication. Seller has paid all taxes, filing fees and similar charges required to be paid by him. Accurate and complete copies of all federal and state tax returns and reports filed by Seller with respect to its last completed fiscal year are attached as Exhibit "_____". No audit is pending or has been threatened against Seller, and no notice of deficiency or adjustment has been received by Seller, by or from any governmental taxing authority. There are no agreements or waivers in effect which provide for an extension of time for the assessment of any tax against Seller.

11. Seller's financial statements with respect to the Publication as at and for the period ending _____, copies of which are attached as Exhibit "_____", fairly present the financial conditions and results of operations of the Publication as at and for the period indicated, and were prepared in accordance with generally accepted accounting principles consistently applied. Between the date of such financial statements and the date of this Agreement, there has been no material adverse change or significant casualty loss affecting the Publication or the Assets.

12. Seller has maintained adequate insurance coverage for Seller's business with respect to the Publication to comply in all material respects with all applicable laws, rules, regulations and contracts. No claims are pending under any insurance policy maintained by or on behalf of Seller.

13. No person or company acting on Seller's behalf is entitled to any brokerage or finder's fee in connection with this Agreement or the transactions contemplated by this Agreement.

14. Seller's social security number is _____-_____-_____. Seller uses no other federal taxpayer identification number in connection with the Publication.

15. All representations and warranties made by Seller in this Agreement, and all information provided to Buyer by Seller in connection with the transactions contemplated hereby and the negotiations with respect thereto, do not contain any untrue statement of any material fact and do not omit to state any material fact necessary to make the statements made, in the context in which made, not false or misleading. There is no fact known to Seller which has not been disclosed to Buyer in writing which has, or so far as Seller can now reasonably foresee will have, a material adverse effect on Seller's business with respect to the Publication or any of the Assets.

The Seller proposed the following for the buyer's representations and diligence:

Representations of Buyer

Buyer represents, warrants and covenants to Seller, as follows:

Inspection. **Buyer has inspected the property, assets and business of Seller and is buying the property, assets and business from Seller on her own examination and judgment and that no representations or warranties, express or implied, have been made by Seller, Sellers agents or representatives, regarding the value of the property, business and assets of Seller, or any of them, the future value of the property, business and assets, the condition of the property, business and assets, or the future profitability of the property, business and assets.**

No Representations by Seller. **Buyer is purchasing the assets to be transferred hereunder based upon Buyer's own examination of all pertinent records, and Buyer has not relied on any representations from Seller, written or oral, nor from any of Seller's agents or employees. Buyer acknowledges and represents to Seller that Buyer is knowledgable in business matters, and has been involved in purchasing businesses in the past, and is intending to acquire the assets described herein solely for the purposes of investment, and that Buyer acknowledges that Buyer may not derive any profits from said assets, or receive reimbursement or return for consideration paid for such assets.**

Buyer waives compliance with the provisions of the Bulk Transfer Provisions of the Uniform Commercial Code in connection with the sale of the assets contained herein, subject to the indemnities of Seller.

Due Diligence

Investigation. **For a period of fifteen (15) days after the execution of this Agreement, Buyer, at Buyer's expense, shall have the right to investigate all representations, if any, made by Seller, to examine all of Seller's books and records, to examine Seller's client lists, and to generally conduct a due diligence investigation into any and all matters deemed necessary by Buyer to purchase the assets to be transferred hereunder. In connection therewith, Seller agrees to provide Buyer with all items reasonably requested by Seller, and agrees to assist Buyer by providing full access to Seller's books and records.**

Time. **At the conclusion of fifteen (15) days from the date of the execution of this Agreement, Buyer's due diligence investigation shall terminate, and Seller and Buyer shall proceed to closing.**

The buyer approached these provisions from a different angle. She refused to take responsibility for tying her inspection of the property into her decision to buy the publication, or to acknowledge that she might not make a profit.

Representations of Buyer

Buyer represents, warrants and covenants to Seller, as follows:

1. There is no litigation, investigation, arbitration or other proceeding pending or threatened against Buyer.

2. No person or company acting on Buyer's behalf is entitled to any brokerage or finder's fee in connection with this Agreement or the transactions contemplated by this Agreement.

3. Buyer's social security number is _____ .

4. All representations and warranties made by Buyer in this Agreement, and all information provided by Buyer to Seller in connection with the transactions contemplated hereby and the negotiations with respect thereto, do not contain any untrue statement of any material fact and do not omit to state any material fact necessary to make the statements made, in the context in which made, not false or misleading. There is no fact known to Buyer which has not been disclosed in writing to Seller which has, or so far as Buyer can now reasonably foresee will have, a material adverse effect on Buyer's ability to perform this Agreement.

Bulk Transfer Provisions

Subject to Section _____ , Buyer waives compliance with the provisions of the Bulk Transfer Provisions of the Uniform Commercial Code in connection with the sale of the Assets.

Obligations of Seller Before Closing

Investigation. For a period of up to fifteen (15) business days after the date of this Agreement, Seller shall continue to permit Buyer, and Buyer shall have the right, at Buyer's expense, to have reasonable access to Seller's offices, to examine and copy all of Seller's books and records, to examine and copy Seller's client lists, and to generally conduct a due diligence investigation into any and all matters deemed necessary by Buyer to purchase the Assets. In connection therewith, Seller agrees to continue to provide Buyer with all information reasonably requested by Buyer, and agrees to assist Buyer by providing full access to Seller's books and records.

Conduct Pending Closing. Between the date hereof and the Closing Date:

a. Seller shall use its best efforts to conduct the business of the Publications in a regular and normal manner, consistent with past practices, not to make any material change in the business practices, and to preserve the business organization intact.

b. Seller shall not (1) create or assume any material lien or encumbrance upon any of the Assets, (2) sell, abandon or otherwise dispose of any of the Assets, or (3) enter into any contract primarily involving the business.

c. Seller shall maintain the Assets in their current conditions, ordinary wear and tear excepted.

You've probably noted that there are no confidentiality or other restrictions on the buyer's use of the seller's records, a necessary item from the seller's perspective. Further, if the buyer wants its corporate accountant to examine the seller's books and records, the buyer needs to bring that person to the seller's place of business; as a business owner, you would not want a prospective buyer to copy your books and records. Also, it would be better to define "adverse changes." Again, the seller's representations, under the buyer's draft, include the negotiations of the parties.

Two things are clear: the parties to this proposed sale had different concepts about the sale, and the parties did not go through a checklist before involving their lawyers. For example, the indemnification provision is critical, because the buyer can set off or deduct any amount that she feels she's entitled to against the installment payments.*

Before I end this discussion of sales agreements, consider this list:

- Know clearly why you want to buy.
- Know clearly why the seller wants to sell.
- Don't rush through a sale. Allow enough time for legal work.
- Specify clearly and distinctly, by serial number, boxes, or some quantification inventory, such as books, copyright registrations, and so forth.
- If you are the seller, do a credit check on the buyer.
- If you are the seller, don't give installment payments without interest.
- If you are the buyer, check other publishing concerns of a like nature to get a feel for the business that's being sold.
- Both parties should give their lawyers clear instructions on making a deal work.
- Communicate all the terms of the sale to your lawyer.
- Review your lawyer's draft sales agreement before presenting it to the other party to make sure it accords with the oral negotiations between the parties.
- Be specific in the negotiations about what you want to keep and what your role will be after the sale of the business.
- Try to balance each party's respective needs for protection when negotiating the final terms of the contract.
- Remember the universal rule about limiting the geography, the time, or the breadth of any provision you find onerous.

It's not often that a lawyer's role in the sale of a concern is acknowledged, but this announcement of a book publisher acquisition appeared in *Publishers Weekly* (January 6, 1989).

---

*Please note that these are random comments about the contracts proposed by both parties. You would need to know the circumstances of that publishing business before you could accurately evaluate all of the contractual provisions. My comments are cursory.

There is sometimes a fine line between a lawyer who is playing devil's advocate for his or her client, and a lawyer who throws up so many obstacles that the deal falls apart—which takes us to our next chapter.

Handling Your
Legal Problems

19

Yes, you can handle certain legal problems, either through your own research or with the help of public agencies.

Enforcing Your Rights

Sometimes a problem arises from a simple misunderstanding or lack of communication. If the problem is fairly straightforward, or too insignificant to warrant the assistance of a lawyer, start the clarification process with a telephone call to the person in charge of the business. Have the documents (receipts, contracts, etc.) concerning the problem in front of you during the telephone call so that you can refer to them. State your case, listen carefully to the response, and take notes. Remember that your presentation of the facts can be crucial to your case.

Case Incident:
Don't do what one of my clients did. She was faced with a copyright infringement claim against some local businessmen who were known for being tough. When she talked with them, they threatened her with bodily harm. Then she wrote a demand letter for $200 and got no response, and she came to see me and wanted to recover several thousand dollars. Tough case.

Keep these points in mind when writing a complaint letter:

- use correct address.
- direct letter to specific person (keep copies).
- state complaint clearly.
- state your demand in terms "if settled now."
- give an action deadline (if letter to wrongdoer).
- indicate where copies were sent.
- attach copies of documents (keep originals).

A sample complaint letter follows:

Righteous Press
Fredonia, Arizona
January 31, 1989

Oh-So-Bad Printer
Key West, Florida

Dear Oh-So-Bad Printers:

This letter confirms our telephone notice to your company this date that your shipment of the 13-page *Comprehensive Guide to Flora and Fauna of Death Valley* was received in good order, except for the short shipment of ten boxes.

As you know, we plan to leave for the American Botanical Society's Conference in Death Valley in five days. This book was specially ordered as a release for the conference. Therefore, your clerk's half-hearted offer to check your warehouse next week and ship any boxes book rate fails to meet our needs and the contract between us.

This letter is being sent overnight express mail and we ask that you extend the same consideration in getting the missing shipment of books to us at your cost.

Sincerely,

Righteous Press

Another complaint letter took this form:

Dear Aksia Printing:

I talked to X on the telephone about the credits left off the jacket cover of *Burro Trails of the Southwest.* Those credits are to the United States Secretary of the Interior and to an ex-president of the United States and are very important. She said there was nothing that could be done until it was reprinted.

Blue Publishing spent over $50,000 in printing with your company last year. While it would cut into the profit of the printing job, your refusal to remedy the problem will eliminate any future printing business from our company. Since you have the preparatory materials, it is clearly easier for you to redo the jacket covers. Before this issue can be satisfactorily resolved, you would need to pay our staff time to open the boxes and rejacket the books.

We are holding off taking other action on this matter for seven days from the date of this letter. We look forward to hearing from you.

Sincerely,

Amerika Publishers

Actually, a press resolved a printing problem with a jacket cover in this manner. The printer air-mailed the jacket covers to the press and press's staff rejacketed the work.

In contemplating your strategy, don't wait until it's too late to go to court. All states have a law, the statute of limitations, concerning the time within which lawsuits must be filed. Generally, a suit for the breach of a written contract must be filed within two to ten years from the time of the breach, depending on your state's law. For the breach of a contract involving the sale of goods, usually the lawsuit must be brought within four years of the breach.

Complain to an Agency

If you can't force a resolution, consider one of the following (depending on the type of problem and assuming it's a small money matter and not a complex issue):

- an agency complaint.
  - private organizations such as:
    - consumer hot-lines affiliated with a local television or radio station.
    - Nader-supported Public Interest Research Group.
    - AT&T's toll-free 800 Consumer Directory, which lists 150,000 organizations that handle complaints.
  - local and state governmental agencies:
    - the consumer-fraud division of most state Attorney General offices.
    - state professional regulatory agencies, such as those for accountants, architects, attorneys, collection agents, contractors.
  - federal agencies:
    - the Better Business Bureau.
    - the Bureau of Consumer Protection, FTC (Washington DC 10500), if there's a pattern of wrongdoing affecting a group.
    - the nearest postal inspector, if mail was used in the wrongdoing.

- the Federal Information Center, for information on where to make complaints.

For a list of federal and state consumer protection agencies request the *Consumer's Resource Handbook* (Consumer Information Center, Pueblo, Colorado 81009).

Here's a consumer fraud complaint form from California:

JOHN K. VAN DE KAMP Attorney General	State of California Office of the Attorney General DEPARTMENT OF JUSTICE CONSUMER COMPLAINT	Public Inquiry Unit Office of the Attorney General P.O. Box 944255 Sacramento, CA 94244-2550 (916) 322-3360 Toll Free—California Only: 800-952-5225

I wish to file a complaint against the company named below. I understand that the Attorney General does not represent private citizens seeking the return of their money or other personal remedies. I am, however, filing this complaint to notify your office of the activities of this company so that it may be determined if law enforcement or legal action is warranted.

PLEASE TYPE OR PRINT LEGIBLY

1. Party Complaining	2. Complaint Against
Name	Name
Address	Address
City State ZIP	City State ZIP
Home Phone Work Phone	Home Phone Work Phone

If product or service advertised
(attach copy of ad if possible):   When _____ (date)

Where _____

NAME OF PRODUCT OR SERVICE INVOLVED: _____

DATE OF TRANSACTION: _____

Was a contract signed?   Yes ☐ No ☐

Have you contacted an attorney?   Yes ☐ No ☐

Have you contacted another agency for assistance? Yes ☐ No ☐

If so, list the attorney's name, address, and phone number: _____

What agency? _____

I will sign a sworn statement regarding these charges if needed: Yes ☐ No ☐

This complaint may be sent to the company complained about: Yes ☐ No ☐

Attach two copies of contract in addition to copies in duplicate of other pertinent papers. (PLEASE DO NOT SEND ORIGINALS; DOCUMENTS CANNOT BE RETURNED.)

Briefly describe events in the order in which they happened. Indicate dollar amount in dispute. If additional space is required, attach pages in DUPLICATE

Signed _____ Dated _____

PIU-3 (REV. 3-87)   **PLEASE RETURN BOTH COPIES OF THIS FORM**   87 82017

Legal Matters You Do Yourself
Other legal matters you may already handle include:

- arranging small loans from credit institutions.
- negotiating routine small contracts with graphic artists and printers.
- registering your copyrights.
- registering your business name with the state.
- obtaining business licenses and permits.
- handling minor traffic complaints.
- handling small insurance claims.

An organization that encourages limited use of lawyers is HALT (1319 F Street, N.W., Suite 300, Washington, D.C. 20077-1335); they publish an "every-day law" series and manuals such as *Small Claims Court* and *Using a Law Library.* These are excellent self-legal guides. (The last subscription notice I received trumpeted that they were fighting "for a legal system that is fair, efficient and works for the people it was designed to serve.")

"You Can't Squeeze Blood Out of a Turnip" or Going to Court
Sometimes it is just not worth bringing a lawsuit, even though right and justice are on your side. If the only people liable for the disappearance of your last shipment of books to the Boston Bookstore are applying for food stamps, it does not make sense to file a lawsuit against them. This chart helps size up your prospects for a successful court suit.

SIZING UP A LAWSUIT

		YES	NO
Adverse Party			
Available for service of papers:		☐	☐
If no proceed no further			
Has Assets:		☐	☐
Recovery Expected			
Estimated Damages (or value of items regained):	_____		
Plus	+		
Filing, service and lawyer's fees (if available from adverse party):	_____		
Minus	−		
Filing, service and lawyer's fees (if NOT available from adverse party):	_____		
Minus	−		
Other expenses (witnesses, discovery et cetera):	_____		
Minus	−		

Counterclaim (if any): Equals Total Estimated Judgment:	=	☐ (if higher than total estimated expenses)	☐ (if lower than total estimated expenses)

If you are still considering filing a suit, answer these questions. Whose name and address are you going to put on the complaint? You might have to find out who really owns the bookstore by checking with the city business-license department or the state corporation commission. If the owners live out of town or out of state, this adds to the difficulty of the suit.

What amount will you get if you win? The amount you sue for in a contract suit is the dollar loss resulting from your opponent's failure to uphold his or her end of the bargain. If money cannot replace the loss, a court will sometimes order that the loser perform some action, such as returning the books.

How much will the lawsuit cost? Will you use a lawyer or can you represent yourself in the local small claims court? All states have a small-claims-type court. In some states, these courts are called "justice" or "magistrate" court. Is the case *too big* for small claims court? Check with your state's Attorney General Office. Can you get legal help free from a local organization? What is the filing fee for a lawsuit? How do you serve the papers on the adverse party and what is the fee for service of the papers? You may have to take time off from work—this also costs money.

At this point, you should consider the possibility of getting a lawyer to send a letter for you. Since the time and expense of sending a lawyer's letter is far less than going to court, this step makes good sense in many cases.

Small Claims*

If, after calculating all the angles and deciding that small claims is the appropriate venue, a lawsuit still seems sensible, it is likely that your case will never see the inside of a courtroom. Eighty to ninety percent of the suits filed in small claims court are settled before a trial is held.

You can decide to use the small-claims-court system by considering the following, and doing your homework. Small claims actions are sometimes a quick and cheaper (lower filing fee and no attorney's fee if you represent yourself) way of getting the courts to help you with your problems. Telephone the clerk of the court and ask about the maximum amount that can be sued for in small claims court. Tell

---

*If you're considering going to court in Canada either with or without a lawyer, see *Making It Legal.* For a discussion of more complicated legal proceedings, see this chapter's section on anatomy of a lawsuit.

the clerk the current business and home address of your adversary and ask if the small claims court would cover his or her location. Stroll around the courthouse when you go down to fill out the forms. Sit inside a courtroom to see what's happening there: who's there, what they are saying, who's winning, what sort of judges preside, and so on. If you feel comfortable with the small claims court, fill out the complaint form, file it, and pay your money. (See the sample small-claims-court complaint form.) The clerk will tell you how to serve the right papers on your opponent. Don't forget that your opponent can file an answer to your papers and in that answer, can charge you with any debts that you may owe him or her. This procedure is called a *counterclaim.*

Be sure to have one person on your staff who is familiar with small claims court and can handle routine matters. If your small claims court has no forms or the forms don't fit your business, having your lawyer develop a set that can be used again and again. After you file the lawsuit, your opponent may finally realize that you are serious and will make a settlement offer.

Here are some Utah forms, used for small disputes. •

CASE NO.	PLAINTIFF	DEFENDANT
		VS.
DATE FILED		
	ADDRESS	ADDRESS

CIRCUIT COURT, STATE OF UTAH

SAN JUAN **County,** MONTICELLO **Department**

SMALL CLAIMS AFFIDAVIT

STATE OF UTAH) ss.
COUNTY OF SAN JUAN)

The affiant undersigned, being sworn, states:

1) DEFENDANT OWES PLAINTIFF THE FOLLOWING SUM: $_____

PLUS COURT COST: FILING FEE . . . . . $_____
ESTIMATED SERVICE . . . $_____
ESTIMATED TOTAL . . . . $_____

2) THE PARTIES LIVE AT THE ADDRESSES SHOWN ABOVE. DEFENDANT HAS BEEN ASKED TO PAY THE CLAIM, BUT HAS NOT DONE SO.

3) THE CLAIM AROSE ON THIS DATE _____ BECAUSE OF THE FOLLOWING:

_____
_____
SUBSCRIBED AND SWORN TO BEFORE ME ON _____

_____   _____
AFFIANT'S SIGNATURE   CLERK OR DEPUTY CLERK

ORDER TO DEFENDANT

YOU ARE DIRECTED TO COME TO SMALL CLAIMS COURT FOR TRIAL AT THE DATE AND TIME SHOWN:

DATE OF TRIAL	TIME OF TRIAL	ADDRESS OF COURT
		SAN JUAN COUNTY COURTHOUSE COURT ROOM MONTICELLO, UTAH

YOU SHOULD BRING WITH YOU ALL WITNESSES, PAPERS, EVIDENCE AND BOOKS YOU NEED TO SUPPORT YOUR DEFENSE.

IF YOU FAIL TO APPEAR AT THE TRIAL, JUDGMENT MAY BE ENTERED AGAINST YOU
FOR THE AMOUNT CLAIMED BY PLAINTIFF (SHOWN ABOVE, PARAGRAPH 1) PLUS COURT COSTS.
PLEASE READ THE INSTRUCTIONS ON THE BACK.

| DATE | | CLERK OF COURT OR CIRCUIT JUDGE |

ENDORSEMENT OF SERVICE
SERVED BY
SIGNATURE _____
TITLE _____
ON DATE OF _____
FEE FOR SERVICES $_____

Small Claims Affidavit & Order

INSTRUCTIONS TO PLAINTIFF

1. **Filing Suit.** To begin an action in Small Claims Court, come to the Clerk's office, and the clerk will prepare the necessary papers for you. The maximum amount you may ask for is $600.00. Claims must be for money only; this court cannot be used to sue for possession of property or to put a tenant out. You may sue a person living in the county where the Small Claims Court is located, or a person living elsewhere if your claim arose in the county. A corporation is treated as a "person." Bring with you the following information:

(1) Amount of claim and what it is for: and

(2) Name, street address, (not P.O. Box) and telephone number of person you are suing.

The debt must be owed to you; you may not bring an action on behalf of anyone else, but an employer may authorize an employee to be his representative. The clerk will prepare the affidavit which states your claim, which you will sign. A filing fee of $12.50 will be charged, as well as a service fee and mileage for service upon the defendant of the order directing him to come to the court to answer your claim.

2. **Trial.** A trial date will be set by the clerk. The clerk will give you a copy of the affidavit, which will have the trial date entered on it. It will be your responsibility to appear at the Small Claims Court on the date set, without further notice, and to bring with you any papers and witnesses to prove your claim. (See "Witnesses" under General Instructions, below.) **IF YOU FAIL TO APPEAR AT TRIAL, YOUR CASE WILL BE DISMISSED.**

INSTRUCTIONS TO DEFENDANT

1. **Trial.** You have had a lawsuit filed against you. If you wish to contest the plaintiff's claim, you must appear on the court date and bring with you any papers, evidence, or witnesses which you need to prove your defenses. (See "Witnesses" under General Instructions, below.) **IF YOU FAIL TO APPEAR AT TRIAL, JUDGMENT MAY BE ENTERED AGAINST YOU.**

2. **Payment.** If you do not dispute plaintiff's claim, you should make arrangements to pay it, either before or after judgment. Include the court costs shown in the affidavit. If plaintiff has to pursue collection procedures through the court, additional court costs will be charged to you.

GENERAL INSTRUCTIONS

1. **Attorney.** Small Claims Court is informal. Parties usually appear without an attorney, but you may hire an attorney if you wish.

2. **Settlement.** If the claim is settled prior to court date, please advise the court.

3. **Witnesses.** If there is someone you need as a witness who refused to attend the trial, you may ask the court to issue a subpoena, which will compel the person to attend. You should request the subpoena, if it is needed, no later than 10 days before the trial date.

4. **Judgment.** If the judgment is for plaintiff, plaintiff will be given a copy of the judgment to send to defendant along with a letter of demand for payment. If the defendant refuses to pay, the plaintiff has, the right to enforce the judgment. The procedures for doing so (garnishment, execution, etc.) are explained on the back of the judgment.

5. **Appeal.** By law, the plaintiff cannot appeal from a Small Claims Court judgment, but the defendant can appeal within 5 days, and a new trial will be held in District Court.

In more serious or complicated matters, remember the old saying: The person who is her own lawyer has a fool for a client.

So When Does My Publishing Concern Need a Lawyer?

You need a lawyer, and sometimes a specialist, in the following publishing business situations:

- deciphering proposed contracts for you.
- before signing an agreement or legal document that you do not understand; for example, a waiver of appearance in court on a major lawsuit.
- in preparing a will and in estate planning.
- in a divorce, annulment, or separation involving as an asset your publishing concern.
- when you purchase real estate or a business.
- when you have a dispute with someone represented by a lawyer.
- in criminal cases when you are accused of a crime that involves jail time, heavy fines, or penalties, such as postal regulation problems.
- if a claim for money damages is made against you or if you have a claim for money damages against someone which involves a serious amount of money.
- if you form a business organization.
- if you want to obtain a patent or sue for patent infringement.
- if you are involved in a legal transaction that is important to your business, profession, or personal life, e.g., a long-term business lease, an exclusive subsidiary rights agreement, a book contract.
- if you are considering bankruptcy or other debtors' remedies.
- if you want to register your trade name or trademark with the patent office.
- if you want to pursue copyright infringement.
- if you have landlord-tenant problems.
- if you have business loss, or had business property destroyed by the fault of another.
- if you cannot resolve a consumer complaint, and the money involved is significant.
- if you have discrimination or wage claims filed against you.
- if you are being audited by IRS for a large amount of money, and the audit may show fraud.
- if a government agency takes or proposes to take action against you that you don't agree with, such as a zoning change, eminent domain, construction of a government nuclear installation.
- other problems or situations of a legal nature that are complex or very important to you.
- if you buy or sell a publishing concern.
- if you need standard contracts for your business.

You need to locate the right lawyer for your publishing concern.

There are many kinds of lawyers. A general practitioner is just that: one who practices law in a variety of categories. Some lawyers specialize in one area: domestic relations, estate planning, corporate, patent work, tax work, criminal. Lawyers represent their clients on legal problems by providing information, giving advice, writing letters, preparing legal documents, making telephone calls, doing legal research, and appearing in court.

Unless you're in a big city, finding someone who specializes in publishing law can be tough. Look for a lawyer willing to acquire expertise in that field.

Finding a Lawyer

Sometimes a lawyer just gives advice, called a consultation; other times, he or she will do more work for you.

If you're in dire straits when you start a newsletter, or a bankruptcy wipes you out financially at the same time the FTC prosecutes you for violating regulations, you may need to find out about free legal services. The public-defender program handles criminal cases for poor persons in some courts. For free legal assistance in non-criminal areas, government-supported legal aid and privately funded organizations (like the ACLU and the NAACP) exist as a service to eligible people, (limited to a certain income level, residence, and type of problem).

Volunteer Lawyers for the Arts, a legal assistance program for the creative person or institution, was organized to meet the needs of people working in the creative arena. The national office in New York can tell you if there's a VLA group in your state, as can California Lawyers for the Arts (for appropriate California lawyers). Both have publications lists. Also, your State Bar Association (it licenses and regulates lawyers) may have a copyright section or intellectual law committee that can put you in touch with lawyers knowledgable about aspects of publishing law.

Law clinics provide routine legal services for a set, advertised fee. Cheap, but unfortunately, most publishing legal concerns aren't routine, simple problems.

Prepaid legal services are available to people affiliated with special groups such as credit unions; they give you lawyer-access for a set fee. I do not know of a prepaid legal services plan specifically for small publishing concerns, although COSMEP has a legal service plan, which is broader than publishing law in application.

Your other choice: a private sole practitioner or a lawyer with a law firm. Begin your search by talking to people you trust for suggestions. Be sure to find out why the lawyer is recommended: were your acquaintances satisfied with the work? what sort of work was done? was the bill reasonable?

The key is a *knowledgable* or *trainable* lawyer in your community. Community is a loose word. The community that draws on my services is the Four Corners area (Arizona, New Mexico, Colorado, and Utah), over to Albuquerque and down to the Arizona–Mexico boundary line. I've never met some of my clients; contact by letter and telephone has sufficed.

Most lawyers won't give legal advice to a stranger over the phone, because advice must be based on an examination of papers and documents, a personal interview (which could be by telephone), and of course, the establishment of a paying relationship.

A consultation with a prospective lawyer helps in the selection process. If the lawyer is lukewarm about the legal problems of publishing concerns, try another lawyer.

Consider these factors in selecting your lawyer:

- ability to explain things simply to you.
- age of lawyer.
- attention and interest in your problem.
- experience of the lawyer.
- fees charged for services.
- your comfort level in the office (remember, all that glitters is not gold).
- interest in books, computer software.
- kinds of clients represented.
- prior involvement in your industry, such as authoring a book.
- specialization in your problem area.
- specialization within the firm.
- the size of the firm.
- willingness to acquire specialty legal texts.
- willingness to not charge you for time she takes to get to know an area.

This selection is quite personal. Some say you need to like your attorney in order to confide in and trust him or her. Others simply don't want to pay someone they can't stand.

An aside: the term "simple explanations" always conjures up the publication by Don Sandberg, *The Legal Guide to Mother Goose* (Price/Stern/Sloan), which retells seventeen nursery rhymes in legalese. "Jack and Jill" becomes an accident report, and when "Jack fell down," he "suffered fractures and contusions of the cranial regions."

"A Lawyer's Time and Advice Are His Stock in Trade." (Abraham Lincoln)

Prepare yourself before seeing any lawyer. Go over your papers and be sure to at least bring them *with* you. Better yet, drop off an extra copy a day or two before your meeting. Read up on your problem if you have access to any information about it. Prepare a list of questions.

Discuss fees before you hire the lawyer for anything more than a consultation. Often, a lawyer can't give you an exact fee for handling your case, because the case's cost depends on the resolution route.

There are several basic fee arrangements:

- hourly rate: tax experts may charge $150 an hour but have the information at their fingertips. The average charge for a lawyer's time is $100 an hour in my community.
- flat rates for routine cases: wills, adoptions, or divorces.

- contingent fee: under this arrangement the lawyer takes a percentage of the amount won in a lawsuit, and gets nothing if the case is lost. The contingent fee is used in cases involving personal injuries, property damage, bill collection, Social Security, etc. Nevertheless, you have to pay the out-of-pocket costs of such cases, i.e., phone, photocopying, filing fees, depositions, and court costs.
- statutory attorneys' fees: examples would be discrimination complaints, certain consumer actions, and in some states complaints based on writings, for these laws permit the recovery of attorneys' fees.

Try to get the best deal and consider other possible fee arrangements. Bargain a little. Suggest a lower percentage on a contingent-fee case. Propose an hourly rate rather than the flat fee if you have a simple, routine problem. Offer to trade for your work or services (taking into consideration IRS regulations on bartering). For example, jewelry, books, repairs, prints, subscriptions, rugs, and pottery have all been traded for legal services at my office. Lawyers are occasionally amenable to half-cash and half-trade proposals. For a small publishing concern, consider offering the lawyer a percentage of your monthly bill in books, if your list is big enough. If appropriate, encourage the firm to trade on the bill for Christmas, birthday, and wedding gifts; your new coffee-table art book of rediscovered Hoopa Indian art could be a good trade item. Or agree to pay a monthly sum fixed at a lower hourly rate.

More than one hundred federal statutes allow the prevailing party to collect attorney's fees; some state statutes do, too. In Arizona, the prevailing party in a contract dispute gets attorney's fees.

Get a commitment from the general practitioner in Wazoo, Michigan, that she'll become knowledgable in the publishing area by a crash self-study course without charge to you. You want to pay for your lawyer's time (well, maybe you don't) and advice, but not schooling. For instance, if a fair-use question comes up, you don't want to pay for the lawyer to read the copyright act *for the first time*. In representing school districts, I always read, at no charge, the district policy manual, the student and teacher handouts, the standard district contracts; I also meet all the department heads—several hours of work, the costs of which I absorb.

Sometimes the lawyer expects a down-payment (a retainer) on the case. The amount depends on the legal problem, the amount of projected work, and whether you're an old or new client. If you're an old client, you may just be billed for the work.

Some businesses pay a set monthly amount as legal fees—sort of a prepayment—against the month the business ends up using their lawyer more than they ever wanted. Some of my clients go quietly along for months, with little or no legal work, and then one month, all hell seems to break loose in their affairs. The resulting hefty bill would be tough to pay at once if they didn't have a trust account already established.

After these discussions, you and your lawyer should contract concerning the specifics of his or her representation of you.

Some ways to save on fees:

- drop off your papers before your appointment so your lawyer can review them.
- completely fill out any forms or interview sheets your lawyer may use, and read carefully any information papers your lawyer may give you.
- write up a detailed narrative of the facts of your problem.
- have names, addresses, and telephone numbers of witnesses and opponents.
- don't repeat yourself.
- keep brief calendar notes of the sequence of events.

I ask all the publishers I represent to provide me a copy of each publication so that I have it at my fingertips if they call with a legal question regarding one of them.

Before you leave the lawyer's office, determine if the lawyer needs more documents or facts, whom you should or should not talk to, what work the lawyer will do on the case, when he or she will contact you, and how you will be kept informed of developments. Be sure the lawyer explains all the alternative solutions available to you on your particular problem. Listen to the lawyer's recommendation on what solution you should use *but* remember that some options may be too expensive for you. Paying a lawyer to file a suit for an unpaid account of $50 just doesn't make sense.

Your lawyer should inform you of developments on your case as they occur. If the lawyer doesn't, request copies of correspondence, most court papers, and development reports—and consider getting another lawyer. If you are involved in a lawsuit, you must be told of offers of settlement.

You have a right to confidentiality. The law regards your conversations with your lawyer as confidential. Even if you reveal your involvement with a past crime or misconduct, your lawyer cannot release this information. Remember that your lawyer cannot give you advice unless he or she has all the facts. Do not lie or hide the facts. Lawyers are pretty hard to shock. Despite warnings about this, it is not uncommon for clients to hide or not admit certain facts that make them look bad and then decide in court to tell those facts. Disastrous.

A lawyer must keep clients' funds (cost-deposit money and recoveries for clients) in a separate account. If you win money, you should receive a statement from your lawyer indicating the costs involved, your share of the recovery, and the lawyer's share of the recovery. The lawyer may not mix clients' moneys with his or her business account. If you have evidence that your lawyer has misspent your funds, report this immediately to the State Bar.

Sometimes clients have problems with their lawyer. Maybe the lawyer works too slowly, misses a deadline, gives you inaccurate advice, or represents you poorly. Discuss this dissatisfaction with your lawyer openly and frankly and try to resolve the matter. If the problem is not resolved, consult with another lawyer. Be sure to tell the consulting lawyer your legal problems first, then your complaint about your lawyer, and ask the consulting lawyer's advice.

Discharge your attorney if necessary. In a court case you may need the judge's permission to do that (as would the lawyer if he or she did not want to represent you further). Sometimes attorneys are reluctant to take over a case from another lawyer.

You should complain to your State Bar Association if you think your attorney has engaged in wrongdoing. As a last and final resort, consider making a malpractice claim if the lawyer made some serious mistake. Of course, you should see a lawyer for assistance with this.

Fee Disagreements

Lawyers are sometimes not paid by their clients. One, Richard M. Rosenthal, sued Jane Fonda in 1984, claiming she'd not paid a $2 million bill for legal advice given to her from 1969 to mid-1980. Based upon written and oral contracts giving him commissions from deferred compensation, the complaint alleged that the lawyer advised her on her anti-war activities, divorce, remarriage, and so forth.

Preventing and Resolving Legal Problems

Faculty at the Practising Law Institute estimated that there were fifty in-house counsel at the various large publishing houses, including twelve at McGraw-Hill, six at Random House, and four at Simon & Schuster (*Legal and Business Aspects of Book Publishing,* May 1988). This means ninety-nine percent of publishing concerns will deal with outside counsel.

Even if you have a lawyer, don't ignore preventive legal measures:

- knowledge.
- lawyer-approved forms.
- review of contract deviations.
- paper records and filing.
- policies and procedures.
- pre-contract and publication troubleshooting.

Invariably there's one staff member with a natural interest in the legal aspects of publishing; staff often refer legal problems to him or her. That staff person is the logical legal liaison.

Decide, before a problem arises, the lines between claimant, author, publisher-editor, publisher's lawyer, and claimant's lawyer. Neither the claimant or claimant's lawyer should have contact with the author. I prefer my author contact to be through the editor to preserve the attorney-client privilege, and thereby confidentiality, intact. Once a claim's made, or in the process of vetting a manuscript, I communicate my needs to the editor, who then secures the information from the author. Most lawyers label written documents to their publishing clients as confidential attorney–client communication.

One major publisher requires the author, when a legal problem rears its ugly head, to sign a letter that certifies that the author has retained the publisher's lawyer to represent him or her on the problem. Although this can affect the warranty-indemnification provision, major houses often cancel lawyer's fees and expenses under the indemnification provisions anyway. As a result, there's not as much concern with any conflict-of-interest created by the publisher's lawyer acting on behalf of the author.

Claims usually start off rather informally, by telephone call or letter, rather than a lawsuit. Don't ignore either one. Handle the telephone claim politely, but tersely, and ask the caller to provide specifics by letter. Get only enough information to respond. *Do not* engage in long telephone justifications about what did or did not happen.

Ask your lawyer to develop a form acknowledging receipt of a written or oral claim, along with a general information request for facts and documents, so that the claim may be appropriately evaluated. This prevents overreaction and a publisher making an inappropriate admission.

Have a policy, even if it's not in writing, that determines:

- who within the publishing house structure must be given copies or notification of claims.
- what your author contract says as far as notifying the author of claims.
- what the notice requirements are under your insurance policy.
- the point of lawyer contact.
- when the publication process is halted.

At some point, claims merit must be evaluated by the publishing concern and its lawyer. Often, if the complaint letter is from a lawyer, it's very general; claimants representing themselves often write windbag complaint letters. Your lawyer will talk with the other lawyer to determine the factual basis of the claim.

Your lawyer will determine:

- the merits of the claim.
- the claimant's finances and ability to litigate the matter.
- the knowledge of the lawyer regarding publishing rights.
- what relief the claimant is looking for.
- relief sought against the cost of litigating the matter.
- the potential outcome of litigation.
- whether the publicity of the lawsuit will be exceptionally harmful.
- what a lawsuit will do to the book's marketing.

Communication on your lawyer's part with the lawyer of the adverse party often will stop the filing of litigation. Over a period of time, a lawyer may convince the adverse party of the merits of the publishing concern's position. Some publishing concerns adhere to a policy of not paying any claims made purely for nuisance reasons, i.e., frivolous claims. Sometimes, a legitimate complaint can be resolved with simply an errata, or a clarification or addition in the work's future editions. Or just a promise to make a change in future editions, like this one from *Publishers Weekly* (June 10, 1988):

405

Harper & Row, Publishers, Inc., has reached an agreement with the American Medical Association to change the attribution for a review from the *Journal of the American Medical Association* that Harper & Row has been using on the jacket of the national bestseller, THE 8-WEEK CHOLESTEROL CURE by Robert Kowalski. The jacket of the updated edition of the book, released in March of this year, carried a quotation which credited only the AMA Journal. This attribution implied that the *Journal of the American Medical Association*, and not the reviewer, recommended THE 8-WEEK CHOLESTEROL CURE. Future editions of the book will carry the same quote ("This book can be recommended") but will be followed by "from a review by David H. Blankenhorn, M.D., in the *Journal of the American Medical Association.*" Harper & Row, though following publishing industry standard practices in citing the AMA Journal, apologizes to the *Journal of the American Medical Association* for violating the Journal's practice of not endorsing the opinions of reviewers whose work appears within their pages.

Harper&Row

A more serious matter may necessitate a recall and revision, or even dropping the work. An offer to pay the claimant a nominal sum, as well as pay his or her attorney's fees, all subject to a non-disclosure agreement, may do the trick.

The "one-dollar judgments" are a defendant's favorite if monetary damages are difficult to prove. The defendant agrees to pay $1.00 in exchange for dismissal of the lawsuit and perhaps payment of some of the attorney's fees and costs. That's a hard pill for the plaintiff to swallow.

There's a host of other decisions to make if you're sued and don't plan to settle:

- whether to proceed with your counsel or associate litigation counsel.
- to what extent you are going to defend the author and how you are going to share the costs of same.
- what licensees you need to notify of the litigation.
- what public statements to make about the matter.
- whether your counsel should try to get the matter dismissed by motion (as soon as possible, always a good choice).

- whether you want to get out of the court where the plaintiff has filed this action because the law is not favorable or the court is too far away.

Once actual litigation has commenced, the more public nature of the wrangling sometimes impedes settlement. Here's a creative settlement on a name infringement case, reprinted with the permission of the National Law Journal.

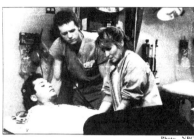

PLUG PULLED: As a result of a suit, NBC will cut a fall story line on its TV show 'St. Elsewhere.'

TV Story Line
Goes Elsewhere

NBC WON'T PULL the plug on any of the stars of the TV drama series "St. Elsewhere," but it will cut off life support to one of the show's fall story lines.

The 6-year-old Emmy Award-winning series about a deteriorating Boston teaching hospital opened the fall season resuscitated by a fictitious new management company called "Ecumena." Lawyers for Louisville, Ky.-based Humana Inc., a real-life hospital corporation, claim the name infringes on that company's trademark and publicity rights.

James R. Cox, a partner in Louisville's Hirn Reed Harper & Eisinger, who represented Humana in the litigation against NBC, says, "We know that [NBC was] aware of Humana, the name."

Now, he explains, "NBC and MTM Productions, the series's producer, have agreed to...eliminate certain references to 'Ecumena' and have agreed to a disclaimer procedure. They have further agreed to ultimately eliminate the name 'Ecumena.'"

Until remaining shows are put under the knife to remove references to "Ecumena," Mr. Cox says, the series will run a disclaimer stating, "'Ecumena' is a fictional company that does not represent any actual company or corporation."

The agreement comes on the heels of a denied request for a temporary restraining order that would have killed the drama's Sept. 30 show, says **Paul Reader**, an NBC spokesman.

NBC lawyer **Donald J. Mulvihill** of New York's Cahill Gordon & Reindel says changes don't mean the show's producers did anything wrong.

And the settlement, he adds, is not a bitter pill to swallow: "Writers enjoy these kinds of challenges."

Rosemary Olander

Reprinted with permission, copyright © The National Law Journal (*The National Law Journal,* October 26, 1987)

Anatomy of a Lawsuit

H. L. Mencken said that a courtroom's a "place where Jesus Christ and Judas Iscariot would be equals, with the betting odds in favor of Judas."

Filing a suit, except on routine collection matters, is a serious legal step. For that reason, when one of my clients considers filing a lawsuit, I provide him or her with the following outline about the steps involved in litigating a case.

STEPS INVOLVED IN LITIGATING A CASE

Complaint: A complaint is a written document that states a complaint that you have against another party. After this document is drafted, often the attorney will want the client to review the complaint, and in some cases, to sign the complaint.

Filing of Complaint: Filing fees for a complaint range from $10 up. A divorce complaint in Arizona costs $92 to file and a complaint for a debt in Superior Court, $50.

407

Summons: When a complaint is filed, the Clerk of the Court issues a summons, and the summons orders the defendant to appear and answer the complaint. Usually the Sheriff's office serves the complaint, but sometimes a process server serves the complaint. The charge ranges from $10 to much more, depending on how hard the defendant is to serve. Before a person can be served, it is necessary to know where that person lives or works. For corporations, you need to find out who the statutory agent is. In most cases, the defendant has twenty days after service to answer, but in some cases, thirty days. The United States Government in Federal Tort Claims has sixty days.

Answer: Once an answer is filed, both the plaintiff and defendant may proceed with discovery. The defendant's answer must admit or deny the plaintiff's allegations, plus make any affirmative defense that the defendant has, such as a release, satisfaction, and so forth. The defendant may make a counterclaim against the plaintiff or may file a cross-claim adding another party to the case.

FOR EXAMPLE: if a publisher sues a printer for failing to deliver the print job due before Christmas until Valentine's Day, the printer might add the paper supplier who held up the printer's paper order in a cross-claim. The printer may have a claim against the publisher for its failure to deliver the work on time or changing the work order. This is a counterclaim.

Interrogatories: Discovery means finding out the other side's story about the incident in question to determine what kind of a case the other party will put on at trial. First interrogatories are sent. These written questions are directed to a certain person or party to find out what they know about the problem. There could be numerous questions.

The other party has thirty days to answer the interrogatories, but often the attorneys agree to extend that time period because it is difficult to contact the person who has to answer the questions, or to find the information, or to get the answers ready.

The answers to interrogatories are reviewed by the party and attorney. These answers give your attorney more information about the other party's position on the problem.

Deposition: After interrogatories, the parties may decide to take the deposition of a certain person or persons. A deposition involves your attorney, the other parties' attorney, and the person whose deposition is being taken. A court reporter takes a verbatim transcript on all the questions asked and all the answers given under each. He or she later types these notes up into a small booklet so that the court can read the answers and questions that were asked during the deposition. It is very helpful to take depositions because you can explore areas of questions more spontaneously than you are able to in written interrogatories; the person being deposed does not have time to carefully construct her answer, and therefore you get more information.

Depositions are, however, very expensive, and run $1.00+ a page for copies. A deposition could cost anywhere from $100 to $300 or even more. If there are many witnesses in a case, or many people who have information about the incident, it is necessary to take several depositions, and the cost of taking the depositions in a particular case could run several thousand dollars.

Motion Practice: Attorneys ask the court to do something by filing a motion. One, a motion for summary judgment, is prefaced on the assumption that there is no factual dispute (a jury determines the facts) and asks the judge to apply the law in a party's favor.

Motion to Set: After the depositions have been taken and the discovery has been completed, the attorneys will make a motion to set the case for trial. In that motion, they list how many days the trial will be.

Pre-Trial Conference: Some time prior to the trial there will be a pre-trial conference among the attorneys. The purpose of the pre-trial conference is to narrow what issues are in dispute among the parties, decide what witnesses will be called, see if a settlement of the matter can be reached and list the exhibits. Other matters are discussed that will make the trial of the case shorter and easier for the judge and the attorneys.

Trial: At a trial, the plaintiff first proves his or her case to the judge or jury. After each of plaintiff's witnesses is called, the other attorney has a chance to cross-examine, or ask that person questions. When the plaintiff is done with its witnesses, the defendant calls its witnesses. At the end of each defendant's witness's statement, the plaintiff's attorney has an opportunity to ask that witness questions. At the close of the evidence, each attorney makes a final argument on the case in which he or she tries to convince the court or the jury that their client is right.

The court or the jury then decides if the defendant is liable to the plaintiff. If the court decides the plaintiff is right, the judge or court decides how much in money damages the plaintiff should be awarded or what relief should be granted.

Appeal: Sometimes one of the parties to a lawsuit does not agree with the court's decision, and may think that there was an error made in handling the case before the court. That party may appeal the case to a higher court.

An in-house checklist that most lawyers follow in some form or other is reproduced below. It's related to Arizona and Federal Rules of Procedure. Remember, for each pleading after the complaint you add anywhere from three to seven days for service of a pleading by mail. It may take a few days to serve the complaint, or a month. A response is made to each motion, then the movant replies to the response. Then the lawyers may ask for additional time to respond. Take into account lawyers' workloads and you can see that each step does not immediately follow the other.

Name: _____

Number: _____

Title of Suit: _____

PLEADING	DRAFT	DATE FILED OR SERVED	FILE RESPONSE BY
COMPLAINT (Rule 7)			
ANSWER OR MOTIONS (Rule 7 & 12) 20 days personal service; 30 days non-resident motorist; 30 days const. service or service out of state			
ANSWER TO CROSSCLAIM 20 days			
REPLY TO COUNTERCLAIM 20 days			
MOTION TO DISMISS DENIED 10 days to answer			
MOTION FOR MORE DEFINITE STATEMENT GRANTED 10 days to cure			
AMENDMENTS (Rule 15) Before responsive pleading served or if none, then 20 days after pleading served (without leave of ct.)			
AMENDED COMPLAINT (Before responsive pleading) 10 days at least to respond to			
RESPONSIVE PLEADING TO AMENDED PLEADING Time left to respond or 10 days, the longer			
RESPONSIVE PLEADING TO SUPPLEMENTAL PLEADING Not required unless ordered			
MOTIONS (Rule 12) Made at least 5 days prior to time set for hearing except M.S.J. 10 days; M.D.J. 3 days			
12b MOTIONS 20 days; venue defect, affidavit and controverting affidavit within 5 days			
MOTION FOR MORE DEFINITE STATEMENT (Rule 12e) 20 days before responsive pleading			

PLEADING	DRAFT	DATE FILED OR SERVED	FILE RESPONSE BY
MOTION TO STRIKE (Rule 12g) 20 days after receipt of pleading			
MOTION JUDGMENT OF PLEADINGS (Rule 12c) After pleadings closed			
MOTION SUMMARY JUDGMENT (Rule 56) 10 days notice of hearing. Claimant must wait till 20 days after service or M.S.J. by adverse party. Defending party, any time			
MOTION FOR DEFAULT JUDGMENT (Rule 55) If defaulting party appeared 3 days notice of hearing on M.D.J.			
MOTION TO QUASH SUBPOENA DUCES TECUM Promptly before time for compliance			
MOTION TO ENLARGE TIME Before expiration of time or after time for excusable neglect			
MOTION FOR CONTINUANCE			
AFFIDAVITS Supporting-served with motion. Opposing affidavits served not later than one day prior to hearing.			
JURY TRIAL DEMAND (Rule 38) Anytime, but not later than date setting case or 10 days after motion to set whichever first. Combined with motion to set.			
MOTION FOR SECURITY FOR COSTS (Rule 65.1) Before trial. P/S affidavit of inability within 5 days after order.			
OFFER OF JUDGMENT (Rule 68) 10 days before trial and acceptance within 10 days			
DEPOSITIONS (Rule 30) Before XN - 20 days notice to perpetuate testimony. After XN - without leave unless before response. Oral exam - reasonable notice 1. 2. 3. 4. 5.			

P L E A D I N G	DRAFT	DATE FILED OR SERVED	FILE RESPONSE BY
WRITTEN INTERROGATORIES (Rule 38) Prompt motion to protect parties. Direct Int - all parties. Cross Int - served on party taking deposition within 10 days. Redirect Int - 5 days. Recross Int - 3 days. Objection to form of interrogatories served within above time. 1. 2. 3. 4. 5.			
REQUEST FOR ADMISSIONS (Rule 36) Any time. Objection within 10 days.			
PRODUCTION FOR INSPECTION (Rule 34) Any time. Notice to all parties.			
PHYSICAL OR MENTAL EXAM (Rule 35) Any time and notice to all parties.			
DISMISSAL WITHOUT ORDER OF COURT (Rule 41) Before service of answer. Stipulation by all parties.			
MOTION TO SET AND CERTIFICATE OF READINESS Issues joined and discovery complete.			
PRE-TRIAL CONFERENCE (Rule 16) Memo filed 5 days prior to conference. (local rule)			
INSTRUCTIONS (Rule 51) Conflict - Rules before close of evidence. Practice prior to trial. See pretrial order.			
JUDGMENT (Rule 54 et seq.) Objection to form within 5 days. Statement of costs 10 days, exceptions thereto 5 days. See ARS § 12-311 346.			
MOTIONS AFTER JUDGMENT (Rules 59-62) Motion to Amend Findings within 10 days; Motion New Trial usually 10 days.			

Lest you think I am beating a dead horse, let me remind you that not only will you be paying an attorney to proceed with litigation, as well as court costs, copying, postage, and other expenses, but this process (as you saw from the foregoing) is going to involve the time and capabilities of your staff, sometimes your entire staff. That also has an hourly value.

Sometimes information provided during discovery in a lawsuit leads to settlement (*Publishers Weekly,* October 28, 1983). The Northern California Booksellers Association reconsidered its suit against Avon upon analyzing a study that showed the practice of giving chains a higher discount is legal because it's justified on a cost basis. In another case, it came out in discovery that a copy-editor wrote on the copy "I don't believe this!" and the statement was published.

Vetting, or Legal Manuscript Review

Prepublication legal review, also called vetting, applies to manuscripts as well as the promotional material and jacket and catalogue copy for those manuscripts. The legal review is usually prompted by an editor who's concerned with problems that surface in a manuscript. Encourage your editors to consider a legal manuscript review if they have *any* question regarding the work's vulnerability to litigation. This vulnerability usually can be found in:

- biographies of living persons, where the content may be unflattering.
- books or works about controversial topics and people.
- works where the copyright of the texts, photographs, or artwork is in question.
- works where the ownership of the book's contents may be questioned.
- a publication that results in embarrassing private facts.
- art books, if someone other than the author owns the copyright to the works.
- fiction books (especially first novels, which tend to be autobiographical).

In vetting, the lawyer looks for the following problems:

- ownership of book's content, i.e., copyright, fair use, etc.
- libel.
- invasion of privacy, including false light, right of publicity, misappropriation of likeness.
- trademark and unfair competition problems.
- contract problems.
- creator's moral rights.
- obscenity.
- warranties (for how-to-books).

Determine whether you want a written or oral opinion from your lawyer. If it's a written opinion, be sure to mark at the top "Attorney-Client Privilege." In the document, the lawyer should not state this sentence or paragraph is libelous, but rather, should inquire about the basis of the statement. The editor would then find out if the author has good reason to believe a statement is true; or would ask the author to provide notes, newspaper clippings, and so forth to support the position; or to do another interview; or to rework it into an opinion. The lawyer will probably suggest that the author remove gratuitously offensive statements; for instance, do not contend that someone's a crook, if it's not necessary. If the statement is needed, again, the lawyer will want to know the basis of the statement.

The PLI book publishing texts contain outlines to guide your lawyer through a vetting.

The End

I'll end this on a semi-humorous note with this copyrighted article from the National Law Journal on a magazine fiasco that probably was poorly organized as to responsibilities, and fell apart.

Magazine Gets Own Divorce?

RELATIONSHIPS gone awry were their specialty, yet they failed to keep their own from splintering rather ungraciously.

Attorney **Daniel Hirsch** of New York's Jones Hirsch Connors & Bull teamed up with investor **Gabriel Safdie** last spring to create Divorce, a magazine designed to address all aspects of divorce for those newly estranged and those contemplating separation. (NLJ, 8-3-87.)

Although matrimonial law is not Mr. Hirsch's area of expertise, personal experience provided inspiration for the magazine. Scheduled for release last October, the bimonthly publication seemed to be on its way with articles in its prototype such as "The Four Year Itch," "The Terrible Truth about Matrimonial Lawyers," and, of course, the latest celebrity gossip.

But, according to published reports, there was a fierce dispute between Messrs. Safdie and Hirsch allegedly over money and who was to pay what bills.

Details are fuzzy, but apparently Mr. Safdie lost his office in Mr. Hirsch's law firm, where Divorce was being run, and a freeze was placed in the editorial department that reportedly left freelancers and vendors shortchanged to the tune of $140,000, according to a story in INC. magazine.

When Mr. Hirsch's office is contacted, the caller is told the magazine no longer exists and there is no forwarding number for it.

Mr. Hirsch refuses to comment on the situation and Mr. Safdie could not be reached for comment.

—Sheryl Nance

Afterword

Legal Step-by-Step: An Overview

T his afterword gives the publisher an overview of step-by-step considerations to setting up a legally sound publishing operation. Some of these steps the publisher takes, others the publisher assigns to staff, the publisher's lawyer, or an accountant.

Getting Started
- Start a legal-business bookshelf.
- Hire an accountant.
- Decide upon your publishing concern's concept and business plan.
- Choose a lawyer.
- Choose a legal structure and do the paperwork.
- Choose a name and logo and protect them.
- Set up a policy book.
- Conceptualize and put in line legal-business training for staff.
- Develop a recordkeeping and processing form for all projects.
- Set up a standard filing system for each book, periodical, or catalogue that is always followed.
- Acquire a block of ISBN—or ISSN for periodicals—numbers from R. R. Bowker.

Contracting
- Open a contract potpourri file for sample contracts.

- Prepare the boilerplate terms for all your contracts.
- Develop an in-house form to check off in evaluating whether to retain someone's services, and a general independent contractor's agreement.
- Check your state's law on written contracts.
- Have your chief financial officer review all standard forms.
- Order Poynter's *Publishing Contracts on Disk.*
- Develop a standard publishing agreement with policy discussions, where necessary, and clauses on:
  - recitals and description of project.
  - satisfactory manuscript and variations.
  - permissions and alternative payment.
  - grant of rights—determine which ones.
  - author warranties—with alternate provisions approved by your lawyer.
  - rights you want to keep.
  - competing works.
  - option policy.
  - proofreading and author's corrections.
  - copyright policy.
  - date, style, and price of publication.
  - advances in installments.
  - royalties.
  - accounting (semi-annual, quarterly).
  - reports.
  - payments.
  - copies to author.
  - author's property—responsibility for negligence, gross negligence, or none at all.
  - revisions.
  - infringement suits.
  - discontinuance of publication.
  - arbitration or not.
  - bankruptcy and liquidation.
  - termination.
  - advertising.

Restrictions on Content

- Know the current obscenity laws if your works touch that area, and contact the National Coalition Against Censorship.
- If your published works include photographs or text of and about living persons, know your state's privacy laws.
- Have your photographers provide you with releases.
- If the work you publish taints some living person's or organization's reputation, consider a legal manuscript review.
- Beware of potentially defamatory statements.

- Proceed cautiously and with legal advice if your work is imitative of another's.
- Pursue your legal remedies against unfair imitation of your work.
- Arrange recalls with legal advice.
- If you have trade secrets, use a written agreement with employees to protect them.

A Hodge-Podge of Contracts
- Develop a graphic artist contract with:
  - parallel grant of rights to your book contract.
  - parameters for payments.
  - determination of artist credit.
  - provision for lost or damaged works.
- Collaboration agreement—have a knowledgable editor or lawyer review any agreement for a large or costly project.
- Ghost writer agreement—same as above.
- Develop a translation agreement if you'll be using translators.
- Review all your backlist contracts on a rotating basis.
- If you publish an anthology, beef up your permission form and enhance your book publishing contract to cover those unique problems.
- If you publish educational texts, incorporate in your book contract the quirks of that field.
  - know the adoption requirements for states to which you intend to market.
  - know how the Manufacturing Standards and Specifications for Textbooks affect you.
- If you distribute software, be sure to adapt your contract to that medium and have a work-for-hire agreement.
- If any particularly troublesome work relationship is a costly one, have your lawyer review the matter.
- For periodical publications, develop at least a check endorsement, preferably a letter agreement.
- If you use consultants, develop a standard form, even a letter agreement, for this relationship.
- For periodicals, develop an appropriate rate card with legal considerations in mind.

The Nuts and Bolts of Copyright
- Order copyright forms, circulars, deposit regulations, and statutes.
- Develop permission guidelines with a disclaimer.
- Review your contracts to see if work-for-hire is appropriate.
- Work out your publishing policy on ownership of copyright (or grant of rights if the author owns the copyright) in text, art work, and jacket covers.
- If a periodical, develop a check endorsement, manuscript purchase state-

ment, and text information form.
- If a periodical or catalogue, set up a prominant location for copyright notice; for books, set up a standard format for copyright page.
- Set up procedure where all flyers, catalogues, published works, and so forth contain a copyright notice.
- Develop a copyright log of each work that has a copyright notice; if you discover a work missing a notice or incorrect, cure the omission.
- Establish a copyright registration procedure, including all forms with instructions, on a filing time line of approximately 15 days after publication.
- Consider opening a deposit account with the Copyright Office if volume of your transactions warrants this.
- Be prepared, if you're a periodical publisher, to confirm or assign copyright.
- Check and see if any of your backlist works need renewals, and calendar them.

Fair Use and Infringement
- Understand, in-house, the principles of fair use.
- Be sure to have copies of all the permissions generated by a given work.
- Review the principles of fair use for educators.
- Consider authorizing in the front of your publications excerpts of a limited number of words.
- Develop a permission request record.
- Check with your authors to ascertain if they have permission for more obvious uses, such as direct quotations, charts, and so forth.

Manufacturing
- Understand the printing processes.
- Get quotations.
- Vary trade customs by using your contracts or amending the printer's— and use standard amendments.
- Avoid alterations.
- Be sure your staff, or you, carefully check proofs.
- Establish realistic deadlines for the printing process.
- Be sure the print contract establishes a standard of workmanship.
- Don't limit liability to merely reprinting.
- If a problem arises, be creative in seeking a resolution and reduce the resolution to a written agreement.
- Approach overseas printing with legal care.
- Reduce any co-publishing arrangement to a written agreement prepared or at least reviewed by your lawyer.

Marketing
- Adapt the agent concept in your publishing concern's operations either by:

- training an employee, or
- retaining an agent(s).
  - review agent contract and negotiate changes.
  - set up in-house procedure to supply agents with catalogues, galleys, and books.
- Actively market book club rights.
  - have your lawyer review any agreements.
- If applicable, pursue movie, television, and dramatic rights.
- Distribution.
  - map out plan.
  - check contracts carefully.
- Consider order fulfillment service.
- Mail order subscriptions:
  - collect and review regulations.
  - determine if you must file a statement of ownership management and circulation.
  - make one staff member a "mail" expert.
  - know the 30-day rule.
- Order one book on legal aspects of marketing.
- Mergers and acquisitions:
  - if major, consult a knowledgable lawyer.
- Be wary and able to justify policies if you don't have one price for all customers.
- Don't provide unequal promotional services.

Subsidized Publishing
- Develop your contracts and in-house procedures.
- Consider legal restraints on vanity publishing.

Desktop Publishing
- Double-check the warranties of the equipment you buy.
- Protect yourself from glitches contractually.
- Use trial periods to determine cost and savings.

Warranties, Disclaimers, and Product Liability
- Avoid express warranties, but make sure your product meets the implied warranties of fitness for ordinary purposes or particular purposes, title, and authorship.
- In situations where a reader would be injured by the use of the text or exposure in the text, review with your lawyer.
- Consider disclaimers.
- Be extra-legal-careful with mixed-media products.
- Consider recall if problems develop.
- Determine your exposure to liability, then find a broker to determine available coverage and costs.

419

- Try to find group insurance rates.
- Consider a media special-perils policy.
- Check the definitions and exclusions in any policy.

Employees
- Hire independent contractors with a contract.
- Use a contract for certain employees.
- Be sure to pay all withholding.
- Be wary of making oral promises for a bonus or a share in the profits.
- Lay the groundwork before firing an employee.
- Be aware of the danger of defamation of terminated employees.

Entrepreneuring
- On acquisition of a book property (or before) consider need for:
  - cash.
  - expertise.
  - other.
- Be creative.

If Your Author Dies
- Review the status of the author's works with your publishing concern and talk to your lawyer.
- Review all legal documents with your lawyer to see if they're in order before making payments.

Handling Legal Problems
- Keep records.
- Complain to state and federal agencies.
- Involve your lawyer early on.
- Work out fees.
- Promptly inquire about questions on bills.
- Understand the lawsuit process.
- Develop in-house procedures and forms.
- Provide staff training to give legal information and so warning lights go off when they ought to.
- Develop a legal claims procedure with your lawyer.
- Attempt resolutions short of litigation.
- Consider mediation or arbitration.
- Vet, or consider legal manuscript review.
- Enforce your contracts.

Buying or Selling a Printing Concern
- Review checklist.
  - modify to reflect your business.

- Make complete notes of sales negotiations.
- Share these with your lawyer.
- Review your lawyer's draft to be sure it reflects what you understand the agreement to be.
- Do a credit check of buyer.
- Be sure the asset-debt list is detailed and complete.
- Consider an amount of contingent liabilities buyer assumes.

Selected Bibliography

Alternative Dispute Resolution Primer. Washington D. C.: American Bar Association, 1983.

American Association of University Presses. *One Book/Five Ways: The Publishing Procedures of Five University Presses.* Los Altos, California: William Kaufmann, Inc., 1977.

Blue, Martha. *Making It Legal: A Law Primer for Authors, Artists, and Craftspeople.* rev. ed. Flagstaff, Arizona: Northland Publishing, 1988.

Bunnin, Brad, and Peter Beren. *The Writer's Legal Companion.* Reading, Massachusetts: Addison-Wesley, 1988.

Chickering, Robert B., and Susan Hartman. *How to Register a Copyright and Protect Your Creative Work.* New York: Charles Scribner's Sons, 1987.

Clark, Charles. *Publishing Agreements: A Book of Precedents.* London: George Allen & Unwin Ltd., 1986.

Curtis, Richard. *How to Be Your Own Literary Agent: The Business of Getting Your Book Published.* Boston: Houghton-Mifflin, 1984.

DuBoff, Leonard D. *Book Publisher's Legal Guide.* Redmond, Washington: Butterworth Legal Publications, 1984 (with 1987 supplement).

Florence, Heather Grant. "Publisher's Liability Insurance," *Book Publishing 1984.* New York: Practising Law Institute, 1984.

Goss, Frederick D. *Success in Newsletter Publishing, A Practical Guide.* Washington D.C.: The Newsletter Association, 1985.

Hale, Robert D. *A Manual on Bookselling: How to Open and Run a Bookstore.* 4th ed. New York: Crown, 1987.

Henderson, Bill, ed. *Publish-It-Yourself Handbook: Literary Tradition and How-To.* 3rd rev. ed. Wainscott, New York: Pushcart Press, 1987.

Hill, Lawson Traphagen. *How to Build a Multi-Million Dollar Catalog Mail Order Business by Someone Who Did.* Englewood Cliffs, New Jersey: Prentice-Hall, 1984.

Hudson, H. P. *Publishing Newsletters.* rev. ed. New York: Charles Scribner's Sons, 1988.

Kamoroff, Bernard. *Small-Time Operator: How to Start Your Own Small Business, Keep Your Books, Pay Your Taxes and Stay Out of Trouble.* rev. ed. Laytonville, California: Bell Springs Publications, 1989.

Kieper, Michael L. *The Illustrated Handbook of Desktop Publishing and Typesetting.* Blue Ridge Summit, Pennsylvania: TAB Books, Inc., 1987.

Labuz, Ronald A. *How to Typeset from a Word Processor: An Interfacing Guide.* New York: R. R. Bowker Co., 1984.

——, and Paul Altimonte. *The Interface Data Book for Word Processing/Typesetting.* New York: R. R. Bowker Co., 1984.

Lee, Marshall. *Bookmaking: The Illustrated Guide to Design, Production, Editing.* New York: R. R. Bowker Co., 1980.

Legal and Business Aspects of Book Publishing 1988. New York: Practising Law Institute, 1988.

Legal and Business Aspects of the Magazine Industry 1979. New York: Practising Law Institute, 1979.

Legal and Business Aspects of the Magazine Industry 1984. New York: Practising Law Institute, 1984.

Lindey, Alexander. *Lindey on Entertainment, Publishing, and the Arts: Agreements and the Law.* 2nd ed. New York: Clark Boardman Co., Ltd., 1982.

Literary Market Place 1990. New York: R. R. Bowker Co., 1989.

Mawdsley, Ralph D. *Legal Aspects of Plagiarism.* Topeka, Kansas: National Organization of Legal Problems in Education, 1985.

Orrmont, Arthur, and Leonie Rosenstiel. *Literary Agents of North America.* 3rd ed. New York: Author Aid/Research Associates International, 1988.

Perle, E. Gabriel, and John Taylor Williams. *The Publishing Law Handbook.* Englewood Cliffs, New Jersey: Prentice Hall, 1988.

Posch, Robert J. Jr. *The Complete Guide to Marketing and the Law.* Englewood Cliffs, New Jersey: Prentice-Hall, 1988.

—— *The Direct Marketer's Legal Advisor.* New York: McGraw-Hill, 1983.

—— *What Every Manager Needs to Know About Marketing and the Law.* New York: McGraw-Hill, 1984.

Poynter, Dan. *Business Letters for Publishers: Creative Correspondence Outlines.* 2nd rev. ed. Santa Barbara, California: Para Publishing, 1985.

——. *Publishing Forms: A Collection of Applications and Information for the Beginning Publisher.* 3rd rev. ed. Santa Barbara, California: Para Publishing, 1986.

———. *The Self-Publishing Manual: How to Write, Print and Sell Your Own Book.* 5th rev. ed. Santa Barbara, California: Para Publishing, 1989.

———, and Charles Kent. *Publishing Contracts: Sample Agreements for Book Publishers on Disk.* Santa Barbara, California: Para Publishing, 1987.

Professional Business Practices in Photography. New York: American Society of Magazine Publisher, n.d.

Publisher's Guide to Printing in Asia, A. Hong Kong: Travel Publishing Asia Limited, 1988.

Remer, John and Stephen Elia. *Legal Care for Your Software.* 4th rev. ed. Berkeley, California: NOLO Press, 1989.

Rice, Stanley. *Book Design, Systematic Aspects.* New York: R. R. Bowker Co., 1978.

Roth, Steve, ed. *Small Press Guide to Computers in Publishing.* Westport, Connecticut: Meckler Corporation, 1987.

Schlain, Barbara. "Errors and Omissions in Editorial Content and Related Torts and New Technologies," *Legal and Business Aspects of Book Publishing 1988.* New York: Practising Law Institute, 1988.

———. "New Technologies: Some Key Issues for Book Publishers and Software Publishing and the Licensing of Electronic Rights," *Legal and Business Aspects of Book Publishing 1986.* New York: Practising Law Institute, 1986.

Scott Paper Co./S. D. Warren Co. *How to Plan Printing.* N.p.: 1978.

Small-Claims Court. 2nd ed. Washington D.C.: HALT, 1983.

Software Protection and Marketing; Computer Programs and Databases; Video Games and Motion Pictures. Volumes I and II. New York: Practising Law Institute, 1983.

Standish, Peter. "Current Antitrust Issues in Book Publishing," *Legal and Business Aspects of Book Publishing 1986.* New York: Practising Law Institute, 1986.

United States Trademark Association. *State Trademark and Unfair Competition Law.* New York: Clark Boardman, 1987.

Using a Law Library. 2nd ed. Washington D.C.: HALT, 1983.

Volunteer lawyers for the Arts and Barbara S. Taylor. *Pressing Business: An Organizational Manual for Independent Publishers.* New York: Volunteer Lawyers for the Arts, 1984.

Writing Business: A Poets' and Writers' Handbook, The. New York: Poets & Writers, Inc., 1985.

INDEX

transport or mailing of, 71

Martha Blue graduated from the University of Arizona Law School and has practiced law in Arizona since 1967, except for a short stint in Micronesia, where she participated in the establishment of a legal-assistance office. She has lectured widely on law for the creative person and publishing law, and has been a featured speaker for the Arizona Authors Association, the Authors Resource Center, Navajo Community College, the National Romance Writers of America, Northern Arizona University, Penwomen, Rocky Mountain Publishers Association, and the Southwest Writers' Conference.

In her law practice, Ms. Blue is involved with publishing, art, and intellectual property matters as well as with Native American- related issues. An advocate for authors, agents, and publishers, she also represents the Havasupai Indian Tribe, whose reservation at the bottom of Arizona's Grand Canyon is accessible only by helicopter or over an eight-mile horse trail.

A partner in the firm of Ward & Blue in Flagstaff, Arizona, Ms. Blue lives with her family in a passive solar house.